Manzoor G.K. Ishani

FRANCHISING
The key to rapid business growth

Foreword by Sir Bernard Ingham

39 Steps To Franchising Successfully

THE CHOIR PRESS

Copyright © 2018 Manzoor G K Ishani

All rights reserved. No part of this publication may be reproduced or transmitted in any form or by any means, electronic or mechanical including photocopying, recording or any information storage or retrieval system, without prior permission in writing from the publishers.

The right of Manzoor G K Ishani to be identified as the author of this work has been asserted by him in accordance with the Copyright, Designs and Patents Act 1988

First published in the United Kingdom in 2018 by
The Choir Press

ISBN 978-1-911589-71-6

For my mother, my mentor, and for my sister Nargis, for her fortitude in adversity.

Foreword

During the 18 years I was president of the British Franchise Association (BFA), the author of this book, Manzoor Ishani, was a member of one of the supporting professions that helped to build ethical business format franchising in Britain.

I reckon the BFA did – and still do – a good job because the sector continues to grow. At the last count franchising was a £14bn business employing more than 600,000 people.

This means that Manzoor Ishani knows what he is talking about. He is worth reading on that account alone. He has now set out clearly in this book what franchising is, how it can be structured commercially and ethically and how it works. It is a handbook for both the company that is thinking of adopting the franchise format and prospective franchisees.

Anyone who doubts his even-handedness should read Chapter 26. He clearly sets out what a franchisor needs to do to make his business ethically operational and what franchisees should look out for in contemplating taking up a franchise.

There are several reasons why firms find franchising ever more attractive. It enables them to penetrate a market without incurring a heavy bill for expansion. It offers a large network of outlets with relatively small office overheads. But most important of all, it enables enterprises to harness the entrepreneurial spirit of those who want to be in business themselves rather than remain as employees.

Franchising has received legal recognition as a marketing method distinct from agencies, distributors and knowhow licences and is seen as pro-competitive by the competition authorities, encouraging the growth of small businesses.

This book is very much about a growth business and I commend it for encouraging its development.

Sir Bernard Ingham
Former Chief Press Secretary to Margaret Thatcher
Former President of the British Franchise Association
Former Non-executive Director of McDonald's UK

Acknowledgements

My thanks to Claudia Bronda for the initial proofreading of the manuscript and to Harriet Evans for editing and the final proofreading, though any errors or omissions are entirely mine, to Annabel Mallan for her keyboard skills and to Lucy Parnell for designing the book cover.

Preface

Franchising has proved to be a very popular method of growing a business. There are several reasons for this. One is that it enables a company to penetrate a market more quickly without the capital costs which would normally be associated with such expansion. Another is that it enables a company to maintain a large network of outlets with relatively low office overheads. But arguably the most powerful reason is that it enables a company to capitalise on the financial resources, drive and entrepreneurship of individuals who are more highly motivated than a company's managers.

In 1986, with a landmark decision of the European Court of Justice in what became commonly known as the Pronuptia Case, franchising in Europe came of age. Effectively, business format franchising received legal recognition as a distinct marketing method in its own right. The European Commission recognised franchising as being an essentially pro-competitive method and one which encouraged the growth of successful small businesses by providing a relatively safe commercial environment.

Rather than omit them, I have dealt briefly with some of the legal issues such as price fixing, restrictions on termination of a franchise and competition rules. Dealing with them in detail would have doubled the size of the book and may have been of limited value given the uncertainty, at the time of writing, surrounding the United Kingdom's resignation of its membership of the European Union. The purpose of these brief references is to bring such issues to the attention of the reader.

This book will present what I hope is a clear picture of what franchising is, how it works and the elements that comprise a business format franchise. The aim is to enable the reader to determine whether expanding his business through the franchising method would be right for his company and, if so, the steps that company will need to take to franchise its business model.

After giving it some consideration, I have thought it best to divide the narrative into 39 chapters dealing with specific topics with each of the 39 steps leading to the next. This has the advantage of enabling the reader to return to the work to address any issue which may arise as his company progresses en route to

Preface

establishing itself as a franchisor. This has inevitably led to repetition across some chapters, which some readers may find mildly irritating, but in my view it is a price worth paying if it results in the work proving itself to be a useful aide-mémoir.

Finally, a note on pronouns. Whilst recognising that not all franchisees are male and not all franchisors are corporate entities, I have used 'he' to refer to franchisees and 'it' to refer to franchisors for reasons of consistency and clarity.

Manzoor G K Ishani
London
March 2018

Contents

CHAPTER 1 What Is Business Format Franchising?   1

   Types of Business Relationship   1
   A Comparison of the Business Format Franchise with
      Other Business Relationships   2
   Types of Franchise Arrangement   6
   Models for Growth   8

CHAPTER 2 Advantages and Disadvantages   14

   Advantages to the Franchisor   14
   Disadvantages to the Franchisor   15
   Advantages to the Franchisee   16
   Disadvantages to the Franchisee   18
   Advantages to the Consumer   20
   Disadvantages to the Consumer   21
   In Conclusion   21

CHAPTER 3 Franchise Statistics: The Hype and the Reality   22

CHAPTER 4 Can a Service Business Be Franchised?   29

CHAPTER 5 Is Franchising Right for Your Company?   32

   Considerations for the Prospective Franchisor   32
   Requirements for a Company to Franchise   38
   Tips for a Prospective Franchisor   39

Contents

CHAPTER 6 Setting up a Franchise Operation — 42

- The Business Concept — 42
- Proving the System Works — 45
- Developing the Franchise Package — 46
- Locating an Outlet — 48
- Developing the Operations Manual — 51
- Selecting Franchisees — 51
- Selling Franchises — 51
- Further Considerations When Setting Up a Franchise — 51

CHAPTER 7 Developing the Concept and Organisation — 54

- Preparing for the Franchise Launch — 54
- Growing the Network — 60
- Innovation — 61
- Monitoring Standards — 62
- Reviewing the Terms of the Franchise — 63
- A Possible Management Structure — 68

CHAPTER 8 Testing the System – Proving It Works — 69

CHAPTER 9 Protecting Intellectual Property — 74

- Trade Name — 74
- Trade Marks — 75
- Copyright — 80
- Know-How and Trade Secrets — 81
- Patents — 82
- Industrial Designs — 82
- In Summary — 82

CHAPTER 10 The Operations Manual — 84

- Fundamental Functions — 84
- Matters Covered in an Operations Manual — 86
- Maintaining and Protecting the Operations Manual — 91
- In Conclusion — 93

CHAPTER 11 Know-How Show-How — 94

CHAPTER 12 Sources of Income — 97

- Initial Franchise Fee — 97
- Franchise Package Fee — 101
- Continuing Franchise Fee — 101
- Mark-up on Products Sold to Franchisees — 102
- Advertising Contributions — 102
- Sundry Services Fee — 104
- Rental Income — 104
- Income from Commission — 105
- Income from Leasing Equipment — 105
- Franchise Transfer Fee — 105
- Avoiding a Shortfall — 106
- A Final Note on Franchisor Income — 107
- Revenue and Income Flows — 107

CHAPTER 13 How Much Can You Charge? — 121

- Initial Franchise Fee — 121
- Franchise Package Fee — 125
- Ongoing Income from Franchisees — 126
- Advertising Contributions — 132
- Reviewing the Financial Terms — 132

Contents

CHAPTER 14 The Financial Aspects of Franchising — 134

    Initial Costs — 135
    Research and Development — 137
    Establishment and Launch — 137
    Continuing Franchise Fees — 140
    Costs and Returns on Investment — 141

CHAPTER 15 Profit Projections — 149

CHAPTER 16 Advertising Funds — 151

CHAPTER 17 Evaluating a Franchise as a Prospective Franchisee — 154

    Considering the Franchisor — 155
    Timeline of Buying a Franchise — 157

CHAPTER 18 Selling Franchises — 161

    Sale of New Franchises — 161
    Sale of Second-Hand Franchises — 165
    Buying Back Franchises — 171
    In Summary — 173

CHAPTER 19 Selecting Franchisees — 174

    Common Issues and Mistakes in Franchisee Selection — 175
    The Franchisee Criteria — 177
    In Summary — 182

CHAPTER 20 Exclusive Territories – Avoiding the Pitfalls — 184

    Legal Issues — 185
    Commercial Issues — 186

CHAPTER 21 Minimum Performance Targets — 190

CHAPTER 22 How Long Should the Franchise Relationship Last? — 194
Franchise Renewal — 196

CHAPTER 23 Price Fixing Within the Network — 198

CHAPTER 24 Managing and Controlling the Network — 201
Maintaining Peace — 201
Franchisee Associations — 206
Research and Development: Involving Franchisees — 210
Franchisee Conferences — 211
Example Structure of a Franchisee Association — 213
Addressing Concerns — 213
Top 10 Tips — 214

CHAPTER 25 The Franchise Agreement — 215
The Importance of the Franchise Agreement — 215
No Negotiation — 217
Legal Matters — 218
Clarity — 219
The Objectives of a Franchise Agreement — 220
Structuring the Franchise Agreement — 221
The Structure of the Franchise Agreement — 222
Length of the Franchise Relationship — 223
Operations Manuals — 224
Obligations and Concerns — 225
Notice of Default — 227
Brand Protection — 227
'Standard' Franchise Agreements — 229
Disputes — 231
In Conclusion — 232
In Summary — 232

Contents

CHAPTER 26 A Franchise May Be Legal, but Is It Ethical? — 235
Ten Rules of Ethical Franchising — 237

CHAPTER 27 Contract Enforcement — 239
Maintaining Uniform Standards — 240
Defaults — 241
Evidence — 250
In Conclusion — 251

CHAPTER 28 Termination: The End of the Relationship — 252
Reasons for Termination — 254
Financial Defaults — 254
Checklist: Preparing for Franchisee Termination — 256
Preventing Competition from Former Franchisees — 257
An Amicable Parting — 262
Suspension — 263

CHAPTER 29 Resolving Disputes Between Franchisor and Franchisee — 266
Causes and Risks of Conflict — 266
Setting the Tone — 270
Alternative Dispute Resolution — 272
Litigation — 278
In Conclusion — 279

CHAPTER 30 Franchisees as Multiple Unit Holders — 280
Advantages of Multi-Unit Franchising — 281
Disadvantages of Multi-Unit Franchising — 281

CHAPTER 31 A Successful Franchisor's Dilemma — 284
Branching Into New Concepts — 284
Branching Into New Countries — 285

CHAPTER 32 Staying Ahead of the Game	287
The Role of Franchisees in Innovation	288
CHAPTER 33 What Happens If a Franchisor Goes Bust?	290
CHAPTER 34 Whom Does the Customer Sue?	296
CHAPTER 35 Co-Branding	299
Reasons for Co-Branding	302
Preparing for Co-Branding	303
In a Nutshell	304
CHAPTER 36 The Problems of Regional Master Franchising	305
The Appeal of Regional Master Franchising	305
Difficulties in Regional Master Franchising	307
A Final Note	310
In Conclusion	311
CHAPTER 37 Franchisors as Landlords	312
The Difficulty of Obtaining Leases as a Franchisee	312
Disadvantages for the Franchisor	313
Advantages for the Franchisor	313
Advantages for the Franchisee	315
In Conclusion	316
CHAPTER 38 Going International	317
Direct Franchising	318
Subsidiary	319
National Master Franchise	320
Regional Master Franchise	323

Contents

Development Agreement	324
Joint Venture	325
Turnkey Franchising	326
Foreign Buy-Back	327
Points to Consider	327
In Summary	332
An Idiot's Guide to International Legal Compliance	334

CHAPTER 39 Regulating Franchising — 335

The Effects of Regulation and Disclosure	338
Is Regulation Worthwhile?	240

APPENDIX A: Trade and Service Mark Classifications — 342

Products	342
Services	351

APPENDIX B: Sample Franchise Application Form — 354

APPENDIX C: Franchisee Preliminary Enquiries — 356

APPENDIX D: The British Franchise Association — 371

APPENDIX E: (i) Case Study: The Ziebart Story — 374

APPENDIX E: (ii) Case Study: The Southern Fried Chicken Story — 376

APPENDIX E: (iii) Case Study: The ServiceMaster UK Story — 380

APPENDIX F: (i) Sample Document: Confidentiality, Deposit and Non-Competition Agreement — 385

APPENDIX F: (ii) Sample Document: Franchise Purchase Agreement — 388

APPENDIX F: (iii) Sample Document: Outline of Franchise Agreement — 400

APPENDIX F: (iv) Sample Document: Franchise Agreement — 413

    Operations Manual Receipt — 490
    Confidentiality Undertaking — 491
    The First Schedule — 492
    The Second Schedule — 493
    The Third Schedule — 497
    The Fourth Schedule — 499
    Schedule A — 503
    Schedule B — 504
    The Fifth Schedule — 505
    The Sixth Schedule — 510
    The Seventh Schedule — 511
    The Eighth Schedule — 512
    The Ninth Schedule — 515
    The Tenth Schedule — 516
    The Eleventh Schedule — 519

APPENDIX F: (v) Sample Document: Outline of International Master Franchise Agreement — 520

    The Schedule — 528

APPENDIX F: (vi) Sample Document: International Master Franchise Agreement — 529

    The First Schedule — 566
    The Second Schedule — 567

References — 568

CHAPTER 1

What Is Business Format Franchising?

> *"If you think information is expensive – try ignorance."*
> Anon

Franchising is a method of marketing goods and/or services. It enables a company ('franchisor') with a branded product or service to increase its sales by granting rights to others ('franchisees') to sell those goods or services in return for a fee. The franchisees offer products or services for sale to their customers under the franchisor's brand and in accordance with their franchisor's established business system.

Although there are many instances where one may claim that the principles of franchising apply, it is generally accepted that the first instance of what is now recognised as a franchise system was the distribution network established in the USA by the Singer sewing machine company following the American Civil War.

Franchising has developed considerably from those times and now involves a franchisor's way of doing business ('business format'), with the result that the world has become increasingly familiar with franchising through many well-known and successful franchise operations such as McDonald's, Holiday Inn etc.

Types of Business Relationship

How does one distinguish between a business format franchise, an intellectual property licence, a distributorship and an agency? The first important thing to remember is that they are all methods, essentially marketing methods, of doing business.

A process of evolution in the various methods of doing business can loosely be traced back to ancient times. Commercial life can be said to have begun with a system of barter where one exchanged one set of goods or services for another set of goods or services. With the advent of money, the most commonplace and enduring form of commercial activity evolved: that of buying and selling. Money became the medium of exchange for goods and services and the system of barter died out until after the Second World War, when it was revived amongst the Communist bloc countries and for those wishing to trade with them.

As trade became more sophisticated the medium of agency was created. In strict legal terms, an agent is a person or company who acts on behalf of another person or company. The person or company appointing the agent is known as the 'principal'.

The agent does not have a direct contractual relationship with the end user (the customer). Whatever the agent says or does will generally bind his principal. In effect, an agent speaks with his principal's voice.

While an agency has a number of advantages, it also has disadvantages (see Chapter 2). There thus grew out of the concept of agency a more sophisticated way of doing business in the form of a distributorship. Whereas the agent acts for and on behalf of his principal, a distributor acts on his own account.

Following on from distributorships came the development of business format franchising. The business format franchise is a stage in the evolutionary development of agency, distributorship, and know-how licences. Instead of being limited to one aspect of business activity, business format franchising entails licensing an entire package comprising all the elements necessary to establish a business to be run by a previously untrained person on a tried and tested basis.

These elements comprise:

1. A complete business concept.
2. Training of the franchisee by the franchisor in every aspect of running a business in accordance with the franchisor's format.
3. Provision to the franchisee by the franchisor of support, training, assistance and guidance on a continuing basis.

A Comparison of the Business Format Franchise with Other Business Relationships

When one compares a business format franchise with some of the methods referred to above, a number of similarities and differences emerge.

Barter

Barter is no longer of commercial significance and is usually absent from a business format franchise.

Buyer and Seller

The buyer and seller relationship is very much present in a business format franchise at both levels of the transaction. There is a buyer and seller relationship between the franchisor and the franchisee in that the franchisor will be supplying services and/or goods to the franchisee, and a buyer and seller relationship between a franchisee and his customer as the franchisee will in turn, be the seller of those goods and/or services to his own customers.

Agency

What the agent does is represent his supplier ('principal') in a commercial transaction. An agent who 'sells' goods does not own them and he sells them on behalf of his principal. It is his principal who owns those goods and who therefore sells them to the customer via its agent.

From the franchisor's point of view, the important point to note here is that the agent, in the course of trading in his capacity as agent, binds his principal, and therefore the principal is liable for the acts, omissions and defaults of its agent.

The agent acts with the authority of his principal. The fact that the terms of his appointment as agent may restrict his authority will not necessarily save the principal from liability if the person dealing with the agent does not know of the limits placed on the agent's authority, or if the action of the agent is ostensibly within the scope of an agent's authority.

Agents are usually paid by their principals on results: the more products an agent sells, the greater his income. In these circumstances, historically, it was tempting for agents to secure a sale by making promises to customers such as an after-sales service to be provided by the principal. Once an agent had made the sale he would move on, leaving the principal to satisfy unauthorised promises and deal with the customer and any complaints. As the customer belonged to his principal, the agent was not necessarily interested in cultivating customer loyalty to his principal's brand.

What Is Business Format Franchising?

Agency is one aspect of doing business which is absent from a business format franchise, save in some exceptional circumstances such as in a parcel delivery franchise. Indeed, franchisors go to great lengths to emphasise to franchisees and specify in their franchise agreements that the franchisee is not the agent of the franchisor and should not represent himself as being one. The fact that the franchisee bears the franchisor's name does not automatically make him an agent of the franchisor, and franchisors go to great lengths to ensure that those dealing with their franchisees are made aware of that fact. As an agent does not own the goods (it is his principal who owns the goods and sells them to the customer via the agent), the customer is the customer of the principal.

Distributorship

Put in its simplest form, in a distributorship the supplier sells the goods to the distributor, who then sells them on to his customer. There is therefore a moment in the buying and selling transaction when the distributor becomes the owner of the goods in question. A distributor does not bind his supplier in the way that an agent binds his principal. Generally speaking, if there is to be any liability (apart from questions of product liability), the distributor will be held liable for his own acts, omissions and defaults.

There is a great deal in common here between a distributorship and a business format franchise, and increasingly less that is uncommon. There are five main factors which distinguish a business format franchise from a distributorship.

1. It is common in distributorships for distributors to have more than one distributorship within the same business. Thus it is possible for someone to be a distributor for Sanyo as well as Sony, Panasonic and Philips radios. In a business format franchise this is generally not permitted. Franchisors insist that franchisees devote their full time and attention to the franchise in question, not engage in any other business and certainly not deal in any competing products or engage in any competing businesses. If the franchisees are permitted to conduct other non-competing businesses, these should not be a part of their franchised business.

2. Distributorships are generally granted to those who have prior knowledge and experience in a particular line of business and who have been running their own businesses. What a supplier will tend to do when looking for a

distributor is seek out, in the area in which they wish to grant a distributorship, someone who has been successfully trading in the same or a similar type of business, with the intention of using that business owner's knowledge of the local market to promote the sale of the supplier's products and/or services.

Franchisors, on the other hand, take an entirely different view. Indeed many franchisors go so far as to refuse to grant franchises to those who have been in the same line of business before. The reason for this is their belief that they have a much greater chance of succeeding with someone who comes to them with a clear mind and who can therefore be moulded into operating a particular business in the franchisor's particular way. Franchisors claim that potential franchisees who come to them with prior knowledge of their type of business are more difficult to train and have greater difficulty in retaining the training they receive than those who have no prior experience or knowledge in the field. So a carpet cleaning franchisor will be reluctant to grant a franchise to someone who has had previous experience as a carpet cleaner. Furthermore, most franchisees will have been employees in their former working life and will never have run a business on their own account.

3. The structure of the financial arrangements between a supplier and a distributor is different from that of a business format franchise. In a distributorship the emphasis is on the sale by the distributor of as many goods or services as possible, and it is common in distributorship agreements to see a minimum purchase requirement or minimum sales targets. The financial arrangements in a business format franchise are generally geared in such a way that the earning potential of the franchisor is inexorably linked to the earning potential of its franchisee. For this reason most franchisors' income is expressed as a percentage of its franchisees' gross turnover to ensure the success of its franchisees. The higher a franchisee's turnover, the greater the income of his franchisor.

4. The level of backup and support given to a franchisee is typically much greater than that given by a supplier to a distributor, though this is now changing as products become more sophisticated. For example, manufacturers now give a very high level of training and support to their dealerships.

5. Distributors generally trade under their own name, whereas a franchisee must trade only under the brand of his franchisor.

Know-how and Other Licences

The term 'licence' is nothing more than a legal term meaning the grant of a right. Thus agencies, distributorships and franchises are all technically licences because they all involve the grant of rights by one party to another. This may include manufacturing rights, selling rights, rights to use trade marks or logos, copyright and so on.

An Intellectual Property Licence is clearly present in a business format franchise, and franchise agreements grant the franchisee the right to use the franchisor's intellectual property such as copyright, know-how, trade marks, trade name and so on.

Types of Franchise Arrangement

Business format franchising was not the result of a single invention by one imaginative individual. It is the result of various solutions developed by businesses in response to the problems they faced.

Over a period of time different types of franchising emerged, involving all levels in the chain from manufacturer to consumer. So we find franchise arrangements between:

- Manufacturer and retailer,
- Manufacturer and wholesaler,
- Wholesaler and retailer, and
- Retailer and retailer (which includes the services sector).

Each of these categories can be identified clearly.

Manufacturer and Retailer

This category emerged from the development of the automotive industry. Charles Mason Hewitt (1956), in his study of the development of automobile franchise agreements, identified the problems with which automobile manufacturers were confronted as the need for:

1. Some rapid means of acquiring retail outlets requiring a minimum of attention, outlay and fixed expense.
2. Some means of making their cars conveniently available for consumer inspection in advance of purchase on a nationwide basis.
3. Some means of coping with the repair problem.
4. Some means of coping with the off-season storage problems.
5. Some means of acquiring a ready market for their goods without having fixed legal commitments for delivery.
6. Some means of acquiring cash on delivery or even in advance if possible.

Attempts to find a solution to these problems led to the introduction of a method of franchise marketing.

By the 1930s franchising was applied in the United States to petrol stations, which also come within this category.

Manufacturer and Wholesaler

This category (also known as product and trade name franchising) seems to have come into existence a little earlier than the adoption of franchising by the car industry when soft drink manufacturers established the practice of franchising their bottling plants.

What these manufacturers did (and indeed still do) was grant to the owners of bottling plants the right, within a defined area, to use a concentrate or syrup manufactured by, and of course obtained from, the manufacturer. The bottler's role was to make up and bottle the drink using the manufacturer's syrups and in accordance with the manufacturer's requirements, and to distribute the resulting product.

Prime examples of this category are Coca-Cola, Pepsi and Schweppes.

What Is Business Format Franchising?

Wholesaler and Retailer

This category is more difficult to identify, but the franchising system does enable a wholesaler to secure outlets for its products, maximising its use of storage and distribution facilities and improving its productivity. It has been used with advantage in such areas as automotive products, drug stores and hardware stores.

Retailer and Retailer

This category principally comprises what are called 'business format franchises'. The techniques of business format franchising have also been applied to the other categories listed above. It has developed from the establishment of a retail operation which is successful and which is then expanded by the use of the franchise method of marketing. This category developed and expanded rapidly in the 1950s and 1960s and established market leaders such as McDonald's, KFC, Burger King, Pizza Hut, Holiday Inn etc.

The growth and development of all these categories of franchise resulted from the realisation that there was a common solution to common problems.

Models for Growth

There are many different growth strategies a business can use, and franchising may or may not be the most appropriate to a situation. So how do the various business growth models compare?

Organic Growth

Advantages	Disadvantages
Retain control of all operational matters	All capital to be funded internally
Control over recruitment policies	Difficulty in retaining good staff
Retain all profits	Profit growth constrained by scarcity of capital
Easy to change direction of the business	Takes longer to exploit the market
Control rate of growth	Requires more management input
Greater scope to try out new products/services	Requires greater overhead base

The presence of the following factors in a business indicates the possibility of successful organic growth:

- Access to adequate capital resources.
- Strength in the depth of the management team to manage growth.
- Stable market to allow time for growth.
- Highly personal service that depends on the direct input of the owners.
- Highly technical service which would be difficult to deliver through third parties.
- A niche market for products/services for which there is limited demand.

Joint Ventures

A joint venture is a partnership between two or more businesses with a common business aim. The partners decide who will contribute the capital, human resources and management skills required to meet the needs of the joint venture.

In most cases the joint venture is controlled by a shareholders' agreement. This defines each partner's position with respect to the joint venture, in terms of capital stakes and each party's powers. It supplements the joint venture's bylaws by setting out the rights of ownership of each party, criteria and procedures for approval of new shareholders, and exit routes in advance of any problems.

Advantages	Disadvantages
Capital funded jointly with partner	Share control of operational matters
Faster growth possible	Profits will be shared
Provides access to key skills lacking in the business	Creates dependency on partner
Can provide access to a new market or customer base	Difficult to disentangle in the event of a disagreement
Can provide access to new technology	Can require compromise on business objectives
Possible synergy with partner's businesses	Risk of training competitors

The presence of the following factors in a business indicates the possibility of successful growth through a joint venture:

- The business has identified a need for additional management skills/technology.
- A business which could be operated in addition to and in tandem with its own business.
- A management team that can operate on the basis of consensus.
- Receipt of direct approaches from third parties to run a similar business.

Franchising

Business format franchising is the replication of a proven business in exchange for an up-front payment plus ongoing fees for an agreed period of time. In essence it is a technique whereby the owner and operator of a business allows and trains a third party to legally copy the *modus operandi* of its business.

Advantages	Disadvantages
Capital is provided by the franchisee	Loss of direct control
Faster growth possible	Profits will be shared
Fewer staff need to be employed	Risk of poor franchise selection
Outlet operated by highly motivated owner	Difficulty in effective communication
Enlarged network enables national customers to be serviced and economies of scale	Market penetration entrusted to third parties
Greater return on capital	The franchise network is only as strong as its weakest franchisee

The presence of the following factors in a business indicates the possibility of successful growth through business format franchising:

- The business is already managed without direct involvement in detail.
- An existing multi-branch network.

- There is sufficient development capital to run a pilot operation (could be £50,000+).
- The margins are high enough to share with franchisees.
- Knowledge easily transferable to a third party, yet there is strong reason for the franchisee to need continued support from the company.
- There exists an identifiable brand or trade mark.

Licensing

Licensing is a growth strategy which allows a company to generate a revenue stream from a product or service which is manufactured or delivered by a third party. Typically, a company will register a patent or other intellectual property on a product or a service it supplies and will provide only limited training and little ongoing support.

Advantages	Disadvantages
No capital requirement	Loss of most forms of control
Revenue stream generated	Profits will accrue mainly to the licensee
Fewer staff need to be employed	Risk of licensee not exploiting the market to its fullest extent
No ongoing management resource needed	Lack of adequate communication
Greater return on capital	No brand development

The presence of the following factors in a business indicates the possibility of successful growth through the licensing of intellectual property:

- A manufacturer which has already received enquiries for its products/services from overseas.
- The business has by-products which are non-core.
- The business involves low-technology processes/services that require no intensive training or back-up support and no business format.
- Products/services with short-term potential.

Agency

An agent negotiates with customers on behalf of his principal, in this case the supplier. The agent is able to bind his supplier to create a legal agreement between the supplier and the agent's customer. The agent receives a commission usually based on the sales value of orders obtained.

Advantages	Disadvantages
No capital requirement	Risk of being tied into poor deals
Revenue stream generated externally without tying up management time	If the agent is non-exclusive, the agent may concentrate on high-commission products from other suppliers
Fewer employed sales staff needed	No brand development
Lower overheads	Lack of adequate communication channels
Payments based on success only	Complex competition laws and regulations
Benefit from local knowledge of the agent	Potentially training competitors by giving them access to customer base

The presence of the following factors in a business indicates the possibility of successful growth using the agency method:

- A lack of internal sales experience.
- The business needs to sell a new, untried product/service.
- The business needs to enter new markets without any direct experience/contacts.
- The business sells products/services with little brand value.

What Is Business Format Franchising?

Distributorship/Dealership

A distributor buys goods on his own account from a supplier and resells them to his customers. It is the distributor who enters into a contract of sale with the customer, not the supplier.

Advantages	Disadvantages
No capital requirement	No control over prices (as minimum resale prices are prohibited)
Allows the company to concentrate on core skills of manufacturing, R&D, product development etc., rather than retail sales	Distributors sell many products; they may concentrate on high-commission products from other competing suppliers
The company has to deal with fewer customers and can impose minimum purchase requirement	No brand development
The company benefits from local knowledge of the distributor	Lack of adequate communication channels

The presence of the following factors in a business indicates the possibility of successful growth by granting distributorships/dealerships:

- The business wants to expand with minimum risk.
- Sales are not dependent on brand perception or image.
- There is a lack of development capital.
- Product/service new to market.

CHAPTER 2

Advantages and Disadvantages

"The chicken was involved but the pig was committed."

Business format franchising, if properly structured and managed, can bring great advantages not only to the franchisor and its franchisees but to the consumer also. However, as in most things, business format franchising has its disadvantages too.

Advantages to the Franchisor

First and foremost, it is always claimed that franchising enables a franchisor to penetrate markets more deeply and more quickly than would be the case if the franchisor chose to 'go it alone'. Franchising is recognised as one of the most effective means of rapidly expanding one's business. It enables a franchisor to increase the number of outlets for its goods and/or services very quickly with the minimum capital investment and with few of the management problems it would otherwise encounter. After all, in business format franchising it is the franchisees who provide the capital and management at the sharp end of the business.

A franchisor is able to benefit from the maximisation of profits from a franchised unit by virtue of the fact that a franchisee is highly motivated and is usually both owner and manager of the franchised outlet. Because a franchisee owns his own business he will be keen to ensure the success of that business in many ways. He may stay open longer hours, go out of his way to make a sale and spend time and energy on cultivating his customers. In theory, a franchisee will work all the hours God sends him to increase his profits.

By contrast, the manager of a company-owned branch is more likely to be concerned with maximising his comfort. He will close the shop at the appointed hour rather than wait until the last customer has left the shop. When not well, he will telephone head office for a relief manager and will stay at home and nurse his cold. An owner-manager, on the other hand, will drag himself into town and open the shop.

A manager is *involved* – a franchisee is *committed*. The difference can best be explained by the illustration of a traditional English breakfast of bacon and eggs. In this case the chicken was involved but the pig was committed.

In a retail operation, quite often a large, well-run franchised network will give the franchisor a captive market into which it can sell its goods.

In a well-structured franchise the projection of a uniform marketing image helps to generate brand awareness. This in turn increases the value of the franchisor's trade marks, trade name and other intellectual property and thus the franchisor's goodwill.

Franchisees within a franchised network are constantly promoting the goodwill of their franchisor whilst promoting their own businesses.

Disadvantages to the Franchisor

Company-owned branches tend to be more profitable for a franchisor than franchised outlets. Whilst franchising may enable a franchisor to open outlets quickly and with a low capital outlay, the return to the franchisor from such outlets is, of necessity, limited. This is particularly true of franchises where the franchisor derives its revenue by means of a royalty-type payment which is expressed as a percentage of the franchisee's gross turnover. These fees range from 7% to 15%, considerably lower than what a franchisor would earn if such a unit were owned by the franchisor and managed by an employee. In those circumstances the franchisor company would take the lion's share of the profit.

Franchisors have to develop particular management skills when dealing with franchisees. This means devoting financial and human resources to manage the franchised network, which are significantly different from those required to manage employees. Franchisees are, after all, owners of their own businesses and need to be treated as such. Franchisors who bark orders at franchisees will seldom succeed in the long run. Employees who do not obey the instructions of their employer can, ultimately, always be sacked. This is not necessarily true of franchisees. Although a franchisor has the ultimate sanction of terminating the franchise agreement if it has just cause, this is a drastic remedy and will more often than not involve the franchisor in a loss. It takes time and money to set a franchisee up in business, and terminating a franchise agreement is usually a last resort and reluctantly done.

Advantages and Disadvantages

Franchisors have to develop the skill of motivating independent businessmen into doing things the franchisor's way. This is not always easy.

For the reasons given above, it is more difficult for a franchisor to 'control' franchised outlets than it is for it to control managed outlets.

Franchisors need to develop sophisticated accounting and monitoring systems, particularly where the franchisor's income is derived from continuing franchise fees based on a percentage of the franchisee's gross turnover, to ensure franchisees report their level of business activity accurately.

Franchisors lose a degree of flexibility in their commercial operations, and franchised outlets can be slow to react to changes in the market. It can take longer to introduce a new range of products/services to exploit market potential within a franchised network than it would in a chain of company-owned branches.

The need for franchisors to maintain a balance between company-owned branches and franchised outlets is critical. When things are going well, franchisors may be tempted to cut back on the number of company-owned branches or indeed to convert most of them into franchised outlets. One of the consequences of such an action is that the franchisor will then become almost entirely dependent on its franchisees for information about various aspects of running the business generally, and about life at the sharp end of selling in particular. This makes it difficult for franchisors to introduce change if the need for such change is not based on the personal experience of the franchisor.

Advantages to the Franchisee

The greatest advantage of franchising to a franchisee is that it reduces his risk of business failure. Because an ethical franchisor will have tried, tested and proven the business concept in the marketplace, most of the wrinkles will have been ironed out and the risk of failure for the franchisee is minimised – *via trita est tutissima*.[1] It is claimed that less than 70% of franchisees fail within the first three years, as compared to over 90% of new business start-ups. Franchisees hit the ground running when they open a franchised outlet as they enter the market with a recognised brand name, proven business system and products and/or ser-

---

[1] The beaten track is the safest.

Advantages and Disadvantages

vices which, having been market tested, come to the franchisee with a certain degree of ready acceptance by the consumer.

Franchising enables a small business to compete with big business. Through franchising, a franchisee can take advantage of economies of scale. All franchisees acting together can buy more cheaply and on better terms than an individual small business. Add to this the franchisor's negotiating skills employed on behalf of its franchisees, and the franchisee should have a distinct advantage over any independent small business competitor.

Through training imparted by the franchisor, the franchisee climbs a very steep learning curve in short order, thereby increasing his chances of succeeding considerably. For example, a fledging entrepreneur who wishes to set up a wedding dress retail business would find it very difficult to get his stock mix right at the outset. A franchisee, however, would have the benefit of an experienced franchisor who will be able to advise him on exactly the range and mix of the stock he should carry: so many size 12 dresses, so many size 14 dresses etc.

No previous experience in a particular business is necessary for a franchisee to operate his chosen business under a franchise, as all deficiencies of know-how are made good by training imparted by the franchisor.

A franchisee has the ostensible backing of an organisation and this is achieved by the pooling of resources, particularly in the field of advertising, marketing and promotions where each franchisee, by contributing a little, can enjoy the benefit of a large fund for this purpose. Franchisees are therefore able to have their goods and services promoted through media which they, as individuals, could otherwise ill afford.

In a well-run and structured franchise, the franchisee is left to concentrate on selling goods or services while at the same time receiving the benefit of continuous market research and development to improve his business and the franchised system.

In many cases franchisees are given exclusive territorial rights and this, in effect, gives them a monopoly over the area allocated to them, certainly in terms of doing business under the franchisor's trade name.

Most franchisors provide back-up and support to assist franchisees in their daily endeavours. This support includes managerial and administrative services,

Advantages and Disadvantages

troubleshooting, product information, marketing, IT support and in some cases bookkeeping, basic accounting and invoicing services.

In summary, the following are generally accepted as being the advantages of franchising for franchisees:

- Lower level of risk.
- Initial and ongoing training.
- Use of a tried and tested business format.
- No need to purchase goodwill.
- The benefit of a branded business.
- The benefit of research and development carried out by the franchisor.
- The benefit of market research and a co-ordinated advertising, marketing and promotions programme.
- Easier entry into business and assistance with setting up.
- Possibly lower capital requirement than starting an independent business.
- Improved opportunities of obtaining finance.
- Benefits from economies of scale.
- Access to operations manuals and ongoing support.
- Communication with franchisor and other franchisees eliminates isolation experienced by most small business owners.
- Scope to make decisions and opportunities to exercise initiative, albeit within the frame of the franchise agreement.
- Status – not an employee.

Disadvantages to the Franchisee

Although franchisees are the owners of their own businesses, they will be subject to controls and regulation by their franchisors which they will not necessarily appreciate or like. The more successful they become in their business, the more irksome they will find the franchisor's directions, controls and regulations.

A franchisee's reliance on the power of the franchisor's trade name may prove to be a disadvantage if the franchisor, through mismanagement or neglect, allows the brand to fall into disrepute.

Substandard franchised outlets can have a detrimental effect on other franchised outlets within the same network. Ultimately a franchised network, it is argued, can only be as strong as its weakest franchisee.

A franchisee's business may suffer as a result of an error on the part of his franchisor. For example, the franchisor may introduce a new product which fails or is not as successful as predicted, or the franchisor may fail to supply its franchisees with products adequately or in a timely manner.

A franchisee may find that his franchisor has sold its business and the new owners of the franchise may have different priorities or take the network in a different direction. A franchisee will have made his decision on whether or not to buy a particular franchise partly on his reliance on the strength and support of the franchisor, which may change if the ownership of the franchisor changes.

Franchise businesses tend to be highly specialised and a franchisee may be exposed to a change in trend to which his franchisor may not permit him to respond, for example by stocking another range of products, instead insisting that the franchisee continue in the narrow specialisation which previously made the franchise business successful.

A franchisee will not have the unfettered right to sell his business to whomsoever he pleases because any such sale will be subject to the franchisor's consent and this can never be taken for granted.

A franchisee may become dependent upon the support of his franchisor to the extent that he may cease to be or never become truly independent in terms of his ability to make decisions, and the franchisee may thus inadvertently, in effect, become a disguised employee.

In summary, the following are generally accepted as being the disadvantages of franchising for franchisees.

- In reality, they may not be entirely independent, instead being somewhere between employed and self-employed.

Advantages and Disadvantages

- They may become dependent on the franchisor.
- The franchisor's ownership may change.
- They will be vulnerable to the franchisor's mistakes.
- Their motives will be slightly at odds with those of the franchisor, the franchisee being profit-driven and the franchisor turnover-driven.
- The failure of the franchisor may bring down the franchisee.
- They will be expected to pay continuing franchise fees irrespective of the level of support provided by the franchisor.
- The terms of the franchise are not negotiable.
- There may be no realistic protection against abuse by a franchisor.
- Their freedom to sell is restricted by conditions requiring, amongst other things, the approval of their franchisor.
- The franchisor or its systems may not meet the franchisee's expectations.
- Their freedom of action after the franchise agreement has been terminated will be restricted by the imposition of non-competition and restraint of trade covenants.
- The type of business chosen or the fact of being a businessman may turn out not to be the franchisee's cup of tea.

Advantages to the Consumer

In theory the consumer should benefit from a franchised business because the consumer will be dealing with an owner and not merely an employee. Franchised businesses tend to offer a much higher level of personal service when compared with managed outlets.

Because of standardisation and uniformity throughout the franchised network a consumer can rightly expect the same standard of goods or services in different parts of the country from members of the same franchised network.

A consumer may take some comfort in the knowledge that should one franchised outlet close, there is a very good chance that other franchised outlets will service that customer's requirements with regard to after-sales service, exchange of goods etc. A consumer who deals with a small, independent business would not have this comfort should the small business close.

Disadvantages to the Consumer

A highly successful franchise could mean the elimination of competition and choice for the consumer as more efficient franchised units drive competition out of an area or out of business altogether.

Where franchisors have granted exclusive territories, a consumer's choice will be limited if he is dissatisfied with the service and/or product he obtains from a particular franchised outlet, or with the way in which the franchisee has dealt with him, as there will be no alternative outlet in his area to which he can go.

In Conclusion

In the final analysis most people will agree that a well-structured and well-run franchised operation can benefit all concerned, even the competition; witness the state of the fast food industry before the arrival of McDonald's.

CHAPTER 3

Franchise Statistics: The Hype and the Reality

> *" So much for statistics. A statistician is a person who deals with numbers and charts but who does not have the personality of an accountant. "*
>
> Anon

In any business activity, the past helps us to better understand the present and to predict the future, and franchising is no different in this respect. In an illuminating paper published as far back as 1997, Professor John Stanworth, David Purdy and Stuart Price compared franchise growth and failure rates in the United States with the United Kingdom and questioned the reality behind the rhetoric surrounding the success of franchising generally (Stanworth, Purdy and Price, 1997).

There has been, with the odd exception (the BFA/NatWest surveys), little by way of research into success and failure rates of business format franchising in the UK. This contrasts with the US, where both federal law and, in many of the states, local law requires franchisors to register their franchises. This enables us to determine more accurately the number of franchisors in existence at any given point in time and to make a comparison with previous years, and thus to make an accurate assessment of growth over the years.

The Stanworth survey serves to highlight a crucial aspect of business format franchising as it relates to the growth of companies.

Those involved in franchising tend to promote, quite liberally, the notion that 'franchises are five times more likely to succeed than other business start-ups' or 'franchisees are five times more likely to succeed than independent start-ups'. These sweeping statements need to be treated with caution.

For a start, a distinction needs to be made between a franchise system failure and franchisee failure. Account also has to be taken of the size of a particular franchisor, with emerging and smaller franchise systems being more prone to failure, thereby rendering franchisor failure rates higher than franchisee failure rates. It is not enough simply to take at face value the dictum that franchising is a good method by which businesses can grow rapidly. It is probably more true to say that business format franchising offers the possibility for a small or medium-sized business to grow into a big business fairly rapidly.

What distinguishes the Stanworth survey from other surveys is that, for the first time, the survey concentrated on survival rates for franchisors. It concluded that only 50% of franchisors survived their fourth year, with overwhelming evidence suggesting that only between 25% and 33% of franchisors survived long enough to celebrate their tenth anniversary. According to the survey, the critical period for franchisors appeared to be during the first four or five years.

The researchers pointed out that:

> *For a small business intent on developing into a credible franchise operation, the strains normally associated with small business growth may well, in fact, be magnified and concentrated, rather than reduced.* (Stanworth, Purdy and Price, 1997)

Although this survey was published in 1997, there is no evidence that the prognosis it suggests would be any better today. In fact, arguably, given the increased competition franchisors face today, the prognosis is likely to be worse.

There are success stories. After all, that is how Kemmons Wilson grew the Holiday Inn chain. The Holiday Inn story is an interesting one. Kemmons Wilson, who was born in December 1912, dreamt up the idea in 1942 when motoring in the United States with his family. He realised that there was no hotel accommodation which catered for families, where children were welcome and which were clean, safe and comfortable. He took the name from the Hollywood film *Holiday Inn*, starring Bing Crosby and Fred Astaire, which contained Bing Crosby's big hit, 'White Christmas', by Irving Berlin. By 1998, although Wilson, then in his eighties, still owned seven Holiday Inns in Memphis, Tennessee, the network had 3,041 hotels with more than half a million rooms in more than 60 countries. Over a period of some 50 years from its inception, this averages out at a growth rate of about 60 hotels a year: something which any company would have found impossible to achieve by means of organic growth. Significantly, 95% of all hotels were franchised.

The company was bought by Bass Plc in 1988. In the financial year ending 30th September 1997, Holiday Hospitality (as it was then known) contributed an operating profit in continuing business of £150 million towards Bass's overall £796 million operating profit. Today the brand is owned by InterContinental Hotels Group. In the case of Holiday Inn, business format franchising certainly helped a small motel business become a big international business relatively quickly.

However, it does not necessarily follow that business format franchising helps *big* business to grow even bigger. There are a number of big businesses that have turned to franchising as a means of expanding the number of retail outlets operating under their brand but have subsequently withdrawn or had second thoughts. These include Holland & Barrett, Sketchley, Dollond & Aitchison and Kalamazoo, to mention just a few.

The reasons for withdrawal, having second thoughts or returning to franchising after having withdrawn are as varied as there are companies. The point to recognise is that business format franchising works for some but not for all. McDonald's is a large company and continues to grow bigger through franchising (albeit internationally), and there are other companies that, although big already, continue to expand successfully through franchising, such as PepsiCo with its chains of Pizza Hut and KFC. Nevertheless they all started as relatively small businesses and succeeded through franchising.

For the first time a debate is now emerging and people are beginning to concentrate on the distinction between the hype and the reality. A good starting point is to look at franchising's track record so far.

For example, the British Franchise Association released the following statement in 1990:

> *Rapidly changing business conditions and the dissolution of EC trade barriers by January 1993 will have a marked effect on planning of UK franchisors. Last year's estimates of £11 billion (turnover) by 1994 has now increased to £12.5 billion by 1995.*

A few months later, in 1991, the annual BFA/NatWest franchise report claimed:

> *Existing franchisors have bold plans for the future. They claim, on average, that they expect to increase to 53 units one year from now (from 43 currently) and to double this number by 1996 ... If these franchisors develop just half the*

number of units they plan, and even if average annual unit turnover grows only to £300,000 (representing an annual growth rate of less than 3%), then in 5 years' time the business format franchising industry will be worth £10.3 billion.

In fact, turnover in 1990 was £5.2 billion and in 1994 was £5.5 billion, a shortfall of 50% on the original estimate of £11 billion. If the 1996 figures are to be believed, turnover in the UK franchise industry in 1996 was around the £6 billion mark (below the £5.25 billion in 1990 if one adjusts it for inflation). This is particularly significant given that 1995/96 saw large-scale conversions by dairies of employed milk rounds men into franchisees.

The more recent franchise statistics from the 2015 annual BFA/NatWest Survey reveal the following, leaving the reader to form his own view as to the future of franchising and whether the reality matches the hype.

The BFA/NatWest Franchise Survey of 2015 shows a steady rise in the number of:

Franchise systems

1988: 244

1998: 568

2008: 809

2015: 901

Franchised outlets per franchisor

1993: 24.9

2003: 33.8

2013: 39

2015: 44.2

Full-time employees in UK franchising

2001: 191,000

2015: 621,000

Franchise Statistics: The Hype and the Reality

The survey places the franchise 'industry's' turnover in 2015 in excess of £15 billion.

Before deciding to go ahead with business format franchising, companies do need to do a comparative analysis of financial projections to see whether it is going to be worth it at the end of the day. For many, it clearly is, because if company operations are more profitable than franchised outlets to a franchisor, why does anyone franchise?

It has to be understood that franchising will *not* solve cash flow problems, turn losses into profits, make up for poor management, beat a recession, buck market trends or resolve problems of undercapitalisation. It *may*, however, help a company to grow more quickly than it might via traditional methods, improve brand recognition, enable faster market penetration, optimise benefits to be derived from enjoying a market lead, eventually increase sales and profitability, and give those involved more headaches, thrills, spills and satisfaction than any other legitimate form of business activity.

However, in a paper entitled 'Assessing the Option' presented at a conference on 'How to Franchise Your Business', Brian Smith warned that franchising could be seen as:

> *A programme for growth, necessitating a cultural fit within the requisite value system, assessed in a limited time frame through a contracting window of opportunity where the downside risk is kept low by a process of loose/tight control on the assumption that critical mass can be reached before the balloon goes up.* (Smith, n.d.)

For those trying to cut through the hype, the mountain of research based on narrow sample bands and the publicity surrounding business format franchising as a method of conducting business (which has a tendency to treat it as a magic formula for success), the publication on the subject by Stuart Price of KPMG entitled 'The Franchise Paradox – New Directions, Different Strategies' is worth reading. Price refers to 'the schizophrenia of franchising':

> *Almost Jekyll and Hyde-like, these are two faces of franchising. The one offering the promise of personal and financial success through a mutually beneficial partnership between franchisor and franchisee and the other, which seeks to show franchisees as victims of outrageous claims, spurious success stories and myths*

and self-deluding images of self-employment made by sometime fraudulent franchisors. (Price, 1997)

Franchise watchers and researchers tend to disagree amongst themselves on a number of points. For example, one group of researchers finds that those franchisors with shorter periods of pre-franchising experience are more likely to withdraw, whereas another group disagrees with this observation and finds instead that young and old businesses are equally prone to withdraw.

Price subscribes to the former view, considering franchisor failure to be high within young businesses:

The regularity of such failures outweigh[s] that of large failures ... and cannot simply be brushed aside by the franchise fraternity, who generally consider the notion of franchisor failure an oxymoron or an anathema. (Price, 1997)

One is often told that more than 70% of franchises succeed. In 1984 the British Franchise Association had 86 members. In 1994 only 28 of the 86 were still members. What happened to 67% of the British Franchise Association membership? For whatever reason, this 67% included Kalamazoo, FastFrame, Holland & Barrett, Sketchley Cleaning, Entre Computers, Cookie Coach Company, Exchange Travel, Ziebart, Curtain Dream, PIP Printing, Marley Paving, Identicar, West Coast Video and Postal Centres. Burger King used to be a member but ceased to be one some years ago. There are others who have not renewed their membership – one wonders why.

The franchise sector can be likened to a large pond, the size of which is growing slowly: a pond which is being constantly fed at one end by new members and which is constantly drained at the other end.

There is a common misconception that franchising is an industry, and it is loosely talked of in the same way in which one may talk of the hotel industry, the steel industry and so on. Nothing could be further from the truth. Researchers will continue to be at odds and those whose interests lie in promoting franchising will continue to talk it up with relative impunity because the very nature of the animal is such that it is not possible to compare like with like.

The franchising sector consists of a wide range of business activities, as diverse as frying chicken, printing, cleaning drains and giving financial advice. Franchisors come in all shapes and sizes, from different backgrounds and with varying degrees of business acumen. They trade in different wares and operate in different marketplaces. Some, such as the Body Shop, have been enormously successful, both for themselves and for their franchisees, whereas others have been less so. What is important is that those thinking of embarking upon franchising as a means of growing their business should do so with their eyes open, having considered all options and taken competent advice. It may not be for them, or it may work better for them than it has done or might do for their competitor.

As one franchisor client remarked to me at the time of withdrawing from franchising:

> Well, despite the outcome I am glad we gave it a shot. We thought we had a good chance at succeeding but at the end of the day we did not. However, we are pleased that we tried, otherwise we would have forever regretted not knowing what might have been the outcome.

- The application of sound management principles should serve to ensure that losses are contained when errors of judgment have been made.

Business format franchising is not a cure for mismanagement; it seldom serves to rescue a company from, and in all probability will accelerate, its failure. Apart from the formula and the proven system, the quality of management is crucial to the success or failure of any franchise. Mediocre franchises have succeeded through the sheer force of personality and management ability of the franchisor. Conversely, franchise systems which looked sure to succeed on paper have come spectacularly unstuck due to bad management. Franchising, after all, is about management. It is about managing systems, managing problems and, above all, managing people.

CHAPTER 4

Can a Service Business Be Franchised?

"Franchising is not the exclusive preserve of the product retailer."

When franchising is mentioned, most people think of fast food. This is because in the sixties franchising was dominated by fast food outlets and also because most of them introduced new concepts even though their products were already known. McDonald's, of course, springs to mind, as does KFC (formerly known as Kentucky Fried Chicken) and the pizza parlours. It was not only that the concepts were new; they also had something else in common in that they were product-based.

Since then people have tended to associate franchising with the sale of products. Until recently it was difficult to convince people that business format franchising involved more than just selling products and that it was also perfectly feasible to sell services through the medium of franchising.

With the success of business format franchising as a method of marketing, it is now obvious to all that this method is just as capable of delivering a quality service to end users as it is of delivering a quality product. Indeed, it can be argued that when it comes to delivering a service, franchising is the best method by which consistency and quality can be maintained.

Service providers have always presumed that because a very high element of personal involvement between the service provider and the service user is essential, the provision of services cannot be successfully delegated. Whilst on the face of it this may appear to be true, closer examination reveals that what makes most service businesses successful is the *modus operandi* of the service provider, not the identity of the person providing the service.

There are plenty of chains of service businesses from tyre and exhaust replacement services to carpet cleaning, operating a large number of outlets across the country and successfully delivering a high level of service to end users through the medium of employees. The originator of the concept does not deliver those services personally. The key, of course, is training. Show an employee exactly how to provide a service and he should be able to go out and do exactly what the founder of the business has been doing. Soon the founder of a successful business realises that, although he has the means of delivering the same service to the same high standards in different locations through well-motivated and trained employees, growth is restricted because of lack of capital. It takes capital to open new branches, service centres etc., and one way to overcome the obstacle is to franchise.

So far, so good. However, what about exporting a business system even if one doesn't franchise domestically?

In the eighties, a number of foreign companies, mainly Australian and North American, entered the market through franchising. Both in Australia and in North America the service industry has been highly thought of, and companies such as ServiceMaster and Molly Maid have done a great deal to raise service standards in the UK.

Until the advent of business format franchising, most people in the service sector turned their backs on export, assuming, erroneously, that one could only export products.

Many companies are reluctant to employ foreign labour, engage in foreign legal and trade practices and run the risk associated with trading overseas – particularly in the case of services, which involve a great deal more than filling containers with products and shipping them abroad. However, if one can operate a successful service business in the UK there is no reason why one cannot franchise a service business overseas. Instead of granting the rights to supply services under one's brand to someone in Manchester, one can give similar rights to a German to do the same thing in Munich. One has to be willing to make adjustments to the business method and the system to accommodate local law, language, customs and trade practices, but the principle is essentially the same. Suddenly through the medium of franchising the possibility of exporting is open to all service providers, from dry cleaners to hairdressers and from those in the hospitality business to carpet cleaners.

Who would have thought that it was possible to export educational services? Yet it has been done with significant success by Stagecoach Theatre Arts, whose core business focuses on providing extracurricular education in the performing arts to 4–18-year-olds. This has been replicated internationally in 10 countries through franchising.

Service providers, even if they do not franchise their businesses in the UK, should consider business format franchising as a means of expanding their business overseas. It could pay dividends.

... and finally ...

The April/May 1985 issue of *Franchise Review* (a US publication) reported:

> *Four men in the US have formed a company to franchise brothels. Chuck Prince, who has a degree from the University of Colorado, Scott Kennedy, a Newport public relations man, and two others have formed Paradise Brothels Ltd and are planning to start franchising. Prince has an expertise in legal prostitution that derives, he says, from two years he spent in a small town in Nevada with a population of 20. He was asked to oversee the rejuvenation of the local garage, casino, bar, restaurant and brothel and he turned what were square, white boxes into what now looks like a Western town. Prince and his partners want to set up similar legal brothels elsewhere. So far the partners have spent around $30,000 on researching state laws governing prostitution and to produce brochures and promotional material. They studied the franchising systems and training manuals of McDonald's and Century 21 among others. 'We are aiming to be the Century 21 of sex,'* [they said,] *with no noticeable tongue in cheek.*

CHAPTER 5

Is Franchising Right for Your Company?

*""Tis not enough to help the feeble up,
But to support him after."*

William Shakespeare, *Timon of Athens*

Considerations for the Prospective Franchisor

Franchising has been lauded as a tried and tested way of growing one's business by using the entrepreneurial skills and capital of others, without incurring debt or interest charges. It has also sometimes misguidedly been promoted as a panacea for ailing businesses. If a company is to succeed as a franchisor, it needs to start from a sound commercial and financial footing.

So what matters should an aspiring franchisor consider?

Competition

A prospective franchisor should investigate who is likely to be competing with it for franchisees. This means researching to see not only who is franchising similar businesses to one's own, but also what other franchises are available for sale at the sort of price one is proposing to charge for one's franchise. Not all prospective franchisees are wedded to the idea of only selling goods or services of the type being provided by a particular franchisor. Many are concerned with starting their own business and approach franchising with an open mind, but with a good idea of what they can afford. They will therefore be looking at franchises within their price range.

A good understanding of the competition is essential if a franchisor is to convince prospective franchisees that it is able to assist its franchisees in beating the competition.

Where the franchise concept is novel, a prospective franchisor should take into consideration the threat from potential competitors which will surely follow *after* the launch of its franchise.

Franchisee Selection

Prospective franchisors need to ask themselves why a prospective franchisee would wish to buy their particular franchise. Franchisees are attracted to franchising for a variety of reasons, principal amongst which are generally one or more of the following:

- The concept itself is appealing.
- Franchising is seen as a relatively safe route to self-employment.
- The business offers the prospects of good financial returns.
- The idea of 'Be Your Own Boss' is appealing.

A prospective franchisor must have a very good idea of what it is looking for in a franchisee. It will need to establish and stick to its criteria for those whom it considers to be suited to operate its franchise; it should not lower its standards in a moment of weakness. (See Chapter 19.)

The Future

A franchisor should ask what it will need to be doing tomorrow that will make its franchisees want to renew their franchise agreements when they expire. Franchising is a long-term proposition and franchisors need to look to the future if their franchise network is to grow and prosper.

Two Businesses

A franchisor has two businesses. The first consists of supplying goods or services to its customers via its company-owned branches. The second is that of franchising. It must not forget that its franchisees are also its customers and that its obligations as franchisor to its franchisees will be different from and a good deal more onerous than those owed to its customers. It should also be aware that the customers of its franchisees will also be the customers of the franchisor, albeit indirectly.

Management Skills

A prospective franchisor cannot be a 'mum and pop' operation. A franchisor must be able to show that it has a strong management team, capable of delivering the required training, support and maintenance services to all franchisees. A prospective franchisor will need to improve its management skills and those of its staff. The big challenge a franchisor's employed staff will face is managing franchisees who are not employees but independent business owners in their own right. Treating them as managers of a branch business will not bring the best out in franchisees and will lead to confrontation (see Chapter 29 for guidance on resolving disputes). The BFA/NatWest Franchise Survey 2015 shows that 91% of those franchisees interviewed were 'mainly' or 'definitely' satisfied.

Support

One of the key obligations of a franchisor is to support its franchisees to the extent that is necessary to sustain them in their businesses. It must seek to gain a reputation for doing what it promises and, more often than not, more than what it promised. A franchisor should never fail to deliver on a promise – franchisees have long memories.

Exclusive Territories

If granting exclusive territories, franchisors need to ensure that the necessary protocols and mechanisms have been established for dealing with turf wars which can break out amongst franchisees.

Performance Targets

If minimum performance targets are to be imposed, a franchisor must be prepared to justify their imposition and the basis upon which they are calculated. Such targets should be reasonably achievable and a franchisor should be prepared to impose such appropriate sanctions as they may have provided for in their franchise agreements in the event that they are not achieved, otherwise a franchisor will lose credibility and have problems in enforcing targets when others fail to achieve them. (See Chapter 21 for more on minimum performance targets.)

Standards

Franchisors should not tolerate substandard franchisees – they affect the whole network and certainly their neighbouring franchisees. Failure by a franchisee to comply with his franchisor's system is a mortal sin. The key to a franchisor's success and that of its franchisees is uniformity: uniformity of business practices, uniformity of marketing image, uniformity of quality, and uniformity of the manner in which products and services are delivered to customers.

Bad May Be Good

It does not necessarily follow that the most demanding franchisees are also bad franchisees. It is often the most demanding franchisees who are also the best in a network. This may be a coincidence or it may be that it is precisely because they are demanding of themselves that they are demanding of their franchisor. Better to have a very demanding franchisee who is firing on all cylinders and growing his business like Topsy than to have a quiet, compliant franchisee who merely chugs along with a tendency to use his franchisor as a crutch.

Feasibility

The object of conducting a feasibility study is to ascertain whether the basic business concept is capable of being franchised and to identify changes which might be required to develop it to its fullest potential. It is quite common for this task to be undertaken by specialist franchise consultants.

Developing the Concept

If the feasibility study indicates that the basic concept is sound and capable of being franchised, the concept will then have to be refined and developed specifically for franchising. This may be an onerous task depending on the nature of the existing business and whether it fits the technical criteria for franchising. If it does, then adapting the business concept can be very straightforward. If not, a prospective franchisor's concept may have to undergo a major revision to make it fit the technical criteria and this will in all probability require additional market research.

Is Franchising Right for Your Company?

The following can be said to be within the scope of any technical criteria:

- How easy the business is to replicate.
- Quality and structure of present management.
- Range of products/services.
- Technology involved.
- Selling the franchise.
- Importance of locations.
- Creation and protection of the brand.

Striking the Right Balance

If a business is not capable of being replicated relatively easily, it is unlikely to succeed as a franchise. However, franchisors have to strike the right balance. Make it too complicated and the franchisor will fail to transfer the know-how to enable a franchisee to operate the business concept in accordance with the franchisor's blueprint. Make it too easy and it will give rise to numerous copycat operations which will undermine the franchisor's network.

There may be good reasons for the franchisor to restrict the product/service range to be offered by franchisees to its customers. In some cases, complicated elements can be provided to franchisees by the franchisor, thereby eliminating from the franchise package the more complicated aspects of conducting a particular business. For example, the franchisor of an office consumables recycling service may have an arrangement with its franchisees whereby the more complicated technological aspects of recycling are carried out by the franchisor in certain circumstances.

The technology employed in franchised outlets must be appropriate to the size of the market (which is usually local), to the profit potential for the individual franchised outlets and to the operating capability of the franchisee. Any technology employed must be:

- Reliable, so that revenue is not lost because of excessive service and repair time.

- Simple, so that the training is not too costly and a wider range of people can be recruited and trained as franchisees.
- Subject to only occasional updating, particularly if the equipment is expensive.

Financial Commitment

Assuming that the technical criteria for franchising are met or can be achieved, a prospective franchisor must be willing to make the financial commitment. This may be small or significant depending upon the tasks to be undertaken. These may include:

- Creating logos, trade marks, trade names.
- Creating letterhead, stationery and signs.
- Website creation.
- Advertising, marketing and point of sale material.
- Shop fitting and layout/acquisition, decoration and fitting out of vehicle.
- Preparing franchise brochures, application forms and promotional literature.

Some tasks can be undertaken by employees but others will require outsourced specialist input, certainly with regard to drawing up the franchise agreement, protecting the franchisor's intellectual property etc.

A franchisor that relies on its income from the *sale* of franchises is doomed to failure. A prospective franchisor must have sufficient capital to enable it to sustain the programme of franchising until revenues start flowing in the form of continuing franchise fees based on its franchisees' turnover, later on.

At the initial stages, employment costs can usually be held in check by franchisors who, if entrepreneurs, usually carry out most of the functions themselves or, if large companies, will probably start either by designating specific employees to specific tasks or by engaging an additional member of staff who will be responsible for developing the franchise side of the operation. A significant advantage in franchising is that office overheads do not rise directly in line with number of trading units and the franchisor's overheads therefore increase gradually. Thus, the increase in administrative costs will usually be proportionately less than the increase in the number of outlets.

Developing the Package

This can be a costly affair and needs to take into consideration the experience of the pilot operation. Developing the package will include preparing:

- The franchise agreement and other documentation.
- Operational manuals.
- Prospectus.
- Franchisee selection procedures.
- Training and franchise marketing.
- Launch package.

Requirements for a Company to Franchise

Having considered the above points, what are the essentials required of a company wishing to franchise?

The following are some of the essential requirements for a prospective franchisor:

1. *A tried, tested and proven system.* A prospective franchisor must have a blueprint of the method by which a franchisee can deliver goods and/or services to customers as consistently and profitably as the franchisor. The system must have been tested under open market conditions, refined and shown to be capable of being replicated.

2. *A strong brand.* A prospective franchisor must be able to show that there is some market recognition for its brand and that it is able to protect its intellectual property against infringement.

3. *An operations manual.* There must be a comprehensive manual setting out the whole business concept and its method of operation in the finest detail.

4. *Comprehensive training.* A prospective franchisor must train franchisees to the extent necessary to enable each franchisee to operate the business from the franchisee's premises in accordance with the franchisor's system.

5. *A franchise agreement* which underpins the whole enterprise. It sets out the rights and obligations of both parties, seeks to protect the franchisor's intellectual property and governs its relationship with its franchisees.

6. *A proven demand* for the prospective franchisor's goods or services.

7. *Developed site selection criteria.* A prospective franchisor must have a very strong sense of the minimum requirements for a retail outlet to enable its franchisees to trade successfully.

8. *A strong relationship with suppliers.* This is essential if the prospective franchisor is going to undertake obligations to supply goods to its franchisees for resale to customers.

9. *An effective system of reporting and accounting.* A franchisor needs to maintain tight control over its franchised outlets and their performance if it is to ensure that it is receiving all the revenue properly due to it.

10. *Research and development.* This is one of the principal obligations of a prospective franchisor. It must establish research and development capabilities so that it is able to develop and improve its business system, products, etc.

11. *Communication.* There must be clear and effective procedures for communicating with franchisees so that both parties can develop their businesses to the benefit of the network as a whole.

12. *Advertising, marketing and promotions programmes.* A programme for advertising, marketing and promotion of the brand and the network's products and services must be developed and updated to meet the changing circumstances of the market.

Tips for a Prospective Franchisor

Case studies of many successful franchisors over the years have revealed a number of elements which they all have in common. When thinking of franchising, they said they already had in mind the need to ensure that they had sufficient funding to see their project through to completion. However almost every successful franchisor admitted having underestimated both the amount of time and the amount of money it would take. Franchising in its formative stages makes very heavy demands on one's senior management time and money, and those contemplating franchising their business should pay heed to this.

So, what else should a prospective franchisor do?

1. *Establish a sound, successful and profitable business* and operate the same business at another location as a pilot operation, which should be run by someone other than the franchisor's existing employees to prove that someone else can operate it in the same way.

2. *Protect all intellectual property* (trade marks, copyright etc.).

3. *Develop a comprehensive training programme* to teach franchisees 'how to do it'.

4. *Develop an operations manual* which contains everything future franchisees will need to know to operate the business. This will be a source book for training programmes and an ongoing reference book for franchisees when their businesses are up and running. It will need to be constantly updated in the light of experience and any changes in the law.

5. *Prepare a franchise agreement* which not only establishes the ground rules but also contains the necessary mechanisms to deal with foreseeable situations (for example, what should happen if a franchisee wants to sell his business). It should also protect one's know-how, brand and business system.

6. *Develop a strategy for recruiting franchisees.* Devise brochures, application forms and an advertising, marketing and promotions campaign. Consider participation at exhibitions. Develop a website. Establish the criteria by which prospective franchisees will be assessed. Do not relax these criteria in a moment of weakness. Resist the temptation to lower standards when recruiting the first few franchisees or if the growth in your network is not keeping pace with expectations.

7. *Establish a system for supporting franchisees* in their franchised businesses on an ongoing basis. Deliver on promises made. The support function will include a programme of continuing training, advice in resolving problems, and spending time and money on developing and improving the business system, concept and products/services.

8. *Ensure uniformity of business practices* and marketing image. Do not tolerate substandard franchisees; they have a detrimental effect both on the franchisor and on other franchisees.

9. *Never forget that a franchisor's franchisees are its customers.*

10. *Look to the future.* Keep asking what will make one's franchisees want to renew their franchise agreements when they expire. Franchising is a long-term proposition and franchisors who do not look to the future will find that their franchise network will diminish in the longer term.

When one looks at a successful franchisor, it all seems so easy, but the road to success is seldom without pitfalls. The trick is to avoid as many as one can.

Over the years, for many, franchising has proved to be an excellent way of expanding their businesses quickly, and experience has proved it to be particularly well suited for medium-sized businesses.

CHAPTER 6

Setting up a Franchise Operation

"Uniformity is the key."

There are six basic elements involved in setting up a franchise, which break down as follows:

1. The business concept.
2. Proving the system works.
3. Developing the franchise package.
4. Developing the operations manual.
5. Selecting franchisees.
6. Selling franchises.

The Business Concept

The move into franchising can arise in two sets of circumstances. The first is when it is decided to expand an existing business by means of a business format franchise. The second, and much more rare, is when a positive attempt is made to establish a business for franchising from day one.

Establishing a business for franchising from day one is not recommended for a beginner and although an experienced franchisor may be able to proceed in this way, few have succeeded. For example, an experienced and successful dry cleaning franchisor may succeed in launching a shoe repair franchise. The usual course is for the owner of an existing business, which has scope to expand at a more rapid rate than its capital and human resources would permit, to turn to franchising as a means of exploiting that potential to the full.

If one intends to franchise, it is essential to keep the business simple, as others will have to be taught to operate it successfully. The more complex it is, the more difficult it will be to recruit, train and sustain franchisees. The *modus operandi* must be limited to a framework which is manageable by others. It is also important to simplify and systemise the way the business is to be conducted.

Take a fast food operation as an example. The more simple the layout of the kitchen area, the more standardised the décor and layout of the restaurant area, the easier it will be to adapt premises to the required design and the easier it will be to establish each operation.

It is also important to keep the menu simple. This reduces the inventory requirements and makes it possible to keep the preparation, cooking and delivery of the food simple and quick and efficient, thereby obviating the need to rely on any one person (say, a chef) on whom the process is dependent. With a simple and limited menu it should be possible to limit the amount of equipment to be employed and thus reduce the business's requirement for space, initial investment and maintenance.

The overall aim should be to simplify control, reduce paperwork, and make the system as foolproof as possible.

A retail outlet is another example of an operation which the franchisor must try to keep simple. Apart from the design, décor and layout, which are all vital, there is the question of the stock inventory. The more extensive the stock, the more complex will be the task of those who have to deal with it, and the greater the likelihood of financial loss through mismanagement.

A classic example of good stock management can be found in a number of convenience store franchises where each store carries a very large range of stock. In a convenience store franchise, the franchisor keeps rigid control over its franchisees' stock and uses software to produce detailed inventories of the stock two or three times a week. This may be an extreme case, but it does illustrate the degree of care which needs to be taken when developing the business concept, paying attention to, for example, the problems of holding a wide-ranging and extensive stock inventory. It is the result of this initial thinking, coupled with the franchisor's experience and support, which no single independent trader could ever hope to match, particularly in a business which is highly competitive and with low margins.

An aspiring franchisor must be able to clearly identify the market at which it intends to aim its business. There is little point in having a good idea if one is dependent on others in the trade (as in the car dealership trade) who do not see the need to deal with one's business, or who are already operating the type of business in which one wants to engage. Nor is there much point in aiming at a customer who is likely to go to the established trade first. This could arise if one is intending to provide a specialist service which may be part of the total service which existing motor traders or garages provide. Having said that, there is always room for a specialist service, if it proves to be truly 'specialist', competitive and convenient – the success of specialist exhaust or tyre replacement service franchises, like Kwik Fit, is a good example.

The prospective franchisor should consider these questions to determine whether it is aiming at the right market:

1. Finance: will it be able to attract franchisees with sufficient funds? If not, will they be able to acquire the required funds?
2. Staff skills: will it be able to attract staff with adequate skills? If not, can such skills be easily taught?
3. Premises: how readily can suitable premises be found at the right price?
4. Consumer demand: is there, or will there be, sufficient market demand for its products/services?

The business must be distinctive in its image. Each successful franchise business has its own innovative concept, which sets it apart from other businesses of the same type. This is what makes people choose to patronise that business as well as, or instead of, others in the same category. The existence of competitors can often be very healthy. It can help to develop the overall market and act as a stimulant to franchisor and franchisee alike.

To protect the distinctiveness of a business image (brand) it is best, if at all possible, to structure it around a trade mark registration. In selecting a trade mark or trade name there are some basic approaches which experience and market research have shown to be successful.

- The trade name should be easy to pronounce and compact; it should roll easily off the tongue. 'Lickety Split' as a name for an ice cream franchise would be an example (though a catering business by that name already exists!).

- The name should take international markets into account. What sounds good in one language may be offensive or counter-productive in another. Some examples of names that run into trouble in English-speaking countries include *Muecas* (a Spanish children's clothes shop), *Slag* (Dutch lager), *Skum* (Swedish confectionery), *Rasch* (Chilean dishwasher powder), *Basterd* (Dutch sugar) and *Puke* (Turkish playing cards).
- The trade mark should be original, rather than being an existing word or phrase, which will make an application for its registration as a trade mark likely to succeed – as in *Kodak*.

A franchisee's business will not only have to provide sufficient profit to give him an acceptable return on his capital and a reasonable salary, but must also provide sufficient profit to enable him to pay his franchisor any levy for advertising, marketing and promotion of the brand and a continuing franchise fee for the support and services which his franchisor will have agreed to provide. Unless the business can generate sufficient profit for these purposes, a prospective franchisor will have to think again. It is essential to have a successful business before starting to franchise.

To give itself the maximum chance of success, the prospective franchisor will need:

- Good timing for introducing the concept to the market
- Available franchisees with cash or access to cash (the banks must be in a mood to lend)
- A climate of confidence in the scheme

Proving the System Works

Having established the business with a distinctive name and image, the next step is to prove that the business system works. This is best done by means of a pilot operation (see Chapter 8). It is essential that at least one pilot operation is established, if not more.

It has been suggested that a pilot operation is not always possible or necessary and that the franchisor can overcome the lack of a proven business system by giving the franchisee a money-back guarantee in the event of failure. This is a dangerous practice and one which negates one of the fundamental principles of business format franchising. Fundamentally and essentially the franchisor is selling a sophisticated package of know-how. If it has not proved the ability to operate that package with success by putting its own money at risk, it should not be selling franchises and prospective franchisees are unlikely to buy its franchises. Nor, indeed, will it have established the goodwill and reputation of the brand which is associated with that package.

It is irresponsible to seek to establish a franchise by trial and error at the expense of initial franchisees. This was also the path chosen in the past by those who perpetrated fraud on the unsuspecting. A guarantee of money back is no substitute for the loss of a business. In any case, how, with an untried and untested concept, does one ensure that the franchisor will be there with adequate money to honour its guarantee and to pay back those who claim? Even if the franchisor and the money are there, there will inevitably be disputes about whether the failure was due to the franchisor's concept/system or to the franchisee's failure to comply with the franchisor's system.

The enormous responsibility borne by a franchisor to its franchisees cannot be emphasised too greatly. These franchisees will be invited to part with their life savings, change their whole way of life and become, to a great extent, dependent on their franchisor and its concept for their future welfare and that of their families.

Developing the Franchise Package

The experience obtained in setting up and running a pilot operation will provide the base on which the various elements of the package are structured. The package should bring together the accumulation of a prospective franchisor's total experience in a readily transmittable form.

At this stage it might be appropriate for a prospective franchisor to consider employing the services of a consultant.

Consultants need to be chosen with great care. There are some established and reputable consultants who offer sound franchise consultancy services. However, there are also any number of 'franchise consultants' whose quality of work is questionable. The difficulty with which one is faced is that there is no formal professional qualification to be a franchise consultant; anyone can set himself up as a franchise consultant. So the best approach is to follow a personal recommendation and to take up references. Prospective franchisors are advised to look for someone who offers practical experience in franchising in return for a fee.

In deciding whether or not to engage the services of a particular franchise consultant, the following 10 considerations at the very least (there are more) should be borne in mind.

1. What is that consultant's specific experience in the field of business format franchising? Is it general, or is it limited to a certain aspect (such as writing an operations manual?).
2. Does the consultant, in particular, have experience in the area in which advice is required?
3. Can the consultant provide references?
4. Can arrangements be made to speak to the consultant's existing and past clients of one's choosing?
5. Has the consultant worked in a franchise company (other than as a consultant) at a senior decision-making level? If so, what was his job?
6, If the consultant offers his services as a salesman of franchises, will he agree that the final decision of whether or not to accept a particular candidate will be exclusively that of the franchisor?
7. How much will the consultant's services cost?
8. Will the consultant work with the prospective franchisor to establish his terms of reference? Do not make any arrangements unless the scope and nature of the services to be provided are clearly defined.
9. Does he belong to any nationally recognised professional body which requires him to comply with a strict code of ethics?

This is not intended to be a complete list of questions but is a guide to the sort of enquiries one should pursue to ascertain the experience of the consultant and what those who have dealt with him have to say.

Locating an Outlet

A prospective franchisor may need to establish the criteria by which potential sites for franchised outlets can be judged. Some franchise operations depend upon advertising to attract customers whereas others depend on a specific type of location to drag in business, such as:

- Primary (high street).
- Secondary (around the corner from a high street).
- Tertiary (where a location is not important because the nature of the business is such that the customer will seek it out).
- Business park.
- Retail park.
- Residential area.
- Industrial estate.

Retail and fast food franchises are typically on primary sites while service-orientated concepts such as drain cleaning, carpet cleaning, etc. are on industrial sites.

Experience with pilot operations will indicate when demand for the products/services is likely to arise: what times of the day or week are likely to produce peaks and troughs in customer demand.

The following considerations should be taken into account when assessing the degree of business activity a particular site may be capable of generating. The requirements will differ in some cases.

1. The type of street.
    - If there is a dual carriageway, is there a central barrier?
    - Is it a local road or a main road?
    - Is car parking available?
    - Is a traffic hazard inherent at the site?

Setting up a Franchise Operation

- Bear in mind that motorway service areas are very expensive and supplies to them are very restricted.
- Do not be misled by the existence of a pedestrian crossing at or near the site. These crossings take people away as well as bringing them towards the premises. If a crossing leads to a town centre or shopping area it could place the premises just out of the main flow of pedestrian traffic.

2. The surrounding area. This is an increasingly important factor in assessing the suitability of a site for the type of business being contemplated.

3. Foot and/or road traffic volume. Do not be misled by the volume of traffic. For example, road traffic may not stop if it is travelling too quickly or if there is too much congestion or risk of congestion. Similarly, foot traffic can be quite large but uninterested for any number of reasons. For example, at a railway terminus, the many passengers in a great hurry to get to work in the morning and to catch a train home in the evening will only stop for a quick purchase. However, such a site may be suitable for a convenience store operation.

4. The extent to which the premises are exposed may be important for some franchise operations, particularly those which rely on customers' impulse purchases: chocolates, flowers etc. However, the better the exposure of the brand to the public, the greater the prospects for business.

5. Landmarks and the business they generate.
    - Museums.
    - Schools.
    - Cinemas.
    - Theatres.
    - Cafés.
    - National brands in a high street.
    - Office blocks.
    - Sports facilities (which may provide business at the weekend and in the evenings).

Setting up a Franchise Operation

- Travel facilities (railway or underground stations, bus stops, car parks).
- Tourist attractions.

Having decided that a particular location is acceptable by the general criteria, one also has to assess the premises for their suitability for the purposes of a particular business. This would be the case, of course, regardless of whether that business is a franchise. Matters to be considered include:

1. The size of the premises, and whether one can fit into them all the necessary fixtures and equipment while providing sufficient selling space.
2. The suitability of the premises for conversion into whatever end product one is aiming at. This must take into account any ventilation, sanitation and safety requirements.
3. The availability or otherwise of the necessary utility services at the premises.
4. The amount of rent and other expenses.
5. The terms and conditions on which a lease will be granted.
6. The cost, assessed by drawing on the experience gained in running a pilot operation, of:
    - Obtaining necessary planning permission.
    - Complying with building laws, fire regulations etc.
    - Complying with any other statutory or local authority requirements.
    - Obtaining landlord's consent.

The experience obtained in running the pilot operation will enable a prospective franchisor to prepare a standardised package which can be amended to fit the requirements of a particular site. The basic requirements in terms of fixtures, fittings and equipment will need to be determined, as will the correct layout. The franchisor should set up arrangements (with shop fitters etc.) to fulfil these requirements. The franchisor will also have to be able to give advice on the décor of the premises to ensure it reflects the established brand image.

It should also be possible, with the information available to the franchisor, to streamline the preparation of any necessary applications for landlord, planning and bylaw consent and to anticipate the problems which may have to be faced.

Developing the Operations Manual

A franchisor must prepare operations manuals which will provide a franchisee with all the information he will require for operation of the franchised business. Any such manual will invariably be used in training and then as a source of reference while the franchisee is running his business. It should be readily available to him at all times so that he can obtain guidance or refresh his memory on any particular aspect of the business.

The manual is an essential part of the process whereby the franchisor transfers to the franchisee its know-how relating to both initial and ongoing operation of the business. Most manuals contain very detailed guidance on the tasks to be performed by each member of the franchisee's staff. For more on the operations manual, see Chapter 10.

Selecting Franchisees

See Chapter 19.

Selling Franchises

See Chapter 18.

Further Considerations When Setting Up a Franchise

A franchisor may make arrangements with suppliers to sell to its franchisees, at competitive prices, basic material or goods in which the franchise business deals. These arrangements may also extend to suppliers of any packaging, bags, boxes or other materials to be used at the point of sale. This material will usually bear the franchisor's trade mark or trade name. Arrangements will have to be made with equipment suppliers to ensure that proper supplies are available to meet the demand of franchisees.

Systems of work will have to be put into clear and concise narrative; job descriptions will have to be prepared explaining all the facets of each employee's activities so as to fit in with the overall scheme.

Promotional literature (in soft and hard copy) including point of sale material will have to be prepared, as will any common form literature and marketing material.

A prospective franchisor will have to set up training schedules and training facilities for franchisees and their staff where appropriate. It will have to prepare accounting procedures and business systems which are to be operated by the franchisees. Franchisees will need to be trained in these systems and methods for two purposes:

1. To ensure that the franchisee has the information to enable him to see whether his operation is going well and, if not, where it is going wrong.

2. To provide the franchisor with the information required for carrying out its troubleshooting, support and follow-up service to its franchisees. It will also provide the franchisor with information which it will need to have readily available for the purposes of selling franchises.

A franchisor should develop its fund of knowledge and skills to enable it to give advice to its franchisees in connection with contracts into which the franchisee may have to enter: contracts regarding the leasing of premises or equipment, contracts with suppliers and those who provide maintenance services etc.

A franchisor may also need to make arrangements with sources of finance so that assistance can be given to franchisees who require loans for acquiring equipment, fitting out the premises and carrying out other necessary work before the franchisee starts trading.

A prospective franchisor should consult its solicitors early about its proposal to franchise, and to discuss the proposed franchise agreement and any other necessary documents (such as deposit and non-disclosure agreements). A franchise agreement is a very complex document dealing with a range of legal topics: commerce, intellectual property, employment, real estate, health and safety etc. The agreement should reflect the franchisor's business practice, methods and systems and should ensure that what is proposed in structuring the package can be achieved in legal terms. In any event, before the franchise package can be sold the form of agreement must be finalised.

It is wise to take advice about trade marks, trade names, copyright and trade secrets at the earliest possible time, probably before establishing the pilot operation. Solicitors should be able to give the necessary advice and a prospective franchisor may also consult a trade mark agent. At the same time advice should be taken to ensure that whatever intellectual property rights are being developed, nothing is done to put them at risk.

All these aspects are brought together into what is commonly referred to as the franchise package, containing all the diverse elements which are necessary to establish a prospective franchisee in his business.

CHAPTER 7

Developing the Concept and Organisation

"The foundations of a successful franchise operation are laid here."

Preparing for the Franchise Launch

As in any business, it is sensible to expand one's organisation gradually as the business develops. It would not be financially sensible to take on too many additional people initially when there are as yet no franchisees. On the other hand, it is essential that all the franchisees (especially the first few) are fully supported, and therefore a franchisor must have properly trained staff available to deal with this requirement and not leave their hiring until too late. So the franchisor will need the timing and judgement to ensure that it has sufficient staff resources to cover the demands of franchising.

The requirements of franchising need to be carefully analysed as it will impose financial demands. There are definitely going to be expenses incurred in establishing and running the new franchising activity before there is any income. Franchising activity will almost certainly produce a net loss in the first couple of years. There will be unavoidable expenses of trade mark registration, production of marketing material, staff salaries, office expenditure, travel, professional advice etc. while the franchisees become established and the continuing franchise fees (usually based on the turnover or profits on the supply of goods) begin to flow to the franchisor.

It is not a solution to charge unrealistically high initial franchise fees. This practice has led to abuse in the past and has damaged the good name of franchising. See Chapter 13 for a more detailed look at how much to charge.

Each franchisee should represent a secure and growing source of income to the franchisor, provided the franchise is a viable system and is kept that way by the sensible management of the franchisor. Furthermore, successful existing franchisees will provide a source of additional expansion for the franchise as they seek to reinvest their profits by opening further units or expanding their territories. It is not uncommon, particularly in the fast food industry, to find existing franchisees open as many as 50% of all new units. Existing franchisees will also provide good leads for other prospective franchisees. Existing franchisees are often the best advertisement and the best salesmen for the franchise. This is the second most popular recruitment channel, visiting a prospective franchisor's website being the most popular.

The long-term nature of a franchise relationship and the revenue it generates is a major advantage over a normal sales operation which needs a large sales force and heavy continuous advertising.

The franchisor will certainly need a few good people who are competent, flexible and hard-working, and who possess the necessary communication skills to deal with franchisees. This is not lightly said, since the franchisees will generally be working long hours, possibly seven days a week, and, having invested their life savings in their franchisor's idea, will expect to be able to talk to the franchisor whenever they feel the need. Managing a franchise network involves a great deal of personal time and effort.

The functions most prospective franchisors need to cover at the outset are:

- Finance (accounting).
- Compliance (legal).
- Marketing (franchise sales and operations).

A new franchisor should be able to cover the finance/accounting function with its existing staff who will already be looking after its own company operations. They must be able to develop a simple bookkeeping system for the franchisee and give advice on this. Regular returns and accounts will be required from the franchisee and it is vital that franchisees understand exactly what is required of them in this respect from the outset. These finance/accounting functions will be important in helping the franchisor to enforce compliance and in evaluating the information being received.

The existing finance and administration staff should also provide guidance to franchisees on matters such as the payment of wages, employment regulations, VAT returns, and the need to retain and raise the necessary finance. These requirements mean that the franchisor's accounting staff will need to be flexible and, above all, interested in the business.

Developing the Concept and Organisation

In time, it may be necessary to have additional accounting staff for the franchise side of the business, but certainly not initially. Indeed there is much to be gained by using existing staff. They will be able to advise from a basis of their knowledge and experience, and doubtless their own understanding of the company's business will deepen in the process.

Discussions with the professional advisors of the franchisees – accountants, solicitors, bankers etc. – should be handled by a senior accountant who should preferably be formally qualified.

Some franchise companies develop in-house computer systems and provide an accounting service to franchisees. These accounting systems and services provide a greater facility, both to the franchisor and to the franchisee, to monitor and control a franchisee's business.

On the sales side, if the prospective franchisor is a small business, the proprietor of the business will initially have to do the selling and marketing of the franchise. In any case, he is the most appropriate person for this as he will fully understand the motivation and worries of a prospective franchisee about to go into business on his own, probably for the first time. 'Selling' in this sense is largely a case of the franchisor explaining the proposition and services being offered and of visiting existing units with a prospective franchisee.

Where the operation to be franchised is part of a large organisation, the head of its franchise division or the managing director of its subsidiary company should similarly devote himself to the initial selling effort.

When extra help is required on the sales side, staff should be taken on one at a time. They should be very carefully screened and thoroughly trained, and should have impeccable references from previous employers. Alternatively, the franchisor may consider transferring someone from its own organisation to assist. The advantage of using in-house personnel is that they have product knowledge and one knows their strengths and weaknesses.

One last word on sales. Any individual specialising in this activity should be paid a good salary, with regular reviews and good conditions of service plus a modest performance bonus. The aim is to attract and retain a career-minded, long-service individual who will produce a steady flow of high-quality results. He provides an essential link to franchisees, who will often consult him as an 'uncle'

Developing the Concept and Organisation

when problems arise. Ethical franchise sales is not about a foot in the door, large bonuses or 'achieve the minimum sales performance or you're out', and therefore such pay scales are inappropriate.

Much depends on the size of the franchisor in determining what level of assistance would be appropriate to carry out the functions referred to above. In the early days of franchising activity it is unlikely that a franchisor will need any specialist additional sales staff for marketing. If the franchisor already has a marketing department for its company operations, it should obviously be used and will be a great help. If an advertising agency has been retained, it should also be briefed on the franchisor's plans to franchise; if not, it is recommended that one be appointed in the fullness of time.

Good design work to establish the image will be needed. Some of this may already exist, but in switching to a franchise it may be wise to take a closer look and perhaps ensure greater distinctiveness. There are specialist design companies that offer such a service. Although these specialist agencies exist, as the franchisor's organisation grows so too will its capacity to do promotional and design work in-house.

Advertisements will need to be placed and PR events/releases to be handled. All these details should be carefully considered, and it is best to start with a modest programme to save unnecessary expense. At this stage, more than any other, it is vital to obtain full value for money.

There is considerable advantage to be gained in discussing marketing and promotional ideas and initiatives with franchisees. A continuous and positive approach to marketing and promotion from within the franchisor's organisation is also good for the morale of franchisees and demonstrates in practice the franchisor's concerned involvement in the success of their businesses.

The franchisor will definitely need staff to help in operations as franchisees will require a good deal of detailed help to implement their new venture, and the franchisor will need to continue to monitor and advise its franchisees and if necessary control them after they have been established in business.

The obvious source for likely candidates will be the internal company operations team. To begin with, it should be just one person, an experienced all-rounder, good both in theory and in practice. He must be able to perform the necessary tasks personally and be prepared to roll up his sleeves and actually work alongside franchisees in the early days. This individual should be made responsible for writing the operations manual. He will need to cover the shop fitting and equipping of new franchised outlets. He must therefore have first-hand experience of these functions. He will need to stay on good terms with the franchisor's existing operational staff in order to obtain help and advice for himself and for training new franchisees.

In the early days, the training of franchisees can be carried out at the company-owned branches by one of the experienced branch managers, using the operations manual. If the company already has a training officer, all well and good, but most new franchisors will not be so blessed and will need to use the limited number of existing operational staff and facilities available. The next stage of development would be the addition of a classroom and possibly dummy equipment. This will often be sited conveniently at an existing company shop/location.

The number of staff involved in operations will expand with the growth of the business and the operational side of the franchise business will develop along a number of paths:

- Training new franchisees and staff.
- Continuing retraining of franchisees and staff. This will mainly be done at the franchisees' premises. Its purpose will be to work out operational flaws or bad habits developed by the franchisees, and/or to introduce new methods.
- The creation and management of a team in the field offering troubleshooting advice.
- A team responsible for product/service development and innovation (all development and innovation should be tried out in the franchisor's company-owned branches).

The size and degree of sophistication of any of the above will depend on the nature and extent of the franchisor's operation. See below for a possible management structure.

Developing the Concept and Organisation

The franchisor's bank may be helpful in providing partial finance to franchisees. According to the BFA/NatWest Franchise Survey 2015, 61% of franchisees needed to borrow money at some point. It is not generally sensible for a franchisor to be involved in financing franchisees itself, either by lending funds or by guarantee. The function of a franchisor should be to introduce franchisees to sources of finance and provide any necessary information to their lenders.

The franchisor's accountants will need to advise on the best methods of monitoring its franchisees, and the receipt and recording of income and expenses. The franchisor's solicitors will need to advise on legal compliance, on protection of the franchisor's intellectual property and on drawing up the complex franchise agreement and other documents.

One can sum up the initial organisational requirements for a prospective franchisor as:

- Franchise sales.
- Proprietor or a very senior individual, plus a PA.
- Marketing of the product or service.
- Advertising agency.
- Operations – one person transferred from existing company operations.
- Shop fitting and equipment.
- External suppliers/shop fitters.
- Existing company operations management.
- Finance and administration.
- Help from the company's bank, accountants and solicitors.

The principles underlying these points are that the franchisor must be fully involved personally since it must be prepared to demonstrate its faith in its business and in franchising, and maximum use should be made of existing company staff for reasons not only of economy, but also of knowledge, experience and dependability. The quality of the initial supporting staff is vital.

Growing the Network

Promoting the Franchise

Promoting one's franchise involves considerations which are different from the above, although there is some degree of overlap.

The franchise itself can be promoted by:

- The visible success of the prospective franchisor's own operations.
- Satisfying the criteria for membership of the British Franchise Association (see Appendix D).
- Membership of any other appropriate trade association.
- Trade press coverage, particularly in trade journals and specialist franchise magazines.
- Presence at exhibitions.
- Business to business news coverage of its 'success story'.
- The PR launch of its own outlets and of the franchise itself.
- Advertising for franchisees.

Promoting the Brand

It goes without saying that a distinctive brand name and house style should be adopted. It must be used consistently – on and in each outlet, on the product, stationery, package, vehicles, point of sale material etc.

Development of the brand name will depend on the promotion of the franchise and of the individual outlets. Of great assistance in developing the brand name is local and regional PR coverage plus advertising in specialist magazines such as *Franchise World* and *What Franchise*. Television advertising is, of course, extremely expensive. Local radio can be effective, as can cinema commercials, which can be tailored to local outlets.

Promoting Individual Outlets

In addition to regional and possibly national promotion of the brand name, local promotional efforts should be embarked upon by franchisees, sometimes independent of regional/national efforts and sometimes as a part of a larger regional or national promotion. The greater the local promotion, the more it will rub off on the national and regional image; consumers are mobile.

Innovation

It is the responsibility of the franchisor to keep the franchise concept up to date and its products/services fully in tune with market requirements.

There must be a positive attitude to innovation. Innovative ideas can come from:

- Market research.
- Research and development.
- Suppliers.
- Competitors.
- Staff.
- Franchisees.
- Trade/professional associations.

Franchisors must be receptive to innovative ideas, and be seen to be so, otherwise franchisees in particular will be frustrated. They must manage innovation within the boundaries of the business concept, otherwise the strength of brand identity may be compromised. Ideas should be tested in company branches/facilities and regionally before the entire network of franchisees is required to introduce change.

Change is vital to the strength and life of the franchise, as it is to any business. A franchisor must remain sensitive to change. Changes should be introduced properly and progressively. They should be fully researched and the following questions (and others) should be asked and answered:

- Will it work?
- Is it legal?

Developing the Concept and Organisation

- Is it practical?
- Will it be profitable for the franchisor?
- Will it be profitable for the franchisee?
- Can it be delivered/serviced?
- Is there enough space?
- Will it improve or slow down service?
- Will it merely draw trade away from products/services already on offer under the franchise?
- Is it available throughout the year?
- Is it available throughout the country?
- Has it been fully bench/lab tested?
- Has it been tested in the franchisor's own branches and regionally?
- Has it been fully communicated to the franchisees?
- Has it been fully demonstrated to the franchisees?
- Has it been promoted and marketed?
- How are franchisees to be persuaded/encouraged to accept the change?
- Has a system of monitoring the change's effects and communicating them to franchisees been established?

Monitoring Standards

Standards must be established and should be defined in the operations manual. These standards can be encouraged by:

- Demonstration (through the franchisor's own operations and personal standards).
- Competition (amongst franchisees and the franchisor's branches).
- Pride (prizes and awards).

The standards can be monitored by:

- Regular site visits by knowledgeable and dedicated field staff (who must have worked in the franchisor's own branches).
- Analysis of data flow.
- Turnover/suppliers/accounts.
- Mystery shoppers.
- Complaints from public/other franchisees.

In addition to monitoring standards (of both franchisor-owned and franchised outlets) it is the franchisor's responsibility to ensure that its systems deliver, in the sense of helping a franchisee establish the business and, having done so, keeping him in business.

The following functions must be covered by the franchisor's system:

- Continuing development and updating of the design and layout of premises.
- Constant development and investigation of equipment sources.
- Striving to ensure that supplies are always available from the best and cheapest sources while still maintaining quality requirements.
- Continuous marketing and promotion.
- Continuous technical research and development.
- Monitoring financial performances and offering guidance.
- Troubleshooting by frequent visits and having staff available to assist with problems.

Reviewing the Terms of the Franchise

Many franchisors will find with experience that they need to revise the financial terms of their franchise. This may result from one or more of the following:

- The original projected figures may prove to be wrong, perhaps because the pilot scheme was atypical.

Developing the Concept and Organisation

- Changes may be desirable to reflect improving or deteriorating market conditions.
- The franchisor may wish to update and/or upgrade the franchise concept itself.

Below is a checklist which a franchisor may wish to consider when reviewing its franchise terms. Once an internal review has been carried out, it may be a good idea to arrange an external review by a suitably experienced solicitor or consultant in case the franchisor's judgement is too strongly influenced by the relatively narrow experience of its own particular franchise.

The Franchise Format

- Should the franchisor reduce/extend the range of products/services offered?
- Does the current equipment specification for franchisees need updating?
- Should the franchisor change its policy on suitable locations or size of franchisees' premises?
- Has there been any significant change in the time/cost involved in producing business/location surveys etc. for prospective franchisees?
- Is there a need to change/upgrade shop fitting specifications (if any)?
- Does the franchisor wish to change the basis of the supply of goods to the franchisee (e.g. from an exclusive to a non-exclusive basis, or vice versa)?

Initial Fees

Consider whether the total initial amount payable by a franchisee (however constituted) is a fair and adequate reward for the franchisor, taking into account:

- The established market reputation of the franchise format and brand.
- The franchisor's related costs (including promoting the franchise to prospective franchisees).
- Whether the launch, promotion and support for each franchisee is adequate.

Developing the Concept and Organisation

- A franchisee's capacity to pay/raise finance.
- The exclusivity of the product/service.
- The know-how/technical input of the franchisor.
- The cash flow implications for the franchisor.
- The fee (if any) for renewing the franchise at the end of the initial term.
- Whether the initial fee structure is clearly understood by franchisees.
- If there is more than one element in the financial package, whether each element (e.g. licence, equipment, launch package) has been adequately priced to reflect value given and to ensure a full recovery of direct costs and overheads.
- Whether any loss is being made on each element of the original package and, if so, whether there are good commercial reasons for it.
- Whether an initial deposit is required from franchisees before signing any agreement. If so, is it sufficient to ensure that there is real commitment? Is there a satisfactory basis for ensuring that expenses directly incurred by the franchisor on behalf of the franchisee can be recovered from the deposit in legitimate circumstances?
- Whether support has been obtained in principle from the key clearing banks to provide finance to suitable franchisees.
- Whether procedures have been established to ensure that a new franchisee settles his financial obligations before trading commences.

Continuing Franchise Fees

The following need to be taken into account when determining the level of continuing franchise fees:

- What are the franchisor's aggregate annual costs of:

    a. Providing continuing field support to franchisees (other than advertising and promotion)?

Developing the Concept and Organisation

    b. Providing advertising and promotional support to franchisees?

- What is the average annual and weekly cost of (a) and (b) above for each franchisee?

- Does the continuing franchise fee income currently exceed the above figures? If not, and the franchise has been operating for at least two years, what steps are being taken to rectify the matter?

- Is a specific proportion of continuing franchise fee income allocated to an advertising fund? If so, can it be demonstrated to franchisees that they are receiving value for money in this area? (It is unlikely that adequate advertising support can be provided in early years by relying exclusively on income from franchisees.)

- If the continuing franchise fee is based on sales by the franchisee, is the franchisor:

    a. Satisfied that franchisees are disclosing all their sales?

    b. Taking full advantage of the opportunity to have franchisees complete a document giving key information about sales trends, profitability etc.?

    c. Operating an effective procedure for ensuring that franchisees pay their fees punctually?

- If the continuing franchise fees are earned by a mark-up on goods supplied (see Chapter 13), is the franchisor:

    a. Satisfied that this is the best method?

    b. Accurately and efficiently monitoring each franchisee's sales?

    c. Satisfied with each franchisee's pricing policy? (See Chapter 23)

- If the franchisor is the landlord of its franchisees, is there a satisfactory procedure for ensuring that the rent is paid punctually and that the franchisees are complying with their obligations under their respective leases?

Other Financial Matters

- Have procedures for dealing with defaulting franchisees been reviewed to ensure that the franchisor will only suffer minimal loss and be able to preserve the credibility of the franchise?
- Is there sufficient capital available to:

    a. Finance any upgrading of the franchise format?

    b. Cover any predicted shortfall between the continuing franchise fee income and the cost of providing advertising and field support?

- Is the balance between the initial franchise fees and continuing franchise fees realistic with regard to likely business trends during the next five years, after which time the network may have reached maturity and therefore the franchisor may be more heavily dependent on its continuing franchise fee income?
- Does the franchisor have:

    a. Weekly trading statistics?

    b. Monthly management accounts?

    c. Annual budgets?

    d. Twelve-month rolling cash forecasts?

    e. Any idea of what its financial circumstances will be in three years' time?

Developing the Concept and Organisation

A Possible Management Structure

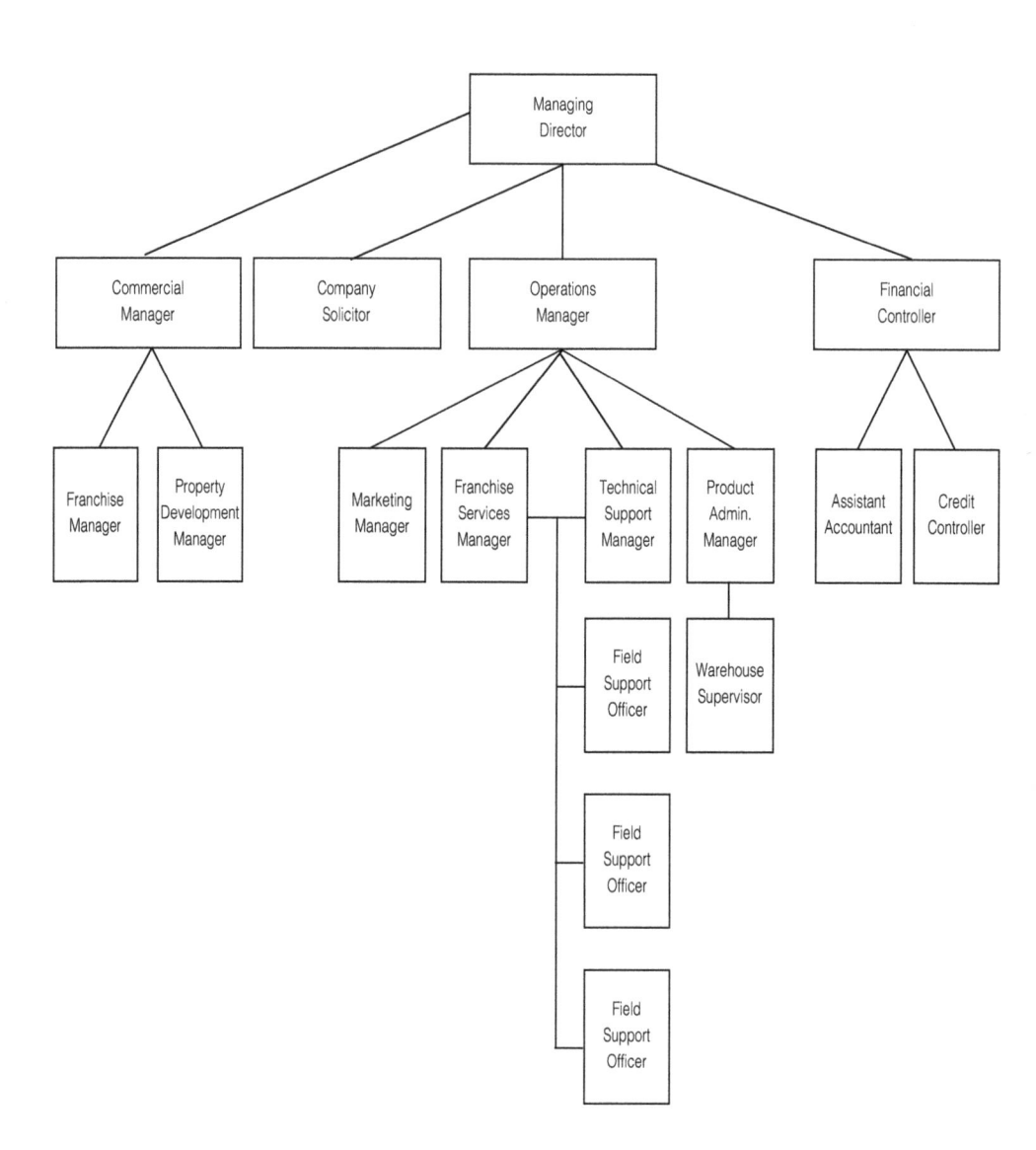

```
                            Managing Director
        ┌──────────────┬────────┴─────────┬──────────────────┐
   Commercial      Company           Operations           Financial
    Manager        Solicitor          Manager            Controller
    ┌───┴───┐                ┌──────┬────┴────┬──────┐    ┌───┴────┐
 Franchise Property      Marketing Franchise Technical Product   Assistant Credit
  Manager  Development    Manager  Services  Support  Admin.    Accountant Controller
           Manager                 Manager   Manager  Manager
                                               │        │
                                           Field    Warehouse
                                           Support  Supervisor
                                           Officer
                                               │
                                           Field
                                           Support
                                           Officer
                                               │
                                           Field
                                           Support
                                           Officer
```

CHAPTER 8

Testing the System – Proving It Works

"The proof of the pudding is in the eating of it."

A franchisor will have spent a great deal of time and resources in developing its business to the point where it thinks it is capable of being franchised. Once the system has been developed, it then needs to be proven to work. This is best done by establishing a pilot operation which should be operated at arm's length. If it is successful, the prospective franchisor will be able to demonstrate to prospective franchisees that its business system can be replicated successfully, and that it is able to transfer its know-how to a third party who can, providing he complies with the franchisor's instructions, look forward, with a high degree of optimism, to operating a successful business elsewhere.

If the pilot operation is to achieve its objective, the prospective franchisor needs to mirror as closely as possible the conditions under which a new franchisee will be operating. Ideally, therefore, franchisors should seek out a guinea pig who is willing to run the pilot operation for a period of at least 12 months, preferably much longer.

The temptation for most prospective franchisors is to convert one of their branch outlets into a pilot operation or, even if they establish a new unit, to operate it under the umbrella of the franchisor's business. In these circumstances, the conditions under which the pilot is operated will be less than 'real' because, however hard the prospective franchisor may try, there will be hidden benefits which the pilot operation will enjoy as a result of being linked to the main organisation.

Another temptation which prospective franchisors find very difficult to resist is to appoint an existing employee as the manager of the pilot operation. In this case, the critical *raison d'être* of a pilot operation will be missing in that the prospective franchisor will not be able to demonstrate that it is capable of communicating the necessary 'know-how': a vital ability for any franchisor. Any such manager will have been pre-trained and will be familiar with the prospective franchisor's business system and *modus operandi*.

Testing the System – Proving It Works

The advantage of having a third party at arm's length operate a pilot operation is that the prospective franchisor will not be able to take anything for granted and will have to handhold and nose-wipe the pilot operator through the initial stages. Approaching the matter in this way gives the prospective franchisor a good indication of the extent to which new franchisees will need support at the initial stages, and this will enable the prospective franchisor to better allocate its resources for this purpose. There is little point in being able to sell franchises quickly if the franchisor is not in the position to support and sustain new franchisees to the extent required.

During the crucial phase of the pilot operation, the prospective franchisor will have ample opportunity to fine-tune its business system and to make such adjustments as are necessary. Matters such as what happens if a franchisee is unable to operate the business due to illness or holidays will need to be addressed. Owner-managers of small businesses do not have human resources on which they can draw to provide cover in an emergency. Solutions to problems such as this need to be thought out by the prospective franchisor, and the pilot operation is the right place for the prospective franchisor to climb a steep learning curve.

All the constituent elements which have made the prospective franchisor's business so successful can be tested in a pilot operation: the operating systems, accounting and reporting procedures, advertising, marketing, merchandising and promotions, stocking levels, range and mix of stock, services to be provided, training, cost of sales, staffing levels, hours of operation, dealing with customer complaints, refunds etc.

In the fullness of time, many pilot operations become training schools and test centres for the franchisor. They can form an important link between the franchisor and its franchisees.

The sale of a franchise is a sale by sample. It is the pilot operation which should be the sample, not a company-owned unit. The franchisor should be able to say with genuine confidence (and with the accounts to back it up), 'Here is a former greenfield site on which we have established and successfully operated our business concept, and, all things being equal, we can do this for you also.'

So far reference has only been made to one pilot operation; however, ideally there should be more than one. Markets differ geographically and prospective franchisors need to take this into account. Just because a prospective franchisor's business is successful in an important shopping area of London and the pilot operation is also successful in a different important shopping area of London, it does not necessary follow that a franchisee will be successful in an important shopping centre in Manchester or Birmingham or, indeed, anywhere else. Something which is successful in London will not necessarily work, or work as well, in another city.

If location is of primary importance, prospective franchisors will need to develop shop layout systems which are flexible enough to accommodate the various problems of laying out and shop fitting inherent to the large differences in the shape and size of premises available.

The layout and configuration of the premises will differ from case to case. Some businesses are very dependent upon the way in which goods are merchandised; others will not be. This point is best illustrated by looking at the fast food business. Fast food establishments will have either a separate kitchen or a 'call bar'. In both cases the layout will have to be carefully planned so that the preparation is conducted in logical steps without the need for staff to retrace their steps, not unlike a car production line. The whole operation of preparation will in all probability be timed, and if the layout demands a few unnecessary seconds per operation it could add up to the need for an additional employee. This could reduce the profitability of the operation and is the sort of costing which could stand between a scheme which could be franchised and one which could not be. In a 'call bar' situation it is important that everything needed is easily within reach to prevent staff from continually getting into each other's way.

Once the pilot operation has proved the concept, the need for continuous 'pilot' operation does not cease. Pilot schemes are usually now carried out in company-owned outlets. If a franchisor is to remain ahead of the game it must be continually experimenting and developing its system, concept, products and services. By being in the field, in the marketplace, it can put these innovations and improvements to the test. It will then be in a position to introduce these into its franchise network as proven and tested. Knowledge gained from experimenting with pilot operations can therefore be put to good use when dealing with individual franchisees.

A pilot operation should also fulfil the following functions:

- The viability of the concept in practice should be established so as to be acceptable and exclusive in the eyes of the general public
- It should identify any problems in at least the following 10 areas, along with other matters that are relevant to the particular type of business:

   a. Marketing.

   b. Acceptability of the product or service.

   c. Methods of selling.

   d. Modus operandi of the business.

   e. Local bylaws (e.g. building regulations).

   f. Fire, health and safety regulations.

   g. Planning requirements.

   h. Staff availability and training requirements.

   i. IT issues.

   j. Taxation (including VAT).

- It should enable the franchisor to experiment with the layout and décor of premises.
- It should offer knowledge gained through actual experience of trading in different locations. This will include, for example, knowledge gained by experimenting with opening hours to discover the optimum hours during which the business should be operating. This should be borne in mind when determining staffing levels, working hours and shifts. Opening at certain times, though desirable, may be uneconomic because of the additional staff costs. In some cases, units in different areas will have different trading profiles.
- Just as training in the operations side of the business is necessary, so of course is training in the business management and accounting aspects. In developing a pilot operation particular attention should be paid to the introduction

of simple and effective systems of accounting, stocktaking and controls (portion and quality controls in a food operation, for example).

- Bearing in mind the need for an operations manual, detailed job descriptions outlining the specific duties of each member of staff and the manner in which they are to be performed should also be developed.

The existence of a successful pilot operation will, of course, have the additional advantage of enabling a franchisor to sell franchises more quickly and with confidence. Investing time and resources in a pilot operation is well worth doing for any business concept. Franchisors should be confident that almost all the teething problems of the business have been sorted out before they embark upon franchising.

CHAPTER 9

Protecting Intellectual Property

"Being copied is the highest form of flattery."

Forms of intellectual property which may be relevant in a franchise arrangement can be divided into two main categories: forms that result from a formal registration process and forms that do not. The former category includes patents, registered trade marks and registered designs. The latter includes copyright, trade names, logos and marks (which are not or cannot be registered as trade marks), get-up and confidential information: trade secrets, know-how etc.

Trade Name

A distinction has to be made between a trade name and a trade mark. Until 1980 there existed a Business Names Registry which kept details of trade names in circumstances where the name under which a business was trading was different from the name of the owner of the business (for example, George Smith might operate a picture framing business as 'Quickframe'). It was thus possible for a member of the public, on the payment of a nominal fee, to find out the identity of a particular business's owner. Without the existence of such a registry or any public declaration of ownership of the business, members of the public would be left wondering who the owner was. However, in the wake of Margaret Thatcher's sweeping reforms designed to deliver the business from the 'nanny state' the Business Names Registry was abolished. It was replaced by legislation which provides that any entity conducting business under a name other than that of its owner must make the name and address of the owner known to those dealing with it.

There is a distinction between a trade name and a trade mark, although the two can overlap. The latter usually takes the form of a word (or words), design, logo or device, but not always. Thus the name 'McDonald's', whilst being a trade name, is also a trade mark. However, the famous 'Golden Arches' of McDonald's qualify as a trade mark but not as a trade name.

The only protection afforded to the owner of a trade *name* against infringement lies at common law. This means that the owner of a legitimate business who finds that a copycat operation has sprung up using the same or a very similar trade name must sue in the ordinary courts and convince the judge that the infringer is 'passing off' its business as being the same as the one it is copying, i.e. pretending to be something that it is not.

Trade Marks

Trade marks, on the other hand, enjoy statutory protection by virtue of legislation. The Patent Office, which contains the Trade Marks Registry, provides facilities for the registration of trade marks so long as they qualify for registration by the criteria laid out in the legislation. An unqualified registration (a registration without any conditions attaching) will give the owner monopoly rights to use the trade mark, making it much easier to prevent infringement.

The owner of an unregistered mark may obtain protection against infringement but, again, at common law if the infringer is deemed to be 'passing off' (see above).

In a franchise operation, the franchisor owns a trade mark but each franchisee is granted the right to use it by his franchisor. If a franchisor (who may own a number of marks) never uses a mark itself but its franchisees do, it could later be argued that one or more of those franchisees should be registered as the mark's owner(s) in the franchisor's place. It is therefore advisable to ensure that the owner is clearly defined, that the 'user relationship' is clearly established in the franchise agreement, that controls and limitations are imposed on the franchisees' use of any mark and, where the mark is a registered trade mark, that the authority of the franchisee to use that trade mark is recorded at the Trade Marks Registry.

Franchisees are concerned to see that their franchisor not only owns the relevant trade marks but has also taken sufficient precautions to prevent infringement by third parties. After all, there is little point in a franchisee paying good money for the use of a recognised trade mark or trade name if the owner of that trade mark or trade name has not taken the necessary steps to protect it, thereby leaving a competitor free to compete with the franchisee using the same or a very similar trade mark or trade name.

Protecting Intellectual Property

There are two ways in which a franchisor can protect its trade mark:

1. By relying on the common law
2. By registering the trade mark at the Trade Marks Registry

So far as the common law is concerned, this does not require the franchisor to do anything until an infringement of its trade mark is brought to its notice. In other words, no action is required until the franchisor discovers somebody using its trade mark, or something that closely resembles its trade mark, in a business which is similar to that being conducted by the franchisor and its franchisees. However, it is advisable for a franchisor to put the public on notice (see below) that the franchisor claims ownership in its mark.

The franchisor's remedy on discovering infringement of an unregistered trade mark would be to sue the alleged infringer in an action for 'passing off'. To succeed in an action for passing off, the franchisor will need to establish the presence of five characteristics, as set out in a House of Lords decision in 1979 in a case which was concerned with the supply of goods (although there is no reason why it should not apply equally to the provision of services):

1. There has to be a misrepresentation,
2. Made by a trader in the course of trade,
3. To prospective customers or ultimate consumers of the goods or services supplied,
4. Which is calculated to injure the business or goodwill of another business, and
5. Which causes actual damage to the business or goodwill of the other trader.

There have been a number of cases in which a franchisor has been successful in preventing others from using a similar name and/or marketing image to those of the franchisor. In a decision in the High Court of just such a case, a franchisor was granted an injunction preventing a franchisee from selling, from his shop, products which were substantially similar to those of the franchisor. As a result the franchisee had to make substantial changes to his shops. Mr Justice Whitford, in his judgement, made a statement worth quoting:

Of course these franchising operations have become a relatively common feature of trading in this country over recent years and everyone is no doubt familiar with concessions which may sell anything from fried chicken to hamburgers, the link between these concessions very often consisting of the use of some particular trading name or style.

If the trade mark is registered, the franchisor's case is much more straightforward and enforcement is relatively simple. To succeed in an infringement action, all the franchisor need do is to invite the court to compare its registered trade mark with that of the alleged infringer and see to what extent the marks are similar. It is no longer necessary for the franchisor to establish that the alleged infringer is confusing the public into thinking he is trading with the franchisor. All the franchisor has to do is satisfy the court that it is the owner of the registered trade mark in question and that the trade mark being used by the alleged infringer bears a close resemblance to its own trade mark.

There is a somewhat bizarre ongoing case between the government of Iceland and Iceland Foods Ltd, the supermarket chain that specialises in frozen food under the name 'Iceland'. Iceland Foods was granted an EU-wide trade mark for the word 'Iceland' in 2014. The Icelandic government launched legal action in 2016, contending that Iceland Foods' trade mark registrations such as 'Iceland gold' and 'clean Iceland' were restricting Icelandic companies from promoting their goods within the EU. Iceland Foods has said, 'We have been trading successfully for 46 years under the name Iceland and do not believe that any serious confusion or conflict has ever arisen in the public mind, nor is it likely to do so.' It will be interesting to see how this plays out. Under EU trade mark law, national flags and emblems cannot be registered as trade marks, but there is nothing in law to stop the name of a country becoming a trade mark – as has happened in this case.

At this stage perhaps a common misconception which surrounds service marks should be clarified. Sometimes the two terms 'service mark' and 'trade mark' are used as if they are two different types of protection. Strictly speaking, a service mark is merely a category of trade mark. The misconception has arisen partly because it is only recently that it has become possible for marks relating to services to be registered in the United Kingdom. Until 1989 registration was only available for marks relating to products. Registration of marks relating to services

Protecting Intellectual Property

was brought into being by amending the legislation relating to trade marks, not by enacting a new Act of Parliament for service marks. Thus, in law a trade mark is any mark which will identify a particular product or a service for a particular trading entity. Logically, trade marks should be divided into product marks for products and service marks for services.

To be registrable a trade mark has to comply with the basic principles of trade mark law. Namely, it must:

- Be distinctive.
- Be non-conflicting.
- Be non-deceptive.
- Be non-descriptive.
- Not be too general in its specification for goods and services to which it is to apply.

Because registration confers a legal monopoly, registration will not be granted for marks which are identical to, or which can readily be confused with, words or symbols which other people trading in the same class of goods or services should be free to use. There are certain words and marks which cannot be registered because they are simply laudatory or commonly used in the industry to describe goods or services. For example, one would not be able to obtain registration of the word 'best' or a money symbol for a bank. Words which describe the business, such as 'Quick Print', would be too descriptive. Essentially the mark must be distinctive, as in the case of the red roof for Pizza Hut or the golden arches of McDonalds.

It is obvious that the mark should not be deceptive or misleading. For example, the mark must not imply that the business is something other than it actually is. In the famous Orwoola case, application was made to register 'Orwoola' to be used in connection with yarn. The Trade Marks Registry rejected the application and held that the mark would not be permitted because it was either descriptive or misleading. If the yarn to which the mark was to be applied was pure wool then, the Trade Marks Registry argued, the mark was descriptive and therefore could not be permitted. If on the other hand it was to be applied to yarn which was *not* pure wool then, the Trade

Marks Registry argued, the mark was misleading as members of the public could be led into believing that the product was 'all wool'.

Perhaps most importantly, the mark must not conflict with the mark of someone else and application for the registration of a trade mark will be refused if there already exists on the register, for the same goods or services, a mark which is the same or very similar.

It is worth mentioning here that when one makes an application for registration of a mark, the application has to be made with regard to a particular category of goods or services. Goods and services have been classified by an international system covering classes from chemicals to insurance. It is possible for an application to be made for registration of a trade mark in more than one class. If a franchisor is engaged in a wide range of activities, it will need to apply for protection in each of the classes within which the activity falls. For example, if a fast food franchisor has a restaurant with a take-away section it should apply in the restaurant service class, in the food product classes for those products in the take-away section, and in the paper products class for its packaging, paper cups etc. bearing its trade mark. A full list of the classifications and the various products and services to which they apply is set out in Appendix A.

The process of applying for registration is a relatively simple one and there is no requirement on the owner to establish prior use. That is to say, it is not a precondition of registration that the owner should have used the mark in the marketplace. This means that those devising new trade marks and logos do not have to go through the lengthy period of market build-up beforehand. However, the intention to use the mark should be present.

There is a unified system of registration in the European Union so that registration at the European Trade Marks Registry will give protection to an EU franchisor within every EU member state.

A prospective franchisor that has done nothing about protecting its intellectual property would be well advised to consider what measures it should be taking at the outset. If it has already registered its trade mark(s), it should keep in mind any other marks which are emerging or have emerged within the business and would benefit from being registered.

Copyright

Apart from trade marks and trade names, the other important intellectual property is copyright. In any franchise operation the franchisor's copyright will exist in a number of important features such as the operations manuals and get-up. Examples of the latter can include packaging, advertising, uniforms, vehicle livery and miscellaneous items such as catalogues, price lists, menus, letterheads etc.

Unlike trade marks there is no copyright registry and no means of formally registering one's copyright ownership to obtain statutory protection.

Copyright arises upon the creation of a literary work. Groves (1997) has defined 'literary work' as 'work which is expressed in print or writing, irrespective of the question whether the quality or style is high'. There is a requirement for the literary work to be 'original', but only in the sense that the work must originate from the author and not be copied from another source. Since 1911, neither registration nor any form of notification of the claim to copyright on copies of a literary, artistic or musical work has been a prerequisite, either of copyright itself or the entitlement to institute proceedings for infringement. All the innocent party need prove is that the infringer has substantially copied his work. It is therefore important that the original work is retained and upon it should be noted the date of its creation and details of its creator.

Copyright essentially means the right not to be copied and arises not from registration but on creation. Copyright is vested in the creator of the work in question (artist, author etc.). Prospective franchisors should therefore take steps at the outset to ensure that they obtain from those charged with the task of creating copyright material (be they employees, consultants or third parties) ownership of the copyright they create.

Copyright is infringed if, without the permission of its owner, another person reproduces the work in whole or substantially.

There is no requirement to exhibit any symbol in connection with copyright work in the UK, such as there is in the United States. However, the 'copyright notice' (the symbol ©, name of copyright owner and year of first publication, e.g. © Manzoor Ishani 2018) is recommended on published works in order to attract copyright in countries where this is a requirement.

Before any matter can gain copyright, it must exist in some permanent form. This means it is not possible to obtain copyright protection for a particular idea. Only when written expression has been given to that idea does copyright protection become available, but only in respect of the way in which the idea is expressed.

Copyright protection can be a much more valuable weapon for the preservation of the franchisor's trade secrets and know-how than is commonly realised. There are many important elements in the franchise package which can be protected by copyright, such as the operations manuals, price lists, menus, training, publicity and promotional material (including point of sale material), premises layout, design drawings etc.

Any franchisor thinking of franchising in another country should take appropriate steps to ensure that it, rather than the translator or its franchisee, owns the copyright for any translations into the language of the relevant country.

Know-How and Trade Secrets

To the extent that know-how is confidential and to the extent that the franchisor has trade secrets, the only way to protect these is through the medium of the franchise agreement and at common law. There is no central registry where such matters can be protected by registration. The importance of non-competition, non-disclosure and restraint of trade clauses in franchise agreements cannot be overstated.

Although most franchisors claim that their system is unique or that they have imparted trade secrets to their franchisees, in reality that is very often not the case. Usually the 'trade secrets' are not secrets in themselves; the information is generally available in the public domain. What, however, is secret is the way in which various constituent elements of the franchisor's system have been put together. It is this 'mix' which the franchisor seeks to protect. The problem of protecting trade secrets and know-how in the United Kingdom, and elsewhere, is proving the 'secret and confidential' nature of the information imparted to franchisees.

If know-how is disclosed to franchisees in confidence, improper disclosure by a franchisee to others may be restrained. However, the ability of a franchisor to

Protecting Intellectual Property

restrain a franchisee is conditional upon the information in question not being in the public domain and the common law doctrine of restraint of trade (i.e. is the restriction on disclosure reasonable?) not intervening.

Although confidentiality will usually cover trade secrets, units of information which are individually in the public domain can also form confidential information when combined or used in a manner peculiar to the business, e.g. customer lists, recipes etc.

Patents

If new, a process or product may be protected by a patent. Compared with the registration of marks and designs, patents require greater expense and time to acquire and to maintain. The use of patents in franchising is very limited. Principally, the foundation of a business format franchise consists of a brand name and/or trade mark, copyright and know-how.

Industrial Designs

It may be possible to protect visual features (e.g. vending carousels) employed in the franchise business as registered designs. Protection for designs by means of registration is available in most countries: for example, in the United States as design patent.

However, as a general rule registered designs do not play a significant role in franchising, and as such, like patents, they are outside the scope of this chapter.

In Summary

The need for franchisors to adequately protect their intellectual property cannot be emphasised too greatly. The intellectual property, after all, is what makes a particular franchise valuable and that is what franchisees will pay their franchisors for on a continuing basis.

Prevention is better than cure, therefore rights should be secured and evidenced by:

- Registration where appropriate.

- Thorough documentation and control of the franchisee's use (regarding both form and manner).

- Retaining and adding to evidence of ownership by the franchisor.

- Giving notice of rights of ownership to third parties:

    a. Where a trade mark is registered, by appending the registered trade mark symbol ®.

    b. In the case of an unregistered trade mark, by appending the symbol ™ next to the mark.

    c. In the case of copyright, by including a copyright notice: ©, followed by the date of first publication and details of the copyright owner.

- Warning off potential infringers and challenging minor misuse or infringement.

- Imposing adequate contractual controls on the use of the franchisor's intellectual property. Establishing mechanisms as to 'who does what' and 'who pays' provisions in the franchise agreement in anticipation of litigation.

- Acting swiftly to exercise the franchisor's equitable rights, especially injunctions, to prevent further/continued infringement.

The subject of intellectual property and its protection is complex and highly technical, and prospective franchisors *must* take specialist advice. The above narrative is not intended to be and should not be taken as legal advice on the subject.

CHAPTER 10

The Operations Manual

"Everything should be made as simple as possible, but not one bit simpler."

The rulebook for a business is commonly known as the operations manual. It should open by spelling out in broad terms the basic nature of the operation, the business philosophy that underlies it and what the franchisor expects from its franchisees.

The operations manual should contain a detailed description of the system, explaining how the operation is set up and how and why the various constituent elements dovetail with each other. The purpose of any business format franchise is to enable a person who is wholly unfamiliar with the subject of the franchise to run a previously proven and tested business on a predetermined basis. Franchisors boast proudly that they have the ability to replicate their business systems and train others to operate them. The business system, which should be ever changing and developing, has to be set down in writing if it is to be successfully replicated. It cannot simply be passed down verbally. The operations manual will contain the A to Z of doing that particular business and will, together with the franchise agreement, form the engine room of the franchise transaction between franchisor and franchisee.

What, then, is it that this bible of the system should contain, which makes it supposedly so significant?

Fundamental Functions

The operations manual fulfils three fundamental functions:

1. It contains the full business format of the franchisor in every detail; if the manual is lost, it can amount to the loss of the franchisor's know-how.

2. It is the instrument by which the franchisee conducts his business in accordance with the franchisor's requirements. In reality the franchisee will first see the manual when he starts training, and the training will be based

The Operations Manual

on the manual. The franchisee should thereafter be required to retain the manual (in whatever form the business demands), which he will use as a source of reference in the day-to-day conduct of his franchised business.

3. It enjoys the benefit of copyright protection and thus forms an essential part of the legal method by which a franchisor will seek to protect its ideas, know-how and trade secrets.

Franchisees make great play of the fact that they are not given access to an operations manual prior to signing the franchise agreement. Franchisors jealously guard the contents of their operations manual, which they claim contains vital secrets about their business system and which, together with the franchise agreement, they perceive as being one of their crown jewels.

Yet it is clear from talking to a number of franchisees and franchisors that, in some cases, only lip service is paid to the operations manual. Indeed, there have been instances where franchisors have been selling franchises while admitting that the operations manual is not yet available because it is 'in the course of preparation'. If one looks at some mature franchise networks, it is apparent that the operations manual has been all but forgotten by the franchisees, sometimes with good reason because it has become hopelessly out of date.

It is hard to believe that franchisors who are serious about their business have no real appreciation of how pivotal a role an operations manual plays in their franchise system and the reliance which franchise agreements place upon it.

On the other side, many franchisees tend to see the operations manual not as an *aide mémoire,* a source of constant reference which should enable them to operate the system more effectively and profitably, but rather as a cumbersome set of rules and regulations which they would much rather ignore.

A general misconception is that a hard copy of an operations manual should consist of one 'book'. That is not the case. There is no reason why hard copies should not run to several volumes; indeed some mature franchise networks have operations manuals which run to sixteen volumes and more, each volume dealing with various aspects of running the business. Furthermore, there will be some material which forms part of the operations manual although it may not necessarily be physically contained within it. For example, in a product retail franchise, the products which are the subject matter of the franchise may be

The Operations Manual

described as those which are specified in the franchisor's catalogue current from time to time. The important thing is that the manual should be readily identifiable and accessible by the franchisee.

Matters Covered in an Operations Manual

An operations manual should address not only issues relating to the operation of the franchised business but also those relating to its pre-opening phase.

1. Introduction.
    - Outline operation.
    - Outline business philosophy.
    - Outline franchisor's expectations from franchisees.
2. Pre-launch.
    - Signage.
    - Checklist.
    - Advertising, marketing and promotions to launch business.
    - Equipment package.
    - Initial stock.
    - Recruiting and training staff.
    - Acquisition and fitting out of premises/vehicle.
3. General rules relating to the operation of the business.
4. The franchisee's management responsibilities.
    - Salaries and wages.
    - Legal aspects – agreements with suppliers.
    - Daily accounting and reporting procedures.
    - Cash book.

The Operations Manual

- Provisions relating to insurance.
- Maintenance of vehicle, property, equipment.
- Procedures relating to the rotation of stock.
- Stock taking procedures.
- Stock ordering procedures.
- Type, quantity and mix of stock to be held.
- Pricing policy (see Chapter 23).
- Quality control procedures.
- Methods and standards of providing services.
- Procedures for dealing with the payment of advertising, marketing and promotions contributions, franchise fees etc.
- Requirements of the franchisor with regard to advertising, marketing and promotions.
- Details of insurance which a franchisee must carry.
- Provisions relating to the use and control of the franchisor's intellectual property including trade names and trade marks.
- A directory with addresses and telephone numbers of all the franchisees within the network.
- Compliance with the franchisor's training requirements.
- Payments to suppliers and other creditors.
- There may be a section setting out standard forms for use by a franchisee, forms for use when dealing with customers, order forms, checklists, work sheets etc. for use in the conduct of the franchised business, forms for completing VAT returns, PAYE etc.

5. Employees.
    - The legal aspects of employment.
    - Recruiting and engaging employees.

The Operations Manual

- Recommendations relating to working hours, rates of pay etc.
- A brief note of the franchisee's responsibilities to staff as an employer.
- Details of staffing levels and the function which each member of staff is required to perform.
- Requirements as to the demeanour and appearance of staff (e.g. use of uniforms).
- Staff schedules and rotas.
- Procedures for recruiting and employing staff and guidance on legal compliance.
- Procedure for disciplining staff and an explanation of the statutory obligations imposed on the franchisee as an employer.
- Staff duties – a detailed job description for each member of staff should be included, setting out not merely the nature and extent of the duties but also the methods and procedures to be adopted in performing them.
- The need to give contracts of employment.
- Forms relating to employment, accident book, holiday rotas, illness etc.
- Staff incentive schemes.
- Staff training.
- Confidentiality agreements requiring managers and/or staff not to use or disclose the franchisor's trade secrets for any purpose except in the discharge of their responsibilities as employees.
- Staff promotion and incentive schemes.

6. Operational matters.
   - Individual responsibilities.
   - Equipment operating instructions.

The Operations Manual

- Provisions relating to preparation, processing and packaging of products.
- Selling methods.
- Operating procedures.
- Opening hours.
- Trading patterns (peaks and troughs).
- Service standards.
- Purchasing policies.
- Guidance on how to troubleshoot basic and common faults (e.g. the electronic tills crashing at a peak time).
- Details of supply and service centres for the equipment.
- Methods and systems for taking payments from customers and for giving refunds.
- Record keeping.
- Dealing with theft/shoplifting.

7. Cleaning and maintenance.
   - Toilets.
   - Keys, locks, alarms etc.
   - Fire extinguishers.
   - Pest control.
   - Background music.
   - Repairs to electrical, mechanical, gas and plumbing equipment.
   - Preventative maintenance schedules.
   - Cost control procedures for consumption of energy and products in the course of operating the business.
   - Provisions relating to climate control, heating, air conditioning, ventilation etc.

The Operations Manual

8. Safety procedures.
    - Loss of stock and personal property.
    - Safety.
    - Equipment.
    - Compliance with health and safety at work regulations.
9. Protection of trade secrets and non-disclosure.
10. Reporting and accounting procedures.
11. Special promotions.
12. Customer complaint procedures.

In addition to the foregoing, depending upon the nature of the business, there may also be a technical section dealing with certain aspects of the operation of the franchised business in detail. For example, a technical section may contain details about the suitability of certain products for certain types of equipment, how food is to be prepared and cooked etc.

13. Technical matters

Fast food

- Recipes.
- Methods of food storage and preparation of food.
- Kitchen procedures and layout.
- Time for preparation, cooking, holding and serving of each menu item.
- Portion quantities, including how many portions one might expect from a given quantity of ingredients.
- Stock requirements.
- Display and merchandising techniques.
- Local advertising, promotion and PR.

- Menu content and variations according to time of day.
- Customer complaints procedures.
- Legal compliance: health and safety regulations, planning, bylaws, statutory requirements.
- Hygiene, litter, night operations, noise, parking.
- VAT.
- Work permits for staff.

Retail

- Stock requirements in terms of quality, quantities and range.
- Shop layout.
- Product display techniques.
- Discounting.
- Special promotions.
- Customer relations.
- Guarantees.
- Customer complaints procedures.

The list could be almost endless as one looks at the variety of franchises on offer; Dyno-Rod, Budget Rent-a-Car, Holiday Inn and Molly Maid are but a few examples. The specific manual requirements of each could well form the subject of a separate study.

Maintaining and Protecting the Operations Manual

All franchisors should be conscious of the need to keep their methods of operation constantly under review and to introduce change and variety so that their operation is at the forefront of its market. Such changes should be reflected in supplements and amendments to the operations manual so that franchisees are constantly kept informed and up to date. This is likely to apply

The Operations Manual

particularly to the advertising, promotions and marketing section of the operations manual.

The most important thing to remember about the manual is that it is ever changing in the light of experience and as a result of enhancement, modification and innovation in the system. Franchisees should be required to make sure that it is kept updated at all times.

All hard copy manuals should be numbered and a receipt obtained from a franchisee when it is handed over. The manual should, of course, be on *loan* to the franchisee, returnable on termination of the franchise for whatsoever reason. Many franchisors have an elaborate error code system which enables them to trace missing pages from any manuals which find themselves in unauthorised hands.

Problems arise when franchisors fail to ensure that their manuals are comprehensive or, if they have set out on the road to franchising with a comprehensive manual, they subsequently fail to update it.

A common provision in operations manuals is a requirement for franchisees to make regular accounting reports to the franchisor in accordance with details 'contained in the manual'. This provision, amongst others, is intended to ensure that each franchisee's accounts are kept accurately and up to date so that he can remit the necessary continuing franchise fees to his franchisor, if these fees are calculated as a percentage of the franchisee's gross turnover. If the operations manual is silent on the matter and not only does the franchisee fail to make the reports as his franchisor expects but the accounts of that particular franchisee are also in a mess, the franchisor can never be sure whether or not it is receiving the correct amount by way of continuing franchise fees. The problem, of course, will generally only come to light when there is a default and the franchisor is seeking to pin down a breach on the part of the franchisee. Whilst things are going well and the franchisee is paying what he considers to be correct continuing franchise fees and the franchisor is receiving what it thinks is the correct amount, the issue is unlikely to surface.

Franchisors should not expect to succeed in any proceedings against a franchisee for a breach of the franchise agreement if the term alleged to have been breached is stated to be contained within the manual but is, in fact, omitted from it. In a franchised retail business where the franchisee is required to buy all his requirements of certain products 'as described in the manual' *only* from his franchisor and the operations manual contains no description of the products in question, the franchisor will find it difficult to terminate the franchise agreement on the grounds that the franchisee has infringed this particular provision in the agreement.

However, franchisees have some responsibility too. They need to keep their copies of the operations manual updated with amendments received from their franchisor. If they fail to do so and as a result end up paying their franchisor less than it is entitled to receive, they should not be surprised to be at the receiving end of a notice of termination of their franchise agreement for breach. Franchisees will only have themselves to blame if they do not ensure that the copy of the manual in their possession is kept up to date.

In Conclusion

The moral of the story, for both franchisor and franchisee, is:

- The value and importance of the operations manual should not be underestimated.
- Care should be taken to make changes to the operations manual in keeping with changes to the system and to ensure all copies are updated.
- The operations manual and its function within the scheme of things should be treated with the respect they deserve.

This chapter has laid out basically what one would expect to find in most operations manuals, but of course there will be certain variations from business to business. In some businesses, one would expect to find other sections, such as a child protection policy, procedures for carrying out DBS (Disclosure and Barring Service) checks,[1] food standards requirements etc., as well as some consequential amendments to the sections mentioned above.

---

1   Previously known as CRB (Criminal Records Bureau) checks.

CHAPTER 11

Know-How Show-How

"A candle loses none of its brightness by lighting another."

One of the proudest boasts of franchisors is that they have the ability to turn a butcher, baker or candlestick maker into a fryer of chicken, dry cleaner or quick print shop operator. Franchising is about three things: passing on the benefit of experience gained in the marketplace, revealing the trade secrets of a particular business format and, arguably most important of all, imparting the know-how of a franchisor to a prospective franchisee sufficiently to enable him to replicate his franchisor's business. This last element is singularly important and its significance cannot be overstated.

A franchisor has to be able to show that its know-how can be transferred into practice. This is done by training. No matter how good the concept, no matter how successful it is, the franchisee's business will not succeed if the know-how/show-how aspect of the business is not conducted successfully by means of high-quality training.

In any franchise transaction, there are three elements to training:

1. *Initial training*, which is imparted by the franchisor to the franchisee prior to the franchisee commencing business.

2. *Ongoing training*, which is imparted by the franchisor to the franchisee on an ongoing basis to keep the franchisee, as it were, 'topped up' with regard to the franchisor's systems, procedures, processes etc. Human nature being what it is, there is a tendency for individuals to cut corners, to have lapses of memory and to succumb to the 'I can do this better' syndrome. Ongoing training is therefore designed to ensure that these negative elements and their influence are minimised.

3. *Further training*, which is usually required as the result of some form of development of the system which the franchisor incorporates into its methods and procedures and which it requires the franchisee to operate.

Although these three aspects of training are primarily the responsibility of the franchisor, the franchisee has an equally important role to play in that he must be receptive and responsive to such training.

There is no better person to impart the know-how of a franchised operation than the person who devised it and ensured its success in the marketplace. This direct training is usually found in new start-up franchises. Engaging the services of professional trainers to do the job is second best.

Professional trainers are generally engaged by the more mature franchisors who have greater resources, whose requirements are somewhat different from fledglings and whose administration is moving from amateur to more professional management systems. What professional trainers will lack is the enthusiasm and in many cases the evangelism of a founder franchisor. However, a well-devised training programme can overcome these shortcomings to some extent by including a non-professional in-house trainer in the training sessions.

So far, so good, but there is another dimension to training which is also very important.

This is training which must be imparted by a franchisee to its employees. In some cases this training requirement may not be too onerous; it may merely be a requirement to ensure that employees behave in a certain way when dealing with customers and have a good knowledge of the product or services being offered. In other cases, however, employees will be applying processes which, however well streamlined, will nevertheless require a degree of expertise (as in a fast food franchise). The level of training required here is obviously much higher.

It is in the area of franchisees training their own employees that problems can arise. What is being increasingly overlooked is that individual franchisees are not necessarily the best people to carry out this function.

The skills required for training a trainer are different from those that are required for training someone to do something. Some franchisors recognise this and do something about it. Others may know that something is wrong but wonder what it is, whilst yet others are not aware of the problem at all. Successful franchisors make the investment and devote the necessary resources to providing the right quality of training to franchisees in their capacity as trainers. Training and presentation skills are not easily learned, and franchisors could do a lot worse than engaging the services of a professional training outfit that can train a member of the franchisor's staff to train franchisees in how to train their employees.

Research has shown that memories fade fast. Immediately following a training session, only 60% of the information imparted is retained by the trainee. One hour after the end of a training session, only 20% of the information is retained, and one week later? Only 10%! If that is a result of professional training, what do amateur trainers think they will achieve without the necessary skills?

Franchisors should review their training programmes regularly and take a slightly longer-term view on their training needs. As business becomes more competitive, it becomes increasingly important for high-quality training to be an integral part of any business that wants to succeed.

CHAPTER 12

Sources of Income

*"There is some ill a-brewing towards my rest,
For I did dream of money-bags to-night."*
William Shakespeare, *The Merchant of Venice*

Franchisors are usually concerned with two main categories of revenue: the initial payment ('initial franchise fee') which a franchisee will be required to pay to the franchisor before he commences to trade, and the ongoing payment ('continuing franchise fee') which the franchisee pays to the franchisor as long as he remains within the franchise network. The purpose of the former is in large measure to reimburse the franchisor for the costs incurred in setting the franchisee up in business and to recover some of the costs of developing the franchise.

A franchisor will have a number of fairly onerous obligations to help the franchisee start up, and the costs of the franchisor fulfilling these obligations are usually met by the franchisee. These are obligations in the nature of training the franchisee, assisting him with site selection, recruiting staff etc.

There are several sources of income available to the franchisor, including one or more of the following:

Initial Franchise Fee

The initial franchise fee is a one-off payment made by the franchisee to the franchisor, usually (but not necessarily) on signing the franchise agreement, and should be calculated to cover the cost to the franchisor of selecting the franchisee, training him and setting him up in business. (See Chapter 13.)

In many cases the payment of the initial franchisee fee is split. A part of it may be paid by way of a deposit before the franchise agreement has been signed, another part paid at the time of signing the franchise agreement and further tranches payable at various stages up to the date when the franchisee commences trading. For example, payments may be made:

Sources of Income

- On signing the franchise agreement.
- On the franchisee commencing training.
- On the franchisee signing a lease for the premises.
- On acquiring a vehicle.
- On delivery of the start-up package.
- On launch of the initial advertising campaign.

A word about taking deposits from prospective franchisees. Not so many years ago it was fairly uncommon for franchisors to require franchisees to pay a deposit as a sign of good faith. Most franchisors were content to entertain applications from prospective franchisees and to take the time and trouble to explain to them what was involved. Although they stopped short of actually training prospective franchisees or disclosing their *modus operandi* in detail, franchisors did impart a great deal of information about their business systems. Franchisees, for their part, tended to be fairly settled in their minds as to the type of franchise they wanted. For them, it was not so much a matter of choosing which franchisor they wanted to do business with as a matter of deciding whether they were suited to the category of business (e.g. quick printing, dry cleaning, fast food) they had chosen. If no deal was done, then, by and large, each party walked away from the other and there were no recriminations.

This idyllic period came to an end with the seventies.

During the eighties franchising grew apace. This led to there being more franchisors in the same category of business than was previously the case. This in turn meant that for the first time prospective franchisees had a choice. In the seventies, if a prospective franchisee had set his mind on, for example, running a convenience store, there would in all probability have only been one franchisor in this business. There were now a number of franchisors operating similar businesses. A prospective franchisee had to pick one amongst many. These were joined in the early nineties by many more. The eighties were also a time when franchisors found it easier to recruit franchisees and there were more prospective franchisees looking to buy franchises than ever before.

The combination of these factors led to franchisees being more analytical in their approach, investigating franchises more thoroughly and shopping around.

Sources of Income

Franchisors also found that they were spending a great deal of time showing around franchisees who did not necessarily sign up with them. Unlike the seventies, franchisees were now investigating not only the concept but also their prospective franchisor. It was not unusual for a franchisor to find, having spent some weeks with a prospective franchisee, that that franchisee had in fact bought a franchise from someone else, and possibly from a competitor. It was also not uncommon for a franchisor to find that a prospective franchisee had made multiple applications to different franchisors at the same time. Franchisors also complained that some franchisees were 'time wasters' or 'giving them the runaround'.

Many franchisors now take the view that the best way to 'sift the wheat from the chaff' is to require prospective franchisees to pay a deposit prior to signing the franchise agreement as a sign of good faith and commitment.

The terms on which such a deposit is taken are as varied as franchisors themselves. The object, however, is the same for every franchisor. They each want to ensure that prospective franchisees take them seriously. Requiring a deposit certainly acts as a deterrent to those prospective franchisees who make multiple applications to different franchisors at the same time.

There is nothing illegal about franchisors taking deposits from franchisees. Whatever the agreement between the franchisor and franchisee in this respect, the law will generally enforce it. Whether or not such deposits are refundable, and if so under what circumstances, is a matter between franchisor and franchisee.

Whether or not taking a deposit is ethical depends entirely on the circumstances under which the deposit is taken and whether or not it is refundable.

There is nothing unethical about franchisors taking a reasonable sum as a deposit if it is fully refundable. Problems only arise when the terms for the deposit's refund are not clearly stated.

Taking a deposit which is not refundable under any circumstances is regarded as unethical, and the onus should be on franchisors to justify taking a deposit on such terms.

Most deposits, however, tend to be partially refundable. That is, the franchisor reserves the right to retain a part of any deposit paid by a prospective franchisee.

Sources of Income

Here, ethics and fairness seem to go hand in hand.

Where a franchisor wishes to take deposits, the following 10 basic rules ought to be observed:

1. A franchisor should be able to justify the taking of a deposit.
2. A franchisor should place the money so taken in a separate (preferably escrow) account.
3. Where the prospective franchisee ends up buying the franchise, he ought to be given credit for the deposit paid towards the payment of the initial franchise fee.
4. Deposits should be fully refundable save in exceptional circumstances.
5. Where deposits are partially refundable, the franchisor should be entitled to retain only that part of the deposit which constitutes a genuine pre-estimate of the cost to the franchisor of its dealings with the prospective franchisee up to the moment when the deposit is refunded. The franchisor should be ready, willing and able to show the prospective franchisee how that figure is arrived at. Without exception the franchisor should be able to justify the amount retained.
6. There should be a fixed period within which a prospective franchisee is required to decide whether he wants to proceed.
7. Where the deposit or a part of it is to be refunded, a date should be agreed by which the refund must be made.
8. It should be clear at the outset who is to get the interest earned on the deposit.
9. The amount of the deposit must be reasonable, bearing in mind the initial franchise fee and the investment the prospective franchisee will be required to make if he purchases the franchise.
10. Any arrangement relating to any deposit must be made in writing.

Most franchisors are now relenting on the requirement for a deposit and are willing to give prospective franchisees the benefit of the doubt. As franchisors mature, they are more able to form a judgement as to whether or not they are dealing with a 'time waster'.

Prospective franchisees who are reluctant to pay deposits to franchisors have, on occasion, suggested that such sums should be paid to the franchisor's solicitors, who are required to hold the money as stakeholders to be dealt with in accordance with the terms previously agreed between the parties. This can work well, but much depends on the nature of the franchise and how much is involved.

In some cases the *quid pro quo* for a franchisor retaining a deposit is that the franchisor has agreed to 'reserve' a territory or location (say an area in a designated town) for a defined period to give the prospective franchisee time to organise his affairs (arranging finance, seeking suitable premises etc.) before buying the franchise. Should the prospective franchisee fail to complete his purchase, the franchisor regards the retained deposit as compensation for loss of opportunity, as it will have withdrawn the territory from sale during the relevant period.

Curiously, the British Franchise Association's guidelines fail to recognise and deal with this issue.

In the final analysis, it boils down to a matter of trust between franchisor and franchisee, the reputation of the franchisor and the ability of the franchisee to look after himself.

Franchise Package Fee

Many franchises offer the franchisee a package comprising different elements to prepare the franchisee to open in business. The franchise package fee aims to recoup the costs of equipping and launching the franchisee and provide a very small element of profit.

Continuing Franchise Fee

As soon as a franchisee commences trading, his franchisor will expect to receive continuing franchise fees from him. These fees should cover the franchisor's provision of ongoing field support and contribute towards the costs of administrating the wider franchise network, but they will also contain an element of profit for the franchisor.

Sources of Income

A prospective franchisor should decide at the outset how it wishes to collect its ongoing revenue from franchisees. This will depend to a great extent on the activities of each franchise, e.g. whether it is a retail or service franchise. Whichever way it is collected, a franchisor must structure the terms of its franchises to ensure a continuing flow of revenue in order to provide the services demanded by franchisees and to perform its obligations under its franchise agreement.

The most common form of continuing franchise fee is based on a percentage of the franchisee's gross sales turnover (excluding VAT). The term 'royalty' is sometimes used to describe this type of revenue, but this is misleading as we are dealing with a payment by the franchisee to the franchisor for services rendered. If it were purely a royalty, it would be a payment for the privilege of using the franchisor's name or idea and no other service would be provided. In a business format franchise this is not the case. To maintain the goodwill and support of its franchisees, a franchisor must provide continuing services.

For more on continuing franchise fees, see Chapter 13.

Mark-up on Products Sold to Franchisees

As an alternative to a regular turnover-based payment, franchisors may take their ongoing fee from a mark-up on products they sell to their franchisees. This is possible if the franchise involves branded products and the franchisee is obliged to buy such products only from his franchisor or suppliers nominated by his franchisor.

For more on mark-ups as a means of deriving revenue from franchisees, see Chapter 13.

Advertising Contributions

Most franchise schemes provide for expenditure on advertising, marketing and promotion by both franchisor and franchisee.

The degree of promotional activity in which a franchisor will engage is very important and the ratio of promotional expenditure to retail sales will vary according to whether a particular business is in its early stages or well established.

One of the advantages that a franchisee obtains in a well-established franchise network is the benefit of national or regional advertising: something he could not achieve if he were on his own. Clearly it is right that the franchisee should contribute to this.

Contributions from franchisees can be calculated as a percentage of sales or a fixed annual payment. For obvious reasons the former arrangement is preferable as this is linked to the ability of the franchisee to pay. The administration of contributions has, in the past, caused considerable conflict between franchisee and franchisor.

Views amongst franchisors vary as to whether promotional costs should be incorporated into the continuing franchise fee structure or whether a separate percentage levy should be made. Nowadays it is more usual for advertising contributions to be kept separate from continuing franchise fees.

The most common approaches are:

- The franchisee conducting his own marketing in accordance with a plan laid out by his franchisor and providing proof that the approved sums have been expended on the activities specified by his franchisor.
- The franchisee submitting the appropriate sum calculated as a percentage of the franchisee's turnover – in my experience the range appears to be between 2.5% and 7.5% – to the franchisor, which then adds it to its own expenditure.
- The establishment of an advertising fund into which all franchisees place their contributions along with those of the franchisor (for example, if a franchisee is required to contribute 5% of its gross turnover, the franchisor should do likewise for each of its company-owned outlets). The advantages of this method are improved purchasing power, more efficient use of funds, co-ordinated programmes, and franchisees participating in decisions on how and when their money is spent.

Where a new franchise has been set up, it is obviously not viable to advertise nationally and it is usually left to the franchisee under guidance from the franchisor to initiate local advertising, marketing and promotion schemes.

Sundry Services Fee

Where a franchisor offers a special service such as bookkeeping, accounting, stock control etc. it is acceptable for the franchisor to charge a fee to reflect the costs of the service with a small element of profit. Use of these services by franchisees is usually optional.

Rental Income

In some cases, particularly when the business of the franchisee involves retail sales or catering and prime locations are required for outlets, the franchisor may have to acquire sites itself and sublet them to franchisees at commercial rents. This usually arises because few franchisees have a track record as tenants, and so a landlord will not find the franchisee's covenant to pay rent acceptable but will be willing to grant a lease to his franchisor.

The rent the franchisee has to pay under the lease or sublease to the franchisor will be a commercial one with some profit usually built in for the franchisor, typically between 2.5% and 5% of the rent paid by the franchisee, to offset the costs of being involved in the property

If the landlord requires the franchisor to pay a premium, the premium element can be dealt with in a number of ways.

- It can be built into the rent paid by the franchisee to his franchisor under the sublease, and can be repaid over a number of years.
- The franchisee can reimburse his franchisor over time for the premium by treating it as a loan repayment, with interest, over an agreed term.
- The premium remains the responsibility of the franchisor.

In the first two cases, where the franchisee has paid the premium, it is only fair that the lease is transferred from the franchisor to the franchisee, provided the landlord has no objection.

From the franchisee's point of view, care must be taken to ensure that the franchisor does not use the lease to impose unreasonable conditions which it would not feel able to insert into the franchise agreement.

For more on franchisors as landlords, see Chapter 37.

Income from Commission

In many franchises an opportunity exists for the franchisor to generate some additional income from commission earned. These opportunities will occur, for example, where the franchise involves the purchase of ventilation systems, shop fixtures etc. or where the franchisor has arranged a special comprehensive insurance scheme for its franchisees through a broker.

In such cases it is important that the franchisor passes on the benefits of its purchasing power to its franchisee. The amount to be passed on to the franchisee should be a reasonable share of the commission received by the franchisor. Should a franchisee find that he can buy cheaper directly from a supplier other than the franchisor, a conflict will almost certainly ensue.

Where the franchisor is a manufacturer and is supplying equipment directly to the franchisee, the price will normally include a mark-up to cover the franchisor's costs in doing so.

Income from Leasing Equipment

Where the franchise involves special equipment and machinery, in some cases the franchisor can arrange for the leasing of equipment to the franchisee on favourable terms, rather than a sale, so as to reduce the cost of the initial package. The franchisor may receive a commission from the leasing company. Alternatively, the franchisor may lease the equipment directly to the franchisee and take its profit on that transaction.

In general terms, there should be no objection to such arrangements provided the franchisee is aware of what is happening and is getting some benefit from the franchisor's buying power. It is important for the franchisee to know the extent to which the franchisor can add to the cost of operating the franchisee's business by taking commission and fees as part of the package.

Franchise Transfer Fee

Franchisors will usually charge an initial franchise fee type of payment for granting consent to a franchisee's sale of his business. It is for the franchisor to decide whether the buyer or the seller should pay this fee. The buyer will subsequently become a franchisee in the seller's place.

Avoiding a Shortfall

It is not only the continuing advertising activities which are likely to incur a deficit during the early years of trading. The franchisor may also be unable to recoup all the day-to-day management and field support costs from the continuing income derived from the franchisees. Therefore, it is important for the franchisor to satisfy itself that, over three to five years, the cumulative income will be sufficient to compensate for any initial shortfall and that there is sufficient capital available to cover it. The franchisor must ensure that, as far as possible, candidates selected as franchisees are capable of building a successful business and the appeal of the product or service is maintained.

A franchisee will generally look in aggregate at the continuing fees and any separate advertising levy, and make a judgement about whether they represent a fair deal. If the fees represent more than 25% of his turnover, the franchisee may feel exploited because there will be little scope for him to generate the scale of reward to which he aspires. In any event, after the first few years there is sometimes a tendency for successful franchisees to become critical of the level of continuing payments made to franchisors. Where this happens it may be because the franchisor has failed to describe adequately the financial benefits being passed on to the franchisee, such as the advantage of its buying power.

In isolated cases, franchisors have attempted to avoid such criticism of fee levels by providing for reducing levels of continuing franchise fees (but without reducing the advertising levy) after a specified number of years. On the whole, however, it is better to maintain the fee level and to apply adequate resources to the continuing provision of services, support and development of the franchise concept.

It is common knowledge that, as years go by, franchisees increasingly resent having to make payments to franchisors. In some cases franchisors, in addition to collecting continuing franchise fees and contributions to a separate advertising levy, may need to recover from franchisees various expenses incurred on the franchisee's behalf. For example, the franchisor may be the landlord of a retail outlet occupied by a franchisee (the franchisor having taken a head lease from the freeholder) because landlords have been reluctant to grant a lease to the franchisee directly on the grounds that the franchisee's guarantee is insufficient. The franchisor therefore has to recover rent payments from the franchisee together with any costs which may be incurred from time to time in dealing with rent reviews, repairing covenants and the like.

Telephone charges are sometimes treated in the same way. The nature of some franchises is such that it is desirable for a franchisor to handle the collection of debts from its franchisees' customers, and in such a case the franchisor will probably need to remit the collections on a weekly basis, probably deducting various amounts due from the franchisee from such remittances.

A Final Note on Franchisor Income

In all cases, without exception, when it comes to franchisor income, the golden rule is *transparency*.

Having looked at the various items of expenditure of the typical franchising company, the franchisor should look at the options open to it regarding income and decide upon a structure.

However, in deciding its fee options it must not neglect the franchisee. A financial structure which ignores the interests of the franchisee will be doomed to failure. Even if it were to attract franchisees, such a franchisor would soon experience problems. Profit margins must be capable of producing attractive profits for both the franchisor and the franchisee.

The financial obligations of both franchisor and franchisee must be drafted precisely in the franchise agreement. It is essential to accurately define the basis on which a continuing franchise fee is calculated and how and when it is to be paid.

Revenue and Income Flows

All references to 'franchisee' mean the developer where the direct franchising method is used.

Sources of Income

Initial Franchise Fees

```
        ┌─────────────┐
        │  Franchisor │
        └─────────────┘
               ▲
               │
               £
               │
        ┌─────────────┐
        │Sub-Franchisor│
        └─────────────┘
```

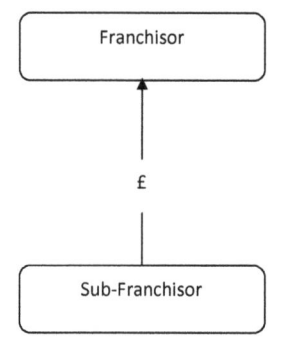

Diagram A: Master franchise fee

```
        ┌─────────────┐
        │  Franchisor │
        └─────────────┘
               ▲
               │
               £
               │
        ┌─────────────┐
        │ (Developer) │
        │  Franchisee │
        └─────────────┘
```

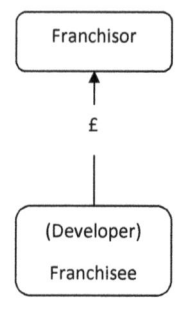

Diagram B: Development grant fee

Sources of Income

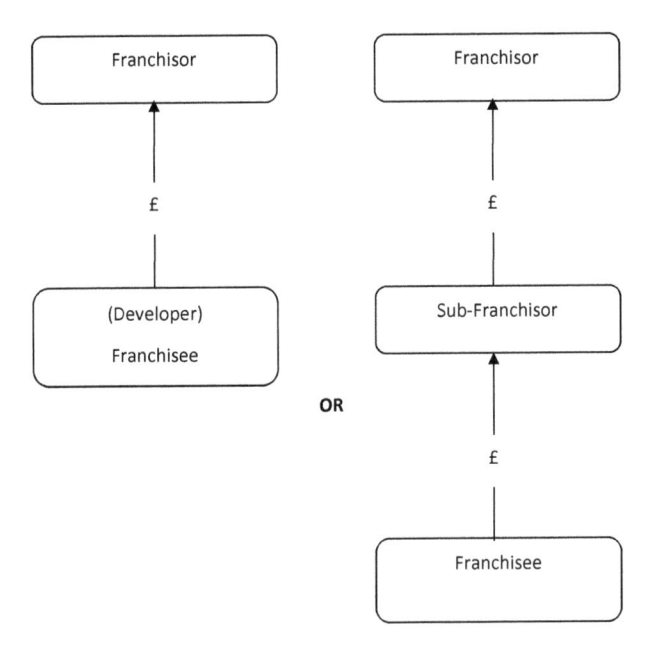

Diagram C: Unit franchise fee

Sale of Initial Franchise Package

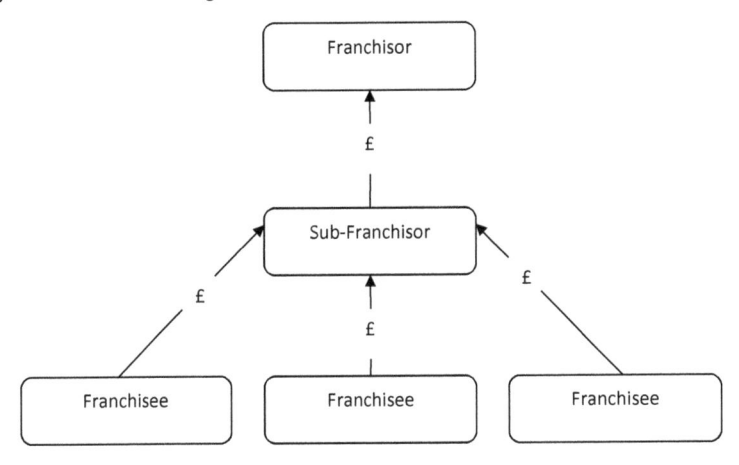

Diagram D: Sale of initial franchise package by franchisor to sub-franchisor, and by sub-franchisor to franchisee

Sources of Income

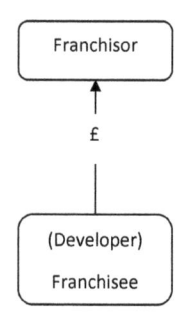

Diagram E: Sale of initial franchise package by franchisor to franchisee

Sale of Equipment

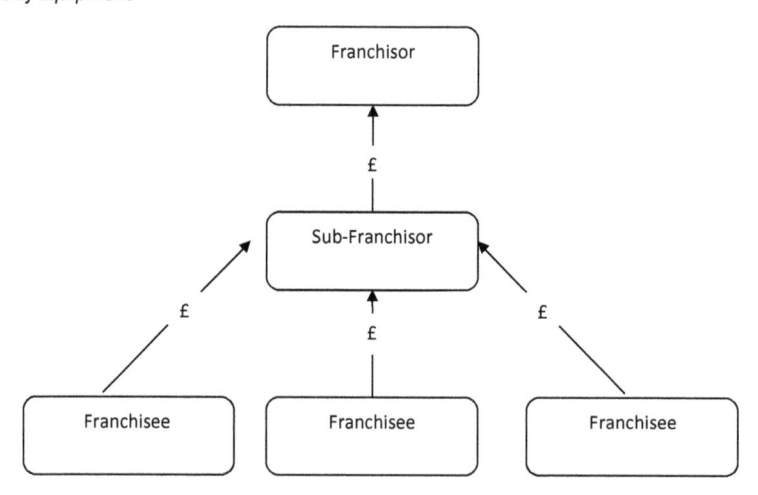

Diagram F: Sale of equipment by franchisor to sub-franchisor, and by sub-franchisor to franchisee

Sources of Income

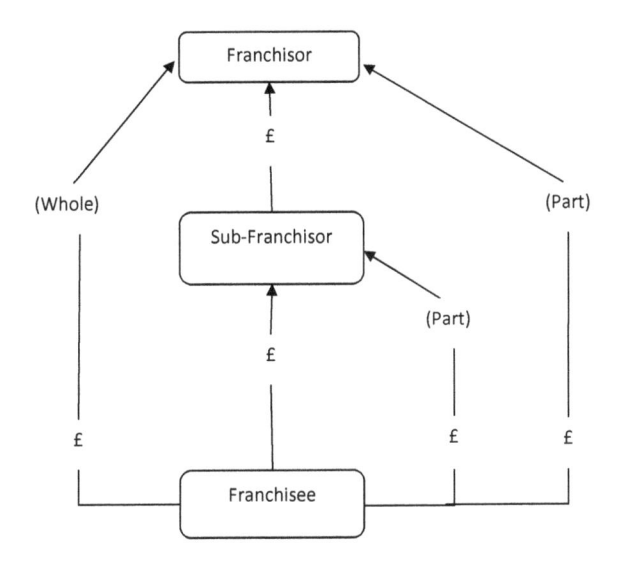

Diagram G: Alternative structure for sale of equipment by franchisor to sub-franchisor, and by sub-franchisor to franchisee

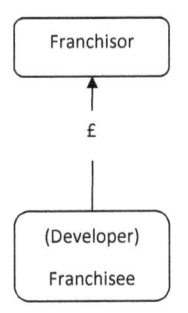

Diagram H: Sale of equipment by franchisor to franchisee

Sources of Income

Leasing of Premises

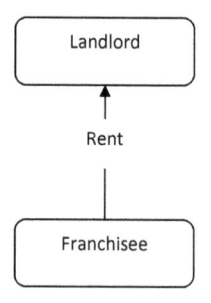

```
        ┌──────────┐
        │ Landlord │
        └──────────┘
             ▲
             │
            Rent
             │
        ┌───────────┐
        │ Franchisee│
        └───────────┘
```

Diagram I: Leasing of premises from landlord to franchisee

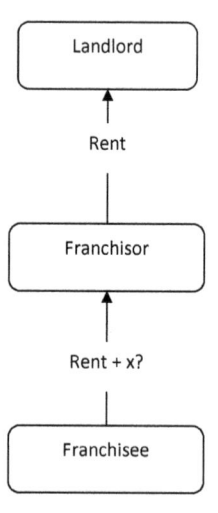

```
        ┌──────────┐
        │ Landlord │
        └──────────┘
             ▲
             │
            Rent
             │
        ┌───────────┐
        │ Franchisor│
        └───────────┘
             ▲
             │
          Rent + x?
             │
        ┌───────────┐
        │ Franchisee│
        └───────────┘
```

Diagram J: Leasing of premises from landlord to franchisor, then franchisor to franchisee (at a profit rental?)

Sources of Income

Leasing of Equipment

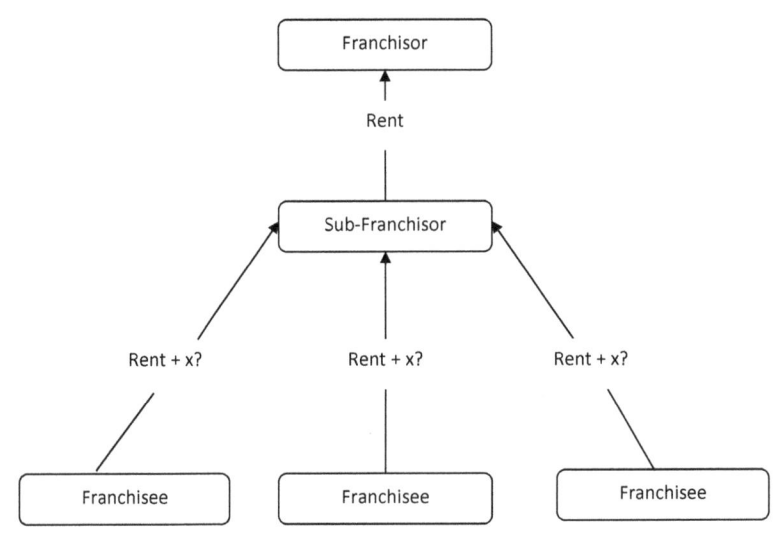

Diagram K: Leasing of equipment by franchisor to sub-franchisor, and by sub-franchisor to franchisee (at a profit?)

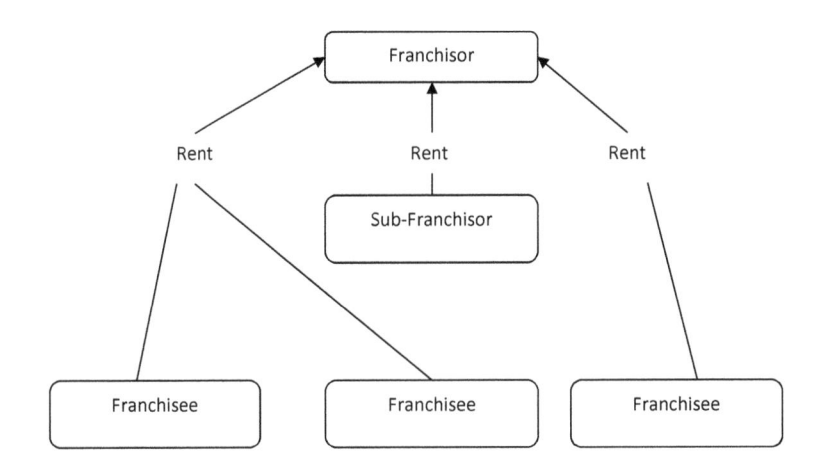

Diagram L: Leasing of equipment by franchisor to sub-franchisor and to franchisee

Sources of Income

Continuing Franchise Fees

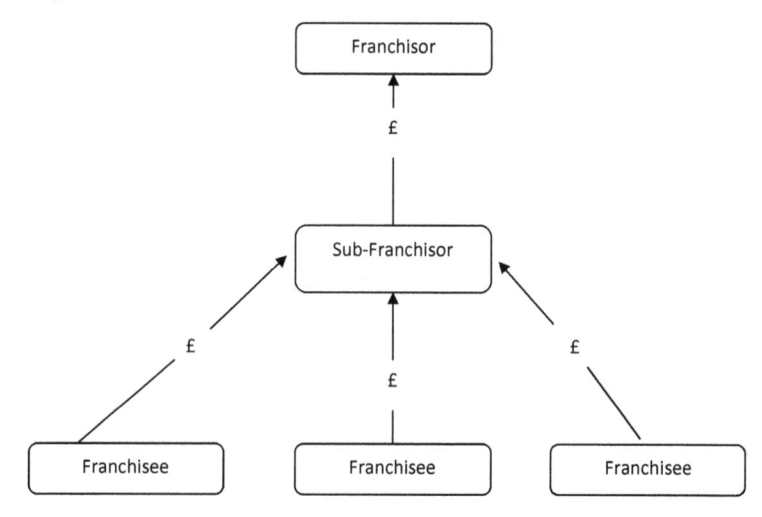

Diagram M: Continuing franchise fees paid by sub-franchisor to franchisor, and by franchisee to sub-franchisor

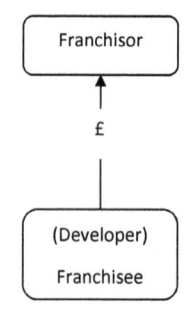

Diagram N: Continuing franchise fees paid by franchisee to franchisor

Sources of Income

Sale of Products

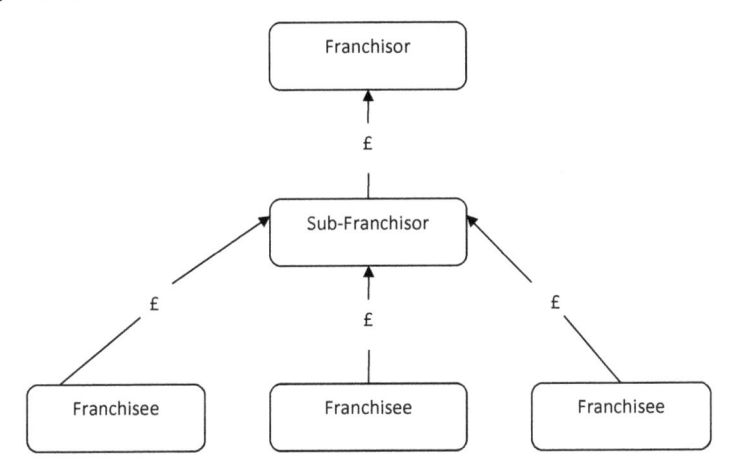

Diagram O: Sale of products by franchisor to sub-franchisor, and by sub-franchisor to franchisee

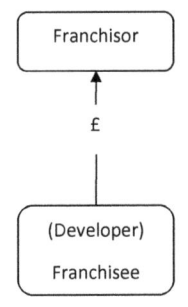

Diagram P: Sale of products by franchisor to franchisee

Sources of Income

Advertising, Marketing and Promotion Contributions

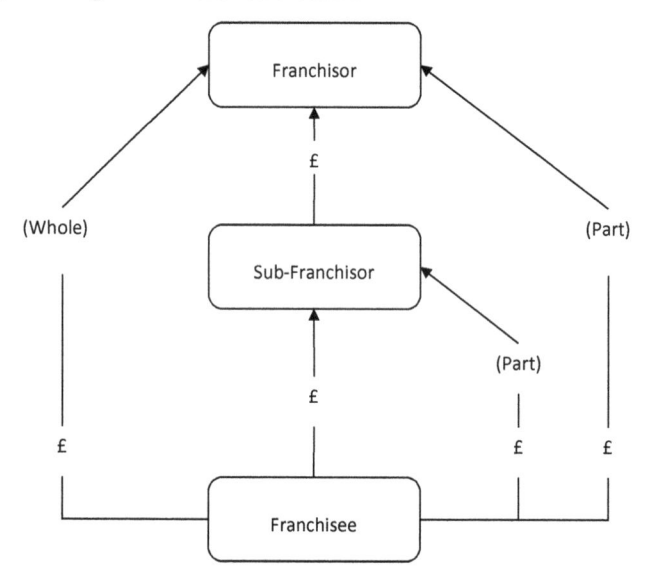

Diagram Q: Contributions made by sub-franchisor to franchisor, and by franchisee to sub-franchisor and/or franchisor

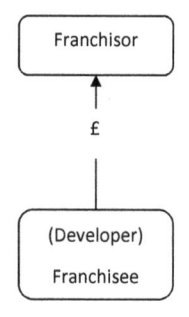

Diagram R: Contributions made by franchisee to franchisor

Sources of Income

Training Fees

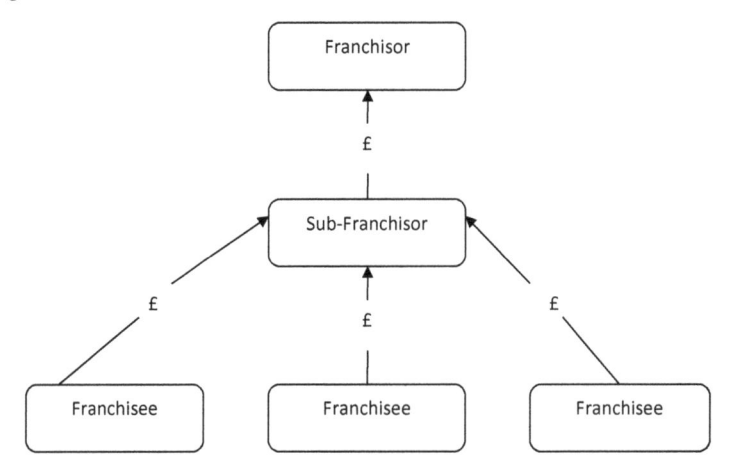

Diagram S: Training fees paid by sub-franchisor to franchisor, and by franchisee to sub-franchisor

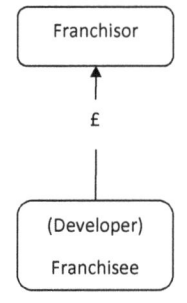

Diagram T: Training fees paid by franchisee to franchisor

Sources of Income

Franchise Transfer Fees

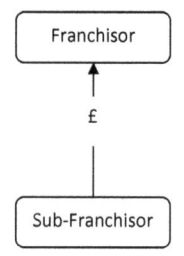

Diagram U: Franchise transfer fees paid by sub-franchisor to franchisor (sale by sub-franchisor)

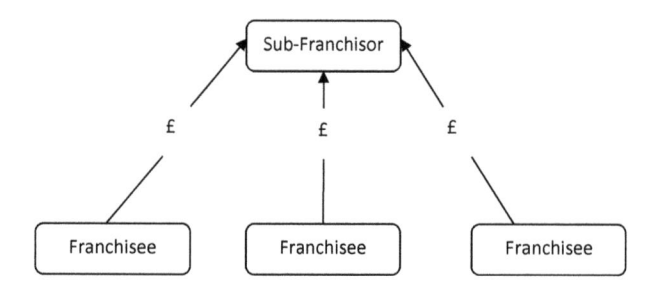

Diagram V: Franchise transfer fees paid by franchisee to sub-franchisor (sale by franchisee)

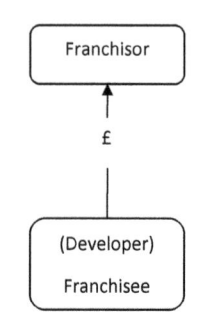

Diagram W: Franchise transfer fees paid by franchisee to franchisor

Sources of Income

Renewal Fees

```
        ┌──────────────┐
        │  Franchisor  │
        └──────────────┘
               ↑
               │
               £
               │
        ┌──────────────┐
        │Sub-Franchisor/│
        │  Developer   │
        └──────────────┘
```

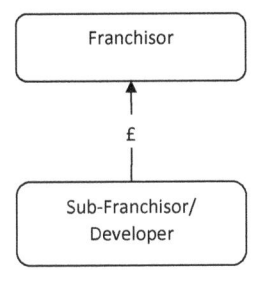

Diagram X: Renewal fees paid by sub-franchisor or developer to franchisor, on renewal of master licence or development agreement

```
        ┌──────────────┐
        │  Franchisor  │
        └──────────────┘
               ↑
               │
               £
               │
        ┌──────────────┐
        │ (Developer)  │
        │  Franchisee  │
        └──────────────┘
```

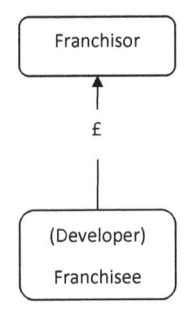

Diagram Y: Renewal fees paid by (developer) franchisee to franchisor, on renewal of franchise agreement by developer

Sources of Income

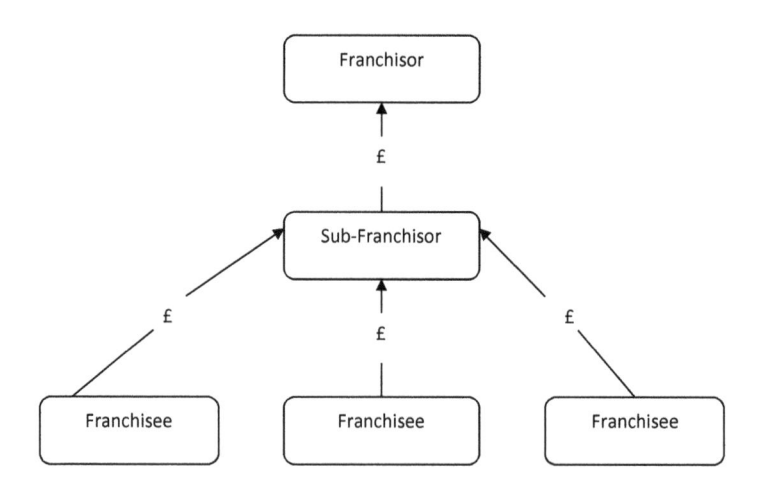

Diagram Z: Renewal fees paid by franchisee to sub-franchisor, on renewal of franchise agreement by franchisee under a master franchise agreement

CHAPTER 13

How Much Can You Charge?

"The fortune of the one is inexorably lined to the fortune of the other."

Franchisors need to be rewarded for their efforts and need to be paid a contribution towards their costs.

Franchisors are usually concerned with two categories of revenue. The first is an *initial payment* which a franchisee will be required to pay to the franchisor before he commences trade, and the second an *ongoing payment* which the franchisee pays to the franchisor as long as he remains within the franchise network.

The purpose of the initial fee is in large measure to reimburse the franchisor for the costs incurred in setting the franchisee up in business and to recover some of the costs of developing the franchise. A franchisor will have a number of fairly onerous obligations to help the franchisee's start-up, and the franchisor's costs of fulfilling these obligations are usually met by the franchisee. These are obligations in the nature of training the franchisee, assisting him with site selection, recruiting staff etc. Once a franchisee's business is up and running, the franchisor should expect to be paid a continuing franchise fee on a regular basis by the franchisee, in return for the franchisor carrying out its obligations to its franchisee on an ongoing basis and also by way of profit.

A golden rule of franchising is that franchisors should structure their franchises in such a way that they stand to make money only if their franchisees make money. This ensures that franchisors have a vested interest in seeing their franchisees' financial success.

Initial Franchise Fee

The initial franchise fee is a one-off payment made by the franchisee to the franchisor, usually (but not necessarily) on signing the franchise agreement, and should be calculated to cover the cost to the franchisor of selecting the franchisee, training him and setting him up in business (see Chapter 12).

How Much Can You Charge?

The initial franchise fee should be calculated to include the following costs to the franchisor:

- A proportion of the setting-up costs of the franchisor.
- Recruiting, vetting and approving the prospective franchisee.
- Training the prospective franchisee and his staff.
- Assisting and advising the franchisee in setting up business. This will cover a range of activities, e.g. helping to find suitable premises, assisting with making planning applications, negotiating a lease, applying to a landlord for a licence to carry out alterations, shop fitting, initial advertising, launch, recruitment and selection of staff.
- In the case of a mobile franchise, providing advice and assistance with regard to the acquisition of suitable vehicles and their fitting out and decorating.
- Providing a start-up package containing a number of items such as stationery, uniforms, electronic equipment (e.g. tills), telephone answering systems etc., the contents of which will vary from one franchise to another.

The received wisdom is that franchisors should only make a nominal profit (if any at all) from selling franchises. Profits for the franchisor should derive from the continuing franchise fees (see Chapter 12). That is not to say, however, that franchisors should not charge a sum in the nature of a premium, providing the franchisor can justify it in ethical terms. There are some franchisors who have a powerful presence in the market and whose brand commands strong customer loyalty, and they therefore consider it to be both ethical and legitimate to charge a premium almost in the form of a 'joining fee'. This also applies to mature franchisors who have been in business for a number of years and who may have an international reputation. Examples of these would be McDonald's, the Body Shop, Holiday Inn, KFC and Domino's Pizza. In many cases, however, one will find that even these franchisors do not charge a large premium for 'membership' of their network.

The amount of any premium will usually be influenced to some extent by such considerations as the exclusivity of a particular product or service, the strength of the franchisor's brand, the readiness of demand for the franchisor's product or services and, sometimes, territory protection (granting exclusivity etc.). In addition, the period of the franchise may have some bearing on this.

Franchises are usually granted for a fixed term rather than for an indefinite period, but it is rare for a franchisor to charge a renewal fee when the initial period expires. There are two main reasons for this. First, franchisors like to avoid introducing new charges which may have the effect of eroding any goodwill established during the initial period. Second, any such fee would usually be taken by the franchisor as pure profit. After all, on renewal there will be very few, if any, initial obligations which the franchisor will have to perform given that the franchisee will already be in business and fully trained.

During the early period of trading by a franchisee, the continuing franchise fees payable to the franchisor are unlikely to cover the franchisor's outgoings, but franchisors should be warned against the temptation to compensate for this by charging an inflated price for the grant of a franchise. Prospective franchisees who seek professional advice will usually be warned off such a franchise on the grounds that they are being asked to pay 'something for nothing'. Indeed, a number of the few notorious cases which have arisen have involved artificially high initial franchise fees.

Calculating the Initial Franchise Fee

Let us assume that the initial development of the franchise costs £100,000. A prospective franchisor must then determine over what period it wishes to recoup this sum.

The initial franchise fee should relate to the initial term of the franchise agreement. If the franchise agreement is to be for an initial term of five years, then the franchisor should aim to recover its true costs within the five-year period. So in this case we have a figure of £20,000 per year.

A prospective franchisor in its research should have determined the number of franchises it hopes to sell over the first five years. If one assumes this number is 100, the franchisor should plan to sell 10 franchises per year and structure its forecasts and budgets accordingly.

We therefore arrive at a figure of £2,000 per franchise to recover the development costs, to which would have to be added the cost of setting up a franchisee in business. Naturally these costs will differ from franchise to franchise, but the principle remains the same.

How Much Can You Charge?

By apportioning the development costs over the franchise term and in proportion to the number of franchisees it plans to recruit, a prospective franchisor is not only budgeting to recoup its costs but it is also doing so in a way that does not artificially inflate this fee in the early stages.

As a general guideline, the initial franchise fee should in practice not exceed 10% of the total cost of the franchise package. Therefore if the total investment expected of a new franchisee is £50,000, an initial fee in the region of £3,000–£5,000 would be par for the course. However, in the case of the smaller and cheaper franchises the percentage may be higher to cover the initial supply of services, and conversely in a higher-cost franchise this percentage may be lower (but not so low as to leave the franchisor with a deficit in terms of the cost of setting up a new franchisee in business).

A franchisor should aim to obtain a strong, widely-spread network of outlets as quickly as possible in order to ensure a good healthy flow of continuing revenue, rather than trying to extract a large profit from the initial franchise fee. Too high a fee will discourage prospective franchisees and cause suspicions, especially if the continuing franchise fees are small. This is because receipts from initial franchise fees will dwindle as the territories available for sale are taken up by franchisees and low continuing franchise fees will be insufficient to provide the franchisor with the income needed to sustain growth.

Too low an initial franchise fee, however, will also cause problems as it will not cover the franchisor's costs. Whilst the initial franchise fee should not be used as a vehicle for overcharging franchisees and making a fast profit, it should be appreciated that in the initial years of the franchise the initial franchise fee will account for an important part of the franchisor's revenue, since income from other sources will take some time to come on-stream and peak. As the network becomes more mature, initial franchise fees are replaced in importance by continuing franchise fees.

It is important to remember that, at least initially, the franchisor is faced with expenses that its income from the franchise will not cover. However, provided its franchise is properly structured, its income should grow faster than its expenses as each new franchisee who commences operation represents additional income.

Once the franchise is established in the eyes of the consumer, the law of supply and demand comes into play. The more successful a franchise, the greater the entry fee the franchisor may be able to charge new franchisees. Given that the franchisor is established, there is little risk of the franchisor charging high initial franchise fees to as many new franchisees as possible and making off with the money. However, again, a franchisor should avoid being avaricious. Excessive initial fees would attract unwelcome competitors and could discourage first-class franchisees who are unable to afford the initial investment but would, if they could afford to buy a franchise, generate high continuing franchise fees through their performance.

Deciding on the level of initial franchise fee therefore takes fine judgement. Franchisors would do well to remember that one of their prime tasks is to help their franchisees make the most of their money and to get them into business effectively while keeping the level of their investment as modest as possible. This attitude will certainly increase the flow of prospective franchisees as well as maximising the receipt of continuing franchise fees.

Finally, there is nothing to prevent a franchisor from reviewing the amount of the initial franchise fee to be charged to reflect inflation and current circumstances. It goes without saying that if such a change is to be made, it usually takes the form of an increase rather than a decrease. Any decrease will cause dissension and protests from those who had to pay more when they joined the network.

Franchise Package Fee

Many franchises offer a franchisee a package comprising different elements, the sum of which will prepare the franchisee to open in business.

If a franchisor wants to charge a franchise package fee, it will need to quantify the costs of equipping and launching the average new franchisee and arrive at a package fee which will recoup these costs and provide a small element of profit.

It would be difficult to include any variable costs in the initial franchise package fee at an early stage: for example, those for the acquisition of premises, structural alterations, building and fitting out, obtaining any planning permission etc. These services would have to be provided as an optional extra. It can, however, include the cost of:

- Assistance with site selection.
- Preparation of drawings and plans.
- Purchase of equipment, shop fitting and stock.
- Selection and training of franchisee.
- Assistance with selection and training of staff.
- Franchisee launch.

Ongoing Income from Franchisees

Although there is no law regulating how much a franchisor can charge a franchisee by way of ongoing income, would-be franchisors should be aware of what is considered to be ethical (see Chapter 26).

Ongoing income is usually referred to as the continuing franchise fee and is obtained from franchisees in one of three ways:

1. Charging the franchisee a percentage of his gross income (net of VAT) on an ongoing basis (see 'Turnover-Based Franchise Fee', below).

2. A mark-up on products which are the subject of the franchise and which have to be purchased by the franchisee exclusively from the franchisor (see 'Mark-up on Products Sold to Franchisees', below).

3. A fixed sum payable by the franchisee at regular intervals (see 'Fixed Fees', below).

It is considered highly unethical for a franchisor to derive income from a franchisee from both a percentage of his turnover and a mark-up on products it sells to him. In such a case the franchisee is effectively being asked to pay twice, once for the mark-up on the products he buys from his franchisor and then again as a percentage of what he receives when he sells them, unless a deduction is made for the cost of those products when calculating the franchisee's turnover.

Turnover-Based Franchise Fee

This is the most common form of payment and is usually calculated as a percentage of the franchisee's gross sales turnover (excluding VAT). It may be on a sliding scale whereby there is a higher percentage rate to start with and as the turnover of a franchisee increases the rate decreases.

The payment system under which ongoing payments to the franchisor are linked to sales has the advantage that the franchisee's and the franchisor's success are closely linked, since the franchisor will only get an income if the franchisee earns an income. It also has the advantage of simplicity.

In determining the percentage rate to be charged, it is unwise to generalise. There is no magic formula for determining this. There is no such thing as a norm. The fee should ideally cover the cost of the services the franchisor provides for the franchisee, plus a profit for the franchisor. A rate of 10% of the franchisee's gross turnover may be adequate for one franchisor but may be inadequate for another. Much will depend on the margins which a franchisee is capable of achieving. In a fast food business with high turnover and relatively modest profit margins, one would expect to see a lower percentage than, say, in a retail franchise with more modest turnover but with higher profit margins.

Some franchisors charge a minimum or fixed continuing franchise fee. There are reservations about such arrangements since the franchisor gets paid irrespective of whether its franchisee is successful or not. (See 'Fixed Fees', below.)

A franchisor should have confidence in the franchisee it has selected and trained. By charging a royalty-type fee, a franchisor is relying on the honesty and efficiency of its franchisees in submitting the *correct* payment at the *right* time. It is strongly recommended that the collection of these fees should be done at weekly rather than at monthly intervals. Not only is this good for the franchisor's cash flow, but it also limits the level of franchisee indebtedness.

Turnover-based continuing franchise fees are an efficient and fair source of income providing they can be properly controlled and monitored. The franchisee knows precisely how much he has to pay and how to calculate it. On the other hand, as he becomes more established and successful and thus more independent, the amount of money he pays to his franchisor will increase correspondingly and he may feel this to be an unacceptable drain on his pocket.

So it is important for a franchisor to justify the fee by the quality of support services it provides.

Mark-up on Products Sold to Franchisees

If the franchise involves branded products and merchandise, and a tied purchase arrangement in the franchise agreement obliges the franchisee to buy such products only from his franchisor or its nominated suppliers, it may be possible for the franchisor to obtain its ongoing revenue from a mark-up on the products or, where a nominated supplier is used, from commission from the supplier.

In effect the franchisor is obtaining its ongoing franchise fee by taking a larger gross profit for the goods than it might otherwise have obtained.

There is usually no objection to this arrangement from franchisees as they are able to buy such products on more favourable terms than they would if they were independent, due to the bulk purchasing power of the franchisor. Furthermore, the franchisees' supplier (their franchisor, in this case) will treat them as valued customers. A small independent business is unlikely to be treated in the same way by a third-party supplier.

In the mark-up method, the fee is absorbed into the price of the goods supplied. Its collection is made easier because the fee is collected at the time of the sale of the goods to the franchisee and there is no need to set up an extra control system. The mark-up on goods will vary from franchise to franchise and probably from one type of product to another, and so it is not possible to suggest a norm.

A possible criticism of this method of payment is that the franchisee can be at the mercy of an unscrupulous franchisor unless some form of protection against abuse for the franchisee is built into the franchise agreement.

Unless the franchisor is a manufacturer or has exclusive rights over products, it is unlikely that it will adopt the mark-up method, if only because of the uncertainty of supply and because there is no guarantee that it will legally be able to force its franchisees to buy only from the franchisor during the whole period of the franchise agreement; competition law is changing all the time.

Choosing a Method

On balance, there is a strong preference for the turnover-based franchise fee method as opposed to the mark-up method. A continuing franchise fee expressed as a percentage of the gross turnover of the franchisee's business is probably a fairer system. The franchisee appreciates that if he pays large sums to the franchisor it is because his turnover is high and he should be doing well, whereas if a franchisee's business is depressed then his franchisor's income will reduce in direct proportion to his own.

A franchisee will probably find a percentage fee more readily acceptable in the knowledge that the franchisor will not be able to unreasonably increase the margin for itself at the expense of its franchisees, whereas in the mark-up method it would be much easier for a franchisor to increase the price of products it sells to its franchisees.

Having said that, a franchisor could be vulnerable in a tied purchase arrangement if, for whatever reason, its franchisees ganged up on it and refused to pay for the goods supplied. This could place the franchisor in a difficult position *vis-à-vis* its own trade creditors.

Whichever method the franchisor chooses, it must budget to ensure that the flow of fees is sufficient to cover its overheads and to make a reasonable profit.

Where the franchisor is the principal supplier of goods to the franchisee, it will probably have to finance stock and provide warehousing and distribution facilities. Furthermore, there will be the need for stock control and, in some businesses, a significant risk of obsolescence. When a product is theoretically suited to the mark-up approach (e.g. flowers, consumables with a limited shelf life), in my experience franchisors and franchisees favour turnover-based continuing franchise fees regardless.

From the franchisor's point of view, the advantage of turnover-based continuing franchise fees is that it can specify a form of weekly revenue report for completion for each franchisee. This enables the franchisor to monitor the performance of the franchisee in a number of key areas, thereby providing valuable feedback to assist in the further development of the business. Indeed, it is possible to devise a weekly report which could also provide the franchisee with a simple estimate of his profit or loss for the period.

How Much Can You Charge?

A possible disadvantage of calculating the continuing franchise fees by reference to the franchisee's sales is that it places a supervisory burden on the franchisor insofar as it will have to be satisfied that the franchisee is disclosing all sales revenue and is not offering unacceptable discounts to customers. This particular difficulty would, of course, be eliminated if the franchisor relied on a mark-up on the goods supplied instead.

Psychologically, the mark-up approach has also been suggested to be less taxing for the franchisee than having to make payments to his franchisor at regular intervals.

There are, however, drawbacks. In adopting the practice of charging a franchisee by means of a mark-up on the supply of goods, is the franchisor:

- Satisfied that this is the best method for both franchisor and franchisee?
- Capable of monitoring the franchisees' revenues accurately?
- Satisfied with each franchisee's pricing policy (see Chapter 23)?

Fixed Fees

In a turnover-based payment, at least the franchisor's income is geared to the level of business conducted by the franchisee, but what if a franchisor requires the payment of a fixed fee from its franchisee irrespective of the franchisee's turnover? Such a structure is not unethical in itself, but it is frowned upon and it does place an obligation on the franchisor to justify it.

One type of fixed fee structure requires the franchisee to pay a fixed sum to the franchisor at regular intervals (usually monthly). Very often the structure provides for some form of increase during the period of the agreement, usually annually and usually by reference to some formula.

The disadvantages of a fixed fee structure are obvious, the main one being that under this type of structure, there is little incentive for the franchisor to support its franchisees. It stands to receive a fee from its franchisees irrespective of their level of business.

However, depending on the nature of the business, there can be some advantages for the franchisor. It does not have to worry about the process of verification or

How Much Can You Charge?

the monitoring of the franchisee's turnover levels. It receives a regular income irrespective of economic conditions and, if it gets the formula right, the effects of inflation will be taken care of.

The franchisee, meanwhile, can treat such a fee as a fixed overhead. This can be a strong motivating factor for the franchisee because the greater the franchisee's turnover, the larger the proportion he can retain.

As long as the franchisor is not avaricious and the fees are fixed at a sensible level, this structure has appeal to both parties. The franchisor accepts the risk that when things are going well, the franchisor will make less money than it would have with a turnover-based fee structure. The franchisee accepts that if things go badly he may be stuck with a high overhead.

But can such a scheme be justified on ethical grounds?

The answer is yes, in certain circumstances and depending on the nature of the franchise. Such a scheme is most commonly found in low-tech franchises which are uncomplicated, where the franchisor has little to give to the franchisee by way of ongoing support once the training is completed and where customers usually pay in cash. Domestic cleaning services are a good example of this.

Another type of continuing franchise fee is where a franchisee is required to pay a fixed sum as a minimum fee, plus an additional payment calculated as a percentage of the franchisee's gross turnover (net of VAT). This is an entirely different matter and should be treated with great caution. Again much depends on the nature of the business and the circumstances, but the burden of justifying such a structure is considerably more onerous for the franchisor. On the odd occasion that one comes across such a structure (and they are rare), the fixed minimum fee is usually extremely low. Furthermore, there is usually a *quid pro quo* in that in return the franchisee will receive some sort of territory protection (see Chapter 20).

Fixed fees are rare, but nevertheless they do exist. Franchisors who are tempted to go the fixed fee route need to be aware that it does not meet with ready acceptance and they will be called upon to justify their choice of fee structure.

Advertising Contributions

It may be difficult to budget accurately at the outset for the cost of advertising and other support, irrespective of whether a specific levy is likely to be made on a franchisee. However, an attempt at budgeting should be carried out because this is an area where wide discrepancies arise between promotional promises made by franchisors and what they can actually afford based on income to be received from franchisees. In many cases, it will be necessary to work on the basis that the advertising activities will operate in deficit for two years or more, rather than curtail promotional support.

For more on advertising contributions, see Chapters 12 and 16.

Reviewing the Financial Terms

Once the financial terms have been agreed between franchisor and franchisee they should, effectively, be written in tablets of stone and not changed without the consent of both parties. It is important, therefore, that the franchisor gets it right. However, that is not to say that the franchisor should not keep the financial terms of its franchise under constant review. An opportunity will present itself to impose revised financial terms upon renewal of the franchise agreement, provided, of course, the franchise agreement has been properly drafted.

Many franchisors will find that they need to revise the financial terms of their franchise in the light of experience. This may be as a result of any or all of the following:

- The original projected figures proved to be wrong, perhaps because the pilot scheme was atypical.
- Changes may be desirable to reflect improving or deteriorating market conditions.
- The franchisor may have failed to update and/or to upgrade the franchise concept itself.

How Much Can You Charge?

Below is a checklist of points which a franchisor should consider when reviewing its financial terms.

1. Is the total initial amount payable by a franchisee (however constituted) a fair and adequate reward for the franchisor? For a list of points to take into account here, see 'Initial Fees' under 'Reviewing the Terms of the Franchise', Chapter 7.
2. Is the initial franchise fee structure clearly understood by franchisees?
3. Where there is more than one element in the financial package, is each element (licence, equipment, launch package etc.) adequately priced to reflect value given and to ensure a full recovery of direct costs and overheads?
4. Is the franchisor seeking to make a marginal loss or profit on each element of the original package and, if not, are there good commercial reasons for it?
5. Is an initial deposit required from franchisees before signing any greement? If so:
   - Is it sufficient to ensure that there is real commitment?
   - Is there a satisfactory basis for ensuring that expenditure directly incurred by the franchisor on behalf of the franchisee can be recovered from the deposit in legitimate circumstances?
6. Has the franchisor obtained support in principle from the key clearing banks for the provision of finance to suitable franchisees?
7. What procedures are in place to ensure that new franchisees settle their financial obligations before trading commences?

Once an internal review has been carried out, it is advisable to arrange an external review by suitably experienced franchise consultants or accountants in case the franchisor's judgement is too strongly influenced by the relatively narrow experience of its own particular franchise.

If a franchise concept is to succeed, the financial terms must be attractive to both the franchisor and the franchisee. They must make the concept profitable for the franchisor, motivate the franchisee and offer both parties a reasonable opportunity to obtain a fair reward for their respective contributions.

CHAPTER 14

The Financial Aspects of Franchising

"Franchising? A licence to print money, surely?"

For those businesses which are considering franchising as an alternative to growing organically, the decision of whether or not to franchise must form an important part of their strategic development plan because it will require resources of time, capital and manpower. In franchising, the investment needs to be made now and the pay-off comes further down the line. It is not a matter of 'show them how to do it and rake in the royalties'.

The following points need to be considered by prospective franchisors:

Although substantial capital will be required to develop and launch the franchise and to finance the operation in its formative years, this is considerably less than the amount which would be required to establish a network of company-owned branches. This is, of course, because a franchisee will be making the capital commitment each time a franchised outlet is opened. Not only will the initial capital outlay for each outlet be reduced for the would-be franchisor, but so will the working capital requirement to meet the day-to-day expenses of operating each franchised outlet.

On the other hand, the profit a franchisor receives from a franchised outlet will not be as great as the profit it could have obtained had that outlet been owned by the franchisor. However, in the majority of cases, the rate of return on capital employed will normally be higher than if expansion were to take place through company-owned outlets.

This is because:

1. The performance of each franchised outlet will normally be better than that of a company-owned outlet because the owner-manager of a franchised outlet will be a good deal more committed than an employed manager.

2. Demands on a franchisor's head office staff are far more modest. The staff required to cope with five franchisees will be able to cope with 25 franchisees, but that is not necessarily true of company-owned outlets. Company-owned outlets require greater support services to manage than franchised outlets, not to mention the need to have surplus management and staff to provide cover for illness, holidays, training etc., all of which, in a franchised network, will be the responsibility of the franchisee of each franchised outlet.

Whilst making a very efficient use of capital, franchising can also improve the liquidity profile of a franchisor because it is the franchisee who makes the capital investment in his own unit.

The balance sheet of a typical franchisor will therefore have different characteristics to that of a company with an equivalent number of retail outlets which it owns.

Many franchisors get involved in the property of their franchisees by taking on leases of retail premises themselves and subletting to franchisees, whether to increase their control over their franchisees, to retain possession of a valuable trading location or simply because a landlord is hesitant to let to the franchisee directly. If they do so they will not be able to take advantage of the cost savings and diminished liability for rent if franchisees were to acquire their own premises directly from the landlord.

The lower capital costs required to open franchised outlets have to be weighed against the substantial costs a prospective franchisor will need to meet in establishing the franchise.

Initial Costs

Before signing up the first franchisee, the franchisor will have to carry out extensive research and testing to establish how to structure the franchise concept to maximise its chances of success. Where the intention is to expand and establish business activity by the franchising method, the development costs will relate mainly to ensuring that the products/services, prices and production processes are suited to franchising and to developing training manuals, legal and commercial structure, promotional material and advertising plans. If the franchise business is starting from scratch, without any record of carrying out the relevant business activity, it will be necessary to invest money in running a pilot scheme under the direct management of the prospective franchisor before commencing the franchise operation in earnest.

Almost invariably the pilot scheme will operate as an initial loss, partly because of the time it takes to build up sales revenue and partly because it will need to experiment.

The profit and cash projections must therefore make full allowance for these initial development costs, together with the costs of initial promotion of the franchise, legal and professional services and financial charges.

In short, the initial costs of setting up a franchise are likely to include the following:

- Conducting a market review.
- Evaluating the feasibility of franchising.
- Developing the concept.
- Conducting a pilot operation.
- Developing the franchise package.
- Selecting procedures for a franchisee.
- Providing training.
- Advertising, marketing and launching the franchise.
- Protecting intellectual property.
- Legal compliance.
- Developing an IT package.

Much, of course, depends upon the size and nature of a prospective franchisor, and the costs of each element will vary from one franchisor to another. The important point is that all elements of the process should be costed and proper consideration given to the cost of engaging in-house resources which could otherwise have been used elsewhere.

Research and Development

It is one thing to have a successful business but quite another to convert it into one which is capable of being franchised and, having done so, to run it successfully as a franchise operation. Costs will be incurred in researching and developing a prospective franchisor's product/service, business and marketing system to the point where it becomes a franchise proposition. This process is a gradual one and requires research and commitment. The importance of the pilot operation, which is discussed in Chapter 8, cannot be emphasised too greatly. The downfall of many franchisors has been caused by their not having made the necessary initial investment to prove the concept before franchising. Where a franchise has been properly piloted, the franchisor will without doubt find it easier to obtain a sensible franchise fee.

Establishment and Launch

Establishment costs will relate to taking the necessary steps to obtain protection for the franchisor's intellectual property and to drawing up the necessary confidentiality agreements, franchise agreement, operations manual and other documentation. Costs will need to be incurred in registering trade marks. Whilst this may not seem important or necessary for a company developing its own network, it certainly becomes very important when franchising, and prospective franchisees will look to see what protection the franchisor is able to give a franchisee against infringement etc.

Before embarking on franchising, most prospective franchisors engage the services of specialists in franchising to conduct feasibility studies and to help the franchisor structure the franchise. The cost of such specialist consultants will, of course, have to be borne by the prospective franchisor.

The initial costs of advertising, marketing and promoting the franchise must also be borne by the prospective franchisor. This will involve the preparation of franchise sales and material which will be used by the franchisor to recruit franchisees.

Apart from advertising and canvassing, many franchisors also participate in the franchise exhibitions taking place at various times of the year, which give franchisors and prospective franchisors an opportunity to display their wares and

The Financial Aspects of Franchising

establish their credentials. Although this is an activity which is left to the last, it nevertheless needs to be planned and budgeted for in advance.

The mainstay of any well-run franchise operation is the operations manual, which sets out in full detail the system and how it is to be operated. The more technically oriented a business, the more complicated and costly will be the compilation and updating of the operations manual. For more on the operations manual, see Chapter 10.

In addition to all of this, there is the cost of the pilot operation, and the prospective franchisor must not forget to budget for legal advice and the cost of producing the franchise agreement and other documentation.

If one is to be realistic, a company establishing a retail franchise operation will need between £50,000 and £150,000 to put the necessary legal, financial, organisational and operational structure in place before it can go to the next phase.

Having established a franchise concept, the next step is to recruit, set up and launch franchisees. Again, these costs will need to be expended by the franchisor up front before it starts generating any income. However, the good news is that once the franchisor starts franchising it will be able to start recouping its initial investment (albeit slowly).

The costs involved in setting up and launching a franchisee include:

- The selection and training of the franchisee and his staff.
- The selection and acquisition of suitable premises/vehicles.
- The acquisition of any equipment.
- The assembly of the start-up package.
- The actual launch of the franchisee.

The costs of selection and training should not be underestimated and prospective franchisors should bear in mind that training does not come to an end simply because a training course has finished. There will be ongoing dialogue with the franchisee on various aspects of running the business.

The Financial Aspects of Franchising

Once a franchisee has been successfully launched in business, there will be *ongoing costs* for the franchisor which will be incurred in the following areas:

- Improvement to the franchise package, product or service range.
- Ongoing support to the franchise network.
- Troubleshooting where franchisees run into difficulty.
- Managing the network and ensuring compliance by franchisees.
- Advising and assisting franchisees who are underperforming.
- Advertising, marketing, promotions and public relations.
- Communications.
- Ongoing and additional training.

These costs will vary according to the rate at which the franchisor is selling its franchises because a franchisor will have to maintain, on a full-time basis, facilities for this task and employ highly skilled and experienced staff who will form a fixed overhead.

All these activities necessitate an in-depth investment in management expertise to deal with such diverse matters as:

- Franchise quality control.
- Franchise department administration.
- Franchisee support.
- Premises.
- Promotion and launch.
- Recruitment and training of senior staff.
- Legal and financial experts.
- Central buying and distribution team.
- Legal compliance.
- Research and development.
- IT.
- Protection of intellectual property.
- Advertising, marketing and promotions.

If one of the most common reasons for small business start-ups failing is undercapitalisation, the same can be said to apply to franchising. If a prospective franchisor is to have any hope of getting the structure right at the outset, it needs to make the correct investment at the initial stages. A franchise which is built on a solid financial foundation is likely to be successful and the network likely to grow rapidly.

It is unlikely that an undercapitalised company can set up a franchise operation successfully. Many companies choose to go the franchise route because they do not have the capital to expand through company-owned operations. In addition to the substantial investment required to set up a franchise operation, the costs of formulating, launching and operating the franchise system will initially be greater than the income generated from the franchise operation, and in the early years the franchisor will probably need to source outside finance to bridge the gap between income and expenditure. Franchising, therefore, is not an easy option in financial terms for a company wishing to expand.

A company which does not lay the right foundations will soon come to grief and suffer from one or more of the following:

- Complaints from franchisees.
- Franchisee failures.
- Litigation.
- Lack of profitability.
- Falling demand for products/services.

That having been said, it should be appreciated that, once a company starts franchising, there should be a steady income stream which increases both as franchisees mature and as the network expands.

Continuing Franchise Fees

As soon as a franchisee commences trading, his franchisor will expect to receive continuing franchise fees from him. These fees should cover the franchisor's provision of ongoing field support and contribute towards the costs of administrating the wider franchise network, but they will also contain an element of profit for the franchisor.

In any business format franchise, the franchisor owns the business format whilst the franchisees own the businesses. Over a period of time, a franchisor may build up a successful franchised network but with few tangible assets. The value of the franchisor's business is thus dependent upon the quality of its franchisees and the income it derives from them by means of continuing franchise fees, thereby increasing the goodwill in the franchisor's business. However, as a franchisor does not share ownership of its franchisees' businesses, the franchisor cannot participate in the equity of the growth in those businesses.

Where prospective franchisors are well capitalised, the franchise option is far less attractive because the absolute level of profit generated from each franchised outlet will be lower than that generated by a company-owned outlet. After all, if the continuing franchise fee is 10% of the gross turnover of a franchised outlet, a franchisor who is well capitalised is better off opening a company-owned outlet and keeping 100% of the profits (or 90% of the profits if one has, say, a 10% profit share incentive arrangement for its managers), rather than receiving 10% of the profits with the franchisee keeping 90%.

A direct comparison of the profitability of expansion through franchised or company-owned outlets can only be made through a financial appraisal.

Costs and Returns on Investment

Having estimated the initial costs to the franchisor of developing the franchise format, the next thing to do is to make some assumptions about the number of franchises likely to be sold.

The profit and cash projections must be realistic because only a few franchisees will commence business in the first year. Whilst it is appropriate for cash forecasting purposes to recognise the initial franchise fee and other items as soon as they are received, income connected with the start-up should not normally be recognised for profit forecasting purposes until the franchisee commences business (and later if the franchisor has not substantially fulfilled his obligations under the agreement at that time).

The franchisor's main source of income is the continuing franchise fee, as discussed in Chapter 12 (and elsewhere). Although there will be other sources of income such as advertising levies, rental of equipment, software licence fees etc.,

The Financial Aspects of Franchising

these should not be structured to yield a significant profit. They are essentially designed to recompense the franchisor for its outlay in providing those goods/services to the franchisee.

Set out below is a financial guide which may give a useful indication of the factors to be considered and the associated costs.

The hypothetic financial model presented in Tables 1 and 2, below, is a highly simplified one covering a franchisor's operation from the pilot through to the end of its fifth year of opening franchises. The costs are purely indicative and should not be used as a guide to the cost of becoming a franchisor. The model could be made more sophisticated by dividing each year into quarters and by incorporating assumptions about when fees are received and when franchisor expenditure is incurred. A complete financial model would also incorporate liability for tax. The model as presented here is an end-of-year cash flow model, and as such does not take account of changes in the cash positions during the year.

The company is a medium-sized one which has decided to franchise an existing business that has developed slowly in its local area. Only three outlets have been opened and, while fairly successful, the existing business has a somewhat old-fashioned and downmarket image. The company's objective is to secure more rapid development of the business without injecting a large amount of capital. The company also does not wish to become too closely involved in managing a chain of company-owned outlets.

The cost of becoming a franchisor in this case is £110,000, as shown in Table 1. The company is able to draw on in-house skills in most areas, but uses professional help for:

- A market review, to survey customer attitudes to its existing offering.
- A franchise feasibility study by a specialist consultant.
- Design for the interior of the shop.
- Design for its logo, signs etc.
- The franchise agreement.
- Protecting its intellectual property.
- Preparing the manuals and systems.

The Financial Aspects of Franchising

- Assistance with establishing a franchisee selection procedure.
- Preparing the franchisee response pack.
- Marketing the franchise.

Table 1

	Professional fees and other payments	In-house staff	Total
Market review	1,000	1,000	2,000
Franchise feasibility	3,000	1,000	4,000
Concept development		2,000	2,000
Design	5,000	1,000	6,000
Pilot operation (using existing premises)			
Shop fitting and refurbishment	45,000		45,000
Staff	25,000	10,000	35,000
Equipment	10,000		10,000
Stock	5,000		5,000
Other inputs	10,000		10,000
Evaluation and experiment		3,000	3,000
Franchise agreement etc.	6,000		4,000
Manuals and systems	6,000	2,000	8,000
Selection procedure	1,000	1,000	2,000
Training procedure		1,000	1,000
Franchise launch and marketing	10,000	1,000	11,000
	£125,000	£23,000	£150,000
LESS			
Income from pilot unit			− £40,000
Total cost			£110,000

The Financial Aspects of Franchising

Financial Projections

Once the franchisor has made the all-important decisions about the financial terms to be applied to the franchise, the franchisor must prepare profit and cash projections, ideally over a period of at least five years.

This is because the first two or three years, however busy they may be, tend to yield relatively low levels of revenue. Consequently the likely capital requirements of the franchisor cannot be realistically assessed without taking a longer-term view.

The company then launches its franchise (see Table 2) and is able to achieve a high rate of opening with 5 openings in the first year, 10 in the second and then 15 per year until by year 5 it has 60 franchised units and one company-owned outlet. By year 5 the need for franchise marketing has declined as the projected number of new openings in subsequent years is low. However in year 5 a major effort is made to develop the product and this raises the overhead costs substantially.

Table 2

Year	0	1	2	3	4	5
Openings						
Pilot	0	1	0	0	0	0
Franchised outlets	0	5	10	15	15	15
Total open	0	6	16	31	46	61
Income						
Company-owned pilot outlet (net)	0	2,000	4,000	50,000	50,000	50,000
Initial franchise fees	0	25,000	50,000	75,000	75,000	75,000
Continuing franchise fee	0	10,000	40,000	95,000	170,000	255,000
Supplies to franchisees (net)		2,000	8,000	19,000	34,000	51,000
Total		39,000	102,000	239,000	329,000	431,000

The Financial Aspects of Franchising

Table 2 continued

Year	0	1	2	3	4	5
Expenditure						
Start-up costs (net)	(110,000)					
Franchise marketing	0	25,000	35,000	25,000	20,000	10,000
Franchise selection	0	20,000	20,000	20,000	20,000	20,000
Location selection	0	10,000	20,000	20,000	20,000	20,000
Franchisee services	0	10,000	30,000	45,000	45,000	40,000
Overheads	0	25,000	25,000	35,000	35,000	50,000
TOTAL	(110,000)	90,000	130,000	145,000	140,000	140,000
Profit (loss) for year	(110,000)	(51,000)	(28,000)	94,000	189,000	291,000
Cumulative profit (loss)	(110,000)	(161,000)	(189,000)	(95,000)	94,000	578,000

The illustration is based on the following assumptions:

- Each franchisee's turnover:
  - Year 1: £40,000
  - Year 2: £80,000
  - Year 3: £100,000
  - Year 4: £120,000
  - Year 5: £120,000
- Initial franchise fee of £5,000.
- A continuing franchise fee of 5% of franchisee turnover.
- Supplies to franchisees produce a net profit of 1% on franchisee turnover.
- The amount for marketing is totally spent in each year.

The pilot operation is expected to continue operating with a turnover equivalent to that of a franchised outlet opened at the beginning of year 1 and yielding a profit contribution to the franchisor equivalent to 5% turnover.

The Financial Aspects of Franchising

It should be noted that the growth pattern will tend to decline as the scope of finding new additional prime locations diminishes.

The franchisor's costs have been calculated on a formula intended to reflect the fact that overheads do not increase to the same extent as revenue from franchisees. For the sake of simplicity it is assumed that the pilot scheme incurred an initial loss of £45,000 and that the franchisor incurred start-up costs (professional fees, operations manuals, corporate identity etc.) of £110,000.

The Results

The company's overall results are shown in Table 2. The cumulative profit performance is typical of a franchise, with large up-front costs and first-year losses being gradually reversed as the number of outlets builds up and the franchisees begin to increase their sales. Year 3 is the peak year for the cumulative loss, and a positive profit position is not achieved until year 4. As can be seen, the return on capital is high.

Points to Consider

This illustration is realistic for the type of company described here. Other companies would have different figures, but there are certain details that tend to be consistent across franchises. For example:

- There is a large up-front investment.
- On a cumulative basis, a positive position is not achieved until around years 3–5 of trading activity.
- The return on capital is high in a successful franchise.

Companies considering franchising because of a shortage of capital must therefore consider the following points carefully, comparing their position with that of the company illustrated in Tables 1 and 2:

- Are there particular reasons why the costs of becoming a franchisor cannot be reduced significantly, without cutting corners? Or would the costs be higher than those shown in Table 1?

- Can the rate of opening of franchised outlets be raised significantly?
- In the case of an operation trading from retail premises which take time to secure, will acquisition of property and recruitment of franchisees be sufficiently rapid to achieve a high rate of expansion? If there is a higher expansion rate this will obviously increase the franchisor's income and expenditure in the financial model.
- Will the sales of franchises be higher or lower than those shown in Table 2, particularly in the first year or two?

Companies are urged to be realistic about their own capability in establishing a franchised network, for only in exceptional cases will a company be able to achieve an earlier positive profit position or significantly reduce its financial exposure.

Although not included in this illustration, a cash forecast would also be prepared for this venture.

In addition to its own profit and cash forecasts, it may be necessary for the franchisor to provide each prospective franchisee with an illustration of the trading results which may be achieved from a typical outlet. Any such illustration should, of course, be accompanied by a vigorous health warning excluding liability.

Special Factors

One factor which must be recognised in profit and cash forecasting is the risk that a small minority of franchises will not come up to expectations, however rigorous the selection and training process.

The practical consequences will be that in some cases the franchisor will need to find a new franchisee to purchase the ailing business. The financial implications are twofold. Firstly, the administrative costs of the franchisor increase (before, during and after the changeover), and, secondly, continuing receipts from the franchisee will be depressed for a while, although usually this situation improves rapidly. Some compensation may be available to the franchisor if the franchise agreement allows for a charge to be made for handling the sale of the business.

In any profit forecast some allowance has to be made for depressed income attributable to 'failed franchisees' and for expenditure incurred on introducing replacement franchisees.

As illustrated in the example above, it can take some time before a franchisor generates accumulated profit (and thus a positive cash flow). The venture would be different if the franchisee were required to pay a far more substantial initial franchise fee, with continuing fees thereafter being substantially reduced or eliminated. However, there are sound commercial and ethical reasons for not charging high initial franchise fees, as explained in Chapter 13.

CHAPTER 15

PROFIT PROJECTIONS

"Turnover is vanity. Profit is sanity. Cash flow is reality."

It is common practice amongst franchisors to produce financial details of their particular franchise for those applying to buy their franchises. These details are called various things: financial projections, business plans, profit projections, financial illustrations etc. Their purpose should be to give a prospective franchisee information not only on how much a franchise would cost to buy and set up, but also on the anticipated income and ongoing costs of running it. These costs would include such items of expenditure as wages, rent, utilities, council tax, purchase of stock, insurance premiums, local advertising and, last but not least, regular payments to the franchisor in the form of franchise fees and advertising contributions.

Given that most applicants have not owned a business of their own previously, they will rely implicitly on these 'projections' and will access their capital requirements on the basis of what they are told by their franchisor. In the absence of any previous experience of running the type of business they are proposing to buy, this is the only information they have upon which to assess the business proposition on offer.

So what do the franchisors base their projections on? In the case of the franchisee's income, a franchisor will estimate, from *its own experience* of running a similar business and from information based on the *actual performance* of its franchisees, what a prospective franchisee can reasonably expect to earn from running the franchised business he is looking to buy.

Ethical franchisors do not offer franchises for sale until they have thoroughly market tested their business concept and shown it to be successful. They draw on their experience of actual costs, expenditure and income to formulate their 'business model'. They use this business model, after adjusting it for local/regional variations (for example, higher wages and rent in London than elsewhere), to produce the projections that they give to their prospective franchisees.

Profit Projections

So far, so good, *but* the business model is only as good as the information on which it is based. All too often, once franchisors have produced the business model, they themselves take it as gospel and forget or fail to update it in the light of changing circumstances. The economic climate and the cost of running a business changes with the passage of time. In addition, some businesses are subject to rising costs of operation by virtue of their nature. A food outlet will have to comply with any new health and safety regulations.

Franchisors should therefore make it a practice to regularly review their financial model and to update it in the light of experience or changing circumstances. Prospective franchisees should not take any projections at face value and should ask searching questions as to the basis on which they are produced, when they were last reviewed and adjusted and how accurate they have proved to be in the past.

Most ethical franchisors own at least one outlet run along the same lines they require of their franchisees. For the franchisee, what better proof of the accuracy of what they are being told than to ask to see the audited accounts of each such outlet?

Franchisors should state on their projections the basis on which they are made. Are they based on the performance of the franchisor's own outlets, or a pilot operation, or the average of all franchisees of longer than one year's trading, or the average of the top 10% of the franchisees, or ... something else?

Franchisors should draw the attention of prospective franchisees to the fact that what they are being given are *projections* and *not* a guarantee that the profit figures stated in such projections will be achieved. Whilst such a warning may not always be efficacious, it is nevertheless worth giving.

CHAPTER 16

Advertising Funds

"Transparency is the key."

One of the golden rules of franchising (there are many!) is that all franchisees should be treated the same, and that is one of the reasons why franchisors don't negotiate individual franchise agreements. Franchise agreements are the same for all franchisees within a franchise. In most franchises, all franchisees are required to pay continuing franchise fees and make a contribution towards the cost of advertising, marketing and promoting the brand.

Where franchisees are required to make a contribution into an advertising fund, this should be on the same basis for all franchisees (and, incidentally, most franchisors also contribute for each outlet owned by them). The franchisor, sometimes with advice from a marketing committee (which usually includes franchisees), administers and manages the fund. The money should be kept separate from the franchisor's money and at the end of each financial year the franchisor should give its franchisees an account (certified by its accountants) of the movement of monies in that fund.

So far, so good. However, there are occasions when one or more franchisees will claim that the franchisor is misusing the advertising money by not spending it for 'its intended purpose'.

It is not uncommon for franchisees who are in dispute with their franchisor to make allegations that a franchisor is misusing the advertising fund. Such allegations, franchisees and their advisors know, are easy enough to make. Advertising, marketing and promotions is by nature a flexible concept, and its benefits can be subjective. Clearly there are items of expenditure out of a franchisee advertising fund which have the effect of benefiting the network as a whole (for example, creating and maintaining a website), and most agree that there is nothing wrong with that.

However, advertising contributions are also spent by franchisors on things such as local or regional advertising. Not all franchisees benefit to the same extent

Advertising Funds

from such initiatives. One franchisee may get good customer response from an advertisement placed in a local newspaper, whereas another franchisee, even one whose territory or trading location is within the circulation area of the same newspaper, may receive a much smaller response. On the other hand, the second franchisee may benefit more than his neighbour from an entry in a trade directory.

Other cases are more complex. A franchisee may experience a downturn in trade because of the arrival of local competition, and in those circumstances many franchisors consider it their duty to help boost that franchisee's turnover by increasing advertising and marketing activity in his area. Some of the cost of this would be paid out of the advertising fund, bearing in mind that such increased activity will have the wider effect of raising the profile of the brand generally.

The purpose of a centralised advertising, marketing and promotions fund into which all franchisees are required to contribute has never been that each franchisee should receive precisely, in terms of advertising spend or value, the equivalent of his contribution. What most franchisees will and should be concerned with is ensuring that money in such a fund is not used for anything other than its intended purpose. The use of such funds by the franchisor for entertaining business associates or suppliers, for example, would be wrong.

As in most things there are grey areas. For example, should a franchisor use the advertising budget to pay for a stand at a franchise exhibition where the main purpose of the franchisor is to recruit franchisees? Some franchisors would argue that this is a legitimate expenditure because the presence of the franchisor at such events enhances the reputation of the brand, meaning that franchisees will ultimately benefit both from the exposure of the brand and from the fact that a successful recruiting programme will enlarge the network. Others would argue that the funds for such a venture should come out of the franchisor's pocket because any benefit accruing to the franchisee is essentially going to be a side effect, rather than the main objective.

If the franchisor suspects that its motives may be questioned, it should sound out franchisees prior to making any large capital expenditure out of the advertising fund.

A straw poll, conducted in 2015 by the author amongst a range of franchisors of various sizes, from small businesses to those quoted on the London Stock

Exchange, revealed that, with the exception of one franchisor, all subsidised their advertising, marketing and promotions fund, in many cases by sums well into five figures. In these circumstances the question of who should bear the cost of a presence at a franchise exhibition would seem to be academic.

What is absolutely clear is that when it comes to dealing with advertising money, transparency is the key.

CHAPTER 17

Evaluating a Franchise as a Prospective Franchisee

*"Nor is the people's judgement always true:
The most may err as grossly as the few."*
    John Dryden, *Absalom and Achitophel*

So what do franchisees look for when evaluating whether to buy a franchise?

- Are there procedures in place for dealing with franchisees who default inancially? Have they been reviewed to ensure that the franchisor will only suffer minimal loss and the franchise's credibility will be preserved?

- Is there sufficient capital available to the franchisor to:

    a. Improve, enhance and develop the concept?

    b. Cover any predicted shortfall between the cost of providing advertising, field support etc. and the continuing franchise fee income to be derived from its franchisees?

- Is the balance between the initial franchise fees and the continuing franchise fees realistic with regard to likely business trends during the next five years, after which time the franchised network may have reached maturity and the franchisor may be more heavily dependent on its continuing franchise fee income?

- Does the franchisor have:

    a. Weekly trading statistics?

    b. Monthly management accounts?

    c. Annual budgets?

    d. Twelve-month cash forecasts?

    e. Any idea what its financial circumstances will be in three years' time?

Considering the Franchisor

Having assessed the essential constituent elements of the business format franchise which he is contemplating buying, the franchisee will examine whether the prospective franchisor satisfies his requirements, considering questions such as:

- Has the franchisor's system been tried, tested and proven? Does the franchisor have a blueprint of the method by which the prospective franchisee can deliver goods and/or services to his customers as consistently and profitably as will be expected of him? The system must have been tested under open market conditions, refined and shown to be capable of being replicated.

- How strong is the franchisor's management? A franchisor cannot be a 'mum and pop' operation. The franchisor must be able to show that it has a strong management team, capable of delivering the necessary training, support and maintenance services to *all* franchisees within the network.

- Does the franchisor have sufficient capital? A franchisor that relies on the income from the sale of franchises is doomed to failure. Franchisors must have sufficient capital to enable them to sustain the programme of franchising until they reach maturity and revenues start flowing from continuing franchise fees.

- How strong is the franchise brand? A franchisor must be able to show that there is some market recognition for its brand and that it is able to protect it against infringement.

- Does the franchisor have a comprehensive operations manual, setting out the whole business concept and its method of operation in the finest detail?

- How comprehensive is the training which the franchisor proposes to provide? A franchisor must be able to train franchisees to the extent necessary for franchisees to operate the franchisor's business from the franchisee's premises, in accordance with the franchisor's system.

- Does the franchise agreement which the franchisee will be required to sign set out the rights and obligations of both parties very clearly and protect the franchisor's intellectual property?

- Is there a proven demand for the goods and/or services which are to be the subject of the franchise?

- How carefully and using what criteria has the franchisor drawn up its franchisee profile? By which benchmark does it propose to select franchisees, and how consistently has this been applied?
- Has the franchisor developed site selection criteria and a very strong sense of the minimum requirements for a franchised outlet?
- Does the franchisor have a good understanding of the competition? This is essential if a franchisor is to convince a prospective franchisee that it can assist the franchisee in beating the competition. Where the franchise concept is novel a franchisor must have taken into consideration the threat of competition from the competitors who will surely follow after the launch of the franchise.
- Has the franchisor developed a strong relationship with suppliers? This is essential if the prospective franchisee is under an obligation to buy goods from the franchisor for resale to his customers.
- How effective is the franchisor's system of reporting and accounting? An effective system is essential if a franchisor is to maintain some control over its franchised units and ensure that it is receiving all the revenue properly due to it.
- What research and development programme does the franchisor have? This is one of the principal obligations of a franchisor. It must have established research and development capabilities so that it is able to improve and develop its business system, products etc.
- Does the franchisor have clear and effective procedures for communicating with its franchisees so that both parties can develop their respective businesses to the benefit of the network as a whole?
- How many franchisees have sold their franchised business to an incoming franchisee?
- How much did the last franchisee sell his franchised business for?
- On average, how long does it take for a franchisee to sell his franchised business?
- What is the average return on investment achieved by former franchisees who have sold their franchised businesses?

- How much does the *average* (as opposed to best) franchisee earn?
- What is the average length of time that a franchisee remains within the network?
- Will the prospective franchisee have unfettered access to a full list of all franchisees and permission to speak to as many of them as he wishes?
- How easy is it for franchisees to obtain a bank loan?
- Does the franchisor have an arrangement with any banks for loans to franchisees?
- How many members of the franchisor's staff are dedicated to supporting its franchisees?
- How does the franchisor treat the fees paid to it by franchisees for advertising, marketing and promoting the brand?
- Has the franchisor developed local, regional and national programmes for advertising, marketing and promotion of the brand and the products and services offered by the network?
- What is the franchisor's record of franchisee failures and terminations?
- How many franchisees renew after the expiry of their franchise agreement?
- Is the franchisor a member of the British Franchise Association?
- If the franchisor is not a member of the British Franchise Association, why not? Is it because its application has failed? If so, why? If not, is it because it does not want to commit to the British Franchise Association's code of conduct for ethical franchising?

Timeline of Buying a Franchise

Any prospective franchisee who seeks professional advice will be advised that once he has made one of the most important decisions in his life, which is whether to start a business of his own, the next decision is almost equally important, which is what sort of business to go into. He will be advised to consider the following matters as a bare minimum:

1. Decide whether you want to be involved in a service or retail business. There are, of course, pros and cons to both. If you are the sort of person who does not want to work anti-social hours, then a retail operation or a business which operates during office hours would suit you better. However, a retail operation from a fixed location does have disadvantages such as having to take on lease obligations, employ staff and carry stock. On the other hand, if you are in the service business, it is quite likely that working office hours alone will not cut the mustard. Much, of course, depends on the type of service business. If you take a carpet cleaning business as an example, this will invariably mean working anti-social hours; on the other hand you are quite likely to be working from home with little or no need to pay rent or carry a large stock of products.

2. Decide how much you can afford. There is now usually a choice of franchises in the same line of business available, and they don't all cost the same. For example, there is more than one carpet cleaning franchise available. So look and see what is available for sale in your price range.

3. Obtain as much detail from the franchisor as possible. Where the franchisor provides financial projections, study these carefully to satisfy yourself that the income shown in those projections satisfies your needs, but always bear in mind that these are only illustrations and may be optimistic. (For more on projections, see Chapter 15.)

4. Whilst reviewing the information supplied by the franchisor, contact your bank if you think you will need a loan and discuss whether, in principle, the bank will lend you the money you require for the type of franchise you are contemplating buying. Most banks now operate fairly sophisticated systems whereby bank loan managers can obtain detailed information about many franchises, which will enable them to make a decision.

5. Consult a solicitor who specialises in franchising to advise you on the franchise agreement.

6. If you and your solicitor are satisfied with the agreement, see your accountant for advice regarding the detailed financial aspects of the franchise. By this time you should have some idea of the sort of premises you will be occupying or the extent of your 'territory' (i.e. your permitted

area of operations) in the case of a mobile franchise. If the franchisor has produced financial projections for your particular business, ask your accountant to verify the likely accuracy of such projections; if not, ask your accountant to help you to put together a business plan. Not only is this an essential tool for the management of your business but you will need it to support your loan application with your bank.

7. At this stage you will probably be asked to sign the franchise agreement. You should be guided by your solicitor as to the timing of signing the franchise agreement, which, where relevant, should be conditional on your securing satisfactory premises and a bank loan.

8. Where there is a requirement to secure retail premises, you should make a serious effort at this stage to secure satisfactory premises and should start talking to your franchisor about the details of converting the premises into a franchised outlet.

9. By this time your bank should have responded to your application for a loan. If the answer is positive, you will be in a position to push those involved into finalising the lease for the premises. It is important that you do not enter into a binding commitment to take on premises unless and until you have your bank's agreement to the loan and the franchisor has signed the franchise agreement.

10. Once you have completed the acquisition of the premises you can go about converting the premises into a franchised outlet and go on the franchisor's training course.

For a more comprehensive list of concerns a prospective franchisee may have, see Appendix C.

From stage 4 the sequence of events up to when a franchisee is ready to open for business will vary depending on the nature of the franchise. The important thing to remember is that there will come a time when a prospective franchisee will have to make significant commitments to *three different parties*:

1. To the franchisor by signing a franchise agreement or an agreement to purchase a franchise.

Evaluating a Franchise as a Prospective Franchisee

2. To the landlord by signing a lease or an agreement to take a lease of the premises (or, in the case of a mobile franchise, signing a lease, hire or purchase agreement for a vehicle).
3. To the bank by taking up the loan.

Wherever possible a prospective franchisee should aim to synchronise these transactions so that he commits to the three parties at the same time.

Having selected a franchise to buy, there are a number of matters to which the prospective franchisee will have to attend before he can open for business. What he will need to do will depend on the nature of the business contemplated. The requirements of a franchise which involves a process to be applied to products before they are sold will be different from one where the products can be sold off the shelf. Nevertheless, the above general guide to the steps, and the order in which they might be taken, will help a prospective franchisee to complete the transaction more efficiently both in terms of costs and in terms of his time and effort.

From the franchisor's perspective, even if it has done many of the right things, ultimately its franchise has to be marketable. It has to appeal to a prospective franchisee. The BFA/NatWest Franchise Survey 2015 revealed the following nine reasons given by franchisees for their choice of franchise:

- Growth potential.
- Well-known brand.
- Interest in field of business.
- Location of the business.
- Success of existing franchisees.
- Affordability.
- Liked the people.
- Low risk.
- Specialist sector knowledge.

CHAPTER 18

Selling Franchises

"There's no law against making a bad bargain."

Sale of New Franchises

It may seem obvious, but the best way of marketing the franchise package is to demonstrate success. As already mentioned, company-owned pilot units should be established to prove the concept in practice. If these units are able to demonstrate success (without which, of course, there is little, if anything, to franchise), this in itself will be the very best marketing tool in the launch of the franchise.

Many franchisors deliberately maintain a low profile when marketing their first couple of franchises. Many have found that editorial matter in the media is very effective. This can, of course, only be achieved if the franchisor or someone connected with it can present a newsworthy and attractive feature to the media. The element of luck has to be taken into account because even newsworthy features get dropped if something better (in the view of the editor) turns up. One can employ public relations consultants, but this is usually expensive, and most franchisors cannot afford the expense at the early stage of their development.

Some franchisors feel that one of the best methods of achieving a feature in a specialist magazine or a local newspaper is to have a gala, or grand opening of one or more of the franchisor's company-owned units. The local or national trade press would normally be invited to a press party at the premises; customers would be attracted by means of discount offers/small gifts, perhaps a minor celebrity to perform the opening ceremony, and staff dispensing drinks with beaming smiles in all directions. The main aim is to create a public event and this can be achieved for a relatively modest cost, but it does take time to organise. One's suppliers can often be persuaded to provide products at specially discounted prices and/or to take advertising space in a special feature in the local paper.

Selling Franchises

Having achieved some measure of public awareness through the visible success of the company or pilot units, the next step is to make public the decision to expand by way of franchising. Again, the best possible marketing technique is that of demonstrated success brought visibly to the attention of the trade and prospective franchisees. It is therefore crucial that the early franchisees and locations or territories are chosen carefully. Prospective franchisors must avoid a false start at all costs.

The success of the franchisor's company-owned units will doubtless have produced some franchise enquiries, particularly if publicity has been achieved in the trade and/or local press.

The launch of the first franchised unit may be approached in the same grand manner as the franchisor's company-owned units.

It is useful to provide the press with thumbnail life stories of the franchisee involved, together with appropriate details of the franchisor and the results to date, so that human interest and personal finance/investment stories can be written. All the facts and data provided must be true and accurate, of course, and must be presented in a direct, positive manner which can be easily assimilated.

It is likely that the opening will be busy and well attended and that there will be little time for a lengthy explanation of any complex details; this makes the written material which is available on the day so important. It will certainly form the basis of most editorial comment that may be made. The more material handed to journalists (photos, draft articles etc.), the more likely it is that the story the franchisor seeks to tell will be published.

This assertive approach does not appeal to all, nor indeed is it necessarily the right approach in every case. However, one fact which is undoubtedly true is that the franchisor must be patient at this crucial stage. It *must not* try to expand further than its capacity to service and support its franchisees. In the end this policy will pay off because the visible success of both the franchisor and its franchised units will produce additional enquiries from prospective franchisees. This and word-of-mouth recommendation from existing franchisees who are satisfied with their investment are the best possible means of producing prospective franchisees.

Most franchisors make contact with prospective franchisees in one of three ways:

1. A prospective franchisee may be introduced by a friend who has taken up a franchise or may become interested after talking to an existing franchisee.
2. A prospective franchisee may have seen a feature in a newspaper or magazine mentioning the franchise.
3. A prospective franchisee may respond to an advertisement in a publication specialising in franchising (such as *Franchise World* or *What Franchise*) or in the business opportunities column of a newspaper.

Trade and business exhibitions may be used to supplement the above methods.

Finally, one must not forget consumer advertising. The franchisor's outlets will be advertising for customers to buy their products/services. This activity by itself will generate enquiries from prospective franchisees.

Franchisors must beware of letting themselves down by gaining good publicity and then, in response to franchise enquiries, producing a tatty piece of paper with some inadequate explanation of the franchise scheme which is on offer.

The material franchisors supply in response to these enquiries will be part of the franchisor's 'shop window' display. It will pay to prepare literature which describes the people involved in the franchise and their experience. The history of the business to be franchised should be given, along with a description of the franchisor's services. Pictures of the business and the people are worth including in such presentation. By this stage a franchisor should have a franchising business of which it is proud and which it will be pleased to explain to others.

Anecdotal evidence suggests that out of every 100 enquiries, 80 will probably never get beyond the initial enquiry stage. Ten will, on submission of personal details, be deemed unsuitable. Ten will be worth meeting and discussing the proposition with, and one or two of them may ultimately be considered suitable and sign. Marketing the franchise requires considerable patience. Its importance cannot be overemphasised.

Any franchisee with pen poised to sign an agreement is likely to be worth having. Again, one needs patience for the lengthy task of explaining the franchise agreement and the reasoning behind its numerous provisions. In the long run, doing this will help deal with any franchisee who complains that he was not aware of certain provisions of the agreement.

It has to be remembered that, for the franchisee, this will be one of the biggest decisions of his life. One should not be surprised if a prospective franchisee who seems ideal gets cold feet at the last moment and does not sign.

It is important to get the sales procedure right. First impressions count a lot, and there is no second chance at making a first impression. A written presentation will tell a prospective franchisee a good deal about the franchisor and how businesslike it is.

When a franchisor receives an enquiry from a prospective franchisee, it will respond by directing the enquirer to the franchisor's website and possibly also sending out a glossy presentation describing the franchise company and its success story. This is often presented in a question and answer format. Some franchisors explain what franchising is. Some find it convenient at this stage to send prospective franchisees a copy of one or more publications on franchising which are available and which may contain an editorial or advertorial about the franchise.

The one advantage which a paper prospectus has over the franchisor's website is that the quality of the printed material can offer the prospective franchisee an indication of the professionalism of the franchisor – something which visiting the franchisor's website will not necessarily give him. Some franchisors also find it helps to put franchising into perspective for franchisees and their professional advisers, who may never previously have had contact with franchising.

The presentation is often accompanied by an explanation of what the franchisor does for its franchisees in terms of assisting them with setting up and in continuing to service their needs and requirements later.

Financial projections are also usually dispatched with the initial material. These should not be presented as a guarantee of what the prospective franchisee *will* achieve. They should illustrate what profits *may* be achieved if certain levels of business are reached and must be accompanied by a warning excluding the franchisor from liability should the franchisee be unable to reach these levels.

This will all be accompanied by a letter inviting the prospective franchisee to contact the franchisor to discuss the matter further. In some cases franchisors follow up with email or phone contact to see whether there is further interest. The prospective franchisee should also be invited to provide the franchisor with details about himself to enable the franchisor to determine whether he is a suitable person with whom to proceed.

The BFA/NatWest Franchise Survey 2015 threw up the following top 10 reasons given by franchisors for not selling a franchise to an applicant:

1. Insufficient capital.
2. Lack of business experience.
3. Lack of experience in their sector.
4. Poor performance at interview.
5. Lack of sales/marketing experience.
6. The applicant viewed it as a job, not as a business.
7. The applicant was unsuitable.
8. The applicant had a poor credit history.
9. Inability to complete application forms.
10. Failure to turn up for appointments.

In the final analysis, the key to successful marketing of the franchise package is the visible and demonstrated success of both the company and its franchise operation. In other words, the franchise proposition should sell itself. Franchisors do not sell; prospective franchisees buy.

Sale of Second-Hand Franchises

Most franchisees buy a franchise with a dream in mind. For some of them that dream is that after a number of years of hard work and dedication they will have built up a business, which they will eventually be able to sell.

Franchisors encourage prospective franchisees in this dream. However, in commerce as in life, things are seldom straightforward. Franchisees who buy on a promise from the franchisor that they will be able to sell often forget that any such promise was made subject to certain conditions. Certainly most franchise agreements are very clear about such conditions. However, at the time of buying a franchise, franchisees are concerned with other things. They concern themselves with whether they have the right to sell only after securing the franchise and starting their business, and even then they do not seem to pay great attention to the fine detail of the conditions.

So what exactly are these conditions?

Most are what one would expect:

- The franchisee must not be in breach of its franchise agreement.
- The buyer must satisfy the franchisor's criteria for franchisees.
- The buyer must pass the franchisor's training.
- The franchisor's costs and (sometimes but not invariably) some sort of franchise transfer fee must be paid by the franchisee or its successor.
- The sale must have the consent of the franchisor.
- In some cases, the franchisor may reserve the right of first refusal.

Most seem innocuous enough, but the devil, as they say, is in the detail. The condition that creates the most difficulty is the one that requires the franchisee to obtain the franchisor's consent.

Franchisors reserve the right to approve the purchaser. Just as a franchisor has the unfettered discretion in deciding whether or not to grant a franchise in the first place, so a franchisor will seek to retain this very same discretion in the choice of a successor to the franchisee who wishes to sell his franchised business. The franchisor will therefore need to be satisfied that the buyer meets the criteria for its franchisees. It will reserve the right to take up references and to approve and train the purchaser.

The franchisor will need to be paid for its troubles in dealing with a franchisee's application to sell his business, but it is considered to be unethical for franchisors to charge a second full initial franchise fee to a purchaser of an existing franchised business. This is because the initial franchise fee includes payment for goods and/or services rendered to a new franchisee which will not be necessary on a subsequent sale. The services are in the nature of site selection, shop fitting, initial advertising and the like.

In return for compliance by the franchisee and his purchaser with the various obligations set out in the franchise agreement, an ethical franchisor will usually (but not necessarily always) grant a new franchise agreement to a purchaser for the full period of the former franchise agreement. In some cases, a franchisor may only be obliged to grant a purchaser the unexpired residue of the term of the franchise agreement originally granted to the outgoing franchisee. This may be, for example, because that is all there is left in the outgoing franchisee's lease and most franchisors are naturally anxious to ensure that they do not grant a franchise which goes beyond the term of any lease enjoyed by a franchisee, leaving the franchisee with a valid franchise agreement but no premises.

In determining the right of a franchisee to sell his business, a balance has to be struck between the needs of the franchisee and the franchisor. The franchisee needs to realise his investment as and when he wants to; the franchisor needs to approve those coming into the franchise network and to prevent those leaving the network (for whatever reason) from continuing to use the franchisor's trade secrets and competing unfairly.

The grant of a new franchise agreement for a full period (accompanied by a surrender of the outgoing franchisee's franchise agreement) has the advantages of:

- Releasing the franchisor and outgoing franchisee from any future obligations to the other (other than any non-competition and restraint of trade covenants which are expressed in the franchise agreement).

- Preserving the franchisee's investment. He is able to offer his business for sale with the benefit of a full period instead of just the reside of the term of his franchisee agreement. For example, if he could offer only the two years left in his franchise agreement he would receive a good deal less for his business.

Many franchise agreements now specify that the franchisor has the right of first refusal if a franchisee wants to sell his business. There is nothing sinister in such a provision, providing it contains certain safeguards for the franchisee. Most franchisees do not really care who their purchaser is, and, so long as the terms of the right of first refusal are equitable, the franchisee will be as willing to sell to his franchisor as to a stranger. In most cases, in fact, franchisees prefer to sell to their franchisor rather than a third party because it makes the transaction a good deal simpler. A franchisor knows and understands the business

Selling Franchises

which is being offered for sale, approval does not have to be obtained, the purchaser does not need to be trained and the franchisee need not waste his time entertaining prospective purchasers, some of whom may well turn out to be timewasters.

Any such right of first refusal, if correctly drafted, will be enforceable at law, which will not look to see whether or not the terms are fair. Thus, in theory, there is no reason why the franchisor should not retain the right to buy a franchisee's business for a nominal sum. However, this would be both inequitable and unethical. A sensible approach would be for a franchisor to retain the right of first refusal upon terms that if the franchisor wishes to buy a franchisee's business, it must do so at market value.

So far as granting consent is concerned, most franchise agreements contain a provision to the effect that if a franchisee wants to sell his business, the consent of the franchisor is required, but that such consent will not be unreasonably withheld.

But what if the franchisor does not *like* the buyer (the incoming franchisee) or feels that the price he is willing to pay for the business is too high?

The point about price is that if the buyer buys at too high a price, he may have a very difficult time of making a success of the business. The margins and the turnover may just not be there to support the purchase price. It may be a case of the buyer having more money than sense, and a franchisor may feel that it has a very strong case, in such circumstances, for withholding its consent to a sale it believes is likely to lead to financial failure.

In any case, where a franchise agreement is so worded, the franchisor will have to show that it has reasonable grounds for refusing to grant consent. Unless the franchisor can reach some accommodation with its franchisee, a judge will have to decide: something neither of them wants. The franchisee is unlikely to have the resources to conduct any litigation and the franchisor is not keen to be seen to be engaged in litigation with a franchisee, nor to have a judge decide who should or should not be its franchisee.

Certainly concerns about the business being overpriced will be easier to prove than concerns about not liking the buyer, but the franchisor will have to 'live' with the new franchisee and so the personality and character of the buyer is important. No franchisor wants a franchisee who has a short fuse or shows a tendency to be disruptive.

Franchisees need to be reminded that one of the prime objectives of a franchisor is to ensure that standards are maintained, and this means ensuring that *all* franchisees satisfy the franchisor's criteria with regard to business ability, management skill, financial strength, character and compatibility. After all, the franchisee selling his business is going to be less concerned about the nature of his purchaser than about the colour of the purchaser's money!

Just as franchisors are very careful in the selection of their initial franchisee, so they are keen to be equally careful in approving an incoming franchisee who buys from an existing one. Were they not so careful, they would soon find themselves with a substandard network of franchisees. It makes sense therefore that all prospective franchisees, irrespective of how they came to be prospective franchisees (and this includes candidates introduced to franchisors by existing franchisees, brokers, consultants etc.), satisfy the franchisor's criteria for franchisees and pass the same rigorous tests.

Franchisees, while accepting the underlying reasons for the imposition of such a condition, nevertheless feel uncomfortable about the franchisor retaining total discretion over whom they can sell their business to. It is a circle that cannot be fully squared and prospective franchisees usually content themselves with relying on the reputation of the franchisor by talking to existing franchisees and doing their homework to see whether or not, in the past, the franchisor has exercised its powers reasonably. Past conduct is of course no guarantee as to future conduct, but it is now by and large accepted that most prospective franchisees rely on the reputation of a franchisor amongst its franchisees.

Despite this tension, a franchisor has little to gain by being obstructive and, in my experience, such a condition is rarely abused.

If consent is withheld for whatever reason, it does beg the question – if a buyer knows that the franchisor is dead against the idea of him buying the business, why would he want to persist in its proposed purchase?

The received wisdom is that if someone is thinking of starting a new business, he would stand a significantly greater chance of succeeding if he started a franchised business as opposed to going it alone. Having said that, no franchisor guarantees success and the best a franchisor can offer is to minimise the business risk. Franchisees do fail, some within a few months of starting up. Prospective franchisees should not forget to assess the risk of franchisee failure when thinking of taking up a franchise.

As franchised networks mature, there will be a growing number of franchised businesses which are available for purchase as going concerns. Of those who leave their franchise network, very few are franchisee failures in the true sense of the word, i.e. their businesses have failed. Some simply do not renew their franchises when they expire, whilst others cease being franchisees for other reasons. These vary considerably from one franchisee to another. Whatever their reasons, when they choose to leave their franchise network, they do not abandon their businesses but rather put them up for sale. There is therefore a growing market in second-hand franchises.

For the faint-hearted or those who wish to increase their chances of succeeding and are willing to invest a little more money, these present an opportunity to avoid the risks attendant upon an initial business start-up while at the same time gaining the advantages of being a franchisee.

By buying an existing franchised business as a going concern it is possible to reduce the business risks associated with new business start-ups considerably. In theory, prospective franchisees should hit the ground running and, if they have chosen wisely, should be in profit from day one. The outgoing franchisee, by selling his franchised business, is fulfilling the expectation based on a promise made by his franchisor at the outset that if he worked hard as a franchisee his business would grow and one day could be sold for a capital gain.

In such circumstances the selling franchisee is able to realise his investment and the incoming franchisee is, to some extent, able to eliminate the fear of not knowing the sort of profit his new business might generate. But what of the franchisor? Is such a transaction to its advantage or detriment?

On the face of it, a franchisor should be pleased to hear that there is a ready market for its franchised businesses and should be ecstatic if, in selling his business, an outgoing franchisee can get a high price. After all, nothing could be of greater advantage to a franchisor than to be able to explain to a prospective franchisee the degree of success enjoyed by its franchisees.

However, it is not always as simple as that. Franchisors need to strike the right balance between recruiting franchisees to run new outlets and the sale of existing outlets. For many franchisors, a key element of their business plan is the growth in the number of franchised outlets, with a good geographic spread, enabling them to penetrate the whole market. In a free market this is not easy to achieve. For example, in a given economic climate, franchisors may find it difficult to recruit franchisees. It can therefore be disappointing for a franchisor to find that prospective franchisees are buying businesses from existing franchisees and not new franchises from the franchisor. Such sales do not help the franchisor to increase the number of its franchised outlets.

Ethical franchisors make a big investment in their franchisees in training them, setting them up in business and supporting them so that their businesses succeed and grow. So they find it painful to see such franchisees leave the network, only to be replaced by an unknown quantity: someone in whom they will have to make a similar investment, but without the advantage of adding any more outlets to their network.

However, when the economic climate is difficult, franchisors can sometimes be relieved to see existing franchised outlets being sold to new franchisees whose enthusiasm may be waning as they wait for territories or premises to become available. This is particularly true for franchise concepts which require retail premises.

How franchisors manage to square this circle depends on the rights, if any, that they have reserved in their franchise agreements. Franchisors who have been advised to bear these problems in mind at the outset are able to deal with the peaks and troughs of the market more equably than those who have not.

Buying Back Franchises

There will come a time when a franchisee decides to leave the network. This may be for any number of reasons. Some franchisees ignore the agreement and just walk away. Others ask to be released because of a change in their circumstances (ill health, bereavement, divorce, relocation, stress etc.). All things being equal, franchisors are loath to insist on such franchisees staying on as a franchisee.

Selling Franchises

One solution, as mentioned above, is to persuade and help such a franchisee to sell his business to a prospective franchisee. Alternatively, a franchisor may buy the business and manage it until a suitable replacement franchisee is found.

In cases where the reason is a failing franchisee business, a franchisor's best option is to accept a surrender from the franchisee and, depending on how rundown the business is, to shut it down without replacing the franchisee, to manage it in order to turn it around and resell it to a prospective franchisee, or to close it down in an orderly fashion and then offer that site/territory as a new franchise to a prospective franchisee. There is nothing unethical in the franchisor charging a full initial franchise fee to a buyer in these cases.

Clearly, trying to turn the business around is not only the most expensive option but also the least desirable. Not only will the goodwill of the outlet be lost, but there may also be a continuing liability for rent, not to mention the negative effect on the credibility of the franchise. News of such a failure spreading to the franchise network may also inhibit possible future sales of franchises.

The best solution is usually to persuade the incumbent franchisee that a sale is in everybody's interests and to allow the franchisor to find a buyer. It may be possible to do this within the terms of the existing franchise agreement, but separate legal arrangements will have to be made if not. Of course, a prospective purchaser may be discouraged by the fact that his predecessor has been unsuccessful. However, if the franchise format itself is a proven success and the location is sound, it should be possible to persuade prospective franchisees that the principal cause of the failure was the limited ability of the outgoing franchisee. Furthermore, there will be an established sales base upon which the purchaser can build.

If a new buyer cannot be found, it is becoming increasingly common (subject to legal considerations) for the franchisor to buy back the outlet, at least until a new franchisee can be identified. This preserves the business as a going concern and enables the franchisor to rectify any shortcomings in the way in which the business has been managed previously. However, the disadvantage of buying back the outlet is that it will cost money to do so. It may also put a strain on the franchisor, who will have to find a suitable person to manage the outlet until it can be franchised again.

The interests of the franchisor and the outgoing franchisee on sale termination are similar, although viewed from different perspectives. Each is concerned with safeguarding his commercial and financial interests. The franchisor will be concerned with ensuring that its brand, system, know-how, and goodwill are protected and preserved, and that it can appoint a replacement franchisee. On the other hand, the franchisee will be concerned with recovering as much as he can financially.

In Summary

The buying and selling of a franchised business as a going concern involves three parties: the outgoing franchisee (the seller), the incoming franchisee (the buyer) and the franchisor.

Any sale by a franchisee to a prospective franchisee can be complicated, involving:

- The sale of business as a going concern (between the outgoing franchisee and the incoming one).

- The surrender of the franchise (between the franchisor and the outgoing franchisee).

- The surrender of the lease if the franchisor is also the landlord of the franchisee (between the franchisor and the outgoing franchisee).

- The grant of a franchise agreement (between the franchisor and the incoming franchisee).

- The grant (or assignment, where appropriate) of the lease (between the franchisor and the incoming franchisee).

What is clear is that franchisors will not be able to sell franchises unless their prospective franchisees have the comfort of knowing that they will be able to sell their businesses when they want to and, all being well, realise a capital gain. These expectations must be based in reality.

CHAPTER 19

Selecting Franchisees

"Many are called but few are chosen."
                                        Matthew 22:14

The selection of suitable franchisees is of crucial importance, particularly in the early days of the franchise. However, the skill of choosing the right individual is, of necessity, developed with experience.

Although each franchisor will have its own criteria for selecting franchisees, there are nevertheless certain qualities which every franchisee is expected to possess. These basic qualities form the foundation on which franchisors add the building blocks to construct their ideal franchisee. The franchisor should take into consideration any special characteristics which may be essential for a particular franchise (such as the ability to absorb technical know-how, as in a franchise for a quick print operation, or the ability to manage people as in a franchise which is labour intensive, such as an office or domestic cleaning business). The art of selecting the right franchisee goes beyond merely selecting the right person for the job.

Apart from specific requirements for specific businesses, a number of qualities can be said to be essential if a prospective franchisee is to be successful in the selection process. These qualities can be broken down into the following broad categories:

- Experience.
- Independence.
- Financial resources.
- Health.
- Trust.
- Management skills.
- Compatibility.

- Individual characteristics.
- Social status.

If one looks at the various statistics for franchising which are available, one of the strongest points to emerge, both in the United Kingdom and in North America, is that a vast majority of franchisees work very hard, usually long hours, and make a comfortable living. Hard work involves stress and strain. A small minority makes a fortune and a somewhat larger minority finds that it is 'just about managing'. In the BFA/NatWest Franchise Survey 2015, more than 50% of franchisees surveyed reported that they were highly profitable.

Many franchisors develop what they call a 'franchisee profile' as the number of franchisees increases. This is the average of the qualities and qualifications of the franchisees they have. As an example, a franchisor may, through experience, discover that a successful franchisee is most likely to be a married man aged 39 to 45, with two children, who has had a useful career in middle management, is fed up with the lack of prospects and is stifled by company policies. He is keen to be his own boss and is supported by his spouse in his ambition but has no previous experience in the type of franchised business on offer. He is adequately funded with fairly good equity in his house on which he can borrow. If only the franchisor knew that on day one.

Common Issues and Mistakes in Franchisee Selection

No matter how careful a franchisor thinks it is in selecting its first half-dozen franchisees, more often than not those early franchisees will be troublesome in the future. As the first few franchisees they will naturally have had lavished upon them time and attention which the franchisor will ill be able to afford as the network grows, and the original franchisees will be left resentful as immediate access to the franchisor becomes more difficult.

Franchisors also need to be aware that, if it is too easy to join their franchise network, quality is being compromised and a price will have to be paid. Generally speaking, the harder the franchisee criteria are to meet, the better the quality of the network. Franchisors have to walk a tightrope between their need to satisfy their roll-out programme (which can more easily be done by relaxing the criteria) and the importance of making sure that they have the right calibre of franchisee conducting business under their brand.

Selecting Franchisees

As in most things, there is a scale of standards for franchisees. At the top end are franchisors with tough franchisee selection criteria, and at the bottom are franchisors who rely on the 'mirror test' when selecting franchisees.

What is the mirror test? It is simply this. A franchisor places a mirror under a prospective franchisee's nose. If after a couple of seconds the mirror clouds over, this is a positive indication that the candidate is alive and breathing, and if that individual also happens to have his cheque book with him, bingo: he is selected! The mirror test satisfies, at least in part, the 'financial resources' and 'health' criteria from the list at the beginning of this chapter. As for the rest, it's pot-luck. If it doesn't work out, the franchisor can always sell another franchise, but for the franchisee it could spell financial disaster.

The idea of having a franchisee profile and selection criteria sounds very grand. They certainly make for good business practice. However, franchisors come in all shapes and sizes; some are more mature than others, some have deeper pockets than others etc. The conventional wisdom has always been that franchisors don't sell franchises; prospective franchisees buy them.

That's all well and good if time is not finite, a franchisor's strategy for growth is elastic and the right quality of prospective franchisees is plentiful. In the real world, of course, franchisors have to grapple with real issues. Established franchisors with a well-known brand will attract franchisees as a matter of course. Relatively unknown franchisors or new start-ups have a tougher time.

What drives a franchisor in the initial stages of franchising is the need to get as many franchisees up and running as possible in the shortest possible time. This is where things start to go wrong.

One of the most common mistakes made by a new franchisor is to be too willing to accept early prospective franchisees and to give them special deals. This is quite understandable, since at this point the franchisor has spent a great deal of money on establishing its franchise and in running its pilot schemes. It is at the point of maximum vulnerability just when it requires the strongest nerve.

It is a great mistake to accept someone who is willing to buy a franchise but does not satisfy the selection criteria. There are many franchisors who, having become established, express a wish to be rid of some of their earlier franchisees whom they accepted at the time simply because they were available. They would not qualify for acceptance now, because the franchisor is established and can afford to be more selective. Would one set up a pilot operation in a totally wrong location merely because it was available, or would one wait patiently for the right site? One would of course wait for the right site. So with the first few franchisees patience is the key; wait for the right person. It will pay dividends in the long run.

The golden rule of 'do not do special deals with franchisees' is often broken by franchisors who are in their initial stages of franchising. Franchisors who give special deals to initial franchisees to lure them in will experience problems later when it comes to exercising control over such franchisees who still rate themselves a 'special case' and thus entitled to 'special treatment'.

Prospective franchisees who are keen to cut a deal with the franchisor should be wary of any franchisor who is accommodating in this regard. The whole ethos of franchising is uniformity. A cornerstone of managing a franchised network is not to discriminate amongst franchisees. Any prospective franchisee who succeeds in wringing concessions from a franchisor may be pleased with himself in the short term. However, sure as night follows day, that very same franchisee will come across another franchisee within the same network who has struck a better deal with the franchisor, with the result that the first franchisee will feel aggrieved.

Franchisors who show willing to make concessions and franchisees who succeed in wringing concessions out of franchisors sow the seeds of their own subsequent failure. It will not be long before the network is full of disgruntled franchisees who will complain that they have been treated unfairly. As with any family, there should be no room for favourites in a franchise network.

The Franchisee Criteria

Experience

A majority of prospective franchisees have had no previous experience in the trade or business of the particular franchise for which they are applying. This is seen by most franchisors to be a positive factor, as it makes training a franchisee that much easier.

Selecting Franchisees

Indeed, there are many franchisors who specifically exclude applicants who have prior experience in their type of business. This is because they wish their franchisee to do things the franchisor's way and not in the way in which they may have learned elsewhere. There are a number of quick print franchisors who will not grant franchises to applicants who have been previously involved in the printing industry. This is not because they would necessarily make bad printers, but because they may not make good franchisees.

The problem is an obvious one. It is very difficult, if not impossible, to untrain a person. The franchisor is not arguing that the applicant's way of doing things is wrong, merely that it is different and it is the franchisor's way of doing things which makes this particular business more successful than its competitors. For this reason franchisors prefer applicants who come to them with an open mind and, as it were, a clean slate upon which the franchisor can imprint its system.

On the other hand, there is the view that a sprinkling of franchisees with prior experience in the trade can help develop the franchise and produce a dialogue leading to the introduction of new methods, products or services.

Independence

A prospective franchisee must be independent enough to be able to manage a business on his own and to be a self-starter. Indeed, making the decision to take up the franchise could be evidence of this. However, he must not be so independent that he will not want to remain within the rules of the franchise or will continually want to break away.

One of the most difficult criteria for franchisors to determine is the degree of independence which a franchisee should possess. Although one of the essential characteristics of a franchisee is that he must be programmable, he should not be a robot. A franchisee should possess a degree of independence sufficient to provide the necessary spark which will make his business successful.

A delicate balance has to be struck between an individual who is too independent and one who shows no independence at all. The former will soon find that he is constantly at odds with his franchisor and challenging the franchisor's system. The latter, on the other hand, will become dependent upon the franchisor's support to the extent that he will show little initiative and find it increasingly difficult to exercise judgment – he will, in effect, have become an employee of the franchisor. A franchisee who strikes the balance between the two extremes is more likely to be successful.

Thus, franchisors seek a franchisee who is not only able to follow a lead, but retains a certain degree of independence that enables him to be active, motivated and innovative, hopefully to the advantage not only of himself but also of others within the franchise network.

Financial Resources

It is important that a prospective franchisee has enough money to get started – but possibly not much more. In other words, the franchisee should be 'hungry'.

Whilst a franchisee may have to borrow some of the required funds, the rest should be his own cash as a sign of his personal commitment. Any borrowing should be arranged over a satisfactory length of time to enable the business to repay the borrowed funds and the interest while leaving enough for the franchisee to live on.

It is worth remembering that if the franchisee has put in no funds of his own or alternatively is 'too rich', he may be tempted to walk away from the franchised operation if difficulties are encountered, rather than work his way through them. An appropriate financial commitment is a considerable incentive and is usually regarded as an essential feature of a franchise transaction.

Health

Given that many franchisees have never formerly owned a business of their own, the strain of running a franchised operation can be considerable. Running a business in the modern world is complicated and becoming increasingly so, and a franchisee is going to have to be able to cope with the stress that goes with it. The nervous strain can come from the entirely novel experience of having his savings and livelihood at stake in the franchised venture. He cannot hold his hand out for wages at the end of the week to anyone but himself.

Quite apart from this psychological strain and the physical strain involved in working long hours, there may be additional demands on a franchisee if the business involves a great deal of physical activity, such as carrying heavy loads or being on one's feet all day. A franchisee therefore needs to be sound in body and mind if he is going to cope with the stresses and strains of running his own business, but that in itself will not be enough.

A franchisee should not be prone to illness. One of the principal reasons why companies franchise is because they place great value on the fact that franchisees tend to be more efficient, as the businesses in which they are involved are owner-operated and not managed. Franchisors do not therefore take too kindly to a franchisee who is too frequently away from the business for reasons of ill health.

Franchisors have a responsibility to their franchisees, as well as to themselves, to ensure that their selection procedures have given sufficient consideration to a prospective franchisee's health. There are a small number of well-advised franchisors who require franchisees to undergo an independent health check before being accepted.

Trust

Mutual trust is essential in a relationship between franchisor and franchisee. A franchisor must be certain that the franchisee:

- Will be honest in his financial returns on which the franchisor's continuing franchise fee income will depend.
- Is someone whom it can trust with its name and goodwill.
- Will treat his staff and customers honestly and fairly.
- Will trust the franchisor.

A franchisor must deserve and earn the trust of its franchisees and demonstrate a successful record of ethical dealing in its business activities.

Management Skills

Can the prospective franchisee organise himself enough to run his own business, probably for the first time?

A franchisor's first couple of meetings with a prospective franchisee should provide some indication of his ability, as will a visit to his home. A franchisor should be able to tell if the prospective franchisee is serious in his approach by the effort he puts into vetting the franchise proposition, for example by asking questions about the franchisor's operation and visiting the franchisor's outlets. How receptive will he be to the training and guidance which the franchisor will be giving him? Does the franchisor feel that he will have the capacity to assimilate and apply the information he is given?

Compatibility

Do the franchisor and prospective franchisee like each other? Since they will doubtless see a lot of each another and will be mutually dependent, it is very important that they can get on with each another and have mutual respect. After all, they will both be working long hours for the same end: the success of the franchise. They really do need each other to be successful. The franchisor's own success and that of its franchisee will be inextricably interwoven.

Individual Characteristics

The 'hungry for success' individual is the archetype of the successful franchisee. However, in some cases corporate entities have made good franchisees, and there are some very successful multiple franchise unit holders, notably in the hotel and fast food businesses. Some franchisors feel that the only way such franchisees can succeed is if their managers have some share of the profits.

The more common relationship is between the franchisor and the individual franchisee, and it is a very personal relationship. The success of this personal relationship is in fact the key to the successful growth of the whole operation.

It is important from the customers' point of view that the franchisee looks healthy, clean and tidy, particularly in any operation where he is required to handle food or beverages. A franchisee who is clean and healthy himself is likely to keep his operation the same way.

It is important to have at least one meeting with the prospective franchisee in his own home. Seeing the way in which he lives and maintains his home (and how he interacts with his domestic partner, if any) can tell a lot about him. Those who live like slobs are likely to run their business in the same sloppy way. Franchisors should not leave this too late to find out.

Social Status

It is important that most prospective franchisees are in a stable long-term relationship. However, the most important question with regard to a prospective franchisee's personal relationship is whether his partner supports him in his intended venture.

In some franchises, domestic partners make an ideal combination with both partners active in the business. Even where this is not required, it is important that the prospective franchisee has the full moral support of his partner. There will be telephone messages to be taken and relayed at peculiar times of night and day, normal mealtimes will continually be missed and there will be widespread disruption of any normal social or domestic life.

Essentially, franchisors must be cautious in their selection of franchisees. They should avoid the great temptation to sign up the first warm body that comes through the door with the franchise fee in hand. The ultimate decision must be made by the proprietor of the franchising company. As the decision has long-term consequences for both parties, the principals on both sides must be happy with the arrangement.

If the services of a consultant are used in the recruitment of franchisees, the consultant must work very closely in harness with the franchisor. He must realise that it is the franchisor who appoints the franchisee and he should want the franchisor to be interested and involved in the recruitment process.

Entering into a franchise relationship is a crucial decision for both franchisee and franchisor. For the franchisee, his life savings and lifestyle will often be at stake. For the franchisor, the reputation of its business, its future income and its ability to sell franchises in the future will be at stake.

In Summary

To be successful in selecting the right individual, franchisors must allot sufficient time and be diligent when conducting their enquiry and background checks. When it comes to selection, the franchisor and franchisee each select the other. Each needs to satisfy its own criteria and each needs to look to the long term.

There is an art to interviewing franchisees, and franchisors who embark upon this exercise for the first time would be well advised to ensure that their staff receive the necessary training to enable them not only to make the most of the opportunity, but also to present their franchise in a way which inspires confidence.

Franchisors are always concerned about the speed with which they can sell franchises. Clearly some forms of marketing are more suitable for some franchises than for others. Whatever the method, the rate of conversion from prospective franchisee to actual franchisee remains extremely low; very few leads (perhaps about 10%) prove to be worth pursuing, and very few of those pursued (perhaps 10% again, i.e. 1% of all leads) actually become franchisees. This is not so extraordinary when one thinks about it. Franchisors tend to be very demanding in their selection, knowing full well that an error of judgement will cost them later. Franchisors should therefore not be too optimistic in assessing the conversion rates or the time it will take to grow the network.

Ultimately, the selection of a franchisee demands the franchisor's ability to select the right person for the right business.

CHAPTER 20

Exclusive Territories – Avoiding the Pitfalls

"A double-edged sword."

It is not uncommon, especially in those franchises where a franchisee travels to the customer (e.g. a man-with-a-van operation), for the franchisor to grant exclusive rights over a defined area (usually by reference to postcodes or redlining on a map) to their franchisees.

But what happens if a franchisee isn't working as hard as he could? There may be a number of reasons for this, but some of the most common are a refusal to employ more people or a lack of ambition, e.g. where the franchisee has a low comfort threshold.

A franchisee's thinking is very clear in such circumstances. After all, it is *his* business, and how much or how fast he grows his business is a matter for him and him only.

A franchisor, on the other hand, is not likely to stand by and watch prospective customers going to the competition. One solution which usually springs to mind is for the franchisor to put a company-owned unit in the franchisee's territory to soak up the business the franchisee is letting go. If the franchisee has exclusive rights over that territory, this is not an option.

The granting of territories, exclusive or otherwise, by franchisors has been the subject of much debate in the past, and the question of exclusivity is unlikely to cease to be topical. Should franchisees expect to be granted territorial exclusivity as a right? There was certainly a time, in the seventies, when franchisees naturally expected this and franchisors felt they had to offer territorial exclusivity if they were going to sell any franchises at all.

Both legal and commercial concerns need to be taken into consideration when deciding whether or not to grant exclusive territorial rights.

Legal Issues

When franchisors allocate an area to their franchisees, they grant exclusive rights, sole rights, protected rights or simple rights.

A franchisee who is granted **simple rights** has the right to operate the franchised business within the designated area or from designated premises and nothing else. In the absence of any legal rights in favour of the franchisee, there is little a franchisee can do if his franchisor opens another outlet, whether company-owned or franchised, next door or across the street.

The grant of **sole rights** means that the franchisor will not grant a franchise to anyone else within the area allocated to the franchisee. However, this does not prevent the franchisor itself from operating a business in that area. The grant of sole rights is rare but is sometimes used by franchisors as a means of maximising market penetration in a franchisee's designated area if the franchisee is unable or unwilling to exploit the area to its fullest commercial potential.

Franchisors often refer to **protected territories**. By this they mean the grant of protected rights whereby the franchisor places a restriction on the franchisee dictating that the franchisee will not actively market or solicit business outside the area allocated to him. As franchise agreements granted by a franchisor to its franchisees should be the same for all, this clause will be contained in all the franchise agreements, and it follows that no franchisee will be permitted to go outside his area. This therefore has the effect of protecting franchisees from other franchisees encroaching upon their territory. However, such restrictions do not protect a franchisee from encroachment by his franchisor, i.e. they will not prevent a franchisor from operating a business within the area allocated to the franchisee or indeed from appointing another franchisee in the same area.

Where a franchisor grants **exclusive rights** to a territory, it agrees not only that it will not grant a franchise for that business to anybody else within that territory, but also that the franchisor will not itself operate that business within that territory.

From the franchisee's point of view, the advantages of being granted exclusivity are obvious. There can, however, be disadvantages in granting exclusive territorial rights for the franchisor, because in so doing a franchisor effectively gives up all rights to that territory.

As a particular franchisor becomes more mature, so the pressure grows on it to find ways of increasing turnover. Also, mature franchisors have less need for capital than before and are capable of opening company-owned outlets. Previously, when a potentially profitable site became available, a franchisor would persuade an existing nearby franchisee to relocate to it or, if no exclusive rights were granted, would try to sell a franchise for that location to another franchisee. Nowadays it is tempting for some of the more successful franchisors to take the location for themselves. This could, if they are not careful, be to the detriment of the franchisee who, in the absence of exclusive rights, is powerless to do anything. Franchisors who are conscious of their public image go some way towards appeasing their franchisees by offering some sort of a deal or by buying the franchisee's business if it is likely to be adversely affected. They will not necessarily pay top dollar for the business and some franchisees in this situation, who have little choice but to accept the offer, feel betrayed and robbed of their business.

On a practical level, franchisees also know that, even if they have legal rights to protect their territory, it is almost futile for them to try to exercise these rights because:

1. The franchisor has deeper pockets than the franchisee.
2. Even if the franchisee could afford to litigate in the courts, it would take forever.
3. The franchisor can make life very difficult for the franchisee on an ongoing basis.

Dealing with the legal issues which may apply to exclusivity is not within the scope of this book, but the reader should be made aware of the potential pitfalls in this area and will need to seek expert legal advice.

Commercial Issues

The commercial arguments for and against the granting of exclusive territories are more interesting. The perceived advantages of granting exclusive territories are readily understood. There are, however, real disadvantages in granting exclusive territorial rights, and these are not always understood by either franchisor or franchisee.

First of all, it is now generally accepted that a factor in considering whether or not exclusive territorial rights should be granted is whether the franchise is a fixed location franchise or a mobile one.

In the case of fixed location franchises, the pressure on franchisors to grant exclusive territories is not so great. For one thing, with a stationary outlet, franchisees draw their customers from the area surrounding the outlet. In many cases franchisees like some assurance that the franchisor will not open another franchised outlet in the vicinity of the franchisee's location. While this desire for assurance is understandable, exclusivity is not essential for the wellbeing of the franchisee's business. The fear most frequently expressed by franchisees is that another outlet will open 'next door' or 'across the road'. In reality, of course, this seldom, if ever, happens. No franchisor is going to be able to sell a franchise 'next door' or 'across the road' from an existing franchised outlet unless it is clear to the prospective other franchisee that his outlet would be drawing its own customers from a different area from that of the existing franchisee. This is sometimes the case, for example where two franchised outlets are divided by a very busy road which is difficult for pedestrians to cross. The result is that each side of the street serves its own catchment area.

Similarly, it is unlikely that a franchisor will open a company-owned outlet in direct competition with an existing franchised outlet. There have been cases where a franchisor and a franchisee have ended up competing with each other, but in these cases it has happened through inadvertence, not by design. Most cases of franchisors competing with franchisees have been the result of mergers or acquisitions. For example, for a number of years Burger King outlets competed with Wimpy outlets. However, as a result of a series of acquisitions, Wimpy and Burger King ultimately became owned by the same parent company. In other cases, franchisors have made an acquisition of retail outlets which may or may not have been competitors of franchisees but which the franchisor has subsequently converted into franchised or company-owned outlets under the same brand. When this happens, responsible franchisors will usually reach some form of accommodation with those franchisees who are adversely affected so that they do not lose out.

When one looks at mobile franchises, the argument for franchisees being granted exclusive territorial rights is more compelling. Experience has shown that the biggest fear amongst franchisees is not that the franchisor will put another franchisee in the same area (who would buy in an area in which a franchisee already exists?) but that franchisees in neighbouring territories will cross the border and poach business from them.

In any franchised territory there are bound to be customers who are considered to be 'plums': they are highly profitable, their custom easy to secure and their needs relatively easy to service. When commercially exploiting a territory, most franchisees will pick the plums first and work to secure business from more difficult customers as time goes on. The temptation for a franchisee to nip across the border and pick the plums in another territory is ever present.

Looking at it from the franchisor's perspective, the granting of exclusive territorial rights for mobile franchisees can create enormous problems of a practical commercial nature. First of all, the franchisor can never be certain as to how large an area to allocate to a franchisee. All the franchisor can rely on is market research, which is essentially only as good as the day on which it was conducted. The franchisor, on the other hand, is being asked to grant exclusive territorial rights for the lifetime of the franchise. Over that period, the market research upon which the franchisor may have relied in determining the size of the franchisee's exclusive territory could, and most probably will, become seriously outdated. Time takes its toll on everything and markets are no exception. What a franchisor may consider to be an optimum-sized territory for a franchisee in one year may, within a short span of years, change. The change could be as a result of inner city decay, a road-building scheme, or the construction of a hypermarket, housing estate or new town. These and a number of other factors all play their part in changing the size of a market.

If a franchisor is going to carve up its market into exclusive territories with any degree of certainty it needs to be not only a clairvoyant, but a good one.

Nor is the argument against the granting of exclusive territorial rights one-sided. Franchisees can similarly face a shrinking market over a number of years within the same territory.

Human nature being what it is, franchisors tend to err on the side of caution. For the most part, when granting exclusive territorial rights, franchisors define territories which are smaller in area than they would have granted had they not

Exclusive Territories – Avoiding the Pitfalls

been granting exclusivity. In some cases, therefore, franchisees have ended up with a very small area with little or no scope for expansion because when they have been ready to expand their businesses, exclusive rights have already been granted to other franchisees in the neighbouring territories. The franchisee is then required to buy another franchise for another exclusive territory which may be some distance from his first territory. In the long run this can be a disadvantage to the franchisees who would prefer not to be restricted within artificial boundaries.

The moral of the story is that franchisors need to get their strategy right at the outset. Changing their strategy after it has been established could prove to be a very costly exercise.

CHAPTER 21

MINIMUM PERFORMANCE TARGETS

> *"Minimum performance targets: a flawed method for dealing with low comfort thresholds."*

A common problem for franchisors is how to deal with the 'comfort thresholds' of franchisees. By granting exclusive territorial rights, discussed in the preceding chapter, the franchisor is in effect selling its right to that particular market. It is therefore important for it to ensure that its franchisee exploits the area he is allocated to its fullest commercial potential. This can be done by imposing minimum performance targets, by motivating the franchisee or by a combination of both.

So far as minimum performance targets are concerned, these are, in practice, little more than a fiction. There is little point in having a minimum performance target unless it can be achieved and at the same time is meaningful in a purely commercial context. A franchisee with a low comfort threshold (and someone who is easily satisfied with his performance) will merely do the minimum and sit back.

If minimum performance targets are not readily attainable, franchisees may not always attain them. In those circumstances, what is the franchisor to do? A franchisor's ultimate sanction for failing to achieve the target set, if that constitutes a material breach of the franchise agreement (which it normally does), will always be termination. However, there may be very good reasons why a particular franchisee has failed to achieve a minimum performance target (a competitor may have opened nearby, there may have been an economic downturn in his area etc.), and the franchisor may be reluctant to terminate his franchise in those circumstances. The same franchisor may not take the same view with another franchisee who has failed to achieve his minimum performance targets for slightly different reasons, but this franchisee and his franchisor may disagree as to the reasons for his failure. A comparison between the two franchisees will not always be black and white. The second franchisee may consider the margin by

Minimum Performance Targets

which he has missed his target not to be material enough to justify the franchisor terminating his franchise for non-performance, whereas the first franchisee will consider himself to have strong mitigating circumstances.

In this scenario, if the franchisor terminates the franchise of the second franchisee and not that of the first franchisee, it may be storing up problems in the future. The franchisor may be accused of being capricious or of discriminating between franchisees for personal, rather than purely business, reasons. Multiply this by the number of franchised outlets and the problem becomes apparent. It is an inescapable fact that if minimum performance targets are to be meaningful, they have to be enforced. Uncertainty and inconsistency in enforcement can breed contempt.

Another problem with minimum performance targets is how a franchisor is to determine what they are to be. The arguments advanced against granting exclusive territories apply equally here. How is a franchisor to know what a minimum performance target should be in year three, year five or year seven of the franchise agreement?

The problem for the franchisor in trying to determine, with any degree of accuracy, a reasonably achievable performance target is made infinitely more difficult if the franchise concept is novel. Kwik Strip is a good example.

Kwik Strip is in the business, amongst other things, of furniture stripping and restoration. When the franchise was first established no such service existed. If a customer had a Victorian pine dresser with six layers of paint on it which needed stripping, the only way he could get the job done professionally was to take it to a restorer. Generally the service was only available to the trade and was quite expensive. With the arrival of Kwik Strip, it became possible for a customer to take that piece of furniture to a local Kwik Strip outlet, have it stripped at a reasonable price and collect it within a few days. In these circumstances, where the size of the market has yet to be determined, how does a franchisor begin to fix minimum performance targets in any meaningful sense?

What franchisor and franchisee have found to be unacceptable is an annual or periodic negotiation between them as to what the franchisee's performance is to be for the forthcoming year(s). It introduces an element of contention into the relationship and for that reason has seldom been successful.

Some would also argue that a franchisee who achieves a certain level of turnover simply because there is a piece of paper which requires him to do so does not make a good franchisee.

The Roots of Underperformance

If minimum performance targets are not a workable solution, this leaves a franchisor with the challenge of motivating franchisees to overcome their 'comfort thresholds'.

Given that motivation is the key to maximising the commercial potential of a franchisee, the problem of comfort thresholds becomes apparent. Most individuals have different comfort thresholds. People work for different reasons. Some people work all the hours God sends because they wish to make lots of money, some because they enjoy indulging in conspicuous consumption, some because they are workaholics and others because they wish to build an empire. Others work for pleasure or see their work as a means to a less ambitious end. They are content to do an honest day's work for a reasonable return and spend the rest of their time with their families, playing golf or pursuing whatever other interests they may have. There is absolutely nothing wrong with that and, as the owners of their own business, it is their privilege. However, franchisors may resent the exercise of this privilege because it has a direct effect on their income.

A franchisor will be faced with a dilemma if it grants exclusive territorial rights to somebody who turns out to be more easily satisfied than the franchisor expected. Having granted exclusive territorial rights to a franchisee, the franchisor has effectively locked itself out of that marketplace. If the franchisee then performs only according to the level of his minimum performance criteria or to the level of his comfort threshold, what is a franchisor to do?

In an ideal world a franchisee should achieve the maximum turnover of business possible from the particular territory to which he has been granted exclusivity. Franchisors will try hard to get the size of a given territory right, with the result that a diligent and hardworking franchisee should be capable of commercially exploiting the area to its fullest potential.

Thus, in granting the exclusive territory, the franchisor would fully expect the franchisee, in the fullness of time, to achieve, say, 100 units of business. However, the franchisee may hit his comfort threshold at 70 units and thereafter refuse to 'bust a gut' to secure the other 30 units of business. He is essentially happy with his lot.

That may be fine for the franchisee, but what about the franchisor? The franchisor sees 30 units of business, of which a part would belong to the franchisor (through the payment of continuing franchise fees or product sales), being lost.

The franchisor may try to motivate the franchisee by making various suggestions as to how the franchisee can increase his turnover. It may, for example, suggest that the franchisee 'put another team on the road', run a promotion or carry larger stocks.

The franchisee may, however, reject the suggestions on the basis that he can do without the added headache of employing more people or financing the purchase of additional equipment/stock and would much rather spend what little spare time he has taking his leisure. In such a situation the franchisor can do very little.

But the problem does not end there. It is quite likely that both the franchisor and the franchisee will suffer in the long term because if there are 30 units of business going begging, sure as night follows day, a competitor, seeing the potential, will step into the market. In so doing it will not only soak up those 30 units of business but may well take another 10 or 15 units of business from the franchisee as well, thereby leaving both franchisor and franchisee worse off.

What needs to be remembered is that, for the most part, franchisors are in business to make money for their shareholders, and as much of it as they possibly can. Franchisees, on the other hand, go into franchising for a variety of reasons. Not all go in only to make as much money as they can.

CHAPTER 22

How Long Should the Franchise Relationship Last?

"Save forever; nothing lasts forever."

Franchise lawyers and consultants are frequently asked how long a franchise relationship should last when advising prospective franchisors. The British Franchise Association and its subscribers spend a great deal of energy on promoting ethical standards and it would seem logical that there should be a standard period for franchise agreements.

In determining the period of a franchise three considerations need to be borne in mind: the law, commerce and ethics.

Although some chapters touch on some general principles of law, it is not within the scope of this work to deal with the legal aspects of franchising for which specialist advice should be sought. The ethics of franchising are generally more demanding than the law or the commercial aspects with regard to the length of a franchise agreement.

From a commercial point of view, no franchisee worth his salt will invest in a franchise if the period of the franchise is not long enough for that franchisee to recoup and obtain a return on his investment. Whilst a franchise that requires little capital investment up front (for example, a simple van-based operation) can be sold as a short-term opportunity for, say, one to three years, any business which requires a significant investment is going to require a longer-term franchise.

A fast food franchise, which these days requires significant capital investment, cannot be marketed successfully unless the period of the franchise is commensurate with the level of investment required and with the expectations of both the franchisor and the franchisee. Similarly, it is highly unlikely that a hotel franchise (given the level of investment required) will succeed unless the franchise is for between 10 and 20 years.

How Long Should the Franchise Relationship Last?

In the EU, at the time of drafting the European Code of Ethics for Franchising there was lengthy discussion about whether or not the code should impose a minimum term for a unit franchise agreement. It was eventually accepted by the various national franchise associations that, although no hard and fast rules could be set down, it was possible to establish a principle (which the European Code of Ethics does) that franchise agreements should be for such a period as is sufficient to enable the franchisee to get his investment back and enjoy a return on it.

Although the debate about the period of the franchise seems pretty straightforward at first glance, complications arise when the same problem is looked at purely from the perspective of either the franchisor or the franchisee.

In some types of business, particularly where the franchised business is heavily dependent upon know-how as opposed to products supplied by the franchisor, franchisors feel vulnerable and therefore seek to grant franchise agreements for a long period of time. Their main fear is that once the franchisor has shown the franchisee how to operate the business, the franchisee will be tempted not to renew the franchise agreement and to go it alone. If, on the other hand, the franchised business is dependent upon products which can only be obtained through the franchisor (or its nominated suppliers), the franchisor is more relaxed about the period of the franchise, knowing that its franchisees will not be able to obtain its products elsewhere and will therefore be beholden to the franchisor, whereas the franchisee will be uncomfortable with a short term. In these circumstances it will be the franchisee who seeks a franchise agreement for as long a period as possible. Going it alone after the initial period of the franchise will not be an option for the franchisee; where is he going to get the products to sell to his customers?

Given that unit franchise agreements are not negotiable, there are a number of mechanisms available to a franchisor to structure the period of the franchise in a way that suits the franchisor's requirements while at the same time allaying the fears of prospective franchisees. Not all such mechanisms will suit all franchise systems and in some cases none of them will, in which case the franchisor will have to be innovative.

A franchisor needs to ensure that its structure encourages its franchisees to stay within the network for the longer term while at the same time giving the franchisor an opportunity to review its franchisees' performance, not only in terms of turnover but also in certain specific areas (such as legal compliance, cleanliness, quality of service etc.), and disenfranchise any franchisee who does not satisfy the franchisor's standards.

From the franchisee's point of view, as already mentioned, he must be afforded some degree of certainty that the franchise will run for long enough for him to recoup his investment and get a reasonable return from it. At the same time, he does not want to feel that he is locked into a particular concept and business system for too long to be acceptable.

In many cases it is necessary to work backwards. The franchisor needs to determine what term will be marketable to its prospective franchisees, not only for its particular business but also bearing in mind what is being offered by any competitor. If the nature of the franchise is such that the franchise agreement has to be for seven years if it is to sell, then a franchisor should be looking to grant franchises for a minimum term of 10 years, or more if it is not going to give its franchisees a right of renewal for a further term.

Franchise Renewal

'Right to renew' is a term loosely used by franchisors and franchisees alike. Franchisees often understand this term to mean that, at the end of the term of the franchise agreement, the franchisee has a right to extend the period of his *current* franchise agreement. That is not what most franchise agreements say. Most franchise agreements provide that when the current franchise agreement expires, the franchisee *may* be able to continue as a franchisee provided he satisfies certain conditions and enters into a *new franchise agreement* with the franchisor. That is not the same as a franchisee carrying on under the old agreement for a further term. It has the advantage of allowing the franchisor to place an existing franchisee under the latest form of its franchise agreement, which will have been amended, in the light of experience and any changes in the law, since the franchisee first signed his agreement.

This generally satisfies franchisees, provided the terms of such option are reasonable. For the franchisor, a fixed period coupled with an option to renew, subject to the franchisee complying with the conditions laid down, has the effect of keeping the franchisee on his toes as he approaches the expiry date of his franchise agreement. Such a provision could also give the franchisor an opportunity to require the franchisee to upgrade his franchised business in order to bring it up to the franchisor's then-current standards.

For the franchisor it is important to retain control over the 'renewal' process of granting a new franchise agreement; franchisors would certainly not wish to be forced into a new franchise agreement in circumstances where a franchisee is in breach of the agreement. It is therefore generally accepted that 'rights of renewal' should be expressed in such a way that the franchisee, if he wants to continue in his franchised business, has the right to do so, but only if he satisfies certain conditions laid down by the franchisor. Franchisors should avoid the pitfall of entering into any arrangement which might give a franchisee an *automatic* right of renewal.

On any such grant of a new franchise agreement, there will be very few *initial* obligations on either party. Many of the services which the franchisor would provide to a new franchisee, such as initial training or launching the business, will not be needed for an existing franchisee who is renewing. Under the circumstances, few franchisors can justify asking franchisees for a fee on renewal. It is true that franchisors will incur some expense in going through the renewal process, but this would be a fraction of the initial franchise fee being charged by the franchisor to new franchisees.

CHAPTER 23

Price Fixing Within the Network

> *"Why was there only one Monopolies Commission?"*

Franchise applicants are well informed and increasingly demanding of their franchisors from the outset. Wherever they go for advice, they are told they must check out their prospective franchisor thoroughly and make sure that 'the figures stack up'. Banks that are approached for loans require business plans, as do other professional advisors. Franchisors are therefore keen to supply as much information as they can, and they in turn are advised by their professional advisors to take great care over any representations they make, particularly those of a financial nature.

A key element in determining the profitability of a business venture has to be price. In a new business start-up there is a great deal of guesswork, sometimes tempered by some degree of experience, in drawing up a business plan.

In the sale of a franchise, however, the buyer relies on the experience of the franchisor, not guesswork. A franchisor with significant experience of running its own outlets should be well placed to produce financial projections which are based on its own experience and which will therefore have a greater chance of proving to be accurate.

From its experience, a franchisor should know what the staffing costs and other overheads are likely to be. It should know the level of turnover that its trading units are achieving. It should know the cost of providing a particular product or service. It can tell, by looking at its own books, the cost of sales, margins and the profit it can achieve if it sells its products/services at a certain price. This is within the control of the franchisor. It decides on the price at which the product or service is to be sold.

As for the other costs, be they interest rates, rents, cost of labour, raw materials etc., the franchisor is pretty much in the same boat as its competitors.

So far, so good. Where things can go badly wrong is if, having produced a business plan based on his franchisor's experience, the franchisee takes it upon himself to depart from the norm for that particular business and starts making unilateral changes to the financial model.

'Franchisees can't do that,' one may exclaim, because in a well-structured franchise the franchisor will have controls in place which will enable it to intervene to prevent any such departure. By and large this is true.

However, there is one area where any attempt by a franchisor to control a franchisee may not only be unenforceable, but may also leave the franchisor open to prosecution for breaking the law. To make matters worse, this one exception is a key element of any business plan or financial projection: price.

All financial projections are based on the assumption that a particular product or service will be sold at a certain price. A franchisor that has experience of selling at a certain price makes this assumption when producing a financial model. It assumes that the franchisee will do as he is told and follow the system. However, if a particular franchisee chooses to ignore the franchisor's price *recommendation*, it will throw the financial model out of alignment.

The law is very clear on this matter. Franchisors cannot force their franchisees to sell any particular product or service at a particular price.

A fundamental principle of competition law is that people should be entitled to determine their own selling prices. Any franchisor who sought to impose a minimum retail price would be breaking the law and asking for trouble. In this regard the franchisor is at the mercy of its franchisees, particularly if the franchise model is such that the franchisee will only make a healthy profit if the products/services are priced at a certain level. A franchisee who discounts the products or services in those circumstances may find himself in financial difficulty.

Some franchise concepts require goods or services to be perceived as being good value and therefore, if a franchisee charges *more* than the price recommended by his franchisor, the product or service could be seen to be expensive and turnover could drop. As things stand at the present, it is possible for a franchisor to insist on maximum prices and therefore to penalise a franchisee who charges more than the franchisor has specified for a particular product or service.

However, the imposition of maximum prices is not permitted if the maximum price imposed by the franchisor is pitched at such a level as to ensure that it op-

Price Fixing Within the Network

erates as a minimum price. In some cases franchisors are able to do this because they know the complete financial model and margins of their franchisee. If a franchisor fixes the maximum price at an artificially low level, the franchisee will have no choice but to sell at that price or sell at a loss. In these and other circumstances, a maximum price fixing structure can be set to operate as a minimum price fixing structure also, making it unenforceable.

So, how should a franchisor deal with a 'maverick' franchisee? One way is for the franchisor to show its entrepreneurial franchisee, by example, why a departure from the *recommended* (not imposed) price list may not be in his best interest in the long run, and that the franchisor will bear no responsibility for consequent deviations from any financial model/projections which it has given to the franchisee, which will be based on the franchisor's recommended price structure.

That having been said, the final decision on pricing must always be that of the franchisee.

CHAPTER 24

Managing and Controlling the Network

"The management of a franchise network is an art, not a science."

One of the key elements of a successful franchise operation is the ability of the franchisor to manage and control its franchised network. No matter how well a franchise is run, there will invariably be problems between franchisors and franchisees as franchisees start to feel more independent.

Disputes between franchisor and franchisee fall into two broad categories: firstly disputes between individual franchisees and the franchisor, and secondly, and more seriously, disputes between the franchisor and the entire network, or a large part of it. In both cases, many of the underlying causes are the same. In broad terms, if disputes with individual franchisees are dealt with properly or, better still, avoided in the first place, disputes with the network are less likely to occur. As with many things, prevention is better than cure.

Maintaining Peace

Even in the most harmonious network, disputes with individual franchisees, from the trivial to the serious, will occur from time to time, and in these cases swift decisive action will need to be taken. Bearing the following points in mind will help in dealing with these disputes.

Trust

The most important element of a harmonious network is the existence of an atmosphere of trust between the franchisees and the franchisor. The franchisor–franchisee relationship is a long-term partnership and, unless there is mutual trust and respect between the parties, the relationship will be difficult. Establishing and maintaining trust with franchisees is therefore a major factor in preventing disputes.

The ground rules for the relationship should be set at the beginning, at the franchisee recruitment stage. Trust will only develop in an open and honest atmosphere, and honesty and openness at this stage will pay dividends later.

In situations where trust with existing franchisees has broken down, or has never existed, time should be taken to build trust. Few, if any, franchisees are difficult and disruptive for the sake of it, and very often there is some underlying worry, concern or misunderstanding causing the problem. If one takes the trouble to find out what the underlying fears and concerns are, the resolution of the dispute will be much easier.

Where appropriate, accept the franchisee's point of view, and if necessary act on it. This will go a long way to reinforcing trust. Fudging the issues or attempting to 'pull the wool' will destroy confidence and trust.

The Good Samaritan is known for what he did. Good intentions in themselves are not enough; actions are what count.

Talking to Franchisees

In any group there will be a relatively small number of opinion formers. It is worthwhile to establish close contact with this group and talk to them regularly. They will almost certainly be an accurate barometer of the mood of the network.

It is important to talk to individual franchisees and tell them what is going on in the network. Simple things like picking up the phone and congratulating a franchisee on securing a valuable customer can have a dramatic effect on the franchisee's morale. It tells the franchisee that his franchisor cares about him and the effort he is making; it tells him that he is not alone, and it makes him feel a bit special. We all like the occasional pat on the back.

Just as important is listening to and trying to understand an individual franchisee's problems. It is a very time-consuming business, but worth the effort. Remember that listening involves understanding, though not necessarily agreeing with, a franchisee's point of view.

Franchisors should explain their perspective on contentious issues to the network. They should be open and truthful; if they do not give franchisees the facts, franchisees will invent them. The fora for these discussions can be anything from the annual seminar to informal local get-togethers.

Firmness

Franchisors should not be afraid to take firm and decisive action. A franchisor has a duty to protect the brand and to act for the good of the network as a whole, and this involves taking tough action on occasion, including disenfranchising where necessary. If the reasons for the action are fair and explained properly to franchisees, they will be accepted. Franchisees will respect a firm, fair line.

Franchisors should not shy away from disenfranchising errant franchisees. If it is justified the network will respect them for it, but trouble should be taken to inform franchisees of why the action has been taken.

Avoiding Precedents

Do not create precedents by allowing individual franchisees to operate outside the franchise system, or by giving way on matters in the franchise agreement. There will be a clamour from other franchisees to be allowed similar relaxations, soon leading to chaos.

Good Guys and Bad Guys

One point which causes unrest is any feeling that the 'good guys' are subsidising the 'bad guys'. If a franchisee is cut some slack, other franchisees will feel that he is being allowed to get away with it. Be firm and fair. If there are valid reasons why an exception is being made, let those reasons be known.

Record Keeping

Maintaining good records of all contact with individual franchisees, including field visits and telephone conversations, is vital. It is remarkable how memories become selective when there is a dispute, and the franchisor's ability to provide detailed evidence to establish the facts will be invaluable. Discussions can then be confined to the dispute, rather than running into constant disagreement over the facts.

A strong and fair franchise agreement is vital. A woolly agreement can cause endless argument.

For more on resolving disputes, see Chapter 29.

Changes Over Time

As a network grows, a franchisor needs to establish some sort of dialogue on an ongoing basis with its network. Most franchisors come to realise that their relationship with their franchisees cannot remain the same as it was when they first embarked on franchising.

The corporate structure of franchisors changes out of necessity. The nature of franchising is such that it enables a business to grow rapidly. Most businesses suffer growing pains, and franchising is no different. What exacerbates this is the speed with which a franchise company can grow. Unless a prospective franchisor is willing to change its corporate structure by taking on suitably qualified managers to perform the myriad of functions which the owner of the franchisor company previously performed personally (relating to finance, marketing, recruiting, training, sourcing products, giving support to the franchise network etc.), the company will quickly outgrow its owner and eventually collapse.

The introduction of management personnel into the franchisor's corporate structure means that the franchisor will at best be one step removed from its franchisees. Franchisees will no longer be able to communicate directly with the franchisor as an individual, and may feel more and more isolated as the franchise organisation grows bigger. Unless the management personnel are extremely well trained and motivated, their attitude towards franchisees will be different to that of the owner of the franchisor company. They tend to be less empathetic and, although in many ways they will be more professional, it is inevitable that they will be less personal in their approach.

One of the main hurdles such personnel have to overcome is the fact that they are employees who get paid every month but are required to interface with business people who run a financial risk every day and do not enjoy the security of a monthly salary. The management of a franchise network is an art, not a science.

If a franchisor's system of communicating with its franchisees is not efficient, the franchisor will be the loser because it will increasingly become out of touch with what is going on in the network and possibly also in the marketplace. Furthermore, the franchisor will be deprived of the franchisee's contribution in terms of feedback, which is vital in the long term if the franchisor is to continue to provide its franchisees not only with support but also with new ideas.

A successful, growing and mature franchise company's franchisees will become more experienced and, by virtue of their increased experience and success, will be less and less willing to be 'managed' by the franchisor or, more accurately, its management personnel. To this has to be added the distortion of the balance of power; the initial weak position of the franchisee will wear off as and when the franchisee's business expands.

As a franchisee's business grows, so he will evolve his own base structure, thereby duplicating to some extent the franchisor's structure. As a franchisee becomes more successful, his marketing management will improve, his commercial management will improve and he will make increasing use of professional advisors.

Whether or not the growth of franchisees (in terms of both number and size) poses a threat to a franchisor will in the end depend on how receptive a franchisor is to its franchisees' ideas and concerns, whether it can adequately communicate with its franchisees, how supportive it is and to what extent it has discharged its responsibilities as a franchisor.

Communication

One of the most important features of any successful franchise is the quality of communication between franchisor and franchisee. Given that communication is a two-way exercise, the mechanisms for maintaining the necessary channels become increasingly cumbersome as the chain grows.

A franchisee who feels cut off or neglected, who feels that his good ideas are being ignored for no good reason, will be a source of friction. Many franchisees can make a valuable contribution to the franchise system with their direct field experience.

The network needs a safety valve, and a workable system of communication.

In any group of people, from the family unit to large multinational companies, communications present problems. There are no simple solutions. However, one can offer some practical advice.

The more communication channels, the better. Seminars, newsletters, regular mailings, franchisee associations (see below) in which the franchisor meets with representatives of the franchisees: all have their place, and the most appropriate vehicle will be dictated by circumstances.

The most crucial factor in maintaining a trusting and happy network is a good communication system. Good communication is of vital importance, and it is therefore essential that existing channels of communication evolve with the growth of the franchisor.

Franchisee Associations

It is by no means inevitable that every franchisor will sooner or later have to deal with a franchisee association, but it is probable and in many cases it may even be desirable.

There are essentially two types of franchisee associations: those which are born out of frustration and dissatisfaction with the franchisor, and those which are formed either on the initiative of the franchisor or jointly by the franchisor and franchisees, as a forum for discussing problems, solutions, new ideas, markets and the like.

A franchisee association born out of frustration will take the form of an action group and will be hostile and in many cases unreasonable in its attitude towards the franchisor. This must be avoided at all costs. If an action group is set up it must mean that the franchisor has failed in one or more of the following areas:

- To adequately communicate with its franchisees.
- To be receptive to its franchisees' ideas.
- To give adequate support.
- To provide the right link between itself and its franchisees.
- In its marketing programmes.
- In its innovative functions – it has failed to keep the system and image up to date with market trends.
- To organise advantageous purchasing arrangements.
- To develop the feeling of mutual trust and dependence which is so vital.
- To be understanding of and interested in its franchisees.
- To discharge its obligations to its franchisees in other material respects.

A franchisee association which develops in these circumstances is symptomatic of the problems; it will not solve them. It is an indictment of the franchisor. The franchise scheme will come under attack and the franchisor may find itself with either a combined legal action or tremendous pressure which could lead to the dismantling of its franchise system. Alternatively the franchisees will try to lead the franchisor back along the path of franchise righteousness. In any event all parties will have suffered in terms of personal relationships, confidence and their financial welfare.

On the other hand, a group formed in the spirit of goodwill, with mutual advantage as its objective, can make an important contribution.

Franchisee associations must not be used as negotiating bodies. One must not forget that there is a contract between each individual franchisee and the franchisor, and nothing must be allowed to get in the way of that relationship.

What, then, are the topics for discussion for such an association?

Franchisee Experience

Franchisee experience in the field can be passed on to the franchisor and methods of coping with problems discussed. There is often a wealth of experience and ability among franchisees which the franchisor would be wise to tap into.

New Ideas

New ideas can be introduced by the franchisor for the association's considered views and reaction. The franchisor can either discuss the views before market testing in company-owned branches or report back its experience in practice after pilot testing has taken place. This would of course include any innovation or improvement in products/services.

Training

The franchisor may discuss training or retraining procedures and facilities with current and former franchisees.

Problems

The franchisee association may investigate and propose solutions to problems facing the network. Not all franchisors are able to cope efficiently with the ever-increasing volume of accounting information with which they have to contend, for example. In such cases, with little additional expense, a full accounting and information service can be offered to franchisees. The introduction of such a service, its scope and its cost can be discussed with an advisory committee to reach a scheme acceptable in its details.

Communication

The style and content of various material can be discussed and improved; for example, suggestions can be made for the improvement of operations manuals where perhaps an explanation is felt to be inadequate. The franchisee association offers an opportunity for a franchisor to discover at first hand, with constructive rather than destructive criticism, why its communication with its franchisees fails to achieve its objective. The association may come to the conclusion that the franchisor should introduce a regular newsletter and may make suggestions for certain topics to be included.

Contractual Changes

Proposals by the franchisor for the introduction of contractual changes and the reason for such changes can be discussed. The franchisor may wish to introduce new provisions to fill gaps, the most common of which, in franchise agreements, is what should happen in the event of the death of the franchisee. Some franchisors also have little or no provision in their agreements for realistic advertising and marketing programmes. If changes must be made to the franchise agreement before a viable programme can be introduced, the franchisee association provides an ideal forum for the franchisor and its franchisees to discuss those changes.

Marketing

This is a wide topic and includes website updating, national advertising, local advertising, point of sale material, promotional activities and public relations. Most franchisees contribute in one way or another towards funding the cost of such activities. They are invariably keen to know how the funds will be spent and how much it might help them individually.

The ensuing year's activities can be discussed with franchisees through the association. A franchisee will frequently have a valid contribution to make because he will be looking at the proposals with his narrow self-interest in mind. This sort of grassroots detail can escape the attention of a franchisor and its marketing advisors.

Promotional activities in the planning of which the franchisees have participated will be greeted far more enthusiastically and will be more likely to succeed than those that have been forced upon franchisees.

It should also be possible to discuss such details as how long before the launch of a promotion franchisees should receive any point of sale material, special range of stock and so on.

Research

As well as marketing plans, there will always be continuing market research and surveys. There will be selective trials of new equipment or ideas by franchisees willing to participate, which can be organised by liaison with an association.

Franchisees have a contribution to make via an association by aiding in such research and surveys. In the course of discussion about the introduction of any research or surveys, franchisees could assist in the compilation of the terms of reference and the scope of the enquiries.

*

The terms of reference of any franchisee association, or indeed any association, should be carefully defined. Such an organisation should at the very least discuss matters such as communication, training and retraining procedures and facilities, accounting procedures, new ideas or modifications to the existing system, the range of products and/or services to be offered, advertising, marketing and promotions.

There are other matters, such as the level of continuing franchise fees, the right of entry into the franchised network and so on, which the franchisor will quite rightly wish to determine itself, and this has to be respected.

No self-respecting franchisor will permit itself to be dictated to by its franchisees. Mature franchisees also resent being dictated to but will respond to systems designed to consult, encourage, motivate and reward.

It is difficult to state when would be the right time in any individual franchise to introduce an association. Obviously in the early stages it will not be necessary or suitable, but once the franchisor is established and has some experienced franchisees in the field the advantage will become apparent.

An association which is created in a spirit of goodwill, with mutual advantage as its objective, will establish a climate of understanding, helping to cement the franchisor and franchisees together in a powerful business alliance. It can act as a positive synthesis of the franchisor and franchisees' entrepreneurial talents for their mutual benefit.

Research and Development: Involving Franchisees

If one of the prime advantages of franchising is that it enables an entrepreneur to get on with the real task of selling goods/services, then someone else (i.e. the franchisor) needs to devote time and resources to ensuring that the franchise concept not only remains relevant to the market but also retains and increases its market share.

The responsibility of improving the system and of innovation rests with the franchisor and, more often than not, this is written into franchise agreements as an obligation of the franchisor. It is also something on which franchisors place a great deal of importance and which they promote as a positive characteristic of their franchise.

However, franchisors cannot work in isolation. Although they may be at the coal face themselves (through their own company-owned branches), few have the sort of geographical spread of company-owned branches which would enable them to assess the true requirements of the market as a whole.

Any research and development policy of a franchisor therefore usually includes an element of franchisee involvement. Most franchisors take one or more of their franchisees into their confidence and use them as a sounding board for their intentions. Franchisors also select certain franchisees to market test an innovation,

Managing and Controlling the Network

after the franchisor has itself tested the innovation in its own company-owned operation.

However, the story does not end here.

Having developed a new product or a new way of doing something, the franchisor then has the very important task of selling it to its franchise network. Although the franchise agreement may give the franchisor rights to insist on franchisees adopting any change, common sense dictates that franchisors will be more successful if they can persuade their franchisees to buy into the change.

This means getting franchisees together under one roof, depending upon the size and nature of the franchise network, either on a regional or on a national basis.

Franchisee Conferences

Franchisee conferences serve a number of useful purposes. Some are designed as 'ra-ra' sessions to enthuse franchisees into increasing their turnovers etc. Some are used by franchisors to explain their future policies and intentions, some as a means of introducing and selling new products or changes to the system to their franchisees, and others to facilitate bonding amongst franchisees and the franchisor's staff. Most franchisee conferences consist of a combination of two or more of the above.

Franchisors also tend to encourage intra-group competition by having their own system of awards for franchisees. They may have shown the greatest improvement in their performance over the previous year, achieved the greatest turnover, landed the biggest contract. They may even have been the most proactive in the business themselves, offering suggestions to their franchisors, as in the case of McDonald's breakfast menu, which was the idea of a franchisee. This sort of feedback is taken seriously by many franchisors and indeed is increasingly being recognised as a means by which franchisees can make a valuable contribution for the benefit of the network as a whole.

If franchisee conferences are all so logical, sensible and constructive, why don't all franchisors arrange them? Why do some franchisors shy away from the idea and why do some of them positively discourage such a gathering? Some of the answers are obvious. Fledgling franchisors usually find it more fruitful to deal with their franchisees on a one-to-one basis regularly and frequently. Some franchisors, however, are just scared. This may be a result of insecurity or a fear that if they get all their franchisees under one roof, the franchisees will start complaining about their franchisor and perhaps even form pressure groups: something which the franchisor may feel it can do without at a particular stage of its development.

On the whole and almost without exception, it can be said that franchisee conferences are a positive force within any franchised network. They help to create an *esprit de corps*, encourage the commercially ambitious to perform better, fire up those franchisees who may be in the doldrums and motivate those who are underperforming. They also provide an opportunity for franchisees to discuss their problems with their peers: an opportunity denied to most independent small businesses, who are unlikely to confide in their competitors.

Franchisee conferences can be a very important tool in managing a franchise network and, if they are well planned and executed, can benefit all concerned. For franchisors, this is not an easy task, but then success seldom comes easily. If, at the end of a franchisee conference, it all seems to franchisees to have been a doddle, the franchisor will have succeeded.

Franchisors who eschew franchisee conferences should be aware that they may be storing up trouble for the future. Unless they provide some forum for franchisees to air their views in an atmosphere which is conducive to producing a constructive outcome, those franchisees will become disgruntled and will form their own discussion groups and set their own agenda, whatever the franchisor's view on the matter.

Finally, many franchisors who hold conferences for their franchisees will tell you that the really frustrating thing about them is that they are most frequently attended by franchisees who are good performers and seldom by those who need to improve, who are the very franchisees who need to attend such sessions the most. Franchisors should therefore think of ways to encourage such franchisees to attend.

Example Structure of a Franchisee Association

One system of association which has been used to very good effect by some franchisors is structured in the following way:

- The association consists of a representative of the franchisor and one or more representatives of the franchisees. The number of franchisee representatives depends on the size of the franchisee network and, within reason, is for the franchisees to decide. The franchisee representatives are required to elect a chairman of their group.

- The purpose of the association is to discuss various matters referred to above. The agenda is set by the franchisee representatives, but the association is chaired by a representative of the franchisor.

- The franchisor provides administration services such as taking minutes, preparing formal agenda, booking and paying for the venue etc.

- Having seen the agenda, the franchisor is required to ensure that those members of staff responsible for departments which are to be discussed (marketing, product procurement, customer complaint, administration etc.) attend the meeting to answer questions, give clarification and discuss issues raised by the franchisees' representatives.

- Where the association takes a decision, such as to embark upon a particular marketing strategy, this is related to the whole network, which is then expected to follow suit. The minutes are drafted, approved by the chairman of the franchisee representatives and then circulated to the whole network by the franchisor, as an administrative function.

Addressing Concerns

Franchisees should also have the opportunity to raise topics. Care should be taken to ensure that the franchisee association only really deals with matters of concern affecting franchisees as a whole. It should not allow itself to be used as a vehicle for the promotion of dissatisfied franchisees' individual complaints. It cannot act as advocate, judge and jury in what would inevitably be a two-sided story. The quality of the relationship between the association and the franchisor should not be placed in jeopardy for the sake of individual problems or disputes.

Managing and Controlling the Network

Therefore a strong chairman who commands respect of the franchisees is essential.

For more on the matter of maintaining control over franchisees, see the opening of Chapter 27.

At the end of the day, if a franchisor is to survive, it will need the goodwill of its franchisees and if it wishes to thrive, it will need their co-operation.

Top 10 Tips

1. Establish trust within the network and with individual franchisees.
2. Establish good communications with a view to ensuring an early warning of possible problems.
3. Make an effort to understand both the problem and the franchisee's point of view.
4. Nip any problem in the bud by taking quick decisive action.
5. Be fair and even-handed in dealing with disputes. Don't be afraid of accommodating a franchisee's point of view – it will not be seen as a weakness if it is handled correctly – but a franchisor should not be afraid of tough action where it is justified.
6. Explain the network policies and the reasons for any action that has been or will be taken.
7. Never forget that one's franchisees are one's customers.
8. Maintain a good written record of all contact with franchisees.
9. Have a strong but fair franchise agreement.
10. Be transparent in *all* financial dealings with franchisees and with third parties (e.g. suppliers) on their behalf.

CHAPTER 25

The Franchise Agreement

"If you sign it, you're bound by it."

When considering franchise agreements, the first thing to remember is that there is no specific legislation for franchising in the United Kingdom. This is both good news and bad news. It is good news because, generally speaking, it means that the franchisor and the franchisee are at liberty to agree whatever terms they choose. The bad news is that, because there is no legislation and because franchising is not regulated, the parties to a franchise transaction are going to have to rely on their franchise agreement. This means that if care has not been taken by the franchisor or the franchisee at the agreement stage, and subsequently events occur which are to the detriment of one of the parties, they will not be able to turn to any franchise-specific legislation for protection. Subject to ordinary commercial law, the parties are expected to comply with their contractual obligations even if they subsequently prove to be one-sided or more onerous than was originally contemplated. Once the franchise agreement has been signed, the parties will be bound by its terms and will be locked in for the duration of the period of that agreement.

Put simply, there is no law in the United Kingdom against making a bad bargain.

The franchise agreement, together with the operations manual, forms the engine of the whole franchise transaction.

The Importance of the Franchise Agreement

If the franchise agreement is essentially what governs the relationship between franchisor and franchisee, then it is important that it sets out clearly the rules which both parties must observe. This means that the agreement should specify in sufficient detail the franchisee's obligations, so that the franchisee, prior to signing the franchise agreement, is given the opportunity of asking himself whether he can perform these obligations and of being informed about the grounds on which his franchisor will seek to terminate the franchise agreement.

The Franchise Agreement

From the franchisor's point of view, bearing in mind that unless it provides the necessary mechanisms for control it may be left powerless in the face of a recalcitrant franchisee, it is important to ensure that the agreement provides the necessary rights and powers to enable it to exercise such control.

Prospective franchisees are sufficiently mature and well informed to realise that the argument often advanced by prospective franchisors that it is not the agreement that matters so much as the franchisor itself, while being essentially valid, is not the whole story. A franchisee will not necessarily rely wholly on the reputation of the franchisor without ensuring that adequate safeguards exist in the form of a property drafted franchise agreement. No matter how big or how benevolent the franchisor is, such notions are no substitute for contractual rights. After all, people change jobs and companies change owners. Although a particular franchisee may have a good rapport with people running the franchise operation for the franchisor, there is no guarantee that they will remain with the franchisor for the duration of the term of franchise or indeed that their job specification will not change during the term of the franchise. With the exception of death and taxes, nothing is certain in this world, and it is a foolish franchisee who makes an investment on the strength of only the reputation of the franchisor or the persons whom he knows within the franchise organisation rather than on the basis of a sound contract.

Franchise networks can change hands at an alarming rate. In the fast food industry, for example, Joe Lyons owned Wimpy, which it sold to United Biscuits. United Biscuits then bought Pillsbury, a US company, which included Burger King in its stable, so this brought two competing fast food hamburger chains in the form of Burger King and Wimpy within the single ownership of United Biscuits. United Biscuits was subsequently acquired by Grand Metropolitan (now known as Diageo), which converted the counter service Wimpys into Burger Kings and sold off the old-fashioned table service Wimpys, with the buyer retaining the Wimpy brand.

New owners may have different priorities. Franchisees may find that their franchisor is no longer as benevolent as it previously was and that the franchise personnel with whom the franchisee dealt previously have departed as the new owners have moved in, or have had imposed on them a different set of priorities and objectives, with the result that there is a significant change in their attitude towards the franchisee.

While it is true to say that large franchise companies, on the whole, do not abuse their franchisees, nevertheless there have been a number of occasions where large companies have taken legitimate complaints from franchisees less seriously than a small franchisor would have done. On the whole, where there has been friction between the franchisor and the franchisee, large companies have tended to be driven by a desire to protect their reputations or, rather, to preserve their reputations, whereas small franchisors have been concerned with the more down-to-earth commercial realities of trying to protect their income. That is not to say that there are no bad small franchisors or that there are no good big franchisors. Big franchise companies contribute enormously towards the welfare and wellbeing not only of franchisees but also of the franchise sector in general by promoting ethical franchising. Nevertheless, most of them will agree that there is no substitute for a good business relationship based on a sound contract.

Once they have been signed, franchise agreements should be put away, never to see the light of day again. Indeed, if either franchisor or franchisee has the need to refer to the franchise agreement it is probably because the relationship has seriously broken down in some way and the parties are left to rely on the written word rather than on the spirit of the agreement. If a franchisor has not addressed foreseeable issues clearly and concisely in its franchise agreement, then it will have the effect merely of further muddying waters rather than clearly spelling out the direction in which the parties should move.

No Negotiation

Although all franchise transactions are subject to the ordinary commercial law, there is one aspect of the franchise transaction which makes it significantly different from any other commercial transaction. Unlike those in most other commercial contracts, the contracting parties in a franchising transaction do not negotiate. Ethical franchising requires that each franchisor is fair and *equal* in its treatment of all franchisees. No franchisee should be treated more favourably than any other franchisees within the same network. The franchise agreement must therefore be the same (save for certain insubstantial changes which may have to be made to take into account details such as the different size and configuration of premises) for all franchisees.

As with any family, there should be no room for favourites within a franchise network. Franchisors are constantly being advised to be on their guard against doing special deals with franchisees. There is nothing more insidious within a franchise network than franchisees discovering that certain franchisees are being treated differently by their franchisor. Any franchisor who negotiates with a franchisee or does a special deal with one or more franchisees will soon discover that it has sown the seeds of future discontent amongst its network. If it keeps any special deal secret, then it is not dealing honestly with its franchisees. If it does not deny or discloses a special deal, other franchisees will demand similar privileges. Would-be franchisees who take pride in their negotiating skills and business acumen will soon realise that, however good a bargain they drive with their franchisor, there will surely be somebody else in the network who has done a better deal, and when they find this out they will feel cheated.

On the other hand, where a franchisor has refused a prospective franchisee's request to make material changes to its standard form of franchise agreement, that franchisee can take some comfort in the knowledge that in refusing his request the franchisor is confirming that it intends to deal evenly with all its franchisees even though each of them is unique – just like all the others.

Human nature being what it is, everyone feels that they are a special case, yet the essence of a business format franchise is uniformity and there can be no uniformity if franchisees are permitted to pull in different directions.

Legal Matters

Although there is no specific franchise law in the United Kingdom, there is a great deal of legislation and case law which has the potential to affect a franchise transaction. Much of it is ordinary commercial law and the common law. But there is also anti-trust and competition law which deals with retail price maintenance, consumer protection, anti-corruption practice, unfair trading, restrictive trade practices, the protection of industrial and intellectual property and last but not least, at the time of writing, the competition rules of the European Union.

Franchise agreements are sometimes inadvertently caught by some of this legislation simply because of the way in which a particular Act of Parliament or regulations made under an Act of Parliament were drafted. In some cases, when drafting legislation, the parliamentary draughtsmen were not conscious of the existence of franchising, and so the wording of some legislation catches certain franchise agreements with dire consequences for those who have failed to appreciate it.

Almost all franchise agreements reflect franchise structures which can be likened to pyramid selling schemes. Whether or not that is the intention of the franchisor does not matter if the transaction falls foul of legislation which regulates such schemes. Ignorance of the law, as one is often told, is no excuse. The penalties which can be visited on a franchisor for failing (even inadvertently) to comply with legislation which applies to it can be severe. In some cases it may amount to a fine; in other cases it may render a part or the whole of the franchise agreement unenforceable. In the case of the law relating to pyramid schemes, breach of the regulations made under the relevant legislation can be a criminal offence. That is the seriousness with which competition authorities see any breach of some anti-trust laws.

Given what has been said about the need to have a standard form of franchise agreement, it follows that the person who is charged with the task of drafting a franchise agreement must be thoroughly familiar with the plethora of legislation that may affect a franchise transaction.

Clarity

If one accepts the fact that franchise agreements are not negotiable, it becomes even more important that the franchise agreement is clearly drafted and leaves no ambiguity. If a particular provision in a franchise agreement is ambiguous, the Judges' Rules on interpretation are clear: when interpreting such a provision, the judge will exercise a strong bias in favour of the party who has had no hand in drafting the agreement in question. As the task of producing the franchise agreement rests with the franchisor, a badly drafted or ambiguous clause in a franchise agreement is very likely to be interpreted by the courts in favour of the franchisee. In other words, if you write it, write it in a way which states clearly what you mean.

Judges do not add words to what is already written to give meaning to an unclear or ambiguous clause. Their common practice in these circumstances is to apply the 'red pencil/blue pencil' rule. If they can make sense of a clause by striking out one or more words (blue pencil), they will do so. However, if, having applied the blue pencil rule, the clause is still not clear, they will strike out the whole clause with a red pencil. If that clause happens to be a fundamental provision of the agreement, the whole agreement may be rendered unenforceable. If that is the case, given that all of a franchisor's agreements are in a standard form, it follows that all its agreements will be unenforceable, with obvious consequences for its franchise network.

The Objectives of a Franchise Agreement

It is important from a franchisee's point of view that the franchise agreement is well balanced in terms of the rights and obligations of the parties and also takes into consideration the franchisee's concerns. Again, in the absence of legislation or regulation which tells the parties what to do and given that the franchise relationship is generally a long-term one, it is important that the agreement spells out very clearly what is expected by and of each party.

If the franchise agreement plays such a pivotal role in giving efficacy to the franchise transaction between a franchisor and a franchisee, what should each agreement seek to achieve and what should it contain?

A franchise agreement must fulfil three fundamental objectives:

1. It should be in writing and accurately reflect the terms agreed on between the franchisor and the franchisee.
2. It should seek to protect the franchisor's intellectual property rights.
3. It should set out the rules which are to govern the franchisor and franchisee's future conduct.

As the law will not generally intervene to provide any term which a franchisor may have omitted from the franchise agreement, and the general principle of 'if you sign it, you're bound by it' applies, the agreement should leave no room for doubt as to what the parties have agreed.

There is no requirement in law for the franchise agreement to be in writing. However, common sense dictates that it should be, because, apart from anything else, it makes it easier to show and, if necessary, prove what the agreed terms of the franchise are. That is not to say that two parties who have conducted business over a period of time cannot be bound to each other even if the relationship is not referred to in writing elsewhere. Under common law, a course of dealing between two parties, even if not in writing, nevertheless constitutes a valid, enforceable and binding contract between them, providing the various terms are readily discernible and can be proven.

The franchise agreement is all-important in determining the rights, obligations and relationship of the franchisor and the franchisee. If difficulties should arise between the franchisor and the franchisee they will need to turn to the agreement to see what, if any, rights and obligations have been provided in the franchise agreement.

Structuring the Franchise Agreement

Unlike Gaul*, a franchise agreement is divided into two parts.

In the first part of the agreement, the obligations of the franchisor are both more numerous and more onerous than those of the franchisee.

The franchisor will be required to train the franchisee in operating a business in accordance with its proven blueprint. It will be required to help the franchisee with a number of matters necessary to set him up in business, such as the acquisition of premises, carrying out alterations, shop fitting, stocking, recruiting and training employees, and in many cases securing finance from banks. Once all this has been done and the franchise is ready to open, the franchisor will help the franchisee with advertising, marketing and promotions to launch his business.

By contrast, the franchisee will essentially be required to do only three things:

1. To attend the franchisor's training course.

2. To do what is necessary to acquire the premises/vehicles required to conduct the business.

3. To pay for the purchase of the franchise and for the costs of setting up in business.

In the second part of the franchise agreement, relating to after the launch, the reverse applies. The obligations of the franchisee are more numerous and

---

* Commentarii de Bello Gallico – Testimony of Julius Caesar – "Gaul was divided into three parts."

The Franchise Agreement

onerous than those of the franchisor. The franchisee will be required to comply with a long list of dos and don'ts and be subject to numerous conditions concerning the way the business is to be conducted, what happens if the franchisee wants to sell his business, what is to happen on termination etc.

By contrast, the franchisor will have three principal obligations:

1. To support the franchisee to the extent needed to sustain him in business.
2. To protect the brand against infringement.
3. To expend the necessary resources to improve, enhance and develop the system and products/services.

The Structure of the Franchise Agreement

Most contracts begin with what are usually known as 'recitals'. Recitals are really preliminary matters which spell out to the reader, in brief, the historical context of the transaction. They, as it were, help to set the scene by very briefly relating 'the story so far'. Thus, the recitals (or preamble) will specify who the owners of the system and the brand are. If, for example, it is a foreign franchise (i.e. a franchise which has been imported into the UK and which the franchisor does not own outright but has the right to operate, and to grant others the right to operate), then the recitals should spell this out. In essence, therefore, recitals are intended to show the reader a chain of events. The recitals will also tell the reader what is involved in the franchise in terms of the trade name, the trade marks, products and so on. If it eventually transpires that the statement as to ownership is wrong or misleading, this may give the franchisee a cause of action against the franchisor.

Next, the agreement should specify the rights which are to be granted to the franchisee. This may be the right to sell the products and/or services under the franchisor's brand and the right to use the franchisor's system to enable it to do so. The franchisee will usually be restricted to exercising those rights only within a particular area or premises depending on the type of business. The area (or 'territory', as it is commonly referred to) within which a franchisee is permitted to exercise his rights may be exclusive or non-exclusive. If exclusive rights are granted, the additional grant of sole rights so often seen in agreements (in the form of 'sole and exclusive') is superfluous. For more on territorial exclusivity, see Chapter 20.

Length of the Franchise Relationship

Most franchise agreements are expressed to be for a term of years. Exactly how long this term should be will depend on the nature of the franchise. There is no law which determines how long a franchise should run for, except where the franchise involves products which a franchisee is required to purchase only from the franchisor. Under English law, such contracts are generally restricted to a term of five years. This is based on some court decisions which were concerned with oil companies' imposition of purchasing obligations on garage forecourt proprietors. The courts considered it unreasonable for suppliers to impose purchasing obligations on a purchaser in excess of five years.

This aside, there are no hard and fast rules. Some franchises are expressed to be for one year only and continue thereafter until terminated by either party, giving to the other whatever notice is provided for in the franchise agreement. This seems to be an unsatisfactory system from the perspective of both the franchisor and the franchisee. From the franchisee's point of view, having made an investment, it is reasonable for him to have some degree of certainty as to the period for which his franchise is to run.

Irrespective of the level of investment, one should avoid any temptation to make franchise agreements terminable by franchisees on notice. A franchisor whose franchise agreement provides that the franchisee may terminate the agreement at any time may be stirring up trouble for the future, even if the franchisee is required to give notice. Franchisees may act in concert and demand concessions from the franchisor with threats of mass unilateral terminations if the franchisor does not comply. In those circumstances the franchisor could lose its whole network overnight.

Franchise agreements usually set out the circumstances under which the franchisor is entitled to terminate the franchise agreement, either immediately or having given notice of default to the franchisee with which the franchisee has failed to comply. Examples of such default are failure by the franchisee to pay continuing franchise fees, to comply with the reporting obligations concerning turnover or to pay nominated suppliers.

There are ethical guidelines on the issue of the term of the franchise agreement. The term should be long enough to enable a franchisee to recover his investment

The Franchise Agreement

in the franchise business and to enable him to obtain a reasonable return on his investment. Irrespective of the earning power of a particular franchise business, franchisees tend to expect the term to correlate with the level of investment: the higher the investment, the longer the term.

Most franchisors do not see the franchise relationship ending on the expiry of the franchise agreement. Franchise agreements usually provide for the renewal of the franchise at the option of the franchisee, but there is no legal obligation for them to do so. It is perfectly legal for a franchisor to have a fixed period franchise agreement which terminates automatically on the expiry of the fixed period, without any legal requirement on the part of the franchisor to renew or to pay any compensation to the franchisee for non-renewal.

A renewal clause is usually expressed in the form of an option to renew in favour of the franchisee. The agreement should then go on to state not only when that option becomes exercisable by the franchisee but also how it may be exercised (e.g. it may be exercised only after, say, two years, and then on three months' notice). Franchisors usually provide time limits within which a franchisee must act if he wishes to exercise his option because this enables the franchisor to plan its franchise marketing strategy.

It is not uncommon for renewal options to be coupled with conditions which a franchisee has to satisfy. These conditions are usually in the nature of requiring the franchisee, again within a stipulated time period, to revamp his franchised business so that it reflects the franchisor's then-current specification for its newly franchised businesses. Of course, renewal is always subject to the condition that the franchisee is not in breach of his obligations under his franchise agreement.

For more on the length of the franchise relationship, see Chapter 22.

Operations Manuals

Almost without exception, business format franchises are heavily dependent on the use of operations manuals which contain details of the franchisor's system (see Chapter 10). If a franchisor wishes to have the right to introduce changes to the system, that right must be provided for in the franchise agreement.

A well-drafted franchise agreement should provide that all mandatory specifications, standards and operating procedures periodically described by the franchisor in its operations manual, or otherwise communicated to its franchisees in writing, constitute provisions of the franchise agreement for the purposes of compliance and enforcement.

The franchise agreement should also make it clear that the operations manual is on loan to the franchisee and that ownership is retained by the franchisor.

Obligations and Concerns

Where a franchise involves the sale of products which have to be purchased from the franchisor, the franchise agreement should contain an obligation on the part of the franchisor to supply the franchisee with all his requirements for such products unless the franchisor is prevented from supplying him for reasons beyond its control. In such an event the franchisee should be permitted to obtain supplies of suitable alternative products as long as the franchisor's disability continues.

A franchisor should seek to impose a host of obligations on the franchisee in the franchise agreement. For the most part, these obligations will be concerned with the manner in which the franchisee is to operate the franchise business, the condition of the premises or vehicles from which the franchise business is to be conducted and the restrictions on the franchisee as to what he can do during the term of the franchise agreement, particularly with regard to any other business interests he may have or his being involved in any competing business.

There should be a separate section in a franchise agreement which deals with the amount of the continuing franchise fees which a franchisee is required to pay the franchisor and how they are to be paid.

The franchise agreement should include provisions which deal with the accounting and reporting procedures with which the franchisee is required to comply. It should also require the franchisee to produce management accounts at regular intervals and statements of his accounts (certified by his accountant as being a true and fair statement of his financial affairs) at the end of each of his financial years. It is not unusual for a franchisor to reserve the right to audit the books of the franchisee where the franchisor thinks this to be necessary.

A franchise agreement should restrict a franchisee from advertising the franchise business without the prior consent of the franchisor. The reason for this is es-

The Franchise Agreement

sentially so that the franchisor can protect what happens to its trade name, trade mark and other intellectual property.

Much depends on the type of franchise, but in some franchises there is an obligation on franchisees to spend a certain amount on advertising at regular intervals and/or contribute regularly to an advertising fund maintained by the franchisor. Any such advertising contribution should be used by the franchisor for the benefit of franchisees. A well-drafted franchise agreement will make special provision for such funds to be kept in a separate account and for the franchisor to account to franchisees at least once a year for the income and expenditure of the advertising fund.

Franchisees buy franchised businesses for various reasons. Usually one such reason is that they wish to make an investment which they expect will appreciate so they can eventually realise a gain when they sell their business. This means that they invariably require the right to sell their franchised business. Franchisors welcome this because one of the ways in which a franchisee can realise his objective is by building up his business, and this is bound to benefit the franchisor. However, franchise agreements seldom contain a straightforward provision which enables the franchisee to sell his business. More often than not, the clause which deals with the sale of business is fairly complicated because although the franchisor will permit a franchisee to sell his business, such permission will be hedged with conditions (see Chapter 18). It is worth noting that franchise agreements do impose restrictions which prevent franchisees from disposing of their ownership of their franchised business, either in whole or in part, without the consent of their franchisor.

Given that franchise agreements are not negotiable, and given that the transaction is deemed to be for a long term, it is important that franchise agreements are reasonable from the point of view of both the franchisor and the franchisee. One indication of whether or not a particular franchisor has considered the welfare of the franchisee is to see what, if any, provisions are contained in the franchise agreement regarding what is to happen on the death of a franchisee, or if the franchisee should be rendered unable to operate his business for health reasons. Clearly, some franchised businesses are such that, on the death of a franchisee, the business can no longer be said to exist because it is very personal in nature. However, there are many other franchises where the business is capable of surviving and carrying on in the absence of the franchisee. In such circumstances ethical franchisors will usually go to some lengths to preserve the value of the business by making arrangements to manage the business in the short term and possibly to buy the business, in the case of death, from the deceased franchisee's executors.

Notice of Default

Franchise agreements will usually spell out the grounds on which a franchisor reserves the right to terminate the franchise, and most ethical franchisors will also provide for notice to be given to franchisees, prior to termination, giving them an opportunity to remedy breaches complained of. The franchisor should review the franchise agreement to ensure that adequate notice of default and, where appropriate, an opportunity to remedy are given to the franchisee.

A franchisor must give careful attention to the preparation of the default and/or termination notice. The default notice should clearly spell out the franchisee's defaults, should specify any money owing, and should list precisely and completely what actions a franchisee must take to cure such defaults and the time frame within which they must be cured.

Furthermore, the notice should give an effective date of termination if defaults are not cured in the time specified and the franchisee's obligations upon termination should be spelt out in detail.

Brand Protection

The termination clause is usually followed by a clause which specifies the consequences of such termination, the principal objectives of which are to secure for the franchisor its goodwill, trade marks, trade name, service marks, specialised equipment, software, machinery, operations manuals and the like. A departing franchisee will therefore be required to make such changes in his business practice, premises and/or vehicles as will ensure that his business no longer reflects the marketing image it previously did. The franchisee will be prohibited from using the franchisor's business system, trade name, trade marks, packaging, signage, stationery, specialised equipment, machinery, software, operations manuals, copyright material etc.

The Franchise Agreement

Franchisors always seek to restrain their franchisees from carrying on the franchise's name or a similar business once the franchise agreement has been terminated, and the franchise agreement will therefore seek to impose restraints on the future business activities of the franchisee to restrict him from unfairly competing with the business of the franchisor or its other franchisees. Such restraints are fully enforceable against a franchisee providing they are reasonable, operating for a reasonable period of time and within a reasonable area. The fixing of reasonable periods of time and areas of operation has to be done by reference to the nature of the business and its area of operation. Obviously, the criteria to be applied for a retail shop in a densely populated city will be different from those which will be applied in sparsely populated rural areas. For more on this subject, see Chapter 28.

In addition to the restraints on trade, franchise agreements also contain a prohibition on the franchisee from soliciting business from former customers usually during a period of one year following termination.

Unless the franchise agreement contains sufficient safeguards to protect the franchisor's intellectual property rights, the franchisor may find that it is unable to prevent infringement of its rights by a third party or an ex-franchisee.

It is not only in the interest of the franchisor that these rights be protected. Franchisees are equally concerned to ensure that the franchisor has done everything that is reasonably possible to protect the intellectual property rights in question. Many franchisees purchase a particular franchise because of the high profile that franchise enjoys in the marketplace. In many cases, a franchisee has the choice of which franchise to purchase in a market sector, and one of the reasons why a franchisee may have chosen a particular franchise is the strength of the brand. It follows, therefore, that franchisees will be anxious to ensure that, in the event of infringement, the franchisor will be able to take such steps as may be necessary to safeguard the ownership of its intellectual property rights and thereby protect the reputation of its brand. If the agreement is weak on this point, franchisees will not consider that particular franchise to be a sound investment proposition because the franchisor will have difficulty in preventing a copycat operation from being set up in unfair competition with a franchisee.

Brand names and trade marks are becoming increasingly important to business; they can increase the asset value of a company and therefore need to be adequately protected. The franchise agreement should not only grant relevant rights to the franchisee and reserve rights for the franchisor, but should also contain the mechanisms necessary for protecting the franchisor's intellectual rights from infringement.

'Standard' Franchise Agreements

Prospective franchisors are prone to ask their solicitors to show them a standard form of franchise agreement. The fact of the matter is that there is no such thing as a standard form of franchise agreement, and anyone who says that there is has failed to grasp the essential nature of the transaction. While it is true that there are a number of provisions which are standard and which do appear in most franchise agreements, there is a great deal in a franchise agreement which is of commercial consequence and has to be tailored to cater for the specific needs of a specific franchise. It does not require a great deal of common sense to understand that the essential terms for a dry-cleaning business are going to be different from those of a fried chicken business, or that the essential terms to be found in a contract for the cleaning of drains are going to be different from those to be found in a franchise agreement for a hotel.

Furthermore, what may seem at first sight to be a standard term in all franchise agreements can subtly differ from one agreement to another. For example, everyone would expect to see a clause in their franchise agreement dealing with the training of the franchisee. However, the training requirements of each franchisor can differ greatly. Some franchisors may involve an element of technical training, others may place great emphasis on training 'on the job' instead of in a classroom environment, whilst others may have genuine need and desire to train not only the franchisee but also all members of his staff. This is particularly true where a franchise involves manufacturing or the application of processes. The extent to which franchisors get involved in further or additional training also varies from one franchisor to another. There is no hard and fast rule about training, or indeed about any other aspect of franchise transactions.

Franchisors usually give financial projections to prospective franchisees. Such projections are expected by prospective franchisees and by those banks who are interested in franchise financing. This means that most franchise agreements contain provisions which seek to exclude liability on the part of the franchisor

The Franchise Agreement

for any statements, representations, advice or explanations which may have been given by the franchisor to the franchisee prior to the signing of the franchise agreement. Such a clause essentially provides that it is only the franchise agreement which is binding on the two parties and that any communication by the franchisor to the franchisee, whether in writing or verbal, cannot be relied on unless it is made a part of the franchise agreement. The importance of this clause cannot be overemphasised.

Franchisees should of course be aware that the appearance of such a clause in a franchise agreement means that the franchisee cannot rely, at a later date, on anything which may have been said or communicated in writing to the franchisee by the franchisor or any of its representatives. Anything the franchisee wishes to rely on must be included in the franchise agreement as a term of the agreement.

From the franchisor's point of view such a clause is essential to protect it from any over-enthusiastic claims which may have been made by a member of its staff at the time when the franchise was being sold. It also introduces a degree of certainty into the relationship of the parties by having the terms agreed on specifically noted in one place. Thus, if a franchisee is under the impression that the franchisor had promised to spend a part of the initial franchise fee on promoting, marketing and launching the franchisee's business, but that particular promise is not reflected in the franchise agreement, and subsequently the franchisor fails or refuses to spend that sum of money for that purpose, the franchisee is going to be able to do very little about it.

Some of the clauses which are standard are obvious. These are clauses which deal with some of the following matters:

Waiver

Most franchise agreements will specify that if the franchisor fails to exercise its rights against a franchisee when the franchisee has breached one or more of the terms of the franchise agreement, the franchisor can nevertheless take action against the franchisee on a subsequent breach of the same terms. In other words, the franchisor does not lose its rights against the franchisee simply because it took no action on the occasion of the first breach. The purpose behind this clause is to circumvent a common law theory that if an innocent party to a contract is aware of a breach by a guilty party, and chooses to do nothing about it, then the innocent party can be prevented from taking action on a subsequent breach by the guilty party. This is based on the reasoning that if the innocent party had considered it important enough to take action, it would have done so in the first instance.

If a franchisor learns of a breach by a franchisee which gives it the right to take action, for example by terminating the agreement, but it does not exercise its right to do so, the franchisor can be deemed to have waived its right to take action on a subsequent similar occasion. In cases where there has been a known waiver, the franchisee should be informed of the fact that the franchisor reserves its rights totally in the event of any future default by the franchisee.

It goes without saying that the stronger a franchisor's case, the more compliant its franchisees will be.

Warranties

This clause usually specifies that a franchisee will not offer any guarantees or warranties other than those which have been authorised by the franchisor. If such a provision were not in a franchise agreement it could have the effect of bringing a franchise network into disrepute simply because a franchisee may, in order to make a sale, make promises beyond those which could be honoured by the franchisee. The failure by the franchisee to make good an 'excessive' warranty could have a knock-on effect on the franchisor and its network, even in circumstances where the customer cannot hold the franchisor liable.

Disputes

Some agreements contain provisions about how disputes may be resolved. The general tendency is for the franchisor either to provide for arbitration in the event of a dispute between franchisor and franchisee or to rely on each party's right to take the other to court. The latter provision usually favours the franchisor because the franchisor has greater resources and is more able than a franchisee to sustain a court action. With this in mind and with a view to encouraging franchisors and franchisees to resolve their differences quickly, privately and with the minimum of cost to the parties, the British Franchise Association introduced, in 1987, an arbitration and mediation scheme with rules which aim to be fair to both parties. The scheme is designed to provide an inexpensive and informal method of resolving disputes between franchisors and franchisees.

For more on resolving disputes, see Chapter 29.

In Conclusion

In the final analysis, a franchise transaction is a complex transaction and the franchise agreement must respect that complexity. For franchisees, it forms the basis for their businesses – it enshrines their rights, and it is therefore important for them to make sure that they have a franchise agreement which is legally binding and which sets out very clearly not only the franchisee's obligations but also those of the franchisor. From the franchisor's point of view, a franchise agreement needs to address all the matters which are reasonably foreseeable to eliminate uncertainty. After all, a franchise agreement should be an income-producing asset, the value of which will ultimately have a place on the franchisor's balance sheet.

If a franchise agreement is well drafted, there is no reason why both parties should not know precisely where they stand in relation to each other. For the reasons outlined above, it is important for both parties to have a franchise agreement which has been professionally prepared by an experienced franchise solicitor, specifically for the franchise in question and with the object of covering all the foreseeable eventualities in that particular franchise. Only then will each party have the comfort of the known rather than the fear of the unknown.

In Summary

A franchise agreement should achieve three fundamental objectives:

1. It should set out clearly what the franchisor has promised.
2. It should seek to protect, for the benefit of both the franchisor and the franchisee, the franchisor's know-how and the brand.
3. It should clearly set out the rules which the parties are expected to observe.

A prospective franchisee will look for promises from a franchisor to:

- Train the franchisee and his staff.
- Supply goods and/or services.
- Be responsible for promoting the brand.
- Help the franchisee, where appropriate, to locate and acquire premises and to have them fitted out and converted into a franchise outlet. Similar considerations apply with regard to the acquisition of vehicles, fitting them out, equipping them etc.
- Assist the franchisee in setting up business.
- Improve, enhance and develop the franchisor's concept and system.
- Provide ongoing support.

A franchisor will wish to reserve rights to:

- Monitor and control the performance of the franchisee.
- Protect itself and its franchisees from unfair competition.
- Protect its know-how and brand.
- Control the use, by the franchisee, of its intellectual property.

If the agreement is weak on protecting the franchisor's intellectual property, franchisees will not consider that particular franchise to be a sound investment proposition because the franchisor will have difficulty in preventing a copycat operation from being set up in unfair competition with a franchisee.

Franchise agreements should be in standard form and best practice requires that all prospective franchisees are offered the same terms with no special deals being done. Franchisors should invite prospective franchisees, in the nicest possible way, to take it or leave it.

The Franchise Agreement

One can imagine the following conversation between a Roman franchisor and a prospective franchisee:

Franchisor: *Ecce pactum. Id cape aut id relinque.*[1]

Prospective Franchisee: *In oppido lusor solus non es.*[2]

Franchisor: *Conventum consuetum est.*[3]

A franchise agreement should clearly:

1. Specify in detail the duties and obligations both of the franchisor and of the franchisee.
2. Deal with the payment of franchise fees and the timing of those payments.
3. State the grounds on which the franchisor will seek to terminate the franchise agreement and what is to happen to the franchisee after termination.

If the franchise agreement is defective, given that it is in a standard form issued to all franchisees, the cost to the franchisor can be the loss of its whole network.

Whatever the reputation of the franchisor, prospective franchisees will look to the quality of the franchise agreement because they know that the franchisor may undergo a change of ownership, personnel or policy.

Once a franchise agreement has been signed, both parties will be bound by it. It can be a double-edged sword and if either party has got it wrong they will have to pay the price.

---

[1] That's the deal – take it or leave it.
[2] You're not the only game in town.
[3] It's a standard deal.

CHAPTER 26

A Franchise May Be Legal, but Is It Ethical?

"One is mandatory; the other is not."

Most franchisors will refuse to negotiate the terms of a franchise agreement but will present it to a franchisee on a 'take it or leave it' basis. It is, therefore, important for a prospective franchisee to give serious consideration to how ethical his franchisor is.

How does one distinguish an ethical franchisor from an unethical one? There are a number of aspects to a franchise transaction which will help to determine whether or not a particular franchisor is ethical.

The litmus test is to see whether what the franchisor is proposing is fair and reasonable. This can be determined by investigating:

- The provisions in the franchise agreement which are legally binding.
- The explanation a franchisor gives for some of the franchise agreement's more onerous provisions.
- Whether the franchisor is a member of the British Franchise Association.
- The behaviour of the franchisor.

As far as the behaviour of the franchisor is concerned, this can be determined by talking to as many franchisees of that particular franchisor as possible to see whether the franchisor acts and has acted fairly and reasonably towards its franchisees. However, care should be taken in basing a determination on this sort of investigation alone, because the fact that a franchisor has acted fairly and reasonably in the past does not guarantee that it will do so in the future. It is also always possible that, later on, the franchisor will sell its business to a buyer who has a different approach and attitude to these matters or the personnel in the franchise company may change, thereby rendering what was previously an ethical franchise an unethical one.

Because the behaviour of the franchisor may change, the franchisee must check that sufficient mechanisms exist in the franchise agreement to ensure that the franchisor, irrespective of any change in ownership or management, is *required* to act fairly and reasonably.

The first thing to look for is the cost of the franchise and in particular the amount of the initial franchise fee which is being asked by the franchisor. It is considered unethical for a franchisor to make more than a nominal profit from *selling* franchises. The simple logic behind this contention is that if a franchisor can make a good profit merely from selling franchises, there may not be a great deal of incentive for that franchisor to support the franchisee after that franchisee has bought the franchise; all the franchisor needs to do is to sell as many franchises as it can for as much as it can get, making money as quickly as it can, and then disappear.

Not making a profit does not mean that a franchisor must make a loss on selling a franchise. What the franchisor should do is seek to recover the costs it has incurred in putting a franchisee into business. It is recognised that some franchisees will cost more to establish in business than others, and therefore a franchisor may lose some money on the sale of one franchise and make a small profit on another. By and large, however, a franchisor should break even over a number of franchise sales.

How, then, can one determine whether a particular franchisor is charging too much? It is generally accepted that if an initial franchise fee is more than 10% of the total set-up costs of a particular franchise, then searching questions should be asked as to why this is so. Where the franchise fee exceeds this percentage, most ethical franchisors should be able to justify it, for example because the franchise fee includes the cost of equipment, uniforms, specialist training etc. The question of how much a franchisor can charge is dealt with in detail in Chapter 13.

Another point for prospective franchisees to consider when determining whether or not a particular franchisor is ethical is how the franchisor derives its income from its franchise network. This is very important. The structure should be such that the franchisor does not stand to make money unless the franchisee makes money also. So any provision in a franchise agreement which requires the franchisee to pay a minimum or fixed continuing franchise fee will be regarded with some degree of suspicion. If a franchisor knows that it will be paid a certain fee irrespective of how well a franchisee is doing, then there will be little incentive on its part to support its franchisees.

Most ethical franchisors obtain their income from franchisees by means of a continuing franchise fee which is expressed as a percentage of the gross turnover of the franchisee. This ensures that the franchisor has a vested interest in seeing that the franchisee's turnover is as high as possible because the higher the franchisee's turnover, the more the franchisor will earn.

A word of caution here: if a franchisee is required to purchase products from his franchisor, care should be taken to see that the franchisor does not make a profit from selling those products to the franchisee as well as taking a percentage of the franchisee's gross turnover by means of a continuing franchise fee. This is particularly important where a franchisee has to buy all his requirements for such products only from the franchisor. Such an arrangement would mean that the franchisor is seeking to take money from the franchisee from both ends of the transaction, i.e. from a mark-up on the products which the franchisee has to buy from his franchisor and also a percentage out of the franchisee's till. In such circumstances an ethical franchisor would choose one source or the other for its revenue, but *not* both.

Membership of the British Franchise Association is an indication that the franchisor is ethical. The British Franchise Association requires its members to comply with its Code of Ethics, and to undergo an accreditation process to qualify for membership.

These are some of the issues which one should look for in a franchise when trying to determine whether or not it is structured in a way that will promote ethical behaviour on the part of the franchisor.

Ten Rules of Ethical Franchising

1. Do not make a significant profit from the sale of a franchise.

2. Do not take a royalty on turnover *and* a mark-up on the sale of products to franchisees.

3. Keep all money received for advertising, marketing and promotions in a separate account and be transparent.

A Franchise May Be Legal, but Is It Ethical?

4. Give franchisees a right to renew subject to reasonable conditions.
5. Give franchisees a right to sell their business subject to reasonable conditions.
6. Do not sell franchises unless the business model and system have been successfully tried and tested.
7. Ensure that your intellectual property is properly protected.
8. Disclose all commissions, volume rebates etc. you receive from suppliers.
9. Provide sufficient training to transfer your know-how to your franchisees.
10. Provide ongoing support and training to the extent franchisees need it.

CHAPTER 27

Contract Enforcement

"It is hard for thee to kick against the pricks."
John 9:5

One of the most troublesome subjects for franchisors is contract enforcement.

In most businesses the right of control arises out of ownership. In franchising, this is not the case, and the sort of control normally exercised by a company through an employer-and-employee relationship cannot be used in the context of a franchise relationship.

In franchising, control is ultimately achieved through enforcement of the franchise agreement, by which time it is quite likely that both franchisor and franchisee have passed the point of no return. The direct exercise of contractual rights is therefore a matter of last resort for most franchisors. In practice, franchisors seek to achieve control through other means, usually by persuasion and motivation.

The skill set required to manage franchisees is quite different from that required to manage employees. Franchisors do not simply issue orders as they might to their own managers and they cannot discipline franchisees in the same way. Franchisees require careful handling and franchisors need to learn new skills in people management. The management of franchisees requires the right combination of an arm around the shoulder and a rap on the knuckles.

The more sophisticated and the larger a franchisor company, the more difficult this exercise becomes. Large franchisor companies need to impart additional and particular skills to their franchise managers who may, until now, have been used to controlling managers and who now have to employ different skills when trying to control people who are owners of their own businesses. Credibility is a key issue here because these managers need to understand and appreciate the business risks which franchisees are taking. Unless the delicate task of controlling franchisees is carried out competently, resentment within a franchised network will soon develop, with franchisees, who do not enjoy the security of a regular income, seeing regional managers as employees who get their pay cheque at the end of each month trying to tell risk takers what to do.

As a franchise network grows and its franchisor grows with it, the nature of the problems changes. An entrepreneurial franchisor will no longer be able to deal with the requests and demands of its franchisees as it previously did. It will increasingly have to delegate those functions to employees who may have 'never run a corner shop', and whose advice and instructions will not necessarily meet with sympathy or ready acceptance from franchisees.

Maintaining Uniform Standards

A successful franchise operation depends to a large degree on uniform, high-quality franchisee-operated outlets and on the public's perception that products and/or services of similar quality can be obtained from whichever outlets they visit. Poorly operated outlets offering substandard products or services will affect both a franchisor's profits and those of other franchisees within the system.

Lack of enforcement of uniform standards by a franchisor and the tolerance of substandard outlets will create resentment amongst those franchisees who follow the franchisor's programme and offer high-quality products and services.

Prospective franchisors who are aware of the commercial consequences of lack of enforcement must bear in mind also that their failure to enforce their rights under the franchise agreement may result in a waiver of their rights (see Chapter 25) and may possibly endanger their ownership of their intellectual property rights.

The uniform and consistent enforcement of contractual provisions and standards, apart from increasing the value and integrity of a franchisor's system, will also:

- Encourage and reward good performance by complying franchisees.
- Send a message to marginal franchisees that substandard outlets, products or services will not be tolerated.
- Serve to protect a franchisor's brand.
- Facilitate the termination of non-complying franchisees' contracts.

Defaults

Violation of a franchise agreement by a franchisee may be the result of a clear breach of a specific provision of his franchise agreement or a failure to comply with mandatory specifications, standards or operating procedures prescribed by the franchisor.

There are various types and causes of default. Set out below are some strategies for dealing with some of them and for enforcing/encouraging compliance.

Types and Causes of Default

There are three main categories of default:

1. Financial.
2. Operational.
3. Product/service.

Another category is the negative/unco-operative attitude of a franchisee; there are no hard and fast rules when it comes to dealing with this kind.

We are very fortunate in that we have little litigation in this country which specifically relates to franchising. However, if one looks at the scene in the United States, one sees that probably the most frequent defaults encountered by franchisors are the failure of franchisees to pay continuing franchise fees or advertising contributions, either on time or altogether, and the failure to submit sales reports on time. Another frequent problem is the understating of sales or revenues, resulting in the payment of lower continuing franchise fees and advertising contributions.

A form of financial default takes place when a franchisee fails to pay his suppliers (which may include the franchisor) and therefore jeopardises his ability to obtain needed products when required.

Contract Enforcement

The causes for these financial defaults fall into three major categories:

1. Dishonesty by the franchisee.
2. A feeling on the part of the franchisee that his franchisor is not providing promised or sufficient services/advertising in return for the franchisee's continuing franchise fees and advertising contributions.
3. Undercapitalisation, which can occur when a franchisee has bought his franchise from a former franchisee at an excessive price.

Operational defaults which have plagued some UK franchisors have arisen from:

- A franchisee's failure to comply with the requirements of his franchisor relating to the décor, cleanliness and sanitation of premises.
- A franchisee's failure to update the premises or to prevent equipment, fixtures, signs etc. from falling into disrepair.
- A franchisee's failure to observe the hours of operation specified by his franchisor.

Some franchisors have also complained of product defaults: for example, franchisees offering unauthorised products for sale, purchasing products from unauthorised suppliers or failing to offer the full range of products required by the franchisor.

In many cases operational and product defaults occur as a result of insufficient training and guidance by a franchisor, poor franchisor–franchisee relations or a franchisor's failure to clearly communicate specifications, standards and operating procedures to its franchisees. That is not to say that a franchisee may not be at fault.

However, the need for a franchisor to enforce and to be seen to be enforcing contractual provisions cannot be emphasised too greatly. Even if operational standards and requirements are adequately communicated by the franchisor and understood by its franchisees, failure by the franchisor to use contractual mechanisms for inspection (and it is surprising how many franchise agreements do not give the franchisor sufficient contractual mechanisms for inspection) may lead franchisees to believe that their violations have gone unnoticed, that they are considered trivial by the franchisor, or that for other reasons they are condoned.

A common error of franchisors is that violations discovered during an inspection are not communicated to the franchisee or, if they are communicated, the franchisor fails to ensure that such violations are corrected.

Apart from financial, operational and product defaults there are a host of other defaults which need to be mentioned, such as the franchisee's failure to use trade marks in an authorised manner.

Other defaults by franchisees include the failure to comply with contractual provisions relating to insurance, maintaining confidentiality of information etc. or to display required signs which make it clear to customers and others with whom the franchisee is dealing that they are dealing with the franchisee and not his franchisor. The absence of such a notice erodes the protection a franchisor has from liability for its franchisees' acts, defaults and omissions.

Dealing with Defaults

As indicated earlier, one cause of non-compliance by a franchisee is a franchisor's failure to clearly and effectively communicate the franchisee's obligations to him.

There are several tools one can use to increase effective communication with franchisees, and it will not come as a surprise to learn that a defaulting franchisee's defence against an accusation of default is often that the matter in question was never mentioned in training etc. Before dealing with a defaulter, therefore, one must ensure that one starts from a sound foundation and that one's house is in good order.

Initially, of course, the franchise agreement should be clearly drafted and set out the franchisee's obligations. Clear drafting is particularly important in the areas of specifications, standards, operating procedures, non-competition, waiver, grounds for termination and the consequences of termination.

A franchise agreement cannot, as a practical matter, spell out in detail all specifications, standards and operating procedures with which the franchisee is required to comply. It is therefore equally important that a franchisor's operations manual is comprehensive. It should cover all important aspects of the franchise business and should be continually updated to reflect current operations, delete obsolete material and implement new programmes.

Contract Enforcement

Any communication to the franchisee with regard to the operation of the system should be in writing. All such material sent by the franchisor to its franchisees should be dated, and copies retained in the franchisees' files. If the material represents a change in policy or a requirement, the franchisor should devise a system whereby, if for any reason it is called upon to do so, it can show that the franchisee received the relevant circulars.

To complete the franchisor's case it is necessary that regular field inspections are performed by field representatives who are thoroughly familiar with the terms and conditions of the franchise agreement, the system, and the current specifications, standards and operating procedures. The primary function of these inspectors should be to *record* and communicate all problems observed. The emphasis is on the word 'record' because this is one aspect which is all too often neglected.

Inspection reports should be filled out on each visit and thoroughly reviewed with the franchisee, and that review should be acknowledged by the franchisee. The report should be signed both by the franchisee and by the inspector and a copy left with the franchisee. The original should be retained in the franchisee's file at the franchisor's head office.

A word of caution: whilst a franchisor may instruct its field representatives that they are authorised to note areas of noncompliance and advise a franchisee that he is in default under the terms of its franchise agreement, they should not be authorised to discuss the consequences of such default. The report should set out, as a matter of fact, the matters which have been observed. This is not the time, place or opportunity for the inspector to discuss possible remedial measures or disciplinary action with the franchisee; that is for the appropriate person within the franchisor's management team (the franchise manager, for example) to take up with the franchisee, possibly after an internal discussion and review of the franchisee's file and history of defaults, if any. Threats of termination or similar statements by a field representative could later work against the franchisor in any termination proceedings.

When an inspection report is submitted, it should be analysed and reviewed by the franchisor. Problems of non-compliance should be addressed with a specific plan and a timetable for correction should be drawn up, and, if relevant, any offer of assistance by the franchisor to correct the problems noted. Any offer of assistance should again be made in writing and should clearly describe both the franchisee's responsibilities and the assistance which the franchisor has offered to provide.

The most important aspect of any enforcement programme is the follow-up inspections and reports relating to the implementation of decisions to correct operational problems.

If the breach or default has not been corrected within the time allocated, a franchisor should look to see whether the franchisee has been unreceptive to offers of assistance or unco-operative in correcting the breach or default. If the franchisee has made a reasonable effort to comply, the franchisor should consider whether further assistance is needed to help the franchisee achieve compliance.

If further assistance is warranted, a revised timetable for correction should be drawn up in writing. Again, a follow-up inspection report and review should be implemented after the allotted time has elapsed.

In practice it may not always be possible to deal with matters as outlined above. In an ideal world it would be. However, it is surprising how rewarding detailed reporting can be once a franchisor makes a habit of the practice. Such a practice has been made considerably easier with the advent of electronic equipment which enables an inspector to record his reports immediately on site or when in transit to his next appointment.

Finally, any inspection (unless unannounced) should be made when it is most convenient for the franchisee, avoiding peak business times, so that the franchisee can give the inspector his undivided attention.

Financial Defaults

Franchisors should provide for and use a number of tools to deal with the various types of financial default.

Again, it is important that these tools are contained in the franchise agreement, because at the end of the day a franchisor will only have such powers as are provided for in its franchise agreement. A franchisor should reserve the right to inspect, audit and copy the business and accounting records of its franchisees.

Contract Enforcement

If a franchisee uses a cash register as a part of his business, the franchisor should consider prescribing a register which provides information useful to it in assessing sales activities. The right type of electronic till will usually do the trick for a franchisor in terms of ensuring accurate sales recording.

In any cash business, numerically sequenced sales tickets or invoices (placing upon the franchisee the burden of explaining any missing tickets or invoices) are another control in franchisee reporting of all revenue, as is a well-advertised offer from the franchisor of a lottery, extended warranty or other incentive for the franchisee's customers, based on the number on the invoice issued by the franchisee. Customers who are drawn to this will insist on an invoice from the franchisee.

Other methods of monitoring a franchisee's sales, such as the use of mystery shoppers, are no doubt familiar to prospective franchisors. Although such programmes are far from foolproof, they can both expose and deter underreporting of revenue.

Non-Compliance with Standards as Grounds for Termination

As mentioned earlier, a good franchise agreement will contain extensive references to the standards and procedures and provide that failure by the franchisee to comply with them is sufficient grounds for termination of the franchise. However, the extent to which such provisions are enforceable will depend on the circumstances. A franchisor will have little chance of success if it attempts to terminate a franchise agreement under circumstances where a franchisee has been in minor as opposed to material breach of his agreement.

One reported French case which deals with the enforcement of standards and procedures, although not a UK case, is nevertheless interesting.

The case of *Dayan v. McDonald's Corporation*, heard in 1984, is a case illustrating that a court will recognise the value of uniform quality controls and operational standards to a franchise system. The simple facts of the case are as follows:

Dayan operated 12 McDonald's restaurants in Paris under a master franchise agreement. The restaurants' cleanliness and sanitation issues, and general operational violations regarding required equipment and prescribed food preparation procedures, were found by the court to be numerous. It is unusual for a franchisor to be presented with such a compelling factual situation.

The court recognised that a non-complying franchisee can affect both the public's perception of the entire system and the attitude of the other franchisees, and stated that a customer who is dissatisfied with one outlet is unlikely to limit his adverse reaction to that outlet.

The court further ruled that:

> If Dayan ... in Paris can thumb his nose at the system and its standards then so too can operators everywhere.

The outcome was that the court held that McDonald's had good cause to terminate the master franchise agreement and the 12 franchises operated by Dayan under that agreement.

Alternatives to Termination

Given that a franchisor has established a strong case against a defaulting franchisee, what are the next steps?

Before deciding to go forward with a termination, the franchisor should consider possible alternatives.

If the remaining term of the franchise agreement is relatively short, the franchisor may want to consider simply allowing the agreement to expire without renewing it.

This approach, of course, must be weighed against the potential damage to the system and to the attitude of other franchisees that may result if a franchisor allows a defaulting franchisee to remain within the system without sanction. It may be dangerous to permit a franchisee to continue trading until his franchise agreement expires despite material default by him, because this approach may possibly diminish a franchisor's rights against another franchisee who commits an even more serious breach of the same or similar obligations.

In general, it is recommended that this approach be used sparingly, especially if a franchisee has renewal rights under his agreement. A well-drafted franchise agreement will have provided a right for the franchisor to refuse a renewal in these circumstances (see Chapter 25).

Contract Enforcement

Prior to a termination, a franchisor should consider whether its franchise agreement contains any post-termination non-competition clauses and, if so, whether such clauses are enforceable (see Chapter 28). If the agreement does not contain such a clause, or if it is thought that the clause is unenforceable, the franchisor must assess the anticipated effect of the franchisee competing with other franchisees. A contractual option to buy a franchisee's business is sometimes used as a contract enforcement device if a covenant not to compete is thought to be unenforceable or of no practical benefit to the franchisor.

Another alternative to termination, used in certain cases, is the temporary removal of a franchisee from the franchise system, i.e. suspension as a franchisee.

This method has been most successful where physical deterioration of the premises and other operating deficiencies are the basis of the default, necessary upgrading can be implemented within a reasonable period of time, and the premises and business are viable and warrant the expenditure of time and resources on the part of the franchisee.

As part of the temporary removal, a franchisee is required to temporarily de-identify itself and its business from the franchisor's system and brand by covering up signs and notifying customers that it is no longer affiliated to the franchisor and its system.

Any rental obligations (for premises, lease of equipment etc.) of the franchisee continue, but continuing franchise fees and other fees are suspended. An agreement by way of an amendment to the franchise agreement is executed reflecting the franchisee's obligation to remedy the defaults complained of and bring the business up to required standards. If a franchisee completes the agreed improvements within the required time period, his suspension is lifted, his business is returned to the system and his status as franchisee restored. If not, the franchise agreement is terminated.

If practicable in a franchise system, this method may avoid the expense and stresses of litigation over a termination. In the event of ultimate termination, the fact of a suspension should go a long way to defeating a contention by a franchisee that a franchisor has acted arbitrarily or capriciously.

A franchisor may wish to consider this alternative, but employing such an alternative without having obtained the agreement of the franchisee is not recommended unless the franchise agreement provides for it. For more on suspension, see Chapter 28.

Another alternative is the sale of the franchisee's business to someone else. The amount of leverage a franchisor is able to exercise on its franchisee in helping him reach a settlement may depend to a very large extent on the provisions contained in the franchise agreement. Options retained by franchisors to purchase expensive equipment and stock can be used successfully in negotiating settlements and purchases from a defaulting franchisees.

Alternative Dispute Resolution

There are alternatives to termination such as conciliation, mediation and arbitration, commonly known as 'alternative dispute resolution' or ADR.

Conciliation is usually an informal process whereby an individual ('conciliator') tries to bring the disputing parties together and to conciliate between them, lowering tensions and encouraging them to accept a mutually acceptable solution. Conciliation has no legal standing, and the conciliator makes no decision or award. The process is usually invoked at an early stage of the dispute when the parties are keen to repair their relationship.

Mediation is often confused with arbitration. There is a distinct difference between the two. Mediation is a dynamic process where an independent person, using special communication and negotiating techniques, assists the parties to a dispute in reaching agreement. It requires the parties to be actively involved in resolving their dispute.

Arbitration is, in fact, a court proceeding in private. It involves the appointment of an individual ('arbitrator') who is neutral and who in effect acts as a privately appointed judge who hears the issues and determines upon them. He makes a decision and an award which is enforceable in the ordinary courts. Arbitration has long been recognised as a method of solving disputes, and is subject to statutory control. In some cases the parties will agree to appoint three arbitrators to form an arbitral panel: one chosen by the franchisor, one chosen by the franchisee, and an independent chairman.

Unlike litigation or arbitration, the greatest advantage of submitting a dispute to conciliation or mediation is that if the process is successful, it does not erode

Contract Enforcement

the underlying relationship between franchisee and franchisor, because an outcome under these processes can only be successful if all parties to the dispute *agree* to the proposed solution. In litigation or arbitration, a solution is imposed on the disputants whether any or all of them like it or not.

ADR has the advantage that the process is conducted in private, meaning that the protagonists do not have to wash their dirty linen in public, and timings can be arranged to suit the convenience of the parties involved.

A conciliator, mediator or arbitrator need not be a solicitor or barrister but he should preferably be someone who had had appropriate training. A conciliator can be provided by Acas, a mediator by an organisation such as CEDR or an arbitrator by the Institute of Arbitrators.

Finally, there is of course litigation when a franchisor may consider suing the franchisee for damages, an injunction or specific performance.

For more on ADR, see Chapter 29.

Evidence

In preparing for termination, a franchisor's primary requirement is the existence of a well-documented file.

A file on each franchisee should be treated, from the beginning, as possible evidence in future judicial or arbitration proceedings. It should contain as a minimum:

- A copy of the initial correspondence passing between the franchisor and the franchisee.
- Signed copies of the franchise agreement and any amendments to it.
- A copy of the franchisee's lease for the premises.
- All bulletins, newsletters, manual updates or other material sent to the franchisee together with signed receipts for such material, where applicable.
- All inspection reports and internal memoranda relating to non-compliance and efforts to correct it.

In Conclusion

To succeed, a contract enforcement programme requires a definite plan and well co-ordinated and continuing efforts by both the franchisor's management team and field personnel.

If a franchisor can get the message across to its franchisees that noncompliance will not be tolerated and that contractual breaches will be dealt with swiftly and effectively, that franchisor will have the greatest tool with which to reduce non-compliance within its system.

Although what has been suggested above sounds simple and straightforward, it is not always possible in a business environment for things to happen in the logical order in which they have been described. Nevertheless, what is important is that franchisors understand that the more closely they follow the procedures outlined above, the greater will be their chances of dealing successfully with a defaulting franchisee.

Put in a nutshell, the method to be adopted by a franchisor when dealing with its franchisees is that of having an iron fist in a velvet glove.

As the old saying goes, nothing makes it easier for a motorist to obey the speed limit than a proper understanding of the reasons for the law, a sound set of personal values, and the sight of a police car in the rear-view mirror!

CHAPTER 28

Termination: The End of the Relationship

"It's not over 'til it's over."

We are often told that once a franchisor and a franchisee sign a franchise agreement they are inexorably locked in for the duration of the franchise agreement. Is that so, or can the agreement be terminated before it has run its full course?

In the absence of specific legislation for franchising, franchise agreements are governed by the ordinary commercial law. In addition, it should be remembered that, at the time of writing, the competition rules of the European Union and regulations of the European Commission also apply.

So far as the law is concerned, there is no statute to which a franchisee or a franchisor can turn which will entitle either of them to terminate a franchise agreement prematurely. There are some provisions which can render commercial agreements or certain parts of such agreements void or unenforceable, but none will come to the aid of either party simply because either of them wishes to pull out of a transaction freely entered into.

Conversely, there is no statute that will force both parties to continue under the terms of a franchise agreement if one or the other refuses or declines to do so. Although a court can order a particular party to perform a contract, such an order is usually only made, if practicable, when it is not possible to award damages for breach of contract or where damages would be an inappropriate remedy.

When a franchisor and a franchisee enter into a franchise agreement, it is potentially a double-edged sword for both parties. Most franchise agreements are for a fixed term. Few are terminable on notice, unless the service of such notice is subject to certain conditions, for example that such a notice cannot be served until, say, five years have elapsed. In being granted a franchise agreement for a fixed term, both franchisor and franchisee have the comfort of knowing that each is bound to the other for the duration of that term and each is therefore able to plan its business strategy accordingly.

Although there is no specific legislation for franchising, there is legislation which has the potential to affect franchise agreements, particularly in the sphere of competition and anti-trust law, both domestic and European. Such legislation, while not necessarily forcing termination of an agreement, could nevertheless render some of the provisions of an agreement unenforceable or void. Much depends upon the nature of the provisions, but if the provisions which are held to be unenforceable or void are fundamental to the agreement, then it is possible that the whole agreement will be held to be unenforceable or void.

What, it may be asked, is the position in law if neither franchisor nor franchisee is able to carry out obligations because of intervening circumstances beyond their control?

The law treats all parties to an agreement in the same way and as such, there are no special rules which should apply specifically to a franchisee or a franchisor. The right of either party to terminate will therefore depend upon the provisions of the franchise agreement.

Where a franchise agreement does provide for its termination, any termination must be in the manner provided for in the franchise agreement if it is to be effective and upheld by the courts. Where the franchise agreement is not expressed to be for a fixed term and there is no specific provision for notice to terminate in the franchise agreement, the law will require the notice to be of reasonable length and sufficiently clear and unambiguous in its terms to constitute a valid notice.

Where franchise agreements are terminable on notice, in most circumstances, the requirement to serve notice is a contractual obligation. However, it is possible to provide for automatic termination without any notice.

A franchise relationship is one which should be capable of subsisting over a long period of time. Nevertheless there will come a time when it will come to an end. How can the two parties extricate themselves with a degree of fairness from a relationship in which they have freely shared each other's business plans and secrets? How can a franchisor ensure that the departing franchisee does not become a competitor to any remaining franchisees or indeed to the franchisor?

Reasons for Termination

Under what circumstances can a franchise agreement be terminated?

- There may be a breach of the franchise agreement by the franchisor.
- There may be a breach of the franchise agreement by the franchisee. Usually the agreement will provide for the franchisee to be given the opportunity to remedy the breach before the franchisor will terminate.
- At the end of an agreement for a fixed term (unless it is renewed).
- The franchisee may sell the business.
- The franchisee may die or become bankrupt.
- The franchisor may go into liquidation.
- In some cases, the law may intervene to terminate the franchise agreement where it is not possible for either or both parties to perform their respective obligations under the franchise agreement without either party being at fault (for example, if a gas explosion destroys a building where the franchise unit is located).

As outlined in the preceding chapter, franchisee defaults which may lead to the termination of the franchise agreement usually fall into one of three categories:

1. Financial.
2. Operational.
3. Product/service.

The financial category is worth examining in more detail.

Financial Defaults

There are three main areas where financial problems arise between franchisor and franchisee:

1. Underreporting of turnover, sales etc.
2. Slow payment or non-payment of fees, rent, advertising contributions etc.
3. Financial failure of franchisees.

Underreporting

There is no foolproof way of ensuring that a franchisee discloses all his income. However, careful and sensible attention to point of sale, stock and margin controls should minimise the risk of underreporting and loss.

Most franchise agreements entitle the franchisor to inspect the records of the franchisee. If the franchisor's suspicions are aroused, an early investigation may be sufficient to discourage the franchisee from continuing to understate his sales.

Payment Defaults

It is clearly in the franchisor's interests to deal promptly with slow payers. Not only will they have a deleterious effect on the franchisor's own cash flow, but slow payment may also convey a signal to the franchisor that the franchisee is running an inefficient operation and may therefore be a danger to the franchise's reputation or that the franchisee is in financial difficulties which may get worse as time passes.

Remittance problems are not always limited to the sums owed to the franchisor. Sometimes, where the franchisor is also the landlord of the franchisee, the franchisee may find that the quarterly rent demand is more than his bank balance can bear, particularly in the early years trading. To alleviate this potential problem, some franchisors arrange to be paid any rent on a weekly or monthly basis at the same time as the continuing franchise fee. This should have the effect of making the payment altogether less painful and reduces the risk of default.

Franchisee Failure

When a franchisee's business fails, or is close to failure, there are at least three possible courses of action a franchisor can take:

1. If legally possible, persuade the franchisee to let the franchisor sell the business on his behalf.

2. Buy the business back from the franchisee or his trustee in bankruptcy.

3. Do nothing and permit the business to fail, take back the franchise and sell that franchise to another franchisee.

Any of these courses of action can lead to a termination of the franchise agreement.

Checklist: Preparing for Franchisee Termination

- Review all operational and legal files.

- Secure additional evidence before sending a termination notice, e.g. photographs, statements of former employees, letters from customers.

- Have similar breaches by other franchisees been treated differently? Can the circumstances be distinguished to avoid a claim of discrimination? How long has the breach continued? Anticipate waiver defences.

- Has the franchisor acted reasonably? Has the franchisee been given any warnings? Has the franchisee been issued with a 'Letter of Concern' drawing his attention to the default complained of and warned of the possible consequences of his failure to remedy the default?

- Can the franchisee be shown as a threat to the system and the public? Any notice of default should refer to the specific clauses of the agreement which the franchisee has breached, the business justification for those provisions, the efforts made by the franchisor to persuade the franchisee to cure the default without termination. The notice of default should place the franchisor as the aggrieved party. Consider whether it is advantageous to include in the notice of default all breaches by the franchisee, not only the major breach which may be the catalyst for termination.

- Ensure that the notice of default is technically correct and ensure that it conforms to the notice requirements of the agreement and where appropriate the law.

- Check files to see if notices are required to be served on third parties: landlords, lenders, guarantors, individual shareholders of corporate franchisee. Draft third-party notices with care to avoid libel.

- Check with solicitors the consequences of any acceptance by the franchisor of fees/rent after termination notice.

- Check files to determine who controls the property.

- Does termination enable the franchisor to exercise rights to take over the franchisee's premises/business?
- Does the franchise agreement contain post-termination/non-competition covenants? Are they enforceable?
- Does the franchisee own other units? Check for cross-guarantees and any general release.
- Does the franchise agreement provide for arbitration?
- If the franchisee is a company, have its shareholders guaranteed its obligations to the franchisor?
- Review the franchisee's application for a franchise to see if it contains any fraudulent statements or material misrepresentations.
- Consider if it is likely that there may be some sort of concerted action by any franchisees. If so:

    a. Is it a real or perceived threat?

    b. Will such concerted action give rise to a libel/defamation case against them?

    c. Can such concerted action induce any of the others to breach their respective franchise agreements?

- Is there in existence a franchisee council or similar association (see Chapter 24) and, if so, would it be the right forum for reaching some form of settlement?

Preventing Competition from Former Franchisees

Most well-drafted franchise agreements will spell out clearly what is to happen on the termination of the franchise agreement for whatever reason.

The post-termination provisions of a franchise agreement will usually deal with the severance of the relationship and the protection of the franchisor's brand, know-how, system, trade secrets, business methods, goodwill, its commercial interests and those of franchisees.

Termination: The End of the Relationship

The franchisor's main objectives will be:

- To ensure that customer contact and continuity of service are maintained with the customers of the departing franchisee. A well-drafted franchise agreement will provide for the transfer of existing contracts between the franchisee and his customers to the franchisor (together with any necessary financial adjustments) on termination.

- To protect its brand by requiring its franchisee to change its business's public image so that it no longer reflects the franchisor's name and goodwill. This will entail, on the part of the franchisee:

    a. Ceasing to use the franchisor's intellectual property and, if necessary, joining the franchisor in making an application to the Registrar of Trade Marks to cancel any registered user agreement relating to the franchisee's use of the franchisor's trade marks or service marks.

    b. Changing the facia, décor and shop fitting of the premises and the livery of any vehicles so that they no longer project their former marketing image.

    c. Returning all advertising, packaging, marketing and promotional material associated with the franchise.

    d. Ceasing to use any material which the franchisor owns or which contains any of the franchisor's intellectual property or reference to the franchise.

    e. Returning the operations manual.

    f. Ceasing use of the franchisor's system.

The franchise agreement should contain clauses with the object of preventing the departing franchisee from using the franchisor's intellectual property, know-how and confidential information imparted to him while he was a franchisee. These are commonly known as 'covenants in restraint of trade' and 'non-competition covenants'. These covenants include a promise from the franchisee in the franchise agreement that the franchisee will not, from the date of termination, compete with the franchisor, or any of its franchisees, for a stated period and within a certain area.

The law recognises the need for such restrictive covenants, but lays down certain rules which have to be observed if they are to be enforceable. The basic rule is that such a covenant will only be enforceable if the person seeking to enforce it can satisfy the court that it is reasonable both as to its time and its area of operation (for example, 'for one year and a radius of half a mile from the franchisee's premises'). So the drafting of an appropriate restrictive covenant is a matter of some delicacy, for it involves a balance between two freedoms: the freedom of the franchisor to protect that which rightfully belongs to it, and the freedom of the franchisee to work in his chosen occupation. Franchisors should therefore be concerned with finding the right period of time and the area within which any prohibition will operate.

In certain cases, time and area will not even be a factor. The franchisor is entitled to prevent a former franchisee for so long as it chooses from:

- Making use of the franchisor's know-how, trade secrets and confidential information. Of course, if any of that information becomes widely and publicly known for reasons other than the fault of the franchisee, the restriction may be difficult to enforce.
- Making any future use of the franchisor's intellectual property.
- Making copies, or any future use, of the franchisor's operations manual.
- Making future use of the franchisor's system.

When a franchise agreement is terminated or just expires and is not renewed, what is the position of the ex-franchisee? Should he be free to continue in the same business even if it is carried on under a different name?

It should be appreciated that to some extent each franchisee is concerned that a fellow franchisee should not break away and engage in unfair competition, making use of the knowledge acquired as a former franchisee. However, difficulties arise in relation to the imposition of restraints on the future business activities of a former franchisee.

As mentioned, such restraints can only apply over a reasonable period of time and area, and whether a period and area is considered 'reasonable' will depend on the nature of the business and its area of operation. Obviously, the criteria applied for a retail shop in a densely populated city will be different from those which will apply in a sparsely populated rural area.

Fortunately there is a great deal of guidance available in the form of court decisions in this matter. The relatively recent case of *PSG Franchising Ltd v. Darby*, decided in the High Court in December 2012, dealt with this very issue. It is worth relating here, briefly, the facts of the case and the judgement because they deal with what should be the most important concern for any franchisor: namely, the protection of its intellectual property and the commercial interests not only of itself but also of its franchisees.

Husband and wife Lydia and David Darby operated a PSG franchise for some years. In 2006 they signed a franchise agreement with PSG Franchising Ltd, for a term of five years. The Darbys claimed that their marriage was deteriorating to the extent that Mrs Darby distanced herself from the franchise in October 2010 and Mr Darby continued to operate the business. Then, in May of the next year, Mr Darby approached his franchisor, PSG Franchising Ltd, and said he'd like to leave the network because he was struggling to make a success of the franchise following problems with his marriage and because he had generally lost interest in the business. After a period of discussions, in August 2011, the parties reached a mutual agreement to bring the franchise to an end. In doing so, the Darbys agreed to be bound by the restrictions in their franchise agreement that prevented them, amongst other things, from competing against PSG for a year after termination.

Shortly afterwards, PSG Franchising Ltd made the alarming discovery that the Darbys had in fact been operating a competing search business since at least September 2011. PSG Franchising Ltd felt understandably cheated by the Darbys. It consulted Barney Laurence, a solicitor with Sherrards specialising in franchise dispute resolution, who quickly wrote to the Darbys asking them to cease their competing business and stated that PSG Franchising Ltd would be bringing a claim for damages for the breaches that had occurred. The case went to a two-day trial, which PSG won on all issues.

Legally, what can a franchisor do to stop franchisees like the Darbys from competing?

Franchisors expect their ex-franchisees not to compete with them or with their franchisees, once they have left the network. Franchisors do not expect ex-franchisees to set up a copycat operation or poach their former customers. Franchisors believe that ex-franchisees should be engaged in a business which is different from the business they ran as a franchisee and should not use their franchisor's know-how.

A franchisor hopes to achieve this by means of various clauses in its franchise agreement which are intended to apply to ex-franchisees on termination. It does this typically:

- By providing in its franchise agreement a promise from the franchisee that, when he ceases to be a franchisee, he will not compete with the franchisor or any of its franchisees and will not carry on any business which is similar to the franchised business from his premises or in his former territory for a certain period after termination, and

- By requiring its franchisee not to use or disclose any confidential information imparted to him while he was a franchisee.

The law recognises the need for a franchisor to extract such promises, but the wording in the franchise agreement has to be clear and the restrictions have to be reasonable if the clauses are to be enforceable.

The enforcement of such clauses is important not only to the franchisor but also to its franchisees, who buy their franchise on the basis that their franchisor will protect them from unfair competition from ex-franchisees. If every ex-franchisee can break away and engage in unfair competition, making use of the knowledge he acquired as a former franchisee, the franchise network could unravel very quickly.

So, how confident can a franchisor be that the non-competition clauses in its franchise agreements are enforceable?

In the case of *PSG Franchising Ltd v. Darby*, the High Court scrutinised the PSG franchise agreement (which was drafted by the author) and examined very carefully and thoroughly, word by word, each clause on which the franchisor was relying to protect itself and its network. The judge ruled in favour of PSG Franchising Ltd on all issues. He concluded that the non-competition clauses which dealt with what an ex-franchisee could or could not do after termination were well enough drafted to enable him to make an order preventing the ex-franchisee from carrying on a similar business.

The case is therefore very important in that it shows that the court will, if it is satisfied that the restriction clauses are enforceable, grant an order to protect a franchisor from the actions of its former franchisees.

The lesson to be learned from this is that one should not take for granted that one's franchise agreements are fully enforceable in such circumstances. When it comes to contract enforcement, one should ensure that the relevant clauses are very carefully worded and furthermore, if the matter should ever come up before a judge, that one engages knowledgeable and experienced lawyers who can forcefully and successfully argue one's case.

An Amicable Parting

By and large, most terminations, even for breach, can be settled between franchisor and franchisee in a civilised way.

Once the relationship has broken down an amicable parting can usually be achieved and will provide the best solution for a franchisee whose business may be bought, either by the franchisor or by a prospective franchisee who is interested in taking it on.

Where the ability to operate from premises in a prime location is important in a particular franchise, it is becoming increasingly common for the franchisor to acquire the premises in question and sublet to the franchisee. In these circumstances, the franchise agreement and lease are drafted in such a way that the termination of one triggers off a termination of the other. The franchisee in these circumstances loses his right to occupy his business premises, but he should be no worse off than he would be given a termination accompanied by effective non-competition and restraint of trade covenants.

Where property does not play a significant part in the operation of a particular franchise, the franchise agreement may nevertheless require the franchisee to sell to the franchisor all its equipment, stock of products etc. on termination.

Such provisions operate for the benefit of both parties. They enable the franchisor to ensure that the franchisee is divorced from the franchise system. The franchisee, meanwhile, is able to obtain a fair price (if an ethical agreement is properly drafted) for his equipment and stock. These would otherwise be of little use to him, given the nature of the non-competition and restraint of trade covenants which will be invoked by the franchisor on termination.

If the franchise agreement is well drafted, there is no reason why both parties should not know precisely where they stand in such a situation and be able to separate amicably.

However, this subject of termination and its consequences does provide yet another illustration of the need by both parties to have an agreement which has been professionally prepared by an experienced franchise solicitor, specifically for the franchise in question, with the objective of covering such eventualities as are foreseeable when the franchise relationship comes to an end.

Termination need not be as traumatic for a franchisor as some might be.

Suspension

A viable novel alternative to termination, touched on in Chapter 27, was pioneered by Holiday Inn in the eighties when it found that the most common ground for termination of its franchises was the failure of a franchisee to maintain the required product quality of his Holiday Inn hotel. This alternative was 'suspension', where a hotel was temporarily removed from the Holiday Inn system until it complied with the franchisor's standards. This procedure is worth examining here.

Morton Aronson, General Counsel of Holiday Inns Inc., said at the time:

> *This new process appears to be meeting with success. In the vast majority of instances, when the temporary removal process has been implemented, the hotel has eventually returned to the Holiday Inn system on the upper end of the standards scale ... the temporary removal process provides an opportunity to the franchisee to continue its business with limitations on its use of Holiday Inn trade marks and service marks, while upgrading its property to meet Holiday Inns Inc.'s product quality standards.*
>
> *At the conclusion of the process, both the franchisor and franchisee find themselves with a quality product. So far, no temporary removal of a Holiday Inn hotel has resulted in the termination of the franchise.*

Termination: The End of the Relationship

The way this system worked was by the drawing up of a temporary removal agreement which provided for removal of the hotel from the Holiday Inn system and required the franchisee to:

- Cover all Holiday Inn signs on the premises.
- Cease all advertising of the facility as a Holiday Inn hotel.
- Cease all other representation to the public that the property is a Holiday Inn hotel.
- Prominently display, in all commercial function areas and in each guest room, signs which clearly reflect that the property is not affiliated with the Holiday Inn hotel system.
- Hand out to customers, at the time they check in to the hotel, notices that the hotel is temporarily not affiliated with the Holiday Inn hotel system while it is undertaking improvements to bring it into compliance with Holiday Inn standards.

The agreement provided for a specific time limit period within which:

> ... the requirements must be complied with and within which the franchisee has to do all that is necessary to upgrade the Hotel to Holiday Inn standards.

If the franchisee failed to carry out his obligations within the stipulated time, the franchise agreement could be terminated by Holiday Inn upon seven days' written notice.

Royalty payment and other fees such as advertising were suspended during the period of suspension, but the term of the franchise agreement continued to run.

While at first sight this system appears to be very attractive, upon closer examination three things become immediately apparent:

1. It is a system which is probably most suitable for capital-intensive service franchises which require periodic injection of capital to maintain a quality product.
2. It has a greater chance of success where franchisees are beholden to their franchisor for providing products (e.g. Body Shop) or services (such as the Holiday Inn loyalty rewards scheme and centralised room reservation system) which are the mainstay of the franchisee's business.

3. It is not a panacea for all ills. It may be tempting to use this system for the wrong reasons (e.g. to put off the evil day when a decision has to be made and decisive action against the franchisee taken). It may provide the franchisee with a God-sent opportunity for reorganising his business at your expense, so that when the crunch comes and his agreement is terminated he can go.

For those franchisors who feel that a similar modified system, suitably tailored to the needs of their particular operations, could be useful, suspension can be a valuable additional option provided it is used with care and with due regard to the long-term as well as the short-term interests of both franchisor and franchisee.

One of the prime advantages of the sanction of termination is its effect on the franchisee's operation. The franchisor can overnight disrupt or prevent the franchisee from doing business.

An injudicious use of this system of suspending a franchisee would diminish the shock effect of the sanction and can have the effect of easing the franchisee into termination.

Careful consideration should also be given to what is to happen to the franchisee's use of the franchisor's trade marks and products (if any) bearing the franchisor's trade names and trade marks. If the franchisor has entered into a registered user agreement (a formal agreement, registered at the Patents Office, authorising the franchisee's use of the franchisor's trade marks) with its franchisee, this will have to be amended to take into account the invoking of the system of suspension.

CHAPTER 29

Resolving Disputes Between Franchisor and Franchisee

"No one really listens to anyone else, and if you try it for a while you'll see why."

Mignon McLaughlin

Chapter 24 has already addressed some ways in which to keep peace within a network, but problems between the franchisor and its franchisees may still arise. The source of these problems can usually be attributed to one of the following:

- Pressure from franchisees for changes in the business.
- Resentment over the payment of continuing franchise fees.
- Development of a 'them-and-us' relationship with a consequent breakdown of goodwill and *esprit de corps*.

Long-term commercial relationships often result in friction amongst the parties from time to time, and franchising is no exception. Serious disputes usually arise from disenchantment and dissatisfaction amongst franchisees towards their franchisor, which is equally unhappy with some or many of its franchisees.

Causes and Risks of Conflict

Some of the franchisees' concerns which give rise to friction are:

- A misrepresentation by the franchisor of the franchise business.
- Disputes over the franchisor and/or nominated suppliers' product pricing.
- Disapproval of suppliers which franchisees are required to use.
- Disapproval of 'kickbacks' taken by the franchisor from goods supplied to the network.
- Disputes about the rate of continuing franchise fees.

- Disagreement about the franchisor's advertising policies.
- Disputes about the use to which advertising funds are put.
- Problems over rights of renewal of the franchise.
- Complaints about the failure of the franchisor to provide support and assistance.
- Failure of the franchisor to control other franchisees within the network.
- Failure of the franchisor to improve, enhance and develop the system and concept.
- Failure of the franchisor to supply products which are the subject of the franchise in a timely way.
- The franchisor supplying products which are not what the franchisee ordered (wrong sizes, quantities etc.).[1]
- Restrictions on the franchisee's future activity following termination.

Concerns which are common amongst franchisors are the failure by franchisees:

- To pay for products.
- To pay advertising contributions.
- To pay continuing franchise fees.
- To buy required products, equipment and other items from suppliers nominated by the franchisor.
- To maintain operating standards.
- To trade exclusively within their allocated territory, instead encroaching on another franchisee's exclusive territory.

---

[1] A handful of examples of the type of problem listed here:
The case, in February 2018, of KFC's distributor failing to supply chicken to KFC outlets for a number of days, resulting in the closure of some 600 (out of 900) outlets.
When bovine spongiform encephalopathy (BSE), commonly known as 'mad cow disease', swept the country in the 1980s and beef for hamburger became difficult to source.
When there was an acute shortage of tomatoes in the 1970s, leading to supply difficulties for the pizza makers.

- To follow the system.
- To preserve and protect the franchisor's reputation and intellectual property.

Although, in theory, both franchisor and franchisee share a common interest in seeing the problem resolved, the parties will often pull in opposite directions in practice when attempting to resolve a particular problem. The franchisor will tend to threaten legal action if the franchisee fails to comply with the franchisor's requirements, playing on the franchisee's fear of retribution and the resultant loss of his investment. The franchisor will also attempt to use its knowledge of the network to its best advantage by isolating what the franchisor considers (rightly or wrongly) 'extremists', 'trouble-makers' and 'radicals', often by exercising its paternalistic influence over the other franchisees.

Many people are attracted to franchising as a result of the representations made by franchisors and increasingly by franchise consultants acting on their behalf. These representations relate to assertions of the 'proven formula' of the franchise, which will 'guarantee' the prospective franchisee's financial success once he has become a franchisee. In some cases, such projections have proven to be widely over-optimistic or unachievable. In those circumstances the franchisee will have to resort to legal proceedings to seek redress and to claim damages.

The franchisor will usually counter these allegations by arguing that the projections were no more than a guide, whereas the franchisee will insist that he relied on such representations, which induced him to buy that franchise. The outcome of cases with which I have been concerned and which have reached the courts generally tend to support the franchisor rather than the franchisee. However, it should be remembered that the terms of the franchise agreement are extremely important in determining the parties' respective rights (see Chapter 25).

More recently, franchisees have increasingly decided to take matters into their own hands because of an alleged lack of assistance and support from their franchisor. The franchisee's initial step is to seek legal advice, after which he may sever his connection with the franchisor if he has been advised that the franchisor's breaches of its various contractual obligations have amounted to repudiation of the franchise agreement.

The franchisee is often in a very difficult position when considering whether or not to take such a step as the franchise agreement normally contains clauses restricting his activities on termination which, if enforceable, may result in the franchisee losing his livelihood in addition to failing in his claim for damages from the franchisor. Following an application by a franchisor for an injunction against its franchisee to enforce post-termination, non-compliance and restraint of trade clauses, the matter will usually be heard on a preliminary basis. Once an interim judgment is given, the parties seldom proceed to a full hearing. It is possible for a franchisor to seek to obtain a temporary injunction against a franchisee from the courts pending the decision of a full hearing, and a judge will grant such an injunction to a franchisor if it can establish a *prima facie* case for its application and if the balance of convenience favours the franchisor.

These post-termination clauses are becoming an area of increasing importance as many franchise agreements which were granted at the beginning of the 2010s are now coming up for renewal. Some franchisees, having run their businesses for many years, believe that they can go it alone and save on the payment of franchise fees and advertising contributions. Such fees often amount to between 10% and 15% of a franchisee's turnover. Whether they are entitled to do this will depend to a large extent on the terms of the franchise agreement. In a number of cases a franchisee has been prohibited from continuing to operate an identical or similar business from the premises or within a certain area of his former franchised business. In some cases the termination provisions of the franchise agreement did not prevent the carrying on of such a business, but required the franchisee to change the marketing image of the premises (debrand). In such cases agreement between the parties has often been achieved.

Costs, of course, have an important part to play in this battle of wits, because the franchisor will usually have deeper pockets. To counter this, the initial idea which usually springs to a franchisee's mind is to try to instigate collective action by his fellow franchisees by harnessing the strength of numbers which franchisees enjoy and sharing costs.

However, experience has shown that collective action is seldom successful. While a disgruntled franchisee will be able to set the wheels of collective action in motion fairly quickly at the initial stages, the franchisee 'action group' will quickly start to lose cohesion as attitudes harden and as individual franchisees look to their own interests, as they usually do where collective action is involved.

The reason for this is very simple. Each franchisee is an independent businessman and has his own priorities. Thus, those franchisees who are doing well will tend to steer clear of, or abandon, the action group, having no desire to rock the boat. Franchisees who are marginally profitable are even less inclined to rock the boat or indeed to spend much-valued resources and time in promoting an action which, whatever its merits, could backfire.

This usually leads to the franchisee engaging 'Plan B' by threatening the franchisor with the public laundering of the issues in question, which could cause harm to the franchisor, its reputation and its public image. So, having failed in his planned collective action, he will find himself acting against the interests of the network as a whole if he embarks upon Plan B.

Any attempt to damage the public image of the franchisor and therefore the network will almost inevitably lead to a termination of the franchise agreement.

Arguably, Plan B is the easiest, cheapest and quickest to carry out. However, it is also the least fruitful of all options open to a dissatisfied franchisee.

A franchisee with a genuine grievance can, and should, consider legal enforcement of the franchise agreement and an action for misrepresentation. This, of course, is the course of action any responsible businessman would take where he has genuine reason to believe that the party with whom he contracted has failed him in some way. Whether or not this is a practical solution to the franchisee's problem depends very much on the nature of the problem. For more on litigation, see 'Litigation', below.

Setting the Tone

Once the sabre rattling is over, there are not many relationships which survive the full rigours of our judicial system as it applies to commercial litigation. However, various mechanisms exist which should enable a franchisor and franchisee to resolve their dispute without resorting to litigation.

Before resorting to litigation, the parties should consider resolving their disputes by means of conciliation, mediation or arbitration. Where the parties are confident that they can have their dispute resolved by an independent third party, they should do so. This is particularly true of disputes over a fact, such as whether or not a franchisee's financial returns are accurate. This is a type of dispute which should be possible for an independent third party to resolve without the process eroding the underlying relationship between franchisor and franchisee.

For the most part, it should be possible for the franchisor and franchisee to agree to refer a matter to arbitration or mediation, or to attempt at conciliation, without dealing a fatal blow to their relationship. For more on these methods of dispute resolution, see 'Alternative Dispute Resolution', below.

The initial reaction of the parties to a dispute will set the tone and determine the course which any attempts at resolution will take. Franchisors sometimes have to be reminded that franchisees are often in a very difficult position when considering whether or not they should take action against their franchisor, bearing in mind the aforementioned clauses restricting the activities of the franchisee on termination, and that termination will usually mean that the franchisee will lose his business. Franchisees have to move with extreme caution because if they get it wrong they could be in a pickle.

In one particular case the franchisee had cause to complain about a breach by his franchisor of certain obligations in the franchise agreement. The franchisee argued that the breach in question amounted to a default by the franchisor which was serious enough to entitle the franchisee to treat the agreement as being terminated, and that under these circumstances the franchisee was no longer bound by the non-competition and restraint of trade clause contained in his now non-existent franchise agreement. The franchisor contested this and sought an injunction against the franchisee to enforce the terms of the franchise agreement which dealt with the consequences of termination. The case went from the High Court (which found in favour of the franchisee) to the Court of Appeal, which found against the franchisee, stating that the franchisee's complaints were not so serious as to amount to a termination of the franchise agreement. Under the circumstances, the Court of Appeal granted the franchisor an injunction enforcing some of the termination clauses in the franchise agreement. These included the return by the franchisee to the franchisor of corporate property, lists containing names and addresses of the franchisee's customers, and ownership of the telephone numbers used in connection with the franchised business. For those reading this, who may be rubbing their hands with glee, it has to be said that in this particular case, the franchisee took unilateral action by ceasing to trade as a franchised outlet on the Friday of one week and then on the following Monday continued the same business under a different, although very similar, name. Not all franchisees are that simple!

Obviously a franchisor should be aware that serious consequences, of both a practical and a financial nature, may follow as a result of wrongful termination. They should at all times be concerned to ensure that termination does not upset the smooth running of their business and that any changeover from the former franchisee to a new franchisee is as seamless as possible.

Before taking any steps to terminate a franchise agreement, it is important for a franchisor to consider these matters very carefully and, in particular, any wider implications which may arise from such termination: for example, any problems relating to the franchisee's premises. The leased premises from where the franchisee operates will be in his name and he may or may not have taken a sublease of the premises from the franchisor. If it is intended that a new franchisee will operate from the same premises, the legal implications need to be carefully considered and, where appropriate, the proper steps will need to be put in hand by the franchisor's solicitors to enable the franchisor or its new franchisee to take possession of such premises.

Alternative Dispute Resolution

By and large franchisors do not take the termination of a franchise agreement lightly. For them it is an admission of failure on their part because, in the final analysis, it was their judgement as to the character, ability and competence of the franchisee which may have been found wanting.

Furthermore, franchisors should realise that it is very important that they comply with the terms of the franchise agreement relating to termination because if it turns out, after the termination, that the franchisee was not at fault, a franchisee could have a substantial claim against the franchisor for damages.

The termination of a franchise agreement, either by the franchisor or by the franchisee, is an admission of failure by both parties. It is a blot on the landscape of the franchisor's corporate strategy for franchising, and an unhappy and expensive, if not bitter, experience for the franchisee. Disputes do arise, and by and large they can be resolved if tackled by both parties constructively and with the right attitude.

As we start to demand a greater say in shaping our own future by becoming more involved in the day-to-day decisions affecting it, so our current legal system – one of adversarial practice, 'winner takes all' – is being questioned. Even the existing system of arbitration as an alternative to litigation is being perceived as being long-winded, costly and simply replacing one binding decision-making process with another.

The reality is that neither party really wants to go to litigation. Except in certain circumstances where precedent case law may be involved, the answer is simply to give both parties a framework within which they can negotiate their own settlement with advice and assistance from a neutral third party. Conciliation, mediation and arbitration are all methods of resolving a dispute without resorting to litigation, commonly known as 'alternative dispute resolution' or ADR.

Conciliation

Conciliation is usually an informal process whereby an individual ('conciliator') tries to bring the disputing parties together and to conciliate between them, lowering tensions and encouraging them to accept a mutually acceptable solution, more casually referred to as 'knocking their heads together to help them see sense'. Conciliation has no legal standing, and the conciliator makes no decision or award. The process is usually invoked at an early stage of the dispute when the parties are keen to repair their relationship. In many disputes involving figures, there is no reason why the matter should not be resolved by the parties concerned with the help of their respective accountants.

Conciliation presupposes a genuine desire by the parties to resolve their differences.

Mediation

Mediation is a voluntary, non-binding, and 'without prejudice' process in which a specially trained third party intervenes (with the consent of all those involved) in a dispute and attempts through negotiation techniques to bring the parties together into a settlement agreement.

All participants in mediation are encouraged to actively participate in the process. Mediation focuses primarily on the needs, rights, and interests of the parties. A mediator facilitates and manages open communication and interaction amongst the parties.

If the mediation succeeds, and over 80% of them do, then it ends with a binding agreement.

If the parties are dissatisfied with the process, either party or the mediator may terminate the mediation at any time. The claimant may then proceed to assert their legal rights through arbitration or the courts.

Mediation is today considered the fastest, most flexible and least threatening of all alternative dispute resolution techniques. It is also the most cost-effective.

For the franchisee's part, he must be reasonable in his demands and appreciate why the franchisor may be unwilling to adopt a solution proposed by the franchisee and insist on a different solution which will produce the same or a similar result.

On the franchisor's part, it requires more than commiseration with a franchisee's problems. An appreciation of his difficulties will not in itself be sufficient. Any proposal put forward by the franchisor should be capable of resolving the dispute in the long term, and not merely a short-term measure designed to keep the franchisee quiet for the time being, without solving the underlying problems which gave rise to the dispute in the first place.

Arbitration

Unlike mediation, arbitration is in effect a private court hearing where the parties accept that the decision of the arbitrator will be binding upon them whether they like it or not. This method of resolving disputes is not new. Arbitration has long been recognised as a method of solving commercial disputes and is subject to statutory control.

The first thing to note is that arbitration can be held in private. This means that one does not have to wash one's dirty linen in public. It is possible for the parties to agree, as a precondition to arbitration, that the arbitration and the decision of the arbitrator will be kept confidential. From the franchisor's point of view, this means that should it lose and an award be made against it, it is less likely to have a knock-on effect within its franchised network than would otherwise be the case.

For some time now, it has been generally felt that arbitration is less costly than litigation. This is still probably true in a local context but is questionable in terms of international arbitration, which can be very costly. Arbitration is usually quicker than litigation because the parties do not have to submit to the long waiting lists of our court system. Arbitrators will usually attend at a time and place which suits the parties concerned.

The ability of the parties to choose an arbitrator also overcomes one of the major drawbacks of litigation. A judge appointed to hear the case may not be *au fait* with the type of matter under dispute (though this is now rare), whereas it should be possible to appoint as arbitrator someone who has the necessary experience of business format franchising to understand the problem which he has been called to determine upon.

In all probability, the greatest advantage of arbitration as a mechanism for resolving disputes is that it can enable the parties to continue in their business relationship not only during the arbitration process, but also after the arbitrator has made his decision. This is something which seldom happens in litigation, which tends to be acrimonious, with the result that it erodes the underlying relationship between the parties concerned. Under arbitration there is an infinitely greater chance that the business relationship of the parties will survive.

As far as enforcement is concerned, where a party refuses to comply with an arbitration order, the award can be enforced by the courts.

The disadvantages of arbitration, although few in number, are nevertheless important.

Court procedures have been laid down as a result of many years' experience and are designed to elicit the facts from the parties concerned and also to safeguard their legitimate interests. The danger with arbitration is that an arbitrator need not follow the procedures laid down for court proceedings. However, this problem can be avoided by the parties if they lay out, at the outset, the procedures which an arbitrator will be required to follow. For example, the Chartered Institute of Arbitrators has a set of rules and there is no reason why those appointing an arbitrator should not make it incumbent upon the arbitrator to follow these rules.

The most serious drawback to arbitration is that an arbitrator does not have the power to grant an injunction. This is an invaluable remedy and one that can be swiftly obtained in the High Court. However, an injunction being equitable remedy, the court will not grant such a remedy (prior to arbitration) to a party if the contract provides that in the event of any dispute, the parties will arbitrate. One of the maxims of equity is 'He who comes into equity must come with clean hands.' This means that a person seeking the equitable remedy of an injunction will not be granted the remedy if he himself is in breach (in this case, for failing to go to arbitration as the contract provides).

If both parties agree in a franchise agreement to arbitrate in the event of a dispute, then they must do so. If one of the parties decides to seek an equitable remedy before arbitrating, the court will not entertain his application. He cannot expect the court to grant him a remedy against his opponent (whom he claims to be in breach) if the applicant himself is in breach by not having arbitrated first. As a judge was once heard to exclaim when refusing an application for an injunction under circumstances where the applicant was himself in breach of the contract, 'A dirty dog gets no dinner here!'

All this does not mean that franchisors, who are usually the ones who seek equitable remedies against franchisees, will always refuse to arbitrate. Indeed there is no reason why the whole agreement should be made subject to arbitration. It is possible for franchise agreements to be drafted in a way which makes only certain clauses subject to arbitration, leaving both franchisor and franchisee to apply for equitable relief in other circumstances.

One should not overlook the fact that arbitration provides flexibility for the parties. The parties not only can choose the arbitrator, but can also set down the procedures to be followed and the powers to be given to the arbitrator.

In the United States, arbitration is increasingly seen as a serious alternative to litigation, particularly in California, where Californians have now taken to hiring retired judges and renting court rooms literally to conduct a court hearing in private! Although the judges don't come cheap, when one considers the speed with which the matters are dealt with and the saving of lawyers' fees as a consequence, litigants find the arrangement cost-effective.

In summary, the main disadvantages of arbitration are that:

- There is always the risk that the arbitrator may be uninformed about franchising and the way in which it operates.
- The arbitrator does not need to follow the procedures laid down for actions in a court of law.
- The arbitrator may do 'rough justice' rather than enforcing the strict letter of the contract.
- An arbitrator cannot grant injunctions and a wide reference to arbitration may prevent one from being obtained in court.

On the other hand:

- Arbitration is private. One doesn't have to wash one's dirty linen in public. (This also applies to conciliation and mediation.)
- Arbitration is generally faster and less costly than litigation.
- The time and place of the arbitration hearings can be organised to suit the convenience of the parties.
- Some of the disadvantages can be avoided by the franchisor insisting that the arbitrator is to have no say in certain matters such as the consequences of termination (contained in the franchise agreement) and by limiting the application of arbitration only to certain provisions in the franchise agreement.
- Arbitration is likely to be less acrimonious than litigation and far more conducive to the survival of the business relationship.
- Arbitration awards are enforceable by the courts.

By using the alternative dispute resolution scheme of the British Franchise Association or that of the Chartered Institute of Arbitrators, it should be possible to appoint as an arbitrator someone with the requisite experience of the problem which has arisen.

If one looks at a franchise agreement there are a number of areas where a genuine difference of opinion might exist:

- Where a franchisee claims renewal and the franchisor wishes to deny him the right to renewal because it asserts that the franchisee has not properly performed obligations in the past.
- Where there is a difference over the calculation of continuing franchise or other fees.
- Where the franchisee feels that the franchisor is not discharging its marketing obligations properly.

On the other hand, there are some areas which a franchisor would not wish to make the subject of arbitration. A franchisor may wish to retain the sole right to determine whether or not its standards are being observed. It may not wish to arbitrate over whether a franchisee should change the name and appearance of his shop after termination. Should a former franchisee refuse to make these changes, a franchisor would want to go to court to obtain an injunction to require the franchisee immediately to cease and desist.

Thus, when disputes arise, a franchisor and franchisee can agree to appear before an arbitrator who could determine the issue, leave the franchise agreement intact and give the parties an opportunity to continue to work together for their future mutual benefit.

Litigation

Conciliation, mediation and arbitration have the benefit of affording the protagonists a chance of resolving a dispute without eroding their underlying relationship: something which is very unlikely to occur in litigation.

There will undoubtedly be cases where the personalities involved are such that one of the parties, if not both or all of them (as the case may be), will be determined to see the other in court. Having said this, not many litigants survive the full rigours of our judicial system unscathed.

There have not been very many disputes between franchisor and franchisee reaching the courts. Such disputes as have reached the courts have largely arisen as a result of an individual franchisee or a group of them becoming dissatisfied with the way the franchisor has purported to carry out its obligations under the agreement. The most common complaints seems to be that the franchisor has failed to give support to a franchisee as required under the terms of the franchise agreement and/or that the franchisee was misled by widely optimistic representations made by the franchisor or those acting on its behalf prior to the franchise being granted.

As mentioned, the franchisee is often in a very difficult position when considering whether or not to take action against his franchisor, particularly as franchise agreements normally contain clauses restricting the activities of the franchisee on termination, howsoever arising.

In Conclusion

Termination should always be an absolute last resort, and there are a number of potential alternatives for dealing with disputes.

The franchise relationship is one which, in theory, at least, and in my view in practice also, should be capable of subsisting in the long term. It is not a short-term arrangement. So long as both parties to the agreement substantially perform their respective obligations, the arrangements should run indefinitely.

Obviously, where necessary, one should be able to terminate and enforce one's rights with the full range of remedies available at law. Naturally, there will be times when the arrangements are re-examined and fresh agreements entered into, reflecting changes in practices and changes in the law, but fundamentally one is dealing with a long-term arrangement.

When one is dealing with a long-term arrangement, one has to establish machinery for resolving disputes within the framework of that relationship, so that the relationship will prove capable of surviving the dispute. Ideally the parties should feel that justice has been done and that they can continue the relationship, possibly on an even better basis than before.

CHAPTER 30

Franchisees as Multiple Unit Holders

"The footprint of the farmer is the best fertiliser."

Which is better: lots of franchisees with single trading units or a few franchisees with each franchisee owning a number of units?

Growing a franchise business is all about increasing the number of franchised units. Given that one of the principal advantages of franchising is that it enables a supplier of goods or services to rapidly penetrate the market, anything which hinders the growth in the number of outlets opened is taken very seriously. Whenever the recruitment of franchisees becomes difficult, franchisors turn to other methods for solving their problems.

Prospective franchisors are advised that they need to establish a franchisee profile on which they can base their selection process for new franchisees. Given that a great number of new franchisors are small or medium-sized businesses, it is unlikely that they have any other option and rare for them to come across prospective franchisees who far exceed the selection criteria in terms of their management expertise and financial resources.

Mature franchisors, on the other hand, have experienced good days and bad days in terms of franchisee recruitment. The redundancies of the early nineties provided a large pool of good-quality prospective franchisees with cash in their pockets. Prior to that, in the booming eighties, franchisee recruitment was a problem, and before that the economic troubles of the early seventies again proved to be a good period for franchisee recruitment at a time when the franchise sector was in its infancy. So mature franchisors are becoming increasingly familiar with what seems to be the cyclical nature of franchisee recruitment.

Those franchisors who are strong and brave enough will upgrade their franchisee profile with a view to giving preference to those prospective franchisees who have the potential to grow their franchised businesses beyond a single unit. The advantages of multi-unit franchisees have not escaped franchisors. As with everything else, there are disadvantages, but, by and large, these disadvantages are overlooked, ignored or considered, on balance, to be outweighed by the advantages.

Advantages of Multi-Unit Franchising

Multi-unit franchisees cost a good deal less per franchise unit opened than individual franchisees. Once a franchisor has done the know-how/show-how bit for a franchisee's first unit, second and subsequent units opened by the same franchisee require a good deal less input from the franchisor, thereby saving the franchisor valuable management time and expense. After all, the franchisee has done it before and is familiar with the franchisor's requirements with regard to shop fitting, stock purchase etc. A good proportion of the initial franchise fee therefore goes directly to the franchisor's bottom line.

Some franchisors offer a discount on the initial franchise fee for second and subsequent units opened by the same franchisee, sometimes as an incentive for the franchisee to open more units, sometimes simply because it seems the right thing to do. However, it is rare for a franchisor to take only a nominal initial franchise fee or indeed none at all.

Even in terms of training, once a franchisee's business has grown to a certain level, the franchisor need only train the franchisee's trainer, who is then responsible for training all the franchisee's staff. Further savings for the franchisor.

Multi-unit franchisees tend to be more sophisticated than individual franchisees in terms of their business acumen, management and administration and therefore require less hand-holding and support from their franchisors. All in all, therefore, it seems to be a good deal for franchisors if they can encourage their franchisees to take on more franchised units.

Disadvantages of Multi-Unit Franchising

There are two principal disadvantages. The first is that unless the franchisor is extremely careful in its selection of the franchisee and keeps a very close eye on the franchisee's managers or supervisors, the ill effects of going against the basic concept of franchising can have a profound effect on both the franchisee and the franchisor's business. One of the fundamental reasons for franchising is that a franchised outlet should be able to generate a much higher level of turnover than a managed outlet and increase its market share because the owner is behind the counter serving the customer. The franchised business is his business, and the profits from that business are his profits.

A multi-unit franchisee cannot be 'behind the counter' of every unit he owns and will perforce have to employ managers. In the case of a managed outlet, the manager will be an employee and, although there may be sophisticated bonus schemes, it is never the same as being the owner of one's own business. If a manager is unwell he will call in sick and nurse his cold. A franchisee, on the other hand, will drag himself out of bed and open the shop. A manager will be anxious to go home at closing time, whereas a franchisee will serve his customers for as long as necessary and close the shop when the last customer has left of his own volition.

The second disadvantage relates to the size of an individual franchisee's business. The larger the franchisee's business, the more demanding that franchisee will be of his franchisor and of his rights. There comes a time when the size of the franchisee is such that he can more or less deal with the franchisor on equal terms, or at least feel he can, even if the franchisor is considerably bigger than him. A multi-unit franchisee's pockets are deeper when it comes to contentious matters than those of a single unit franchisee. A multi-unit franchisee will be more questioning of the franchisor's policies and more challenging of the franchisor whenever the franchisor introduces changes to the system.

Multi-unit franchisees are commonplace in the United States and there is now increasing litigation between multi-unit franchise holders and their franchisors. Some have scored notable successes.

Clearly the strength of the franchisor is crucial when planning a strategy for multi-unit franchise holders. They are certainly a good way of expanding the number of franchised outlets. However, as in all things, a balance has to be struck. If a franchisor encourages multi-unit franchise holders in circumstances where it does not have a sufficient number of company-owned outlets as a counterbalance, it may be storing up trouble for the future. Once franchisees, whether multi-unit franchise holders or individual franchisees, realise that the franchisor is beholden to its franchisees for a substantial part of its income, the rules of the game change and the balance of power begins to shift.

There is no doubt that multi-unit franchising can catapult a franchisor into a different league in terms of the numbers of outlets operating under the franchisor's brand, but such a strategy needs to be carefully planned and executed if it is to be successful in the long term and not eventually derail the franchisor.

CHAPTER 31

A Successful Franchisor's Dilemma

"Stick with what you know and go abroad."

Franchisors who have been franchising successfully for a number of years find that they reach a stage when they have sold as many franchises as they are likely to. Although there remains room for growth through franchise sales, it becomes increasingly difficult to sell franchises as the locations or territories still available for sale are more remote.

In such circumstances, what can the franchisor do to generate additional revenue?

Branching Into New Concepts

In many cases, franchisors in this situation look to either developing (using their own resources) or acquiring (by means of buying rights to) another concept.

To take an example, let us assume that Fictitious Carpet Cleaners is a very successful franchise. It operates a mobile carpet cleaning service and the franchisor is now in a position where it has sold most of the territories available. It therefore decides to grow by buying the rights to an existing concept, which may complement its current business, like cleaning curtains and upholstery, or may alternatively be something completely different, such as a mobile windscreen repair service.

If the new concept is similar to the current business, there is the advantage that it can be sold to existing franchisees as another business concept which they could operate alongside their existing successful franchise. This carries with it the advantage of providing for each of them a way to expand their business and therefore generate additional income. This has a reasonably good chance of succeeding, particularly where the franchisor has acquired rights to such a concept as opposed to having developed it from its own resources. This greater chance of success is because developing a new concept from its own resources would take time and probably cost a lot more than paying someone for the rights to a tried and tested system. As long as there is a strong enough synergy between its original business and the new concept, such a strategy could work.

This is different from co-branding, where it is more common for the franchisors of each brand to enter into some sort of joint venture. In such a venture, neither franchisor is acquiring rights to operate the business concept of the other. For more on co-branding, see Chapter 35.

What appears to have been singularly unsuccessful is a strategy where a successful franchisor acquires rights to or develops a concept which is quite different from that of its core business, as with the windscreen repair business referred to above. The history of franchising in the UK is littered with such failures. In the past some franchisors whose brands were household names have failed in their attempts to expand their business by this means, such as Dyno-Rod (which tried Texon, a car respray service), Prontaprint (which tried Jucy Lucy, freshly squeezed orange juice, and Fudge Kitchen), and Pronuptia & Youngs Formal Wear (which tried La Mamma, clothes). In the case of Youngs, the franchisor went into receivership.

Usually, the choice of developing a different concept is based more on arrogance than on common sense. Just because a particular franchisor is very good and successful at cleaning carpets, it does not follow that it can be equally successful in franchising a business which involves repairing car windscreens. Yet, despite the history, franchisors continue to make this mistake.

Branching Into New Countries

Another option for the franchisor would be to continue doing elsewhere what it has done successfully in the UK. It should consider expanding its brand overseas. The franchisor would have a lot going for it: a sound business, a successful concept and an income flow. Given the right advice, it should be possible for a franchisor to do in Germany what it has done successfully in the UK, providing, and it is a big proviso, the franchisor does not *automatically* assume that because it works in the UK it will work in Germany. Hence the emphasis on taking sound professional advice. So far what the franchisor has proven by its success in the UK is that it can:

- Transfer its know-how to a third party, enabling that third party to establish and operate successful businesses.

A Successful Franchisor's Dilemma

- Manage a network of franchisees.

It can take these strengths abroad. Whether or not it can succeed in replicating what it has done in the UK will depend in part on:

Its method of entering the foreign market (master franchising, direct franchising, joint venture etc.; see Chapter 38).

- Its choice of partner.
- The country into which it makes its first foray.
- The quality of professional advice it seeks, receives and accepts.
- Most of all, flexibility: its ability to make changes to the original concept to accommodate the differences in law, culture and commercial practice in the foreign country.

There are good examples of how this can be done successfully, mostly from the United States. Once US franchisors have achieved the level of market penetration they are comfortable with, there is a tendency for them to take their concept abroad instead of trying to do something different at home.

For more on international franchising, see Chapter 38.

CHAPTER 32

Staying Ahead of the Game

> *"In our rapidly changing society we can count on only two things that will never change. What will never change is the will to change and the fear of change."*
>
> Harriet Lerner, *The Dance of Intimacy*

Prospective franchisors who are successful in their business know already that it is tough enough reaching the top but it is even tougher staying there. If this is true of most independent retail concepts, franchising is no exception. Franchisors are under intense pressure to increase their market share and to retain their market lead, and, unlike independent retailers, the pressure comes not only from their shareholders but also from their franchisees.

In a sense, franchisors have two very different categories of customers: the purchasers of their goods or services and those who are its franchisees. Franchisors who forget that their franchisees are also their customers will not succeed in the long term. They will fail to attract new franchisees who, although they may be attracted by the success of the concept, will shy away from locking themselves into a long-term agreement with a franchisor who has a reputation for having little respect for its franchisees' wishes.

Franchisees rely on their franchisors for a number of things, principal amongst which is the obligation to expend human and financial resources towards research and development. This is not something which franchisees are able to do for themselves. Unless franchisors can demonstrate to prospective franchisees their commitment to research and development, any market lead enjoyed by their franchise will soon diminish.

Franchisors should therefore have a programme of innovation and seek to improve, develop and enhance their methods of operation, products/services, delivery etc. It is the fruits of their labours in this respect which will eventually determine whether or not a particular franchise concept will retain its pole position in the market. Success breeds imitators and franchisors need, and are expected by their franchisees, to keep ahead of the competition.

The Role of Franchisees in Innovation

It is accepted that franchising involves a close relationship between franchisor and franchisee: a form of partnership, where both parties share a common interest and common goals. So, although the primary obligation for developing the franchise rests upon the franchisor, franchisees nevertheless have a role to play in the process. The franchisor cannot do it alone.

Given that the strength of business format franchising is uniformity, it does not make sense for franchisees to modify the franchise concept in the light of their own experience on an individual basis. For this reason, franchisors should prohibit franchisees from making any change to the system or the business model without the prior approval of the franchisor. On the other hand, ethical franchisors should not use their franchisees as guinea pigs for introducing changes to the system without the franchisor having first tested and proven the efficacy of such changes itself, usually through its own company-owned outlet and sometimes with the express consent of its most highly regarded and successful franchisees.

Franchisees are at the coal face and, based on their experience, should be able to provide franchisors with market intelligence as to what the consumer is looking for, likes, dislikes and might be persuaded to buy.

The importance of franchisors listening to their franchisees cannot be overemphasised, because in many cases the gut reaction of a franchisee is as important as that of his franchisor. Franchisors do not always know best and do not always get it right. For example, some years ago, McDonald's launched a range of beef, chicken and fish menu items under the name 'Arch Deluxe'. This was a product of two years' research and an alleged expenditure of $2 million. Notwithstanding this, the menu items were not successful. This is not the only franchisor-led product innovation which has failed to succeed. Earlier, both 'McPizza' and 'McLean' menu items failed to attract customers. On the other hand, McDonald's has enjoyed success with new menu items in the form of 'Egg McMuffin', 'Hot Apple Pie', 'Filet-O-Fish' and, of course, the 'Big Mac'. All these were born out of ideas proposed by franchisees to whose suggestions McDonald's, as a responsible and progressive franchisor, was receptive.

The point is that successful companies like McDonald's do not ignore suggestions from their franchisees but, rather, treat them as valuable assets. By the same token, they take their obligations as franchisors seriously and do not rely on their franchisees to produce new ideas but make the necessary investment in research and development. True, they have had some failures, but so what? If one is not prepared to make mistakes or accept that sometimes things will not work out as hoped, one will not make anything. It's that simple.

Not all ideas will work and not all ideas will be suitable, but if the name of the game is staying ahead of the competition and maintaining a market lead then attention needs to be paid to innovation, improvement and development in every aspect of the business.

"If you spend your time avoiding risk, you are unwittingly taking the greatest risk of all – failure to adapt."

John Harvey-Jones, *Troubleshooter*

CHAPTER 33

What Happens If a Franchisor Goes Bust?

"Things work out best for those who make the best of the way things work out."

John Wooden

There are probably as many reasons why franchisors go bust as there are franchisors. Franchisors, of course, are not infallible and there are a number of different reasons why a franchisor may fail.

Principal amongst these are:

- The franchisor may be very good at running its business, but not at being a franchisor.
- The franchisor may be undercapitalised.
- The franchise may be badly structured.
- The business concept may not have been market tested and proven to the extent necessary.
- The franchisor may have set its continuing franchise fee lower than it should have and may therefore be starved of income vital for fulfilling its obligations to its franchisees.
- Although the franchise business may be sound, the franchisor may subsequently make mistakes or bad policy decisions
- A change in the law or regulations may make it difficult for franchisees to continue as before. It may entail changes in the system and/or may require franchisees to make additional capital investment, thereby rendering what was previously a profitable franchise marginally so or unprofitable.

The consequences to the franchisee of a franchisor's failure will vary according to the circumstances of the failure.

In some cases a franchisee will go bust with the franchisor. This is particularly true of franchises that rely on products which can only be obtained from the franchisor and where alternative products will not do the job as well, or where the franchisor's ongoing support is essential to the franchisee and an integral part of the franchise system.

In other cases all may not be lost and the franchisee will be able to pick up the pieces and carry on, eventually recovering his loss (if any) and making a profit.

It goes without saying, of course, that prospective franchisees must thoroughly investigate their chosen franchisor. Prospective franchisees are now far better informed than ever before and have available to them a great deal of information about franchising, not only in the form of books and articles, but also in the form of information packs distributed by the major banks, major franchise consulting firms, solicitors and the British Franchise Association.

When a franchisor goes bust, the first two questions franchisees usually ask are:

1. How does it affect the franchisees' businesses?
2. Do they have to cease trading immediately or can they carry on trading?

To address these concerns, one has to see what it is that the franchisor owns *vis-à-vis* the franchisees' business. The franchisor will be the owner, amongst other things, of the following:

- The franchise system in accordance with which its franchisees operate their businesses.
- The know-how associated with the franchise business.
- Confidential information, which may include trade secrets.
- A trade name, trade marks and/or service marks and the goodwill associated with them.
- Copyright material, usually in the form of advertising, marketing and point of sale material, the operations manual etc.

When a franchisor fails, none of the above disappear. Nor will the franchise agreement automatically come to an end unless there is an express provision in the franchise agreement which provides for this. All the above form the assets of a franchisor's business. Assuming that the franchisor is a limited company (which is usually the case), it will go into receivership or liquidation. In either case, the liquidator or the receiver will take control of these assets and these assets will be subject to rights granted to the franchisees.

One of the primary obligations of a liquidator or a receiver is to protect the assets of a failed company. In most cases, of course, the franchise agreements will be income-producing assets (not unlike leases of premises) in that they will previously have produced an income for the franchisor and will now produce an income for the liquidator. Therefore, it is usually in the interest of a liquidator to ensure that the franchisees continue operating their businesses and continue paying the continuing franchise fees.

Another obligation of the liquidator is to obtain the best possible price for the assets in question. This means that he will be very keen to keep the franchise network alive because so long as it is alive it will have a value to the liquidator. In most cases the obligations of the franchisor under the various franchise agreements are such that a liquidator will be able to perform them as long as he retains some, if not all, of the franchisor's staff.

However, a liquidator does have the right to disclaim franchise agreements if he considers the obligations of the franchisor under the franchise agreements to be too onerous. This could arise if one of the causes of the franchisor's failure is that it has failed to provide for sufficient franchise fees to enable it to perform such onerous obligations.

Generally, it is rare for a liquidator to disclaim franchise agreements because most franchise agreements do not impose unduly heavy obligations on the franchisor once the franchise is up and running. Although franchisors have numerous onerous obligations at the front end of the transaction (i.e. when setting a new franchisee up in business), a franchisor's obligations are relatively easy to perform once a franchisee has opened for business, unless, of course, the franchise system is such that the franchisee is wholly dependent upon the franchisor's continuing support. This would be the case, for example, where a franchisor is a manufacturer of products which are the subject of the franchise. In such a case it could be that the manufacturing arm of the franchisor has brought down the franchisor's business.

Given that a liquidator will be looking for a buyer to buy the failed franchisor's business and franchised network for the best price obtainable, who, one may ask, would want to buy a failed franchisor's business assets?

A purchaser could be a competitor of the franchisor, which may or may not already be a franchisor itself. If it is already a franchisor, it may be a little reluctant because of the complications which would necessarily ensue as a result of its buying a failed competitor's network. For one thing there may be a certain amount of duplication of sites with the result that the buyer may now have two franchisees competing with each other, whereas previously there were two different franchised outlets. Secondly, if the original franchisor's decline has been slow and painful, the buyer will have the problem of integrating its competitor's franchisees into its own network in circumstances where they may not be in the mood to deal with yet another franchisor. Most purchasers from failed franchisors insist on having at least one meeting with the franchisees to canvass views, gauge opinions and determine whether or not there could be a basis for a successful long-term relationship.

A second type of purchaser could be one or more of the franchisees themselves. This has been done in the past with some degree of success. It works best if franchisees are quick off the mark to take legal advice when the first signs of trouble appear. In one particular case I was approached with, a group of franchisees were experiencing a deterioration in the services provided by their franchisor. This, together with other signs, such as the shedding of some staff on the franchisor's payroll, led the franchisees to believe that all was not well. A contingency plan was drawn up which could have been put into effect at a critical moment with the object of ensuring a seamless transfer of ownership. Such a plan need not be expensive. However, the success of implementing such a plan will depend on the reaction of the franchisor and/or its receiver/liquidator.

Such a purchase may prove to be a relatively low price to pay for franchisees, particularly if the cost is shared out amongst the network, compared to losing one's business or finding oneself as a franchisee of a strange franchisor.

It should not be forgotten that if the franchisor, in its death throes, has reached the point where it is in breach of its franchise agreement obligations, it is always open to a franchisee to terminate his franchise agreement for breach of contract and make a claim against his franchisor for damages.

The problem with this course of action is that it could precipitate the liquidation of the franchisor if others followed suit. Alternatively, such a claim may not be worth pursuing if the franchisor is in financial difficulties. Furthermore, termination by a franchisee would mean that he would thereafter, in all probability, be prevented from using the franchisor's system, know-how, trade secrets, trade name, trade mark, trade service mark, goodwill and copyright material. In addition to this, there will invariably be non-competition and restraint of trade clauses in the franchise agreement which, depending on the way it is drafted, could restrict the franchisee's future activities.

It is, of course, always possible that a franchisee may be able to negotiate his way out of this difficulty by trading off his claim for damages against being released from the non-competition and restraint of trade covenants. In the past, some have succeeded, but the road of negotiation can be long and tortuous and is not recommend to franchisees other than those who have the financial stamina and are stout-hearted.

The principal advantage in planning a strategy to buy out the franchisor before the proverbial fertiliser has hit the fan is that it enables franchisees to plan things in a rational manner. Franchisees quickly realise that amongst them there are people with varying degrees of ability, views on what to do and willingness to become involved in running the franchise operation. They are more likely to succeed in organising themselves at an earlier stage than when the pressure is on and the clock is ticking. Not all franchisees will wish to be involved, but there is no reason why only a handful of franchisees should not take over the mantle of the franchisor.

The vehicle used by franchisees in these circumstances would normally be a limited company structured in such a way that the franchisees become shareholders and those who have agreed to take an active part become its directors. The company would take a transfer of the franchise agreements from the failing franchisor and then fulfil the role and the obligations of the franchisor. To the extent that it lacked expertise in certain areas, the company would have to engage personnel with the expertise needed.

Once franchisees have decided on their own internal structure they can concentrate on the best means of acquiring their franchisor's assets. When they come to negotiate with a receiver or liquidator, there may be more than one purchaser in the frame and they will, therefore, need to negotiate better than any other prospective purchaser the liquidator/receiver may be considering.

So far, it is assumed that the franchisor's business and assets will be sold. It is always possible that there will be no buyer for such assets. If that is the case, then

Christmas may have come early for the franchisees. In those circumstances they should, at the very least, be able to purchase from the liquidator some of the essential features of the franchise, such as copyright in the operations manual, trade mark, trade name etc., at a relatively low price. The cost, if shared out amongst the whole franchise network, would be negligible, and franchisees would thereafter be free to carry on the business as previously. However, whereas they had previously relied on their franchisor's support, they would now have to swim for themselves. Here, again, franchisees see merit in co-operating with each other, even on a limited basis, because they recognise the benefits to be derived from a uniform marketing image, communal advertising, bulk purchasing etc. With this in mind they can 'club' together and buy the assets and operate their network as a cooperative, paying a reduced level of continuing franchise fees to the entity engaged by their cooperative to manage the cooperative and provide such services.

Very few franchisees seem to have lost out significantly in circumstances where a franchisor has gone bust. If they have lost out, it is because they have failed to take the right advice and appropriate action at the critical time. A well prepared and organised group of franchisees can drive a very hard bargain with a liquidator. After all, who would buy the assets of a failed franchisor in the face of organised opposition from franchisees to whom that person is going to look for his future income?

In the final analysis, whether or not franchisees are organised, it seems that when a franchisor does fail, it is seldom bad news for its franchisees. At best, they may end up owning their own franchisor company or becoming franchisees of another franchisor, which, having made a cash purchase, is likely to take its investment more seriously and show greater enthusiasm towards its franchisees than their former failing franchisor. At the very worst they may end up having to change the name and style of the business and going it alone, but carrying on more or less as previously, without having to pay franchise fees.

Whether franchisees who are a part of a co-operative or are going it alone will succeed in the long term will depend entirely upon the resources, imagination, creativity and ability of the franchisees, but if they do fail, they will at least do so knowing that, this time, they have no one but themselves to blame for their failure.

CHAPTER 34

Whom Does the Customer Sue?

"With rights come obligations and responsibilities."

One of the questions which is usually uppermost in the mind of a prospective franchisor is 'Could a customer or anyone else dealing with my franchisee hold me liable for the acts, omissions or defaults of my franchisee?'

Most franchisors go to great lengths to establish that the relationship between the franchisor and the franchisee is an independent one and not that of an agency, partnership or employment. Provided a franchisor has been careful in its dealings with its franchisee and in the way in which it has structured the franchise transaction, it is unlikely that a relationship of agency, partnership or employment could be brought into being. That said, it is usually easier for a franchisor to prevent a relationship of partnership or employment with its franchisee than it is to prevent an agency from arising.

For a third party (say, a customer or supplier) to make a franchisor liable (within the framework of existing law) for an act or default of its franchisee, he would have to establish that the franchisee was an agent of the franchisor.

This can happen in either or both of the following ways:

1. By the third party being able to establish that the franchisee is a duly appointed agent of the franchisor. This is unlikely to happen if the franchise agreement is properly drafted and, more importantly, the franchisor's directions as to how to operate the business carefully followed.

2. If the franchisor or franchisee led the third party to believe that the franchisee was the franchisor's agent, and that third party entered into a transaction with the franchisee in that belief.

In such circumstances, the franchisor may be prevented from denying the agency, and may therefore be held to be liable. It seems, therefore, that if a franchisor wants to avoid the creation of an unintended agency, the franchisor has to be careful about the sort of message it delivers to the public about its relationship with its franchisees. Both franchisor and franchisee must make it clear to the public (in general) and to customers, suppliers and others dealing with the franchisee (in particular) that the franchisee is not a representative of the franchisor but acting on his own.

However, could it be argued that, by virtue of common advertising, signage, mode of operation, manner in which the product/services are delivered to customers etc., by obeying the directions and instructions and by virtue of the controls imposed by the franchisor on the franchisee, the franchisee is so deprived of independence that he effectively becomes a partner or representative, if not the agent or employee, of his franchisor?

It was determined as far back as 1885 that the directions given by A (franchisor) to an independent contractor B (franchisee) who is engaged by A to carry out work will not generally give A such control over B as to make A liable for B's acts and defaults, provided that such directions do not amount to instructions as to the *manner* in which such work is to be done. So if the franchisor of a quick print operation shows a franchisee how to run a quick printing business but not the manner in which the franchisee does the printing for customers, it is unlikely to be held responsible for its franchisee's defaults unless, of course, the franchisor's system is defective.

The theory that a franchisee is an agent of his franchisor may appear attractive to a customer of a franchisee who is contemplating suing the franchisor, because of the emphasis it places upon the control exercised by the franchisor. However, upon close examination, it is evident that this theory is unlikely to apply to a franchisor–franchisee relationship. This is not only because the franchisee cannot be said to be working for the franchisor, but also because the definition of an independent contractor can, by implication, be said to require a person who already has special skills of his own which are required in the performance of the work that he is engaged to do. Most franchisees, meanwhile, bring with them few if any skills in conducting the franchised business. The necessary skill and knowledge is imparted to the franchisee in training by the franchisor. This is one of the primary factors which distinguishes a franchisor–franchisee relationship from that of a principal and agent or supplier and distributor, or indeed possibly employer and employee.

It would seem therefore that if a franchisor wants to avoid the creation of an unintended agency (and therefore liability for the acts, omissions or defaults of its franchisees), it has to be very careful about the structure of its concept and about the sort of message it delivers to the public about its relationship with its franchisees.

The above narrative is not intended to be nor should it be taken as legal advice. Its purpose is to draw the attention of the reader to the matter discussed. A franchisor must take legal advice to determine the true position in law as it applies to its concept and franchise structure.

CHAPTER 35

Co-Branding

"A way for franchisees to increase their turnover on the coattails of others?"

Franchising, like any other business activity, continues to evolve. Over the last few years there have been a number of advances within business format franchising. One major development has been the evolution of the concept of co-branding, sometimes referred to as dual branding when the operation involves only two concepts.

Franchisors are always looking at ways to increase the turnover of their franchisees. A franchisor will sometimes receive an offer to 'team up' with another franchisor who is in a similar (not the same) line of business, but whose business is not as successful.

The offer is not for the more successful franchisor to buy out the less successful one, nor to merge the two businesses. The idea put forward is for both of them to do some sort of joint venture whereby their respective franchisees, in addition to selling their own products/services, would also sell the other franchisor's products/services under the other franchisor's brand.

By way of illustration, let us assume there are two franchises: one selling pizzas and the other ice cream. The pizza franchise is more successful than the ice cream one. The proposal calls for the pizza franchisees to be allowed to also sell ice cream under the ice cream franchisor's brand and, sometimes, vice versa. At first glance, the idea has appeal: the two brands side by side feeding off each other's customers. What the ice cream franchisor is suggesting is a co-branding operation and there are indeed advantages, but the parties should give full and careful consideration to some of the potential pitfalls.

The concept being discussed here is different from the concept of concessions in the retail sector, for example where a cosmetics company occupies space within a department store or a food court. In the case of a concession, owners of various businesses operate from the same location under their own brand, franchised or otherwise. Each operation, therefore, trades under its own brand but shares with the others the same trading location and amenities such as lighting, heating and opening hours. Generally speaking, in the case of concessions, the one thing which all traders have in common (apart from sharing premises etc.) is that they have similar business concepts, e.g. cosmetics or fashion wear.

Co-branding is difficult to define precisely, partly because of its complexity in some cases and partly because any attempt at precise definition would have the effect of limiting the flexible nature of the concept, which embraces a wide range of possible structures and relationships.

Essentially, co-branding involves the juxtaposition of two or more different brands, each providing different goods or services and each of which has a different owner. At its most basic, the sale of Coca-Cola at a McDonald's outlet can be said to be a co-branding operation. The nature of the relationship between the different owners of the brands may be limited; it may be consensual but not contractual; it may be a franchisor–franchisee relationship or some simple or complex form of joint venture.

In business format franchising, a distinction also needs to be made between the different owners of the brands involved and the owner of the operator of the co-branded business.

Co-branding comes in all shapes and sizes. For example, co-branding operations may exist under one roof at a single location, generally referred to as a 'shop within a shop'. A good example of this would be a quick printing operation stationed within a stationery/office supplies shop. Co-branding operations may alternatively exist side by side, as in a one-stop shop adjoining a petrol station, where both operations (which may or may not be commonly owned) share facilities such as parking.

The degree of integration may also vary, with some co-branded operations being partly integrated while others may be fully integrated. An example of a partly integrated co-branded operation would be a petrol station which contains within its shop a bakery product merchandiser such as Dunkin' Donuts. In such a case, the co-branded operation would share personnel, storage space etc.

A fully integrated co-branded operation is one where, for example, a restaurant chain is integrated within another concept. A TGI Fridays restaurant concept within a Holiday Inn hotel would amount to a fully integrated co-branding operation if not only personnel, storage space etc. are shared but also food preparation facilities, telephone reservation systems etc.

A very simple form of co-branding which is now commonplace but was introduced some years ago is the issue by various institutions of credit cards under the MasterCard or Visa brand. A number of clubs, educational institutions and others issue their own credit cards, and one therefore sees credit cards displaying both the Visa or MasterCard symbol and the trade mark of the issuing institution.

In some cases, single brand operations evolve into co-branded operations where no formal contractual relationship exists between the brand owners but the evolution takes place by tacit understanding. An example of such a concept would be certain music systems in certain makes of cars.

Particular care needs to be taken by brand owners when considering co-branding in terms of franchising. Given that the fundamental nature of franchising requires a uniform system and marketing image, one needs to guard against the possibility of increasing encroachment on one branded system by another brand. Co-branding also has a tendency to throw into disarray the traditional justification of restricting franchisees from being involved in other businesses. Each brand owner will be concerned to ensure that its particular brand is adequately protected and that each receives the anticipated benefits from being associated with the other. It is for this reason that any co-branding is best done if planned and contractually secured by the brand owners, rather than developing casually.

Although co-branding involves two or more distinct brands, it does not necessarily follow that the owners of the trading unit must also be the owners of one of the brands involved. One could have two individually branded but different business concepts being operated under one roof by someone who owns neither brand, as in the case of a convenience store concept within which is placed a dry cleaning operation. In these circumstances it would be usual for the franchisor of the convenience store concept to have a contractual arrangement with the owner of the dry cleaning brand under which the franchisor of the convenience store concept is granted the right to sublicense the dry cleaning brand to its franchisee. Under such an arrangement there will be no contractual relationship between the convenience store franchisee and the owner of the dry cleaning brand. Alternatively, the franchisor of the convenience store concept may consent to its franchisee acquiring a dry cleaning franchise directly from the owner of the dry cleaning brand. In a co-branding exercise such as this, the convenience store would sometimes be referred to as the 'host' and the dry cleaning concept as the 'guest'.

Reasons for Co-Branding

So, what compelling reasons persuade owners of different brands to engage in a co-branding exercise?

The reasons for co-branding are, in many cases, obvious. Where prime locations are scarce, it makes sense for two or more companies whose brands are compatible and whose products complement each other, as in the case of, say, hamburgers and ice cream, to get together and share space which might prove to be too large for only one concept. In these circumstances, failure to co-brand may mean the opportunity to sell their products from that location is lost. By the same token, entering into a co-branding arrangement may also serve a franchisee well in that it would enable the franchisee to make efficient and profitable use of surplus space.

Cost savings are, of course, an obvious advantage that comes from shared space, facilities and operating costs. Another advantage is that by choosing a co-branding partner carefully, the operator of a business may benefit from increased revenue. This is one of the arguments which has been advanced for siting sub-post offices or pharmacies in convenience stores, but the oft-cited example of National Lottery outlets in retail premises is more akin to the granting of concessions than co-branding. Furthermore, co-branding may help a business to become more competitive by offering a wider range of goods or services instead of operating under a single brand.

Finally, co-branding is a means by which a single brand business can be further developed. A restauranteur serving only lunch and dinner, wishing to expand to serving breakfast, may find it more sensible to form an alliance with an established breakfast operation than to develop its own menu, thus benefiting from the experience and brand recognition of its co-branding partner.

Preparing for Co-Branding

Anyone proposing to enter into a co-branding operation needs to give careful consideration to the legal and operational issues involved before making a commitment. Regard has to be had, of course, to ensuring that one's intellectual property is protected and one's own brand is not cannibalised or its reputation eroded. The contractual issues may be quite complicated, depending on how many brands are to be the subject of a co-branding operation, whether they have a common owner or separate owners and whether the trading outlet is franchised or company-owned.

Careful consideration also needs to be given to setting out the rules of operation. Some of the most obvious issues which spring to mind are:

- Exterior cleaning.
- Repair and maintenance of premises.
- Hours of operation.
- Storage areas.
- Product processing, preparation and packaging areas.
- Whether the premises should be divided into exclusive retail areas for each brand.
- Rules relating to the serving of customers and taking of payment.
- Human resources issues.
- Insurance issues.
- Accounting and reporting procedures, particularly where separate licence fees are to be paid by the operator of the business to different owners of the brands.
- Advertising, marketing and promotion of the business.
- Special provisions relating to the occupation of the premises and landlords' requirements.

Finally, the more complex the business, the more complicated will be issues surrounding termination.

Consideration needs to be given to what happens in the event that a cobranding venture has to cease for whatever reason. What, for example, is to happen if a franchisee, operating a co-branding business, is in breach of an agreement relating to one of the brands but not the other, or if a franchisee wishes to sell his business and his purchaser is acceptable to one brand owner but not to another?

What is clear is that the concept of co-branding operations has gained wide acceptance. The success enjoyed by food courts is testament to the fact that if carefully thought out and implemented, co-branding can be a powerful marketing force, benefiting not only the owner-operator of the trading unit and the owners of the brands involved, but also the consumer.

In a Nutshell

Reasons for co-branding:

- Access to locations.
- Cost savings.
- Shared facilities.
- Increased turnover – the customer of one brand driving business to the other.
- Raising of profile.

Disadvantages:

- Complexity.
- Restrictions on operation.
- Vulnerability to substandard partner.
- Reliance on franchisee commitment to the partner brand: 'If I wanted to sell ice cream, I'd have bought an ice cream franchise.'
- Complications on termination.

CHAPTER 36

The Problems of Regional Master Franchising

"A case of too many cooks spoiling the broth?"

One of the most common methods of franchising internationally is by means of national master franchising (see Chapter 38). This involves the grant of franchise rights by a franchisor directly to a franchisee in another country. These rights include the right for the franchisee to own and to operate his own franchised outlets and for him to grant franchises to others to do so also, as shown in Diagram AA. For example, under such an arrangement, the UK franchisor grants a national master franchise for Germany to someone who will become the national franchisor in Germany and who will have his own franchisees in Germany.

The method of regional master franchising, whilst sharing many of the features to be found in national master franchising, differs from it in that, instead of granting a single entity the right to franchise in the whole country, the franchisor grants the right to franchise within only a part of a country to different entities. Thus a regional master franchisee receives franchise rights for only a region in a country.

In the UK, these regions would be areas such as the Midlands, the South East and South West of England, Wales, Northern Ireland and Scotland. As shown in Diagram AB, each regional master franchisee would have the right to open his own company-owned units and sub-franchise to individual franchisees in his territory.

The Appeal of Regional Master Franchising

Increasingly, franchisors have found that they are able to spread the risk of possible failure and increase their revenues by engaging in regional (as opposed to national) master franchising.

The rationale of the franchisors is that by adopting a regional master franchise structure they would be able to expand and penetrate the market much more quickly than by selling individual franchises themselves. Also, in the case of international franchising, they would not have to rely on one national master franchisee to sell individual franchises.

The Problems of Regional Master Franchising

Some franchisors believe that by selling a number of regional master franchises they would take in more money by way of initial franchise fees than by selling one master franchise for the whole of the country. Unlike the sale of individual unit franchises, the sales of regional master franchises are negotiable and there is nothing unethical about either party driving a hard bargain.

These franchisors work on the principle that if they were to divide the UK into, say, 10 regions and sell a regional master franchise for an up-front fee of £100,000 for each region, they would make a total of £1 million for the country. If, on the other hand, they tried to sell a conventional national master franchise, it is highly unlikely that anyone would be prepared to pay £1 million up front.

A regional master franchise structure therefore appears to make sense as a commercial proposition and, although at first sight the £1 million looks like a high figure, on closer examination it does not appear that the franchisor would be making excessive profits at the expense of its regional master franchisees. A fee of £100,000 for the exclusive rights to the Midlands, for example, does not look unreasonable for a territory in which the regional master franchisee could sell individual franchises for, say, around £20,000 each. He would only need to sell five single unit franchises to recoup his original investment.

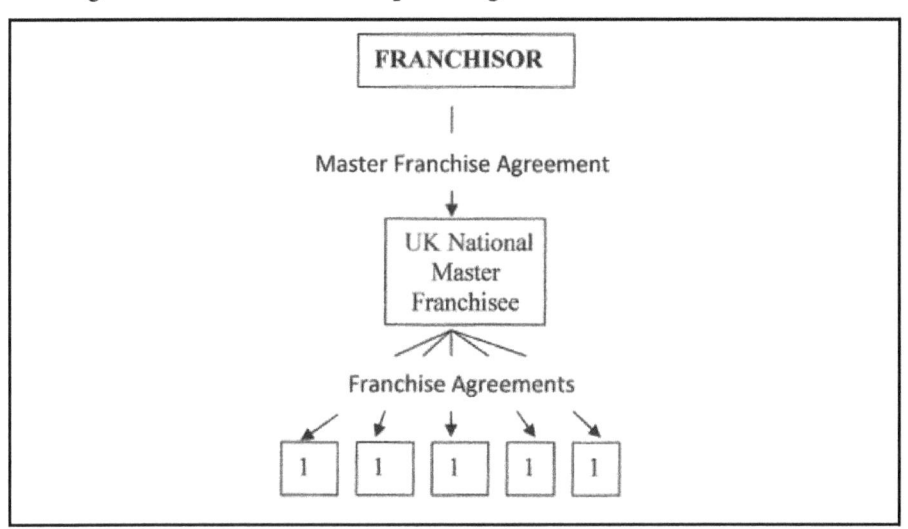

1 = Individual franchised units, or units owned and operated by the master franchisee

Diagram AA: Conventional master franchise structure

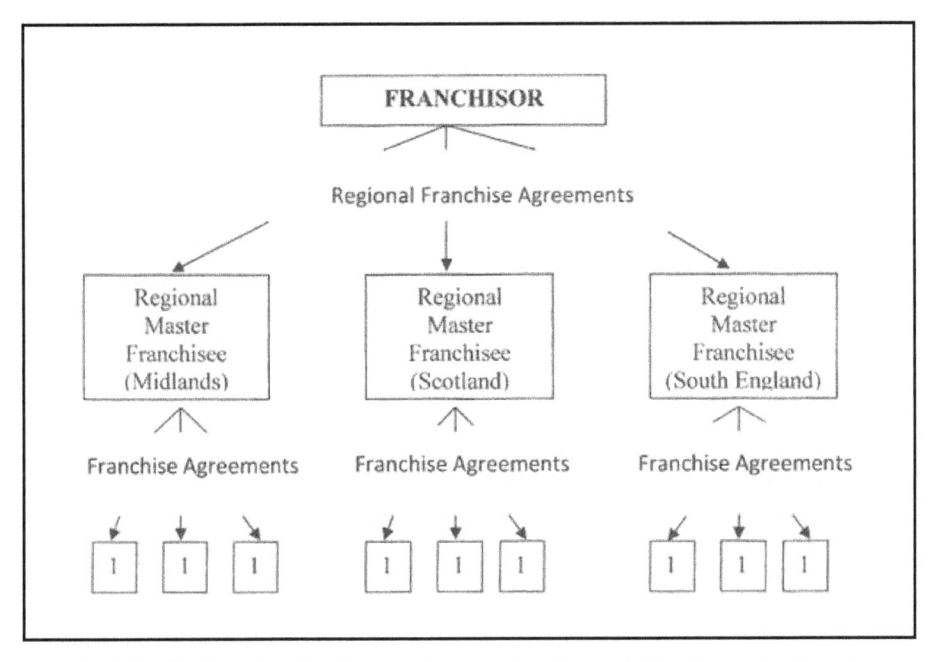

```
                        FRANCHISOR
                           │
              Regional Franchise Agreements
        ┌──────────────────┼──────────────────┐
        ▼                  ▼                  ▼
    Regional           Regional           Regional
    Master             Master             Master
    Franchisee         Franchisee         Franchisee
    (Midlands)         (Scotland)         (South England)
        ↑                  ↑                  ↑
  Franchise Agreements  Franchise Agreements  Franchise Agreements
   [1] [1] [1]          [1] [1] [1]          [1] [1] [1]
```

1 = Individual franchised units, or units owned and operated by the regional master franchisee

Diagram AB: Regional master franchise structure

Difficulties in Regional Master Franchising

However, there are some inherent problems with a regional master franchise structure. As in any complex transaction, the disadvantages are not always apparent at the outset. Much, of course, depends on the nature of the franchise and the type of business, but the following difficulties are likely to be encountered in most systems.

Problem of Control

The most obvious problem is the loss of control that would be felt by the franchisor. With a conventional national master franchise agreement (Diagram AA), the franchisor only has to deal with one national master franchisee, who in turn controls the whole of the franchised network in the country concerned.

The Problems of Regional Master Franchising

Under a regional master franchise agreement, the franchisor would have not one but several regional master franchisees to control and deal with on an ongoing basis and would have to devote considerable management resources to advising, supporting and motivating each of them.

This could prove to be particularly costly if the franchisor is franchising overseas. It may be forced to open an office in the foreign country. This would negate one of the basic advantages of national master franchising. If the franchisor has to have an office presence there, it might be more attractive to sell individual unit franchises directly to the unit franchisees in that country itself and take the initial franchise fees from the individual franchisees.

Inconsistency

Another problem is that there would be more than one entity in the country controlling the different regional groups of individual franchisees. Some regional master franchisees will be better at running their business and at controlling their individual unit franchisees than others. This will lead to a lack of consistency and uniformity across the national franchised network. In a network of 10 regional master franchisees, each with his own corps of individual unit franchisees, something is bound to get lost in the translation.

The focus of training, for example, provided by one regional master franchisee to his individual unit franchisees may differ from that of his colleagues in the adjoining regions. One may place greater emphasis on the quality of his franchisees' work, whilst another may feel that it would be more profitable to concentrate on the speed with which his franchisees get the job done. End users would therefore find that the service offered by a business which, on the face of it, looks to be one national network, would in fact differ from one franchised unit in one region to another elsewhere. This runs contrary to the very essence of franchising – uniformity of service and quality over the whole of the network – and it would have a serious detrimental effect on the value of the system and the individual businesses of all those involved in it.

Differing Standards

Usually, a national master franchisee stands in the shoes of the parent franchisor – the master franchisor. For example, the Burger King franchise in the UK is operated by a national master franchisee of the USA franchisor. However, for all intents and purposes, the UK company which grants individual unit Burger King franchises is considered to be the Burger King franchisor in the UK. Under a multiple regional master franchise arrangement there would be more than one franchisor in the UK of the same concept and brand. It is easy to see why this could cause problems.

It has always been accepted that a franchise network is only as strong as its weakest franchisee. In a multiple regional franchisee arrangement, one bad regional franchisee could seriously affect the others and, in turn, the individual franchisees of the whole network throughout the country.

A particular regional master franchisee who is having problems in achieving his business plan or development schedule (which is likely to form a key part of the deal with the franchisor) may be forced to drop his standards and recruit franchisees of a calibre that would not be acceptable to the other regional master franchisees, nor, indeed, to the parent franchisor itself. The result would, of course, be a gradual (or even an accelerated) deterioration in the franchised network within a particular area of the country, with predictable consequences for the other regions.

When one looks at developing a franchised network and the uniformity of that network's provision of products or services to customers, the problems become more complicated. For example, it is generally accepted practice (and was a requirement of the European Commission's franchise block exemption regulation) that franchisees honour guarantees to consumers, irrespective of which particular franchisee provided the product or service. If all franchisees are under the control of one franchisor, this is relatively easy to manage. What happens, however, in circumstances where they are all perceived to be members of the same franchised network, but where control is exercised regionally by different regional master franchisees? If one particular regional master franchisee's network is substandard, how long will the franchisees of the other regional master franchisees be happy to continue honouring the guarantees issued by those in the substandard region?

The Problems of Regional Master Franchising

Advertising Levy

One of the big advantages of franchising is that it enables the franchisor to advertise and market the franchisees' businesses on a scale which would not be available to them if they were independent small businesses. Under normal franchising arrangements, franchisees are required to make a contribution to the franchisor towards the costs of advertising, marketing and promoting the network.

Under a regional master franchisee arrangement, if the parent franchisor is foreign, and if the system is to work properly, the advertising situation becomes fairly complicated.

Either all franchisees would be required to make their contributions directly to the foreign franchisor, which would then undertake all advertising and marketing from its own country overseas (an added burden on the foreign franchisor which it would not have to carry had it chosen the traditional national master franchising route), or alternatively contributions would be paid by the individual unit franchisees to their regional master franchisee. All the regional master franchisees would then have to have some mechanism for co-ordinating advertising, marketing and promotions, under circumstances in which each would be anxious to ensure that he got at least his fair share of the resulting benefit.

Less Independence

At best, all regional master franchisees would lose a degree of independence in how they each run their business. Furthermore, they may not be able to respond in the way in which they would wish to the particular demands of their local market, which might be different from those of the other regional master franchisees.

A Final Note

These are some of the problems which need to be borne in mind by those considering regional master franchising, but that does not mean that one should drop all plans for such a scheme.

Regional master franchising is used very successfully in the USA, although it should be noted that the USA is a vast country. Some of the problems outlined above do not necessarily apply in large countries like the USA, Canada or Australia but do apply in geographically small countries like the United Kingdom. For example, a blunder by a regional master franchisee in New York may not have any effect on a regional master franchisee two thousand miles away in California, but the distance between Birmingham and London is not so great.

Prospective regional master franchisees need to be reminded that they will not own any of the intellectual property (in the form of trade marks, know-how, copyright, the brand name etc.) in the franchise concerned, which will remain vested in the parent franchisor.

In Conclusion

Regional master franchising is fraught with difficulties but, in the right circumstances and with a carefully worked-out structure, such arrangements can and have been made to work.

However, very careful consideration needs to be given to such schemes, and their potential challenges and risks should be fully understood and accepted at the outset. Expert professional franchise advice is imperative for anyone contemplating this route.

CHAPTER 37

Franchisors as Landlords

"A franchisor with two hats."

Those involved in retailing will know the importance of the right location for their business. The acquisition of the right property is therefore crucial.

Selecting the right location is not easy and acquiring the right property even less so. Perhaps it is stating the obvious, but, recessions apart, retail property in this country is scarce. Prime positions (high streets) are even more scarce. Generally speaking, such properties are owned by institutional or similar landlords who, to a large extent, can afford to be selective in their tenants because:

1. The owner is reasonably financially sound and not desperate to obtain an income.

2. There will be no shortage of high street retailers anxious to secure a lease.

Such a landlord is more inclined to take a medium-term or long-term view rather than a short-term view, because the focus of the property owner's thinking is the effect that granting a lease will have on the investment value of his property. It does not necessarily follow (although of course it does help) that the higher the rental income, the higher the freehold value of the property. In the investment property market, the strength of the tenant's covenant (i.e. his ability to pay the market rent promptly and to comply with the conditions in his lease without giving the landlord a headache) and the location and condition of the property are as relevant to the freeholder as the actual rental income.

The Difficulty of Obtaining Leases as a Franchisee

Given the high demand for the right property, a small businessman (in this case a franchisee) is unlikely to obtain a lease of a property, because he just cannot compete with established retailers in terms of his personal promise to be a good tenant ('covenant') and, sometimes, the rent he can afford.

Therefore, one will usually find in practice that the franchisor, being an established company with a proven track record, will stand a better chance of acquiring the desired property than the franchisee. The effect of this is that a landlord will only grant a lease to the franchisor, because the franchisor can offer the calibre of covenant sought by the landlord to maximise his investment value.

For prime property, it is therefore likely that the decision as to whether or not to get involved in the property will be made for the franchisor by the landlord. For properties in secondary locations it is quite likely that a franchisor will not become involved in the property at all, and a landlord will grant a lease directly to the franchisee.

It is possible for a franchisor to negotiate the grant of a lease by a landlord directly to a franchisee with the franchisor acting as guarantor, but clearly, from the franchisor's point of view, this approach has little to recommend it. In such a situation the franchisor will inherit all the disadvantages of being a tenant without any of the advantages. The franchisor could also find itself liable for obligations of which it was unaware, although the close relationship between the franchisor and the franchisee reduces the chance that these will arise.

Disadvantages for the Franchisor

Briefly, the main disadvantage to the franchisor of being involved in the property of a franchisee is that the franchisor will incur property obligations as a tenant. In cases where a franchisor gives a guarantee, although it will not be directly involved, it will not have any direct control over the property either, nor over what goes on under the terms of the franchisee's lease which it will be guaranteeing.

At the end of the day, if there has been an error of judgement in the choice of location or if for any reason the franchisee fails to make a success of the business being operated from the site, the franchisee may walk away, leaving the franchisor to pick up the pieces. It is highly unlikely that a franchisor will sue a franchisee who is more than likely to be a man of straw.

Advantages for the Franchisor

Apart from being able to secure a site for a franchisee, the franchisor may also enjoy other advantages if it chooses to get involved in its franchisee's property.

Profit Rental

Effectively acting as a franchisee's landlord can give the franchisor a means of deriving profit from the franchisee's operation. This can be achieved by the simple device of letting at a profit rental. The profit rent does require a special mention because in practice it can cause problems to landlords who do not generally allow underletting other than at current market rent. Some, however, do not object because they intend, sometimes successfully, to use the profit rent to their own advantage on rent review.

Franchisees who are asked for a profit rental are advised to consider all the implications very carefully. Much, of course, depends upon how large the profit is. Generally speaking, it is considered unethical for a franchisor to take from its franchisee anything in excess of the market rent. Usually any profit element is expressed as a flat fee (say, approximately £250 per annum) or a percentage (anything up to 2%) of the rent under the franchisee's lease, which should be the same as the rent under the franchisor's lease. In return for this 'profit rental' the franchisor undertakes to deal with the superior landlords on behalf of the franchisee in connection with various matters arising under the lease, such as the repairing and decorating obligations of the tenant, and in negotiating rent reviews to the best advantage of the franchisee.

In any circumstances where a franchisee is offered premises for a sum or sums in addition to the market rent, he will tend to proceed cautiously and investigate thoroughly.

Control

Getting involved in a franchisee's premises gives the franchisor control over the premises in question. Usually the franchisor will, on termination, be able to force the franchisee to change the shop fittings etc. so that the premises no longer reflect their former public and marketing image. If the franchise agreement is well drafted, the franchisor may also be able to prevent a former franchisee from conducting an identical or similar business from those premises.

However, that may not be sufficient for a franchisor. After all, a franchisee cannot be prevented from disposing of his lease to a third party who may well be a competitor. If this should happen the franchisor will suffer financial loss.

There are various schemes which a franchisor can use to ensure that upon the termination of the franchise, the franchisor is able to regain possession of the premises, eliminating delay and consequently financial loss to the franchisor in setting up alternative premises. Once it has regained possession of the premises, the franchisor can put in a manager or another franchisee and thereby continue the franchise's presence in the marketplace.

Given our present landlord and tenant legislation and the security of tenure which most franchisees enjoy, such schemes tend to be complicated.

If the principal aim for the franchisor becoming involved in its franchisee's property is to control the premises, there are other ways in which the franchisor can achieve the same result without becoming the franchisee's landlord. The reader is advised to consult a solicitor specialising in franchise property schemes to explore this. Much depends upon the nature of the franchisor and the type of business being franchised when determining whether franchise property-related schemes are of any benefit to a franchisor.

Advantages for the Franchisee

The concept of the franchisor getting involved in its franchisee's property is not without merit in the eyes of the franchisee. In some cases it makes a particular franchise more attractive. After all, why should a franchisee who may never before have been in business on his own account – who feels he is taking enough risks already and who is to a large extent relying on his franchisor for his future success – commit himself to a ten-, fifteen- or maybe even twenty-year lease (with rent reviews) when he may only have a five- or seven-year franchise agreement, albeit with an option to renew it?

The franchisee will tend to take comfort in the fact that, if it does not work out for him, at least he can walk away from the whole business at the end of the term of his franchise rather than being left with an ongoing commitment in property terms. This is particularly relevant, of course, if the reason for the franchisee not wishing to renew his franchise agreement is the fact that the location is poor or over a number of years has declined in terms of trade. In such circumstances, a franchisee who holds the lease may see himself as being saddled with premises which may not be easy to dispose of, which in all probability will be subject to certain restrictions on use and which may well give the franchisor additional leverage against him when negotiating termination.

In Conclusion

Franchisees seldom have a choice of whether or not they are to become a tenant of the franchisor. In many cases, the franchise package includes a property package and the franchisee is asked to take or leave it. Some franchisors find that they are able to be more flexible in their approach by insisting on being their franchisees' landlord in some cases but not in others.

What is important is that franchisors should give due consideration to the problems of property ownership from both the franchisee's and the franchisor's point of view, and should establish some policy on the matter.

CHAPTER 38

Going International

> *" The right partner but wrong country: there is a chance you will succeed. The right country but wrong partner: there is a chance you will fail. "*

Franchisors would be ill-advised to franchise internationally until they have established themselves in their home market. This means:

1. That they are a successful franchisor domestically.

2. That they have established their operating standards, training and manuals in writing. This is a must for domestic franchising and is even more critical when attempting to communicate internationally. Prospective international franchisors can save a lot of future problems if they make sure that they have addressed this aspect thoroughly before even thinking about international operations.

3. That they have significantly commercially exploited their domestic market. It is always easier to be a success in one's home market than crossing borders, which creates new problems.

Once the franchise business has been established, what options are there for franchising internationally?

If a franchise has established its franchise business by granting individual unit franchises, the first and most obvious approach would seem to be to franchise individual franchise units in the foreign market.

However, wherever one expects to have multiple locations because of the market potential, one will discover two things:

1. The servicing (meaning continuous training and communication of know-how) is very difficult with individual franchisees in a foreign country.

2. The type of franchisee suitable for an individual franchised unit has a different degree of sophistication from one capable of running a national

network of franchisees ... so don't expect to easily convert one to the other at a later time.

International franchising can bring rich rewards, and not only financial rewards.

- McDonald's established the fast food category in most of the world.
- Denny's defined coffee shops in Japan.
- 7-Eleven redefined convenience stores for the Japanese market.

Being first can provide one with enormous advantages and great potential for growth, if one is in the right place, at the right time, with the right business proposition. The only way to ensure that one will be in the right place at the right time is to ask the right questions and get the right answers: the truth. The truth may not set one free, but it could help keep one solvent!

However, establishing a new business concept in a country is likely to be more costly, more time-consuming and more difficult in the early stages of development than one thinks.

There are a number of different ways in which an international franchise arrangement can be structured. Each has its advantages and drawbacks.

Direct Franchising

Direct franchising involves the grant of franchise rights by a franchisor directly to a franchisee in another country. Much depends on the size of the territory into which the franchisor is thinking of franchising. If a territory is capable of sustaining only one outlet (for example, Malta), the franchisor will usually grant a franchise agreement directly to the prospective franchisee. If the territory is capable of sustaining a number of outlets, there will usually be a two-tier arrangement: a development agreement between franchisor and franchisee (see 'Development Agreement', below) which will require the franchisee to own and open a number of outlets within a given time, and a franchise agreement under which he will be required to open each unit.

For the franchisor, there is no sharing of fees with anyone else. The franchisor gets the whole amount of the initial fee and the continuing franchise fees, and it has greater control over its franchisee because there is a direct relationship between franchisor and franchisee.

On the other hand, direct franchising requires the franchisor to expend greater financial and manpower resources, time and commitment. The franchisor may suffer from a lack of local market knowledge, will incur higher costs (travelling etc.), and may take longer to penetrate the local market. The franchisor will also have to overcome language and cultural difficulties and will incur obligations to the franchisee under the various franchise agreements in the same way as it would for its UK franchisees.

Advantages

- No sharing of franchise fees.
- Greater control over franchisees.
- Direct relationship between franchisor and franchisee.

Disadvantages

- Requires greater financial and human resources, time and commitment.
- Lack of local market knowledge.
- Higher costs incurred in establishing local presence, travelling etc.
- May take longer to penetrate local market.
- Differences of language, culture, customs and commercial practice to overcome.

Subsidiary

This involves the establishment by a franchisor of a subsidiary in another country. The subsidiary would then grant individual franchises in that country. The difference between direct franchising and going the subsidiary route is that in direct franchising the franchisor remains abroad, whereas in this case the franchisor has a local presence.

This approach requires a considerable commitment of both financial and staff resources. In addition, the franchisor will acquire local marketing know-how by hiring at least some foreign national staff, plus national advisors for advertising

Going International

and public relations. A prospective international franchisor will also need local legal and accounting advice on incorporation, tax and the usual 'conducting business' regulations.

Even though the risk is the highest using this approach due to one's increased exposure, the potential for success may also be the greatest because one can more closely direct the effort. As with a direct franchise, the franchisor will have a personal relationship with the franchisee and will retain total and direct control of the franchise system.

In the long run, this is probably the most profitable route. However, it will be more costly for the franchisor, the franchisor will have to comply with corporate and other local laws, and there may possibly be adverse tax consequences.

Advantages

- Personal relationship with franchisees.
- Total and direct control over franchise system.
- Probably the most profitable method in the long run.

Disadvantages

- More costly.
- Responsibility for legal compliance.
- Potential adverse tax consequences.

National Master Franchise

This is the most common route, and, experience shows, the least successful. One hears a great deal about the successes, but little is known or said about the failures.

National master franchising involves the grant, by a franchisor to a local business entity in another country, of franchise rights for the whole of that country. These rights include the right for the local business entity to operate its own outlets and to grant franchises to other local business entities. Under this arrangement, the person to whom the franchisor grants a master franchise will become the national franchisor and will have his own franchisees (Diagram AC).

Note that a national franchisee/franchisor is very different from a regional franchisee in one's domestic market who basically follows the franchisor's marketing programme. The difference lies in the responsibility that the foreign national franchisee/franchisor has to adapt the international franchisor's domestic market approach to his market. This adaption will not be limited to language changes, but may include different selling propositions more suited to the foreign market. A great deal is written about 'global marketing', but there is much that needs to be said with regard to making sure that the local marketing approach meets the local needs.

The national franchisee/franchisor also has the responsibility for sub-franchising within his territory, with all its inherent legal and marketing implications. This situation may be further complicated if his local legal advisor has little understanding of the franchised concept, perhaps believing it is some form of trade mark licensing.

It is important that a prospective international franchisor understands that these wider responsibilities imposed on its national franchisee will necessitate a lower continuing franchise fee rate than that paid by its domestic franchisees. The foreign franchisee/franchisor must be compensated for his higher costs, thereby making it possible for him to charge his sub-franchisees a similar continuing franchise fee to that the international franchisor charges in its home market, which is good, because information about fee levels tends to become common knowledge.

Going International

```
         FRANCHISOR
             ⇩
    MASTER FRANCHISE
        AGREEMENT
             ⇩
        NATIONAL
         MASTER
        FRANCHISE
        AGREEMENT

    UNIT FRANCHISE AGREEMENTS
        ☆ ☆ ☆ ☆ ☆

    ☆ = Individual franchised units
```

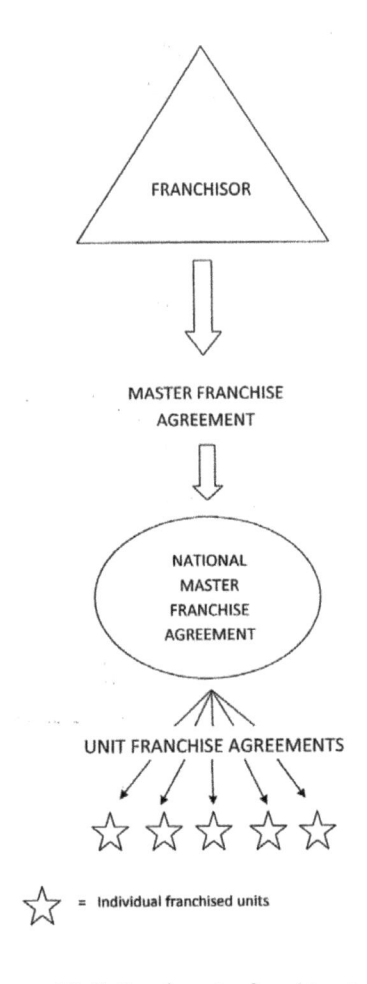

Diagram AC: National master franchise structure

The main advantages to the franchisor are that this method makes efficient use of someone else's financial and manpower resources, and it reduces the risk to the franchisor. Also, in theory, there should be a higher degree of success in adapting the franchisor's system to the local market due to the input of the local franchisee, enabling quicker penetration of the market.

The disadvantages to the franchisor are that it has less control over the unit franchisees and it has to share revenues; the continuing franchise fee (and possibly also the initial franchise fee) will have to be shared between the franchisor and the national master franchisee. Additionally, there are potentially greater risks to the franchisor's intellectual property due to lax control or misuse by the national master franchisee. It is also a relatively complicated transaction and poses problems on termination (for example, what is to happen to the franchisees of the national master franchisee?).

Finally, it is not easy to select the right local partner.

Advantages

- Efficient use of someone else's financial and human resources.
- Lower risk.
- Quicker penetration of local market.
- Access to local know-how.
- Higher degree of success in adapting the system to the local market due to input by local franchisee.
- Less hand-holding and nose-wiping.

Disadvantages

- Less control over individual unit franchisees.
- Sharing of revenues.
- Potential risk to franchisor's intellectual property.
- More complicated transaction.
- Problems on termination.
- Difficulty in selecting the right local partner.

Regional Master Franchise

The principles of international regional master franchising are similar to those of domestic regional franchising discussed in Chapter 36.

Going International

Diagram AD (below) shows the structure commonly used in international regional master franchising, giving the example of a UK franchisor franchising into the USA.

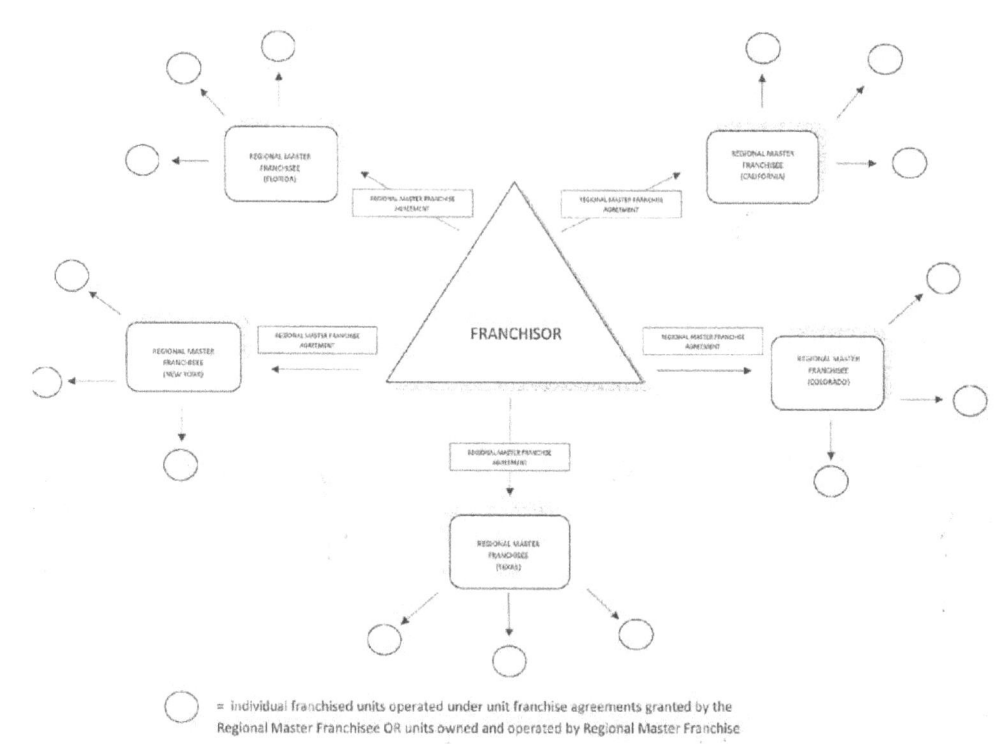

Diagram AD: International regional master franchise structure

Development Agreement

This involves granting a franchisee the right to roll out company-owned franchised units to be managed by managers. The franchisee would have no rights to sub-franchise.

Advantages

- Faster growth.
- Low capital requirement.

- Less administration and management.
- Scope for successful franchisee to grow.

Disadvantages
- Difficulty in motivating franchisee.
- May need to pay finder's fee to recruit a suitable partner.
- Controlling franchisee more difficult than controlling individual unit franchisees or managers.

Joint Venture

In this scenario, a franchisor establishes a joint venture with a local business entity. A master franchise is then granted to the joint venture, which becomes the national franchisor. This is a combination of forming one's own foreign subsidiary and granting a master franchise to a foreign partner.

This approach gives one more control, but will also require greater human and financial resources than granting master franchise rights to a foreign partner. It is also important not to be too confident about the degree of control, because it diminishes in relation to the distance from one's home base.

The net effect is that the degree of risk for a franchisor in a joint venture is greater than if it has its own foreign subsidiary, but the degree of commitment may be smaller, thus resulting in less financial exposure.

As Jan Hartmann of Ziebart (Appendix E (i)) said at a conference:

> *We used this approach in Japan, but 10 years later we ended up buying out our foreign partners in order to get the control we needed to institute the marketing programs necessary to succeed in such a changing market.*

In a joint venture there is a closer working relationship with the local partner, and therefore much more about the local partner is revealed during the negotiation process, and there will possibly be a higher return to the franchisor because it shares the profit from the joint venture operations as well as the franchise from the national master franchise agreement.

The downside is that this will require an initial capital outlay from the franchisor and the franchisor runs the risk of financial losses.

One way to ameliorate the initial capital outlay required by the joint venture company could be to make the franchisor's share of the contribution by way of waiving or reducing its initial master franchise fee to the joint venture company, with the joint venture partner making its share of the contribution in hard cash.

Whatever the legal arrangements, in all probability, the *de facto* control will be with the local partner and any termination will be complicated by the fact that, apart from the franchise arrangements, the joint venture may also have to be unravelled.

Advantages

- Closer working relationship with a local partner.
- More about local partner revealed during negotiation process.
- Possibly higher return due to profit share from joint venture operation as well as franchise fees from individual unit franchisees.

Disadvantages

- Initial capital outlay.
- Risk of financial loss.
- De facto control will usually be with local partner.
- Problems on termination.

Turnkey Franchising

Under this system, a franchisor establishes a local subsidiary and this subsidiary opens its own outlets. The franchisor later sells the whole subsidiary, including the outlets, to a local business entity and grants that entity a national master franchise. In this way the local business entity becomes the national franchisor of a network which has already been established and which it can expand further by increasing the number of company-owned outlets and/or by selling franchises.

Foreign Buy-Back

This usually applies to a mature franchisor who, after entering a foreign market via some form of franchising, buys out the local business entity and then runs the local franchised network as its own outlets. This is obviously not an option which is available to a new international franchisor but is something which may be considered by an established company in certain circumstances.

Points to Consider

Before embarking on any form of international franchising, a franchisor needs to do its homework thoroughly.

The franchisor needs to go to great lengths to ensure the establishment of the foreign franchisee as an independent contractor, and to ensure that the franchisee has no power to bind the franchisor and is not its agent, partner or employee. The trap of not taking local law seriously and of basing decisions on assumptions should be avoided.

It is important to examine what the attitude of the government of the relevant country is towards franchising and to the import of know-how and trade secrets.

Review local law in relation to the following:

Competition

Local competition laws should not be ignored. In the US they are such an important factor as to almost overwhelm franchise agreements.

Intellectual Property

In some countries, one needs to have *used* a trade mark for a specified period before one can obtain registration. In other countries one needs to use a trade mark for which registration has been granted within a specified period, failing which the registration will be lost.

Steps must be taken to protect trade marks before the first steps are taken to go international. Success breeds imitators.

Going International

One's trade mark should be registered in every country one is considering entering. Otherwise one may find oneself buying back one's own mark from a local entrepreneur.

Here's a question: will one's trade mark have initial, widespread consumer recognition and marketing impact, or will one have to reinvest locally in building an effective consumer image and franchise? KFC (Kentucky Fried Chicken) was known as PFK (Poulet Frit Kentucky) in France.

Maury C Roe, vice president of the Coca-Cola Company, said when addressing a meeting of the International Franchise Association in Washington DC in 1985:

> Back in 1928, when Coca-Cola was introduced in China, it became obvious that the trade mark had to be transliterated into Chinese characters. Out of something like 40 thousand characters, there were more than 200 that would approximate the sounds of the four syllables 'Coca-Cola'.

> While our lawyers and language specialists were wrestling with the problem... trying to come up with characters that not only sounded right, but which also conveyed a proper meaning... some of our customers – Chinese shopkeepers – were also working on the problem.

> One of their home-made signs sounded okay but the Chinese characters actually translated to 'bite the wax tadpole.' Not exactly the image we had in mind!

> Today, of course, the Chinese idiograph for Coca-Cola translates roughly to... 'permit the mouth to rejoice.' A real improvement!

> The point, though, is to be careful with your trade mark. It's a major business asset, and you must be able to protect it.

Trade Name

Remember that this is not necessarily the same as a trade mark, and be aware of a literal translation of a trade name into a foreign language.

Copyright

Methods and effectiveness of copyright protection in the various jurisdictions into which one intends to expand should be explored.

Design Rights

Secure the necessary legal protection.

Translations

Appropriate steps need to be taken to ensure that copyright in any translations into the language of the relevant country vests in you and not in the translator or your franchisee.

Ownership

Take steps to secure your ownership of the following:

- Domain name.
- Telephone numbers.
- Corporate name.
- Patents.

Corporate Laws

Apart from the taxation implications, consider local corporate laws to see whether some form of incorporation is necessary or desirable.

Special Franchise Laws

Check carefully to ensure that you comply fully with such disclosure, registration and/or franchise relationship laws as may apply.

Special Industry Laws

Investigate to see whether the relevant country has any laws which concern or affect the type of operation in which you are proposing to engage.

Going International

Property Law

Laws affecting freehold and leasehold property vary from country to country. What may be permissible in one country may not be in another.

Contract Law

The law of contract will, of course, differ from country to country. Take note of different legal systems: the common law system, the civil law system. Even where the same systems apply, there may be different legislative approaches which lead to differences in the legal requirements. These have to be considered and taken into account.

Planning Law

Careful investigation has to be made to discover any restrictions on the use to which premises can be put, building requirements, building regulations etc. which may affect the proposed scheme.

Employment Law

There is a wide variation in employment law, and a wide range of add-on costs on employers, depending upon the degree of social security available in the foreign jurisdiction.

In several countries special rules govern contracts where agents qualify as 'employees' or more generally where agents are assimilated to the status of employees.

In 2016, McDonald's faced the question of whether it could be considered to employ workers at its franchise restaurants:

> McDonald's Corp has agreed to pay $3.75 million to settle a lawsuit claiming it was liable for labor law violations by a California franchisee, marking what lawyers said was the first time the company has settled legal claims by a group of U.S. workers at one of its franchises . . .
>
> The settlement, which must be approved by a federal judge, comes as McDonald's faces claims before two U.S. agencies that it is a "joint employer" of workers

at franchise restaurants, a designation that could make the company liable for legal violations by franchisees and require that it bargain with workers who unionize ...

The 2014 lawsuit claimed McDonald's and the franchisee, Smith Family LP, violated California law by failing to pay overtime, keep accurate pay records and reimburse workers for time spent cleaning uniforms. The franchisee previously settled the claims for $700,000.

[In 2015], a judge ruled that McDonald's was not the plaintiffs' joint employer under federal and state laws. But he said the company could still be held liable if the workers believed McDonald's was their employer. (Wiessner, 2016)

Exchange Controls

Some countries impose restrictions on the import and export of currency. There may be a requirement that consent is given to inward investment only on certain conditions. Assess the risk of any exchange rate movement in an unfavourable direction.

Taxation

The taxation effects on the franchise scheme have to be considered. There may be local sales taxes to bear in mind and certainly, in operating the pilot scheme, care has to be taken to ensure that the effect of local tax laws on the scheme is fully taken into account.

With regard to international tax, one should commence by investigating whether double taxation agreements exist between the UK and the relevant country, to determine its effect.

Customs and Excise Duties

When considering the cost of importing material and equipment, one must take into account, in addition to shipping costs, any excise or other duties which may be levied on them in the relevant country.

Import/Export Controls

Some territories have restrictions on what may be imported or exported, and also require compliance with certain standards. Certain countries impose quotas limiting how much can be imported from other specific countries.

Restrictions on Payment of Royalties

In some countries, usually coupled with exchange control requirements, there can be limits imposed on the rate of royalties which can be paid to a foreign franchisor.

In Summary

1. **Acquire the different skills and resources** which are required from those in one's own country depending on the type of arrangement envisaged (national, regional, master, developer, franchisor).

2. **Consider the level of initial fees.**

    - Be realistic about the initial fee to be charged. Justify the level and be sensible. Ask too much up front by way of an initial franchise fee and the franchisee will be starved of much-needed capital to establish the franchise and grow the business.

    - Budget for low income in the early years. During the first two to three years of the foreign partner's operation he will have few units and low turnover, so expect little or no return on investment.

    - Don't underestimate the initial expenditure.

3. **Be realistic about imposing performance targets.**

4. **Protect all intellectual property** at the earliest stage possible.

5. **Get to grips with legal compliance** at an early stage.

    - Disclosure/registration.

    - Cooling-off periods.

    - Codes of conduct (voluntary/mandatory).

6. **Take language problems and definitions seriously.** Be clear and take care to avoid ambiguity. When granting rights to a country or territory, for example, accurately defining that country or territory is important. What does one mean by England, Great Britain[1], the United Kingdom[2] or the British Isles?[3] Do any of them include the Channel Islands or the Isle of Man? Or what does one mean by France? Be aware of the differences between Continental France[4] and Metropolitan France.[5]
7. **Send in the first XI.** Send the most experienced people to assist the foreign partner. If one is direct franchising, maintain a senior presence in the territory – *do not* try to manage the operation from head office. All too often one sees second-tier management assigned to overseas operations which are in their infancy when what is required is for the franchisor to put its best foot forward.
8. **Be mindful of cultural differences.** Be flexible (just because it works in the UK doesn't mean it will work in the same way elsewhere) and never underestimate the problems posed by a different language.
9. **Seek verification.** People are people the world over – don't trust those in one country any more than you would anyone else! Seek verification of assurances and information about growth prospects given by the foreign partner.
10. **Adapt training** to train the foreign partner to be not only an operator but also a franchisor.
11. **Ring fence UK assets and operation against foreign liability.**
12. Think very carefully about **termination.** It can cost more to leave a country than to enter it.

---

[1] Great Britain is defined in the Union with Scotland Act 1706 as England, Wales and Scotland. It does not include Northern Ireland, the Channel Islands or the Isle of Man.
[2] The United Kingdom is defined in the Royal and Parliamentary Titles Act 1927 as Great Britain and Northern Ireland. The United Kingdom includes the Isle of Man and the Channel Islands in some but not all statutory provisions.
[3] The British Isles are defined in the Interpretation Act 1889 Section 18 (1) as the United Kingdom, Channel Islands and Isle of Man.
[4] Continental France is France in Europe without the island of Corsica.
[5] Metropolitan France is France in Europe plus the island of Corsica but does not include overseas French departments and territories (Martinique, Guadeloupe, French Guiana, Tahiti, Saint-Pierre and Miquelon, New Caledonia etc.).

Going International

... and finally, finally ...

An Idiot's Guide to International Legal Compliance

- In the UK, everything is permitted unless it is expressly prohibited.
- In Germany, anything that is not prohibited is compulsory.
- In Switzerland, everything is prohibited unless expressly permitted.
- In France, nothing is prohibited even if it is not permitted.
- In Italy, everything is permitted; nothing is prohibited!

CHAPTER 39

Regulating Franchising

"Regulation can, at best, deter – it cannot prevent."

Consider this: a former UK franchisee immigrates to the USA and is considering buying a franchise of the same concept from the master franchisor of his former UK franchisor. Although the franchise agreement is more or less the same length as the one he signed with his UK franchisor, the paperwork which accompanies his US franchise is very different.

His US franchisor has produced an 80-page document entitled 'Franchise Disclosure Document' which contains details of the full history of the company, its directors, the number of franchisees, the number of franchisee failures, the number of terminations, past and current litigation with franchisees etc. In essence it contains chapter and verse about the company and its trading history, and also a copy and summary of the franchise agreement. By contrast his UK franchisor had produced half a dozen pages of narrative containing what the franchisor considered to be the principal facts about itself and its system, which was considered to be sufficient for the purposes of the Code of Ethics of the British Franchise Association.

Why such a difference? The answer is very simple. Franchising is heavily regulated in the United States and it is not regulated in the UK. Indeed it is illegal for anyone to offer a franchise in at least 15 out of the 50 states in the USA without having prepared a bulky document which complies not only with federal law but with franchise laws, and worldwide there are some 57 countries which have some form of regulation. No such franchise-specific legal requirement exists in the UK.

Any franchisor thinking of exporting its goods or services abroad through franchising, after hearing about the way in which franchising is regulated in the USA, can be forgiven for thinking that with all the talk about harmonisation and the single market within the European Union, it would be easier to look to the European market instead of the North American one. Whilst this may be generally

Regulating Franchising

true in terms of franchising law and regulation, franchisors seeking to enter the European market should be aware that each member state still has its own peculiarities and in some cases franchise-specific legislation or other legislation which can affect a franchise transaction.

France was the first European country to introduce franchise legislation and was followed by Spain. Italy joined them later but imposed a more onerous regime. Whereas the legislation in France and Spain is concerned with giving franchisees cooling-off periods and requiring franchisors to register their agreements, the law which came into force in Italy on 25th May 2004 is more specific, laying down rules and regulations for franchising. For example, both franchisor and franchisee are required to act in good faith with each other, and the franchise agreement must be in writing and must contain, as a minimum, information in eight categories (such as the specification of know-how, conditions of renewal, limits of possible exclusive territorial rights etc.).

Nor is franchise regulation proliferating only within Europe. For example, there is an obligation to make disclosure and to register franchise agreements in Indonesia, Malaysia, Mexico and Taiwan, and franchise agreements must also be registered in Saudi Arabia. In the cases of Australia, Brazil, China, Indonesia, Japan, South Korea, Romania and some provinces of Canada, franchisors are under an obligation to make disclosure and one suspects that it is only a matter of time before they introduce some form of registration.

All this is quite apart from what are known as 'franchise relationship' laws, which seek to regulate some aspects of the relationship between franchisors and their franchisees. Korea, Lithuania, Malaysia, Romania and Russia are examples of countries with such laws.

In addition to the above, there are voluntary codes of practice in countries such as New Zealand, the United Kingdom and some of the other EU member states of which one should be aware. In many countries where there is no franchise regulation, voluntary codes and their observance can make a significant difference to the success or otherwise of a franchise operation. The Code of Ethics for Franchising of the European Franchise Federation (as adopted by the British Franchise Association) is a case in point. In Texas, business opportunities laws have the potential to affect a franchise transaction.

As if that weren't enough, beware of the regulation of franchising by stealth! Ask about franchise regulation in Germany and you will be told that there is no legislation for franchising there. However, a decision of a regional court in May 2004 awarded damages to a franchisee for breach of a duty of care by his franchisor.

'Duty of care': where did this spring from? Well, it derives from a general principle of liability for culpable acts performed during contractual *negotiations* which has evolved in German case law (and in this case was applied to a franchise agreement).

The implications of this court decision should not be underestimated. A failure on the part of a franchisor to provide information at the pre-contractual stage could result in the franchisor being required to repay to the franchisee the initial franchisee fee, all continuing franchise fees and the costs incurred by the franchisee as a result of entering into the franchise agreement. Essentially, the franchisee can ask to be put back into the position he would have been in had the breach by the franchisor not occurred.

The lesson to be learned from this is that one should never lose sight of the big picture. There is a tendency to concentrate only on franchise legislation to the exclusion of other law which may have the potential to affect franchise transactions.

Finally, what of the countries not mentioned? The answer is that international franchisors should always keep one eye on the future. For example, Sweden, Belgium and one or two others, including Tajikistan (yes, Tajikistan!), have proposed or are contemplating legislation to regulate franchising in one form or other. Whether there is need for regulation in the UK is debated from time to time.

There is much loose talk about regulation and it might help to be a little more precise. Those who speak of regulation may also mean pre-sale disclosure. The two are not necessarily the same. Discussion of 'regulation' here refers to statutory (legal as opposed to voluntary) pre-sale disclosure and/or regulation.

In the USA there is a duty to disclose details about the franchisor in the terms referred to at the beginning of this chapter. In many cases there is also registration (the need for a franchisor to register its franchise agreement with a government agency or department) and/or regulations which regulate the franchise relationship. In California, not only must one disclose, but there are also laws which regulate how a franchisor must conduct itself. In some of the US states a franchisor cannot terminate a franchise agreement without showing 'just cause'. In other states, in certain circumstances, a franchisor may be required to compensate a franchisee for loss of his business on termination; this is also true of Germany, if a franchisor wishes to enforce post-termination non-competition clauses in some circumstances. In Australia franchises are regulated to the extent that, irrespective of what the franchise agreement says, a franchisor may, in certain circumstances, be at the receiving end of heavy fines.

As for the UK, the British Franchise Association seeks to regulate its members by means of a voluntary code. This code applies only to its members, and one does not have to be a member of the British Franchise Association in order to franchise. That in itself eliminates the British Franchise Association as a possible statutory regulator, quite apart from the fundamental question of whether, as presently constituted, it would be suitable for such a role.

It follows that prospective franchisees, when contemplating buying a franchise in the UK, have to act as responsible purchasers because the golden rule of 'buyer beware' applies. If, having made their purchase, they discover they got less than they bargained for, or have been ripped off, they are unlikely to find redress in the absence of fraud or misrepresentation. In any case, if there has been a misrepresentation, making the allegation is one thing; proving the misrepresentation and recovering one's loss is quite another matter. From this it is clear that those who are seriously considering the purchase of a franchise should treat it no differently from the purchase of any other business and they will be doing themselves a disservice if they do not take proper legal, accounting and financial advice.

The Effects of Regulation and Disclosure

Those who suggest that some form of statutory regulation/disclosure may be inevitable may find it is useful to look at the effects of franchise regulation in the US and in other jurisdictions where franchising is regulated.

In the USA it has been shown that there are four effects of regulation:

1. Practical:
   - The franchise agreement becomes a public document. This is unpalatable to many UK franchisors who jealously guard the confidentiality of their franchise agreements.
   - A requirement to file any important changes means that franchise sales may have to be put on hold until the process is completed.
   - Franchisees are deluged with more information than they would otherwise receive, leading to information overload in some cases.
   - Franchisors feel a lesser need (than their counterparts in the UK) to join the trade association of US franchisors: the International Franchise Association. This is so called, it is alleged, because, at the time of its formation, it had some Canadian franchisors as members. It is not, as its name implies, an association of franchisors internationally!

2. Legal:
   - Franchisees have greater legal rights and remedies than under common law.
   - Some of the states in the US have enforcement and investigative powers.

3. Economic:
   - The whole process is much more expensive for franchisors and as a result franchisors tend to be better capitalised and prepared than in the UK, where there is little to discourage a cavalier attitude to franchising by those with limited resources.

4. Franchisor–franchisee relationship:
   - US regulation is said to have a positive effect on franchise relationships in that there is greater openness about the franchisor, its track record and its network.
   - However, the principal disadvantage of disclosure is that any disclosure document will only be a snapshot of the true position, i.e. it is only accurate on the day it was written and therefore again places the onus

of investigation on the prospective franchisee. A prospective franchisee presented with a disclosure document is more likely than not to assume that the document is up to date. Most matters required by any disclosure regime can be ascertained by a prospective franchisee's solicitor, but the production of a disclosure document tends to make prospective franchisees less inquisitive.

One of the most positive effects in many countries where there is franchise regulation (Australia, Germany, France etc.) is the provision of a cooling-off period where a franchisee is entitled to change his mind about going ahead within a given period after signing the franchise agreement, usually 10 to 20 days after signature.

Is Regulation Worthwhile?

The important questions are: what is the mischief which franchise laws are designed to prevent and to what extent have they succeeded?

Franchise legislation by and large seeks to prevent franchisors from ripping off franchisees. The truth is that success is limited. Confidence tricksters are expert in the art of lying and there is no real evidence that a disclosure regime will prevent confidence tricksters; if they are determined to give false information, they will do so. It seems that whilst legislation may deter some conmen, it will certainly not turn conmen into straight men.

The reality:

- Are UK franchisors clamouring for regulation? No, they are not.

- Are UK franchisees clamouring for regulation? No, they are not.

- Is the British Franchise Association clamouring for regulation? No, it is not (in fact, quite the contrary).

- Has there been widespread (or even significant) abuse by franchisors? No, there has not.

- Has there been any demand for regulation from anyone other than some franchise consultants or lawyers? No, there has not.

Ask another question: who stands to gain most, financially, from the added cost of compliance if there is regulation? Franchisors, franchisees, franchise consultants or lawyers?

Legislating against abuse does not in itself prevent abuse any more than legislating against theft prevents theft. At best it has the effect of minimising the offence the legislation seeks to prevent. Conmen continue to practise their 'art' in other market sectors which are regulated; they ignore regulation and take the money.

That in itself is not an argument for not legislating with a view to preventing or indeed minimising abuse, but, in the present case, regulation seems to be a wholly disproportionate response. The simple fact is that, in the history of franchising in this country, there has been relatively little abuse to merit intervention by Parliament. The British Franchise Association is not a statutory body, it does not represent all franchisors (though it punches above its weight), and those expressing views, one way or another, on regulation in its various fora represent but a handful of UK franchisors. Neither the British Franchise Association nor any other body can legitimately claim to be the voice of franchising in the UK. At best, the British Franchise Association can only claim to be persuasive.

The track record of various regulatory bodies in the UK such as the pensions regulator, the financial services regulator etc. is woeful in the minds of the public.

One has to decide whether one is to be responsible for one's own actions, or whether one should expect the state to intervene and provide redress for those who have been less than diligent in their purchase. Any franchise legislation is bound to make franchising more expensive, the cost of which will invariably be passed on to franchisees.

In the final analysis, nothing will prevent fraud – least of all legislation. If one is minded to perpetrate a fraud on another, neither legislation nor self-regulation will prevent it. Both, in their own way, can be said to be a deterrent. In the case of legislation, if the deterrent fails, there is at least sanction; self-regulation may not be a realistic solution in the long term unless it has statutory support.

APPENDIX A

Trade and Service Mark Classifications

Trade Marks

Class 1

- Chemicals used in industry, science and photography, as well as in agriculture, horticulture and forestry.
- Unprocessed artificial resins, unprocessed plastics.
- Manures.
- Fire-extinguishing compositions.
- Tempering and soldering preparations.
- Chemical substances for preserving foodstuffs.
- Tanning substances.
- Adhesives used in industry.

Class 2

- Paints, varnishes, lacquers.
- Preservatives against rust and against deterioration of wood.
- Colourants.
- Mordants.
- Raw natural resins.
- Metals in foil and powder form for painters, decorators, printers and artists.

Class 3

- Bleaching preparations and other substances for laundry use.
- Cleaning, polishing, scouring and abrasive preparations.
- Soaps.
- Perfumery, essential oils, cosmetics, hair lotions.
- Dentifrices.

Class 4

- Industrial oils and greases.
- Lubricants.
- Dust absorbing, wetting and binding compositions.
- Fuels (including motor spirit) and illuminants.
- Candles, wicks.

Class 5

- Pharmaceutical, veterinary and sanitary preparations.
- Dietetic substances adapted for medical use, food for babies.
- Plasters, materials for dressings.
- Material for stopping teeth, dental wax.
- Disinfectants.
- Preparations for destroying vermin.
- Fungicides, herbicides.

Appendix A: Trade and Service Mark Classifications

Class 6

- Common metals and their alloys.
- Metal building materials.
- Transportable buildings of metal.
- Materials of metal for railway tracks.
- Non-electric cables and wires of common metal.
- Ironmongery, small items of metal hardware.
- Pipes and tubes of metal.
- Safes.
- Goods of common metal not included in other classes.
- Ores.

Class 7

- Machines and machine tools.
- Motors and engines (except for land vehicles).
- Machine coupling and transmission components (except for land vehicles).
- Agricultural implements.
- Incubators for eggs.

Class 8

- Hand tools and implements (hand operated).
- Cutlery.
- Side arms.
- Razors.

Appendix A: Trade and Service Mark Classifications

Class 9

- Scientific, nautical, surveying, electric, photographic, cinematographic, optical, weighing, measuring, signalling, checking (supervision), life-saving and teaching apparatus and instruments.
- Apparatus for recording, transmission or reproduction of sound or images.
- Magnetic data carriers, recording discs; automatic vending machines and mechanisms for coin-operated apparatus.
- Cash registers, calculating machines, data-processing equipment and computers.
- Fire-extinguishing apparatus.

Class 10

- Surgical, medical, dental and veterinary apparatus and instruments; artificial limbs, eyes and teeth.
- Orthopaedic articles.
- Suture materials.

Class 11

- Apparatus for lighting, heating, steam-generating, cooking, refrigerating, drying, ventilating, water supply and sanitary purposes.

Class 12

- Vehicles.
- Apparatus for locomotion by land, air or water.

Appendix A: Trade and Service Mark Classifications

Class 13

- Firearms.
- Ammunition and projectiles.
- Explosives.
- Fireworks.

Class 14

- Precious metals and their alloys.
- Goods in precious metals or coated therewith (not included in other classes).
- Jewellery, precious stones.
- Horological and chronometric instruments.

Class 15

- Musical instruments.

Class 16

- Paper, cardboard and goods made from these materials (not included in other classes).
- Printed matter.
- Bookbinding material.
- Photographs.
- Stationery.
- Adhesives for stationery or household purposes.
- Artists' materials.
- Paint brushes.

Appendix A: Trade and Service Mark Classifications

- Typewriters and office requisites (except furniture).
- Instructional and teaching material (except apparatus).
- Plastic materials for packaging (not included in other classes).
- Playing cards.
- Printers' type.
- Printing blocks.

Class 17

- Rubber, gutta-percha, gum, asbestos, mica and goods made from these materials (not included in other classes).
- Plastics in extruded from for use in manufacture.
- Packing, stopping and insulating materials.
- Flexible pipes, not of metal.

Class 18

- Leather and imitations of leather, and goods made from these materials (not included in other classes).
- Animal skins, hides.
- Trunks and travelling bags.
- Umbrellas, parasols and walking sticks.
- Whips, harness and saddlery.

Class 19

- Building materials (non-metallic).
- Non-metallic rigid pipes for building.
- Asphalt, pitch and bitumen.

Appendix A: Trade and Service Mark Classifications

- Non-metallic transportable buildings.
- Monuments (not of metal).

Class 20

- Furniture, mirrors, picture frames.
- Goods (not included in other classes) of wood, cork, reed, cane, wicker, horn, bone, ivory, whalebone, shell, amber, mother-of-pearl, meerschaum and substitutes for all these materials, or of plastics.

Class 21

- Household or kitchen utensils and containers (not of precious metal or coated therewith).
- Combs and sponges.
- Brushes (except paint brushes).
- Brush-making materials.
- Articles for cleaning purposes.
- Steelwork.
- Unworked or semi-worked glass (except glass used in building).
- Glassware, porcelain and earthenware (not included in other classes).

Class 22

- Ropes, string, nets, tents, awnings, tarpaulins, sails, sacks and bags (not included in other classes).
- Padding and stuffing materials (except of rubber or plastics).
- Raw fibrous textile materials.

Appendix A: Trade and Service Mark Classifications

Class 23

- Yarns and threads, for textile use.

Class 24

- Textiles and textile goods (not included in other classes).
- Bed and table covers.

Class 25

- Clothing, footwear, headgear.

Class 26

- Lace and embroidery, ribbons and braid.
- Buttons, hooks and eyes, pins and needles.
- Artificial flowers.

Class 27

- Carpets, rugs, mats and matting, linoleum and other materials for covering existing floors.
- Wall hangings (non-textile).

Class 28

- Games and playthings.
- Gymnastic and sporting articles (not included in other classes).
- Decorations for Christmas trees.

Appendix A: Trade and Service Mark Classifications

Class 29

- Meat, fish, poultry and game.
- Meat extracts.
- Preserved, dried and cooked fruits and vegetables.
- Jellies, jams, fruit sauces.
- Eggs, milk and milk products.
- Edible oils and fats.

Class 30

- Coffee, tea, cocoa, sugar, rice, tapioca, sago, artificial coffee.
- Flour and preparations made from cereals.
- Bread, pastry and confectionery, ices.
- Honey, treacle.
- Yeast, baking powder.
- Salt, mustard.
- Vinegar, sauces (condiments).
- Spices.
- Ice.

Class 31

- Agricultural, horticultural and forestry products and grains (not included in other classes).
- Live animals.
- Fresh fruits and vegetables.
- Seeds, natural plants and flowers.
- Foodstuffs for animals, malt.

Appendix A: Trade and Service Mark Classifications

Class 32

- Beers.
- Mineral and aerated waters and other non-alcoholic drinks.
- Fruit drinks and fruit juices.
- Syrups and other preparations for making beverages.

Class 33

- Alcoholic beverages (except beers).

Class 34

- Tobacco.
- Smokers' articles.
- Matches.

Services

Class 35

- Advertising.
- Business management.
- Business administration.
- Office functions.

Class 36

- Insurance.
- Financial affairs.
- Monetary affairs.
- Real estate affairs.

Appendix A: Trade and Service Mark Classifications

Class 37

- Building construction.
- Repair.
- Installation services.

Class 38

- Telecommunications

Class 39

- Transport.
- Packaging and storage of goods.
- Travel arrangement.

Class 40

- Treatment of materials.

Class 41

- Education.
- Providing of training.
- Entertainment.
- Sporting and cultural activities.

Class 42

- Providing of food and drink.
- Temporary accommodation.
- Medical, hygienic and beauty care.

- Veterinary and agricultural services.
- Legal services.
- Scientific and industrial research.
- Computer programming.
- Services that cannot be placed in other classes.

APPENDIX B

Sample Franchise Application Form

1. Full name.
2. Address.
3. Date of birth.
4. Marital status.
5. Number of dependants.
6. Details of present employment.
7. State of health.
8. Education.
9. Have you ever been convicted of a criminal offence?
10. Have you ever been involved in a bankruptcy or liquidation?
11. Have you ever been involved in any litigation or legal action?
12. Employment history.
13. Business history.
14. How much money are you prepared to invest from your own resources?
15. State source of investment funds.
16. How much do you intend to borrow?
17. Will you actively operate and manage the proposed franchise on a full-time basis?
18. Do you have the full support of your partner or spouse?
19. Do you intend to trade as a sole proprietor, a partnership or a limited liability company?

Appendix B: Sample Franchise Application Form

20. If you are seeking to take business partners, please provide their details.
21. If you intend to trade as a limited company, please provide:
    a. A copy of its memorandum and articles of association.
    b. A list of all shareholders and the percentage of the issued shares each shareholder holds.
    c. A list of the directors of the company.
    d. A copy of the last three years' audited accounts.
22. Please provide a map indicating the proposed location of any premises or the extent of the area for which a franchise is sought.
23. Please provide a statement of your assets and liabilities.
24. Please provide details of the following from whom we may obtain a reference:
    a. Bank.
    b. Accountant.
    c. Two individuals (to give personal references).
    d. Your current landlord (if any).
25. Why have you chosen this particular franchise?
26. Why do you think that this franchise would be successful in the area which you have chosen?
27. Are there any competitors to this franchise in the area which you have chosen?
28. Are you at present or have you been a franchisee before? If the answer is 'yes', please give details.

APPENDIX C

Franchisee Preliminary Enquiries

This is a list of questions prospective franchisees may wish to know the answers to. Not all enquiries will be relevant. The nature and number of enquiries will depend on the nature and size of the franchise business. In most cases, much of the information requested in the list below will have been supplied piecemeal in material previously delivered to the prospective franchisee by the franchisor.

1. What is the address of the principal place of business of the franchisor?
2. What is the registered office and company registration number of the franchisor?
3. What are the franchisor's full contact details?
4. Is the franchisor resident in the UK?
5. What is the franchisor's parent or holding company (if there is one)?
6. Is the franchisor or its holding company a member of the British Franchise Association (BFA)?
    a. If the franchisor is a member of the BFA, please confirm that it complies with the code of ethics promoted by the BFA.
    b. In which ways (if any) does the franchise agreement which the franchisor intends to use in its proposed relationship with the franchisee differ from the recommendations and standards of the BFA?
    c. Has the franchise agreement been disclosed to the BFA? If not, please set out the departure from the draft actually disclosed to the BFA.
7. Give details of the intellectual property which will form the subject matter of the franchise.
    a. Does the franchisor own all rights?
    b. If any rights are used by the franchisor under licence, who is the licensor?

Appendix C: Franchisee Preliminary Enquiries

    c. When does the franchisor's right to use those rights expire?

    d. Please produce evidence of the franchisor's right to grant this proposed franchise.

    e. Please provide a copy of all relevant documents.

    f. If essential rights are used under licence, please state what will happen to the franchisee if the licence is suspended, is terminated or expires. Does that licence contain provisions whereby the rights of the franchisor under its franchise agreements automatically revert to the licensor upon termination or expiry of the licence?

8. What will be the result (in respect of that licence referred to in (f) above or any other document agreement or arrangement) on the insolvency of the licensor or the franchisor?

9. Which, if any, of the intellectual property rights mentioned in your reply to question 7 above are protected by registration? Give details including date and place of registration.

10. Has any opposition been lodged or have any proceedings been taken against the registration or use of any of the intellectual property mentioned in your reply to question 7 above?

11. Is the franchisor aware of any actual or potential claims or proceedings involving other entities in which allegations of invalidity or infringement of those intellectual property rights are or might be made?

12. Are the intellectual property rights mentioned in reply to question 7 above subject to any agreement or arrangement with any other party which in any way limits or controls their use other than by any licence disclosed in reply to question 7?

13. If the franchise includes the name of a well-known person, has his consent and has licence to use that name been given to the franchisor? Please produce evidence of this.

14. If the franchisor has provided a statement of the projected earnings of the business to be franchised, what is the source of information on which that projection was based? In particular:

Appendix C: Franchisee Preliminary Enquiries

      a. Have those figures been calculated by reference to the actual performance of franchised or company-owned businesses? If so, over what period?

      b. Have those figures been based on a business which is similar in terms of size, location and demographic characteristics to the proposed business of the franchisee?

      c. Do those figures represent trading once the business has achieved maturity or take into account start-up and development time?

      d. How accurate have the franchisor's projections have been in the past?

      e. How many franchisees have been obliged to put more money into their businesses due to shortfalls between their actual and projected performance, and in what circumstances? What has been the average additional injection?

      f. If any franchisees have achieved their projected performance later than anticipated in their projections, what is the average delay?

      g. Has the franchisor any evidence of performance by franchised or company-owned units after the period covered by the projections? If so please state if there has been any reduction in performance in any case and whether any changes in management have had an adverse effect upon performance.

      h. Are any franchised or company-owned units trading unprofitably or below their current targets?

      i. What, if any, significant regional variations or trends have appeared?

      j. Which assumptions have been made in the projections?

      k. Which risk factors would the franchisor and its advisors consider appropriate to draw to the attention of potential investors if the projections formed part of a prospectus?

15. Please provide an audited set of the latest accounts relating to the franchise business.

      a. What portion of the gross income of the franchisor was derived from payments made by franchisees?

Appendix C: Franchisee Preliminary Enquiries

    b. What part of such portion was derived from continuing franchise fees based on franchisees' gross takings? From initial fees received from franchisees or prospective franchisees? From sales of items to franchisees?

    c. What amount was spent during the last twelve months on advertising, marketing and promoting the franchise business and its outlets? Exclude from this figure any sums spent advertising for new franchisees.

    d. Have there been any material changes since these accounts were prepared? If so, give details.

16. Who are the directors of the franchisor company and what is their business experience?

17. What is the business experience of the senior management responsible for the day-to-day running of the franchise operation?

18. Have any of the persons named in 16 and 17, above, been involved in any bankruptcy, liquidation, receivership administration or insolvency? If so, please give details.

19. Have any of the persons mentioned in 16 and 17, above, been convicted of an offence involving dishonesty during the last 10 years?

20. Have any of the persons mentioned in 16 and 17, above, ever been declared bankrupt?

21. Have any of the persons mentioned in 16 and 17, above, ever been party to a civil action in which allegations of fraud or misrepresentation have been made against them?

22. Have any of the persons mentioned in 16 and 17, above, ever been disqualified from holding office as a director or other officer of a company for any reason?

23. How long has the franchisor:

    a. Conducted a business of the type to be operated by the franchisee?

    b. Offered or sold franchises for such business?

Appendix C: Franchisee Preliminary Enquiries

24. Have the franchisor or its participators, directors or managers at any time operated any other business in which the intellectual property rights set out in 7, above, have been used? If so, is such a business still in operation? Give details.

25. Have the franchisor or its participators, directors or managers ever operated any other franchise business? If so, give particulars.

26. The information and advice provided by the franchisor contains many representations which will materially influence the judgement of the franchisee in his decision of whether or not to proceed with this proposed arrangement. Was that information and advice compiled by some of those persons mentioned in 16 and 17, above? Please provide the names of those persons who are, were or will be responsible for:

    a. Projections.
    b. Site selection.
    c. Size of territory.

27. Has the franchisor been convicted of any offence during the last 10 years?

28. Has the franchisor ever been party to a civil action in which allegations of fraud or misrepresentation have been made against it?

29. Has the franchisor ever been involved in litigation with present or former franchisees? Action taken by the franchisor under summary judgment procedure may be ignored.

30. Give details of all franchisees whose franchise agreements have expired without being renewed, or have been terminated for whatever reason.

31. Provide a full factual description of the franchise business, including the historical development of the business.

32. In the case of a new franchise business, please provide full details of pilot schemes operated by the franchisor.

33. Why does the franchisor consider its franchise package to be superior to other franchises in the same business sector (if any) currently on offer?

Appendix C: Franchisee Preliminary Enquiries

34. What payments of any kind must be made by the franchisee in order to obtain and commence the franchise business (including initial fees, deposit, purchase or rental of equipment)? Under what conditions are any such payments returnable?

35. What recurring payments of whatever kind will the franchisee have to make in order to continue to operate the franchised business?

36. Will the franchisee need to purchase any goods or services from the franchisor or any other person affiliated with the franchisor? If so, please give details.

37. Is the franchisee required to acquire any specialist equipment from the franchisor?

    a. If so, what are the terms of such acquisition?

    b. If such equipment is hired or rented to the franchisee during the term of the franchise, what happens on expiry or earlier termination of the franchise agreement?

38. Is the franchisee required or advised to hire or purchase any other equipment or materials needed to operate the franchised business from the franchisor or other specified supplier? If so, please specify the materials and provide a list of the names and addresses of any specified suppliers. Are any such suppliers affiliated with or owned wholly or partly by the franchisor?

39. Will the franchisor or any person connected with the franchisor receive any payment or other consideration for goods, services, property or finance supplied to the franchisee by persons other than the franchisor itself? If so, please give details including the basis on which such payments will be calculated.

40. What advertising policy does the franchisor pursue:

    a. With regard to the business as a whole?

    b. With regard to the opening of new outlets? If there will be any material departure from this policy in relation to the present outlet, please specify.

Appendix C: Franchisee Preliminary Enquiries

41. Will the franchisee need to acquire any freehold or leasehold property from the franchisor or from any other person affiliated with or owned by the franchisor? If so, please give details, and in particular:

    a. Will any lease of such premises terminate on expiry or termination of the franchise agreement?

    b. What will be the permitted use of the premises under such lease?

    c. What rent review provisions are included in the lease?

    d. Is the valuation for rent review purposes limited by any restriction of the use of the premises, or is that restriction specifically excluded from consideration in such valuation?

42. What training in the business is provided by the franchisor to new franchisees?

    a. Is this included in the fees payable by the franchisee?

    b. What additional training facilities are made available by the franchisor during the term of the agreement and at whose expense?

    c. Is the franchisee obliged to attend further training when required by the franchisor?

43. Will the franchisee be subject to any restrictions:

    a. As to the goods or services he may offer for sale?

    b. As to the persons to whom he may sell or supply such goods or services?

    c. As to the geographic area in which he may offer such goods or services?

44. In what way will the franchisee be protected against competition from:

    a. A business operating under the same trade name and/or marks, whether in the same or in a different field of activity?

    b. A business operating in the same or similar fields of activity which is in any way connected with the franchisor?

Appendix C: Franchisee Preliminary Enquiries

45. What will be the extent of such any such territorial protection?

46. In the case of border areas dividing territories, does the franchisor insist on strict adherence by each franchisee to the border demarking his territory or will it permit franchisees to make arrangements between themselves?

47. What is the attitude of the franchisor to orders from customers in one territory made to a franchisee in another territory if the goods or services are supplied by that franchisee to that customer:

    a. In the territory of the supplying franchisee?

    b. In the territory in which the customer is located?

48. If the franchisee is permitted or obliged to undertake his own local advertising, what is the attitude of the franchisor to advertising by a franchisee in media which covers not only his territory but adjoining territories as well (e.g. local press or radio)?

49. Does the franchisor permit joint local advertising by adjoining franchisees?

50. How does the franchisor resolve territorial disputes between its franchisees?

51. Does the franchise agreement contain the right on the part of the franchisor to reduce any territory, exclusive or other, granted to the franchisee? If so:

    a. In what event may that right be exercised?

    b. Has it been exercised in the past?

    c. If it has been exercised, for what reasons?

    d. If it has been exercised, what was the effect of that reduction on the gross turnover of the business whose territory was reduced?

    e. Does the franchisee whose territory is to be reduced have the right of first refusal to open a further franchised business in that part of his territory which is about to be split from the part retained by him?

Appendix C: Franchisee Preliminary Enquiries

52. If the franchisee is not granted an exclusive area, will there be a maximum number of franchisees within an area specified by the franchise agreement? If so, please give details.
53. If the franchise business deals in the supply of goods, please confirm that the franchisor does not and will not operate a mail order service.
54. Will the franchisor confirm that any enquiries from potential customers located close to the proposed business outlet of the prospective franchisee will be referred to the franchisee as soon as possible after receipt?
55. Will the franchisee be permitted to operate only within a specified area or from a specified location? If so, please give details.
    a. If the franchisee is only permitted to operate from a specified location, please advise what criteria are applied by the franchisor in the selection of such a location.
56. Will the franchisee be required to participate personally in the franchised business? To what extent?
57. What are the usual business hours of a franchised business?
    a. Will the franchisee be obliged by the franchisor or by practical considerations to work longer than the hours mentioned above?
58. May the franchisee use the premises from which he undertakes the franchised business for any other business venture?
59. If the franchisee is to receive financial assistance from the franchisor or any person connected with the franchisor, please confirm that the franchisee will be provided with all information which would be required if the provisions of the Consumer Credit Act 1974 applied to the agreement, whether or not that Act in fact applies.
60. Does the franchisor have a particular relationship with any banks which may assist the franchisee with loans or other financing for the proposed franchised business? If so:
    a. Which banks?

Appendix C: Franchisee Preliminary Enquiries

    b. Upon what terms are loans usually made, with regard to percentage of total funds required, interest rates, security, duration, capital repayments?

    c. Do those banks usually require the personal guarantees of directors of franchisees that are corporate entities?

61. Please confirm that the franchise departments (if any) of the potential lenders mentioned above have received a copy of the current version of the draft franchise agreement.

62. What is to be the duration of the franchise agreement?

    a. Is it renewable, and if so upon what conditions?

    b. Under what conditions may the franchisor refuse to renew or extend the agreement?

    c. In what circumstances may the agreement be terminated or varied unilaterally by the franchisor?

    d. When is the franchisee entitled to terminate the agreement?

    e. What will be the obligations of the franchisee (including obligations under any lease or rental agreement entered into with the franchisor or any person connected with the franchisor) following the termination of the franchise agreement by the franchisor itself?

    f. Under what conditions may the franchisor repurchase the franchised business and how will the price be calculated?

    g. Under what conditions may the franchisee sell or assign all or any interest in the franchised business, or the assets of the franchised business?

    h. Under what conditions may the franchisor assign in whole or in part its interest under such agreement?

    i. What steps to carry on the business will the franchisor take to ensure business continuity in the event of the death or incapacity of the franchisee?

    j. What rights will accrue to the franchisee's next of kin or estate in the event of his incapacity or death?

Appendix C: Franchisee Preliminary Enquiries

    6.3 If the franchisor is to approve the site of the franchised business, how long a time usually elapses between the signing of the franchise agreement and other documents to secure the site selected?

64. If the franchisor is to provide the operating outlet, how long usually elapses between the signing of agreements relating to the franchise and the commencement of the franchisee's business?

65. What is:

    a. The total number of outlets at present franchised by the franchisor?

    b. The total number of company-owned outlets operated by the franchisor?

66. What are the names, addresses and telephone numbers of all the franchisor's franchisees operating businesses near to the proposed franchised business? Will the franchisor consent to the franchisee discussing the proposed franchise with its other franchisees?

67. What are the addresses of company-owned outlets adjacent to the proposed franchised business?

68. Give details of:

    a. The number of franchisee agreements voluntarily terminated or not renewed by franchisees within the last two years.

    b. The number of franchises acquired by the franchisor within the last two years.

    c. The number of franchises which the franchisor has refused to renew within the last two years.

    d. The number of franchises which the franchisor has cancelled or terminated during the term of the agreements within the last two years. Please give reasons for such termination.

69. Will the franchisee be restrained from carrying on any similar business after the termination of the franchise? If so, give details.

70. If the franchisor requires its franchisees to make payment to an advertising or marketing services fund:

Appendix C: Franchisee Preliminary Enquiries

  a. Who will be responsible for deciding what advertising or promotional programmes will be commenced or maintained?

  b. If the franchisor is responsible for such decisions, who will receive advertising discounts or commissions?

  c. If the franchisor administers the fund, what management fees (if any) does it charge for so doing?

  d. How is the fund audited?

  e. Will the fund be maintained in a bank account of its own and kept separate from the franchisor's money?

  f. Please confirm that no advertising for recruiting franchisees will be charged to the fund.

  g. Will the franchisor be entitled to recoup excess expenditure on advertising from the fund?

  h. Please confirm that, if advertising expenditure by the franchisor in any period exceeds the amount then in the fund, there will be no additional levy on franchisees.

71. Is there an association of franchisees of the franchisor?

  a. If so, who is the secretary and what is his address? Please confirm that the proposed franchisee may contact him.

  b. If there is no such association, does the franchisor hold regular meetings with all its franchisees, or groups of its franchisees? When is the next such meeting?

72. If the franchisor has company-owned outlets:

  a. Are they profitable?

  b. Do they pay the standard franchise fee?

  c. Do they pay the normal advertising contribution?

  d. Are their managers freely permitted to attend any meetings of franchisees to discuss business or problems?

Appendix C: Franchisee Preliminary Enquiries

73. How many company-owned pilot units have been operated before franchising has commenced? In what areas were they situated?

74. What are the franchisor's requirements with regard to alteration, refurbishment or updating of franchise outlets or equipment during the term of the agreement or on renewal? Are all its franchisees subject to the same obligations in this respect?

75. How does the franchisor ensure that all its franchisees maintain high standards in their business?

76. Does the franchisor supply its franchisees with an operations manual? If so:

    a. Is it updated?

    b. Who owns it?

    c. Does each copy have a serial number?

77. Is the franchisee required to conduct his business subject to standard accountancy and bookkeeping practices stipulated by the franchisor? If so:

    a. Are these methods acceptable to the Institute of Chartered Accountants (or its equivalent in Scotland or Northern Ireland) for audit purposes?

    b. Are these methods set out in detail in the operations manual?

78. Has the franchisor the right to nominate the auditors of the franchisee? If so:

    a. Which form will be nominated?

    b. Are those auditors chartered accountants?

    c. What would be their charge-out rate and the anticipated amount of annual fees for a franchisee?

79. If the franchise business involves the production of goods or any process of altering products, please confirm that all steps in such production or alteration process comply in all respects with government or other regulations.

Appendix C: Franchisee Preliminary Enquiries

80. Please confirm that all wage rates recommended by the franchisor comply with any relevant minimum wage regulations and that the profit projections supplied by the franchisor take such regulations into account.
81. To what extent is the business dependent on part-time or casual employees?
82. Has the franchisor effected an insurance for employers' and public liability?
    a. Will the franchisee be obliged to insure against employers' and public liability with an insurance company nominated by the franchisor, under the terms of a policy agreed by the franchisor with the insurance company?
    b. If so, will the franchisor be covered by that policy?
    c. In what way is the franchisee covered against claims by third parties against the franchisor?
83. Is the franchisee required to offer credit to his customers? If so:
    a. How is this financed?
    b. Is there any special relationship with a finance house?
    c. Who receives any commission payable by such finance house upon the introduction of business?
84. What is the VAT number of the franchisor?
85. Is any part of the sums payable by a franchisee to the franchisor subject to VAT?
86. Has the franchisor submitted the draft of the franchise agreement to the Office of Fair Trading? If so, what was the result?
87. If the proposed franchised business does not perform satisfactorily (or the franchisee or its key director is incapacitated or dies), does the franchisor have the right to install its own management? If so:
    a. In what circumstances?

Appendix C: Franchisee Preliminary Enquiries

b. Who pays?

c. If the franchisee pays, what is the current charge?

d. What management resources has the franchisor to cover emergencies and poor performance?

e. Has the franchisor installed its own management in a franchised business in the past? If so, why? What was the result?

88. If the franchised business depends upon the performance of specialist employees, does the franchisor assist in recruiting them at the start of the business? Throughout the duration of the franchise agreement? Is recruitment charged to the franchisee?

89. Is employee recruitment advertising a charge on the advertising fund?

90. In the event that the franchisee wishes to dispose of his franchised business:

    a. Is it now the policy of the franchisor to purchase the business of franchisees who wish to sell?

    b. If so, have any been purchased by the franchisor in the last two years?

    c. If so, was the price reached by agreement or independent professional valuation?

    d. If by valuation, on what basis was the valuation made by the accountant?

    e. If the franchisor was the lessor of the location, did the franchisor claim a discount because of the terms of lease?

    f. Have any franchises been assigned to a new franchisee in the last two years?

    g. If so, what were the charges for vetting prospective assignees?

APPENDIX D

The British Franchise Association

1976 marked a major milestone in the history of UK franchising with the formation of the British Franchise Association.

The franchise concept had, however, been employed as a successful and popular business technique for at least 16 years prior to this date, with major companies such as J Lyons and Co. operating franchise businesses throughout the UK. Wimpy, for example, was busy opening one franchise outlet per week from the mid-1960s to the mid-1970s.

So what was it that possessed eight major UK companies employed in very diverse franchising sectors to come together in 1976 and form the BFA?

First, it was the desire to present and promote ethical franchising as a bona fide business technique in a rapidly expanding market, and second, it was to counteract the quite erroneous and damaging impression that franchising and pyramid selling were somehow the same.

The declared objectives of this new association were to promote, protect and further the interests of properly constituted franchising companies, and by these means to establish and maintain a clear definition of ethical franchising standards to assist the press, members of the public, prospective investors and government bodies in distinguishing between sound business practices and any suspect investment schemes.

To further these aims, a code of ethics and strict set of criteria for membership were established, both of which were structured, amongst other things, to ensure that a prospective franchisee was offered a viable business opportunity.

To help ensure that franchising developed ethically, eight leading companies incorporated the British Franchise Association Limited (a company limited by guarantee) in 1997.

Appendix D: The British Franchise Association

These eight companies were:

- Budget Rent a Car (UK) Ltd.
- Dyno-Rod Plc.
- Holiday Inns (UK) Inc.
- Kentucky Fried Chicken (GB) Ltd.
- Prontaprint Ltd.
- ServiceMaster Ltd.
- Wimpy International Ltd.
- Ziebart Mobile Transport Services Ltd.

The reader will recognise some of these companies as having their origins in the USA. Only DynoRod and Prontaprint can be said to be home-grown, although the principal and owner of Dyno-Rod is an American.

The aim of the British Franchise Association is to develop and continuously improve standards of good practice in franchising, to accredit franchisors who meet those standards, to promote good franchising as represented by the association's accredited franchisors to the general public, business community, government and media, and to provide prospective franchisees with information and education to help them decide on the best franchise for them.

In joining the British Franchise Association, members, be they provisional, associate or full, commit themselves to complying with the Advertising Standards Authority's code of advertising practice and with the following policies and procedures, as published by the British Franchise Association:

- The code of ethical conduct.
- The disciplinary procedure.
- The complaints procedure.
- The appeals procedure.
- The terms of annual re-accreditation.

Appendix D: The British Franchise Association

In addition members are required to provide the British Franchise Association with such nonconfidential information relating to their franchise business as may be requested by an authorised official of the British Franchise Association.

www.thebfa.org

85f Park Drive, Milton Park, Abingdon OX14 4RY

01235 820470

APPENDIX E (i)

Case Study: The Ziebart Story

Ziebart is a worldwide leader in car care and protection services. It was founded by Kurt Ziebart, a penniless émigré from Germany, who arrived in Detroit in 1953. He got a job at a car dealership repairing cars damaged in accidents and while doing so made his first attempt at rustproofing body panels.

Ziebart perfected his sealant product and in 1959, together with his former employer, opened his first rustproofing outlet in the Detroit area. The quality of the product overcame consumers' initial scepticism and he struggled to satisfy demand. The only solution was to open additional rustproofing service centres. He did this by franchising, selling 18 franchises.

In 1963, Kurt Ziebart sold his now prosperous business to corrosion expert Roger Waindle, who renamed it Ziebart Process Corporation.

The Ziebart success spread across the border into Canada and in 1965 the first international master franchise was sold for Canada. By 1969, the business had spread its wings to the Far East with the grant of an international master franchise for Japan.

The Ziebart success story is in part driven by its advertising campaign with advertisements appearing in *Life, Look, Time, Newsweek* and other US magazines. The famous actor Rod Serling (of the TV series *The Twilight Zone*) appeared in Ziebart's national 'it's us or rust' TV advertising campaign in 1975.

Ziebart launched an aggressive franchise sales programme in 1980 both in North America and internationally and in 1982 bought back the Canadian master franchise. Between 1982 and 1990, Ziebart concentrated on expanding its range of products and services, acquiring the 'Tuff-Kote Dinol' franchise system with 130 outlets in North America and securing the worldwide rights to 'Tidy Car', including its franchise and trademarks, which were then marketed under a comprehensive business plan.

Between 1991 and 1993, Ziebart engaged in a review of its brand and made changes to its image. In the following year, 1994, Ziebart International Corporation was bought by its employees by means of an employee share ownership plan. Upon the successful employee buy-out, Ziebart launched an effort to return to is core services.

During the next nine or ten years, Ziebart was engaged in a number of corporate ventures generating corporate and franchise profits. These ventures included expanding its product range, aggressively expanding its sale of franchises, introducing a new exterior marketing image, and selling its manufacturing facilities and the Ziebart Products Group subsidiary.

In 2006, Ziebart's profits were negatively impacted when many US dealers diversified into non-Ziebart products, and in 2007 Ziebart sold a master franchise for Canada to an investment company. In the following year, Ziebart simplified its franchising format, and between 2012 and 2013 it improved, enhanced and extended its product range.

In 2014 Ziebart made its largest marketing effort in decades and relaunched its brand with a national public relations programme to promote the company's products, services, and franchise opportunities.

In 2016, Ziebart rolled out its new point-of-sale software, 'iBart', designed to enable the company to better understand its customers and to improve sales reporting. In the same year it also opened a new master franchise in Thailand.

APPENDIX E (ii)

Case Study: Southern Fried Chicken

The Southern Fried Chicken business was founded by Arthur Withers, who was born in London. In the early 1970s, when he was visiting South Carolina, he was served fried chicken. It was at this time that he came across the concept of fast food. When he was in the US again in the 1980s he witnessed the growth of the fast food business there and realised that there was nothing similar in the UK. He came to the conclusion that small independent food restaurants operating along traditional lines were not going to survive in the wake of competition from US fast food companies who were beginning to enter the UK market.

In the 1980s Arthur Withers came up with a brand: Southern Fried Chicken, which continues to the present day as SFC Express. The famous steamboat logo came about because, when in New Orleans, he had seen a steamboat with the sun setting in the background, and this had reminded him of the first time he had eaten southern fried chicken. The original business supplied catering equipment and seasonings to end users under a loose licence arrangement.

Withers put together a fast food chicken concept embracing the complete package of equipment, packaging and ingredients. He chose chicken because it was a cheap product to which value could be added by the use, in its preparation, of coatings and flavourings. Also, a chicken could be divided into nine separate pieces, the value of which was significant compared to the base price of one whole chicken.

During the first ten years the company developed a branded restaurant in the UK. In its operation they realised that they needed better controls and standards if they were to expand successfully and quickly.

'During the early days of our growth, we did everything wrong and eventually we got it right and by 1996 we had developed sufficient controls to implement a business format franchise system and gradually, the franchise grew,' said Andrew Withers, the present chairman of the company.

Appendix E (ii): Case Study: Southern Fried Chicken

By 1990 there were more than 400 licensed fast food establishments providing the company with exceptional income streams from their purchase of equipment and seasonings. This licence arrangement, although very successful, fell short of providing the company with the mechanisms required for ensuring quality control.

As any suggestion to licensees to adopt standards proved difficult, a decision was made to offer fully franchised options internationally in the 1990s. The company also grew its core business of supplying equipment, seasonings and other branded products by granting international distributorships.

In the 1990s the company also acquired its own UK manufacturing facility to work in synergy with the distributorships. The manufacturing facility is now supplying blue chip companies with quality catering equipment as well as providing core equipment for every new franchise site that opens.

From the turn of the millennium, various rebranding exercises were carried out piecemeal over the years. In 2009 the well-known 'Steamboat' logo and associated trade marks were updated to the new look that is available today.

Although the international business grew at a slower rate than the UK licensed sites, the gradual growth of single site owners and small multi-site operators changed the dynamic of the company over the following years. By 2017 Southern Fried Chicken had developed over 200 sites internationally and had 150 re-branded restaurants operating.

Currently Southern Fried Chicken restaurants serve over one million pieces of chicken every week and employ over 10,000 staff.

Timeline of development of Southern Fried Chicken:

- 1973: Arthur Withers establishes Fast Food Systems Limited after a trip to Greenville, South Carolina, where he spots an opportunity for southern fried chicken after being served it in a local hotel restaurant.

- 1973–1980: Fast Food Systems imports mainly American products.

- 1980: Fast Food Systems starts manufacturing its own products and equipment under the Vizu brand. The first two products, Vizu Chip Dump and Vizu Burger, are manufactured under licence by third parties.

Appendix E (ii): Case Study: Southern Fried Chicken

- 1983: Creation of Southern Fried Chicken brand.
- 1984: The company starts co-branding with UK fish and chip shops.
- 1990: The number of restaurants in the UK using the brand grows to 300.
- 1992: The first international restaurant opens in the UAE.
- 1994: The company launches its international franchise strategy.
- 1995: Fast Food Systems manufacturing is founded, with more than 20 products being manufactured in-house.
- 1996: The company develops a business format for its concept with a view to franchising.
- 1999: The AJ's Piri Piri brand is added to the Fast Food Systems family.
- 1999: The first Southern Fried Chicken (SFC) restaurant opens in Russia.
- 1999: Fast Food Systems reaches a turnover of £5 million, of which 40% is achieved via exports to five continents.
- 2000: The company develops 10 additional Quick Service Restaurant equipment models, bringing the number of Vizu products being manufactured in-house to 65.
- 2005: The 40th SFC restaurant opens in Russia.
- 2008: SFC restaurants are open in 30 countries worldwide.
- 2009: The company revitalises the brand with an image overhaul. An important stage in the brand's growth was to consider the brand image and whether it was still current in the marketplace. Attention was paid to colours and styles which were now being well received by customers frequenting a quick service restaurant. The new branding was designed to incorporate natural material (woods, ceramics and brick) to convey a message that Southern Fried Chicken restaurants only used non-processed fresh foods. This was a big change from when red and yellow and lots of plastic were used in the fast food industry in 1980. A large investment was made in writing a range of manuals to standardise all processes, with the goal of ensuring that customers could expect the same service and menu wherever in the world they stepped into a Southern Fried Chicken restaurant. A new set of guidelines were also drawn up, which included a range of acceptable

Appendix E (ii): Case Study: Southern Fried Chicken

standards which franchisees were required to adhere to. These standards were monitored and controlled by constant auditing worldwide.

- 2010: Master franchise sold for Nigeria with openings at seven locations.
- 2011: The company starts a refranchising programme in the UK.
- 2011: The first company-owned restaurant opens in Whitley Wood, Reading, UK.
- 2013: The company's CEO, Andrew Withers (son of the founder), appears on the Channel 4 business documentary *Undercover Boss* to audit the brand in the UK.
- 2013: The company buys the Contact Grill Company a new range of grills.
- 2015: By now, 70 SFC restaurants are open in Russia and CIS countries.
- 2016: Master franchise is sold for Senegal with three SFC restaurants opening.
- 2016: Master franchise for UAE is sold.
- 2016: Master franchise for Martinique is sold.
- 2016–2017: A new franchise development program is introduced for Russian and Indian markets to promote breaking up the countries into smaller regions to enable multiple master franchises, thereby allowing greater growth within these countries.
- 2017: Master franchise for South Africa is sold.
- 2017: The company produces a film documentary to showcase what it really takes to open an SFC franchised restaurant.
- 2017: Master franchise is sold for Hyderabad, India.
- 2017–2018: The company embarks on a major franchise sales drive concentrating on Asia and Africa, with exhibitions in Singapore, South Africa, Azerbaijan and Thailand.

APPENDIX E (iii)

Case Study: The ServiceMaster UK Story

The ServiceMaster story began in 1929 when an ex-professional baseball player and insurance salesman called Marion E Wade started a mothproofing business. At this time a large proportion of carpet cleaning was done by lifting carpets up and taking them away. He saw the need for carpets to be cleaned where they were: at home. However, the main obstacle to this was the absence of the right equipment and detergents. Working with chemists in the search for a solution, Wade achieved a major technical breakthrough by producing a detergent which would be suitable for cleaning carpets as they lay on the floor. He also developed equipment which could handle the detergent safely, as the chemicals he had used were volatile; in 1937 they had exploded and he was seriously injured and hospitalised.

In 1946 he started cleaning carpets on-site and his business as a sole proprietor turned over $45,000 in that year.

In the following year, he persuaded two young men from his church to join him. In that year they did $129,000 worth of sales, and in 1948 $200,000 worth of sales.

Wade believed that the people who worked with him should have the opportunity to share the excitement, the risks and the rewards of running their own business, as he had done when he and his wife were in business on their own. So in 1952 the first franchise agreement was signed. In this sense, Wade's reason for franchising was different from that of most franchisors, who embark upon franchising as a means of growing their own business.

In the early years mothproofing played a major part of the business, as carpet cleaning was still commonly done by lifting carpets up and taking them away. However, as bigger carpet looms were developed in the industry and techniques for mothproofing fibres prior to carpet manufacture became available, so close-covered wall-to-wall carpeting became an increasing market. This led to the need for developing ServiceMaster services, which were soon extended to the cleaning of fabric-covered upholstery.

The successful operation of the business by Wade and his two church colleagues led them to develop their own marketing, operating and accounting methods,

Appendix E (iii): Case Study: The ServiceMaster UK Story

all of which culminated in the development of a business format for their franchise package.

As ServiceMaster's business developed throughout the United States, the difficulty of communications and the problems of extensive travelling became acute, and so ServiceMaster evolved the Master Franchise Coordinator concept. This consisted of granting rights to a large area to approved individuals who effectively became mini-franchisors, responsible for setting up and licensing new franchisees and acting as a distributor for products and equipment. The coordinator was responsible for coordinating his franchisees' reports and reported to ServiceMaster head office. It was a bold move, but one that paid off.

ServiceMaster reduced its fee from 10% to 5% so that the coordinator shared half of the fee income. In addition, the coordinator was given a substantial discount on products to encourage him to warehouse and store them for his own franchisees.

This had the effect of considerably reducing ServiceMaster's overheads, as ServiceMaster itself now carried a smaller inventory and dealt with fewer franchisees. ServiceMaster only dealt with the coordinators, which freed up its resources to concentrate on developing a smaller group of people. One of its mantras was 'train the trainer'. ServiceMaster trained the coordinators who in turn were responsible for training the franchisees.

This concept was extended in 1958 when ServiceMaster in the United States signed its first overseas agreement with Raymond Crouch, from the UK, whose family business of Humphrey & Tapling was involved in carpet wholesaling. Ray Crouch was a man of vision who saw that the trend towards fitted carpets in the US was spreading to the United Kingdom and that there would be a need for an on-location carpet cleaning service. In 1958 there were very few, if any, who offered such a service and it was certainly not available throughout the country as a whole. ServiceMaster sold Ray Crouch the Master Franchise Coordinator Licence for Europe to operate along the same lines as a master franchise coordinator in the United States.

Crouch followed the textbook practice of appointing a general manager to set up a pilot operation in the Hammersmith Road, London. Using his contacts with carpet and fibre manufacturers, he was able to give demonstrations and obtain recommendations from major carpet and fibre manufacturers in the UK. The

Appendix E (iii): Case Study: The ServiceMaster UK Story

detergent originally developed by Wade and much improved since then was unique at that time in the UK and found quick acceptance with carpet manufacturers.

These carpet and fibre manufacturers' endorsements gave strong credibility when Crouch approached both commercial and domestic potential customers in the London area, and many prestige accounts such as Marks & Spencer, the House of Lords, and royal palaces soon became ServiceMaster customers.

As well as developing its own cleaning systems ServiceMaster also developed methods of marketing, one of which was to work through retailers. At that time US and UK retailers were offering an excellent service. They employed their own carpet cleaners, carpet fitters, cabinet makers, upholsterers etc. Customers tended to remain loyal to a particular department store or carpet retailer and they would go back there for all their cleaning, repair, alteration etc. needs.

ServiceMaster in the USA had a nationwide agreement with the Sears Group to carry out carpet cleaning as the Sears ServiceMaster department. This marketing technique was used to good effect in the London operation, once again by making use of the Crouch Humphrey & Tapling company contacts. In addition, ServiceMaster in the USA had developed a marketing method for securing domestic customers in concentrated areas, and this too was used.

The plan was to penetrate the UK market by means of franchising once the London pilot business was operating successfully.

When ServiceMaster in the UK started looking for franchisees, its first franchisee, not unnaturally, was one of its London employees who had been training carpet cleaners and who had moved to Guildford. He bought a franchise for Guildford.

In 1963, Dr Brian Smith joined the company as the franchisee for Leicester and moved there from his home near London to start the business. He had previously worked in advertising and had also worked overseas.

In 1963 the service of cleaning carpets on location was almost unheard of in the UK. On Smith's first day of calling on 27 carpet retailers, 24 of them told him it was impossible to clean carpets on the floor. The other three were delighted to learn of the service. One produced immediate business as he worked with a local brewery, supplying and fitting all their carpets. The other two also produced individual business.

Appendix E (iii): Case Study: The ServiceMaster UK Story

Given that ServiceMaster was 'the only show in town' – the uniqueness of the service did not require any special selling or marketing techniques – there was no competition. By the same token, there was no great volume of business. Few customers were willing to risk having their carpets cleaned *in situ*, having had previous experience of a well-known DIY product which at the time was based on coconut oil and led to rapid re-soiling of the carpet.

Rather like Dyno-Rod, who were the very first to have power drain cleaning, the uniqueness of the service in itself, if marketed in only a moderate way, generated sufficient business from customer recommendations, referrals and repeat business to build up a viable operation.

In the 1960s business format franchising, as it is known and understood today, was by no means completely developed. ServiceMaster relied very heavily for promotion on its carpet cleaning specification sheet and manufacturers' testimonials. Neither Smith nor either of the two other franchisees at that time had any regrets about not having fully laid down procedures to follow. Smith recalls a manual of some 25 pages, but by the mid-1980s the manual had expanded to some 600 pages!

In 1971 Smith, who was still a ServiceMaster franchisee in Leicester, was invited to join the franchisor organisation. ServiceMaster franchisees had an annual conference and received bulletins, but at the time there was little communication between franchisor and franchisee or amongst franchisees themselves, who numbered about 20 at that time.

Smith discovered that the majority of the franchisees were excellent craftsmen running small but successful businesses, but they did not really understand the selling or accounting side of the business. It was obvious that ServiceMaster needed to develop a total business format which franchisees could follow.

Smith initially devoted his attention to the accounts side of the business and ran a series of seminars entitled 'Management for Growth'. This was aimed at developing the management and administrative side of the business, and in particular developing an accounting system which franchisees could use and understand. It was designed to manage and operate a business rather than satisfy the needs of the auditors or HMRC!

Although this may appear to be a digression from how the franchise business developed, it is relevant in the case of ServiceMaster to show how the system

Appendix E (iii): Case Study: The ServiceMaster UK Story

evolved whilst it was up and running rather than having been developed during the pilot operation of the franchisor. It is not something I would recommend today.

In 1976 the ServiceMaster organisation in the UK was restructured. A new company, 'ServiceMaster Limited', under the control of ServiceMaster Industries in the United States, was established, and Smith was appointed managing director.

The carpet cleaning industry changed dramatically and by the mid-1980s a conservative estimate of the number of carpet cleaners in the UK was put at 2,000. As with all good ideas, the ServiceMaster idea was copied and the market changed; fitted carpets were to be found everywhere and there was now a good deal of competition.

ServiceMaster spends millions on research and development, improving its equipment, products and methods of carrying out its service. It has developed far more sophisticated marketing techniques and continually improves its administrative and franchisee management processes and procedures.

A franchisee joining ServiceMaster today gets a true complete business format. Every aspect of the business is covered in manuals and training is given in all areas, both in the initial training process and in continuing training sessions.

ServiceMaster is continually researching and developing new methods and techniques not only for cleaning carpets and upholstery, but also in other areas. Considerable development has taken place in the field of disaster restoration and smoke odour removal. Care is taken to see that these services are offered by franchisees in addition to their existing services so that there is real growth rather than merely exchanging, say, carpet cleaning pounds for smoke odour removal pounds.

For ServiceMaster, the market research carried out in the early stages was vitally important for growing its franchise business and for reaching the number of franchisees it needed to penetrate the market whilst ensuring the success of individual franchisees.

APPENDIX F (i)

Sample Document: Confidentiality, Deposit and Non-Competition Agreement

This is NOT nor is it intended to be a legal document and should NOT be used as such.

The reader is strongly advised to seek legal advice before its use.

The author accepts no liability for its content or use.

This Deed is dated the day of 2009 **BETWEEN** _____ of _____ ('Prospective Franchisee') and **FRANCHISOR LIMITED** (Company Registration No ____) of _____ ('Franchisor')

(A) The Prospective Franchisee wishes to become a franchisee of the Franchisor in the Territory

(B) The Prospective Franchisee requires from the Franchisor accounting, financial, technical and commercial information relating to the Franchisor's franchise concept which is secret and confidential to enable the Prospective Franchisee to obtain finance and/or evaluate the Franchisor's concept and business methods for the purpose of determining whether or not to become a franchisee of the Franchisor

(C) The Prospective Franchisee has received and will be receiving Information which is confidential and valuable to Franchisor

1. DEFINITIONS

THE following Initial Periods shall have the following meanings:
'#####': the business of _____

'Business': utilising the Intellectual property
'Intellectual Property': the Franchisor's trade marks, trade names, know-how, business systems, methods of operation and Information used in the operation of a **##### Business**

Appendix F (i): Sample Document: Confidentiality, Deposit and Non-Competition Agreement

'Deposit': £___

'Information': trade secrets and other confidential information (written, oral, visual and electronic or in whatever other form) concerning the ##### **Business** which is the property of the Franchisor

'Initial Period': from the date of this agreement until the __ day of ____ 20__

'Territory': _____

'##### Franchise Agreement': the standard form of franchise agreement of the Franchisor in the agreed form attached

2. FRANCHISOR'S OBLIGATIONS

IN consideration of the payment of the Deposit by the Prospective Franchisee to the Franchisor (the receipt of which Franchisor acknowledges) and of and subject to the Prospective Franchisee's agreements warranties and undertakings set out in this agreement, the Franchisor agrees that it will not grant a ##### franchise to anyone else in the Territory during the Initial Period

3. PROSPECTIVE FRANCHISEE'S OBLIGATIONS

IN consideration of the Franchisor agreeing as set out in paragraph 2, the Prospective Franchisee agrees with and warrants and undertakes to the Franchisor as follows:

3.1 not to use the Information for any purpose other than for deciding whether to become a ##### franchisee

3.2 not at any time to disclose any of the Information to any person without the prior written approval of the Franchisor

3.3 unless the Prospective Franchisee becomes a franchisee of the Franchisor:

    3.3.1 immediately upon demand by Franchisor to destroy or permanently erase all records or copies of the Information and such business plan

    3.3.2 for a period of one year from the date of this agreement not to engage directly or indirectly in any business which competes or which would compete with any ##### **Business**

Appendix F (i): Sample Document: Confidentiality, Deposit and Non-Competition Agreement

    (i)   anywhere in the Territory; or

    (ii) operated by Franchisor any of its franchisees or prospective franchisees anywhere in the United Kingdom

3.4 that the Prospective Franchisee is not:

    3.4.1 directly or indirectly connected or associated in any way with any person or entity who or which is engaged or intends to become engaged in a business similar to the ##### **Business**

    3.4.2 engaged in any discussions with or has an option to take up a franchise from such a person or entity

3.5 that the information disclosed by the Prospective Franchisee to the Franchisor in his/or her franchise application form and in any discussions with Franchisor are true and correct

4. FURTHER AGREEMENT

IT is further agreed between the parties that:

4.1 the Deposit is not fully refundable and is subject to deductions by the Franchisor of all costs relating to the transaction contemplated by this agreement and the Franchise Agreement including but not limited to all property costs

4.2 if the Prospective Franchisee enters into a ##### Franchise Agreement with the Franchisor:

    4.2.1 the Deposit shall form part of the Initial Franchise Fee (as defined in the ##### Franchise Agreement) then payable by the Prospective Franchisee; and

    4.2.2 the ##### Franchise Agreement shall supersede this agreement except for paragraph 3 of this agreement which shall remain in full force and effect

4.3 this agreement will expire at the end of the Initial Period for which time shall be of the essence

Executed as a Deed by the parties, etc.

APPENDIX F (ii)

Sample Document: Franchise Purchase Agreement

This is NOT nor is it intended to be a legal document and should NOT be used as such.
The reader is strongly advised to seek legal advice before its use.

The author accepts no liability for its content or use.

Contents

Clause Page
Product Distribution
Service Business
Fast Food
Sale of Package
Confidentiality of Information Supplied
Premises
Company's Obligations
Your Obligations
Consequences of Default in Payment
Acknowledgement as to Advice Given
Consequences of Not Proceeding
Assignment
Schedule – Start-up Package

Appendix F (ii): Sample Document: Franchise Purchase Agreement

THIS AGREEMENT is made the __ day of ____ Two thousand and __ **BETWEEN Franchisor Limited** (Company Registration Number _) of _____ ('Company') and _____ of _____ ('You' or 'Your').

WHEREAS
[PRODUCT DISTRIBUTION]

(A) The Company has expended time, effort and money in developing and in obtaining and acquiring knowledge about the distribution merchandising and promotion of the sale of _____ ('Products') and has established a demand and goodwill for the Products under the trade name _____ ('Trade Name') and a substantial reputation and goodwill in the Trade Name and its associated trade marks.

(B) The methods of distribution used in or in connection with the sale of the Products ('System') sold under the Trade Name are secret and confidential and are the exclusive property of the Company.

(C) The Company has granted and may from time to time grant franchises to certain franchisees to sell the Products under the Trade Name.

(D) You wish to enter into a franchise agreement in the agreed form (annexed) ('Franchise Agreement') with the Company to enable You to sell the Products under the Trade Name at _____ or at such other address within _____ as may be approved in writing by the Company ('Premises').

[SERVICE BUSINESS]

(A) The Company has expended time money and effort in developing and in obtaining and acquiring knowledge about the conduct of the business of _____ and has established a demand and goodwill for the said business under the name _____ ('Trade Name') and a reputation and goodwill in the Trade Name and its associated trade marks.

(B) The methods of conducting the said business ('System') are secret and confidential and are the exclusive property of the Company.

(C) You wish to enter into a franchise agreement ('Franchise Agreement') with the Company to enable You to operate the System under the Trade Name from _____ or at such other address within _____ as may be approved in writing by the Company.

Appendix F (ii): Sample Document: Franchise Purchase Agreement

[FAST FOOD]

(A) The Company has expended time effort and money in developing and in obtaining and acquiring knowledge about the manufacture preparation distribution merchandising and promotion of the sale of _____ and related products ('Products') and has established a demand and goodwill for the Products under the trade name ('Trade Name') and its associated trade marks and a substantial reputation and goodwill in the Trade Name.

(B) The formulae, ingredients, specifications, recipes, processes and methods used in or in connection with the preparation making service and sale of the Products ('System') are secret and confidential and are the exclusive property of the Company.

(C) The Company has granted and may from time to time grant franchises to certain franchisees to make serve and sell the Products under the Trade Name.

(D) You wish to enter into a franchise agreement ('Franchise Agreement') with the Company to enable You to make serve and sell the Products under the Trade Name at _____ or such other address within _____ as may be approved in writing by the Company ('Premises').

NOW IT IS HEREBY AGREED as follows:

1. SALE OF PACKAGE

1.1 The Company agrees to sell to You and You agree to buy from the Company on and subject to the terms of this agreement the Start-up Package listed in the attached Schedule for the cash price of £___ (+ VAT) [of which £___ has been paid as a deposit to the Company on signing this agreement.]

1.2 You agree to pay [the balance of] the Initial Franchise Fee by instalments as follows:

    1.2.1 £___ on the execution of a lease or underlease of the Premises or upon You taking possession of the Premises if earlier.

    1.2.2. £___ on signing the Franchise Agreement.

    1.2.3 £___ 2 weeks prior to the date scheduled for the commencement of Your training under Clause 4.

1.3

    1.3.1 You will pay the Company [the balance of] the purchase price for the Start-up Package [£___] within 10 days of the Company's written notice to You of the Company's willingness to deliver and install (where appropriate) the Start-up Package on payment of the purchase price.

    1.3.2 The purchase price referred to in clause 1.1 does not include delivery charges to the Premises or Value Added Tax or any other tax payable which will be payable by You.

    1.3.3 Property in the Start-up Package will not pass to You until You have paid to the Company all sums which may be payable under the terms of this agreement.

1.4 You and the Company agree to enter into the Franchise Agreement at least 2 weeks prior to the date scheduled for the commencement of Your training.

2. CONFIDENTIALITY OF INFORMATION SUPPLIED

2.1 You warrant to and undertake with the Company that the operations manual or manuals and its contents and the information divulged to You in the course of training will remain confidential and will not be divulged whether before or after the termination of this agreement.

2.2 You further agree that You will not directly or indirectly in any manner whatsoever make use of any of the Start-up Package, operations manual or manuals or any information contained in it or derived from it or in training except insofar as is necessary for the purposes provided in the Franchise Agreement (if entered into).

3. PREMISES

3.1 **IF** the Company owns the freehold interest in the Premises then (subject to the obtaining of the Court Order hereinafter mentioned unless the Company waives this requirement) the Company will grant to You and You will accept a lease of the Premises ('Head Lease') in the form of the draft annexed for a term of years equal to the term of the Franchise Agreement (and commencing on the date of commencement of the Franchise Agreement) at the rent (payable from the date specified by the Company but not being a date earlier than the date of commencement of this agreement) which will be such sum as the Company's Valuers certify as being the full market rent for the Premises having regard to current rental values and on the basis of:

3.1.1. a letting by a willing landlord to a willing tenant

3.1.2 there being ignored any restrictions on the use to which the Premises may be put and

3.1.3 a term of years equal to the term of the Franchise Agreement.

3.2

3.2.1 If the Company holds a lease of the Premises ('Lease') then (subject to the obtaining of the consent of any requisite Superior Landlord and the obtaining of the Court Order mentioned below unless the Company waives this latter requirement) the Company will grant to You and You will accept from the Company an underlease of the Premises ('Underlease') in the form of the draft annexed with such modifications (if any) as may be required by any superior landlord.

3.2.2 The term of years granted by the Underlease will either be equal to the term of the Franchise Agreement or equivalent to the residue of the term of years granted by the Lease less the last 10 days (whichever is the shorter) and in either case will commence on the date of the commencement of the Franchise Agreement.

3.2.3 The rent payable will be the same as that payable under the Lease or market rent (if higher) (subject to review in the manner set out in the Underlease) and will commence upon the date specified by the Company which shall not be prior to the date of the commencement of this agreement.

3.3

3.3.1 If the Company does not hold a freehold or leasehold interest in

Appendix F (ii): Sample Document: Franchise Purchase Agreement

> the Premises then the Company will at Your request use its reasonable endeavours to acquire a freehold or leasehold interest in the Premises (upon terms acceptable to the Company).
>
> 3.3.2 If the Company acquires a freehold interest then the provisions of clause 3.1 will apply.
>
> 3.3.3 If the Company acquires a leasehold interest then the provisions of clause 3.2 shall apply.
>
> 3.3.4 Any premium payable for the acquisition of such leasehold interest by the Company will be reimbursed by You to the Company forthwith upon demand by the Company.

3.4 [The Company and You shall forthwith or so soon after the signing hereof as may be possible and practicable apply to the relevant Court for an Order contracting Your Lease or the Underlease or (as the case may be) out of the provisions of Sections 24 to 28 (inclusive) of the Landlord and Tenant Act 1954. In the event of the Court refusing such an order the Company shall be entitled to terminate this agreement within four weeks after receiving notice of such refusal from the Court and in that event the Initial Franchise Fee shall be repaid to You but You will comply so far as the same may be applicable with the provisions of clause 8.]

3.5 If the consent of any superior landlord is required to the grant of the Underlease the Company hereby undertakes to endeavour to obtain such consent as quickly as possible and You hereby undertake to provide all references and other information as may reasonably be required to obtain such consent and to enter into any licences and provide such personal guarantees as may be required by any superior landlord.

3.6

> 3.6.1 If You are allowed into occupation of the Premises prior to the grant of Your Lease or Underlease (as the case may be) it shall be as licensee only and no tenancy will be created and such occupation will be on the same terms and conditions as if Your Lease or the Underlease (as the case may be) had been granted (except for those which are inconsistent with the terms of a licence) and You will pay

to the Company a licence fee equivalent to the rents and all other monies which would be payable under Your Lease or the Underlease (as the case may be).

3.6.2 If the Company gives written notice to You to vacate the Premises You will forthwith vacate and deliver them up to the Company.

3.7

3.7.1 If six months from the date of this agreement [the Court Order or] any requisite superior landlord's consent has not been obtained for the grant of the Underlease the Company will have the right to terminate this agreement on serving fourteen days written notice on You.

3.7.2 The Company will repay to You all sums paid by You to the Company under the provisions of this agreement (other than Continuing Franchise Fees and advertising, marketing and promotional contributions) plus a sum equal to the value of Your sound saleable stock fixtures fitting and equipment at cost price against their delivery by You to the Company less:

3.7.2.1 expenses incurred by the Company in Your respect from the moment of Your first contact with the Company. The amount of such sum (which shall not exceed any sum paid by way of Initial Franchise Fee).

3.7.2.2 a licence fee calculated in accordance with clause 3.6 for such period of time as You have been in occupation of the Premises; and

3.7.2.3 a sum equal to the cost to the Company of any repairs decorations or replacement of equipment fixtures and fittings not wholly attributable to fair wear and tear.

3.7.3 For the avoidance of doubt any profit or loss made by You while operating the business under the Trade Name during your period of occupation of the Premises will belong to or be suffered by You.

3.8 Your Lease or the Underlease (as the case may be) will be completed within four weeks from [the date of the said Court order] or the grant of consent by any superior landlord (if necessary) [whichever shall be the later].

3.9 You will procure the execution by a person or persons acceptable to the Company and any superior landlord (if any) as surety for Your Lease or the Underlease (as the case may be) upon its completion.

3.10 You will enter into such form of agreement permitting the alterations and/or fitting out works to the Premises by You as the Company or any superior landlord shall require and (if applicable) You will at Your own expense assume the obligations of the Company (in respect of such works) to any superior landlord in accordance with the directions of the Company and to the reasonable satisfaction of the Company.

3.11 You will pay all reasonable and proper costs charges and expenses (including value added tax and disbursements and whether incurred as principal or by way of indemnity to a third party) incurred by the Company in and giving effect to the terms of this clause including and without prejudice to the generality of the foregoing those incurred

   3.11.1 in the acquisition of a freehold or leasehold interest by the Company (including all professional fees) in accordance with clause 3;

   3.11.2 in the grant or obtaining of any licences under clauses 3.5 and 3.10; and

   3.11.3 in the grant of Your Lease or the Underlease (as the case may be).

3.12 [The Company may by written notification direct that the provisions of clause 3.4 will not apply.]

4. COMPANY'S OBLIGATIONS

4.1 **SUBJECT** to the provisions of clause 5 the Company will provide or make available to You the following services:

   4.1.1 Consultation and advice as to the location suitability and acquisition of the Premises;

   4.1.2 Consultation and advice with regard to alternations refurbishment renovation any further equipment required or other work necessary for the conversion of the Premises so that they are fit for use for the purpose of conducting the _____ business from them;

Appendix F (ii): Sample Document: Franchise Purchase Agreement

    4.1.3 General supervision of the said conversion [not] including day to day or immediate supervision which will be provided by [Your] architect builder or surveyor;

    4.1.4 Delivery and installation (where appropriate) of the Start-up Package at the Premises;

    4.1.5 Consultation and advice with a view to enabling You to open Your _____ business including advice and consultation with regard to the purchase of materials the selection training and supervision of staff accounting book-keeping advertising and the day to day operation of the business;

    4.1.6 Advice on the stocking of the Premises prior to the commencement of the business;

    4.1.7

        4.1.7.1 The Company will train You in the operation of the System. Such training shall be provided to You without further charge but You will be responsible for paying any travelling food and accommodation expenses which You incur during the period of training.

        4.1.7.2 If at any time during the period of training it becomes apparent to the Company that You do not satisfy or meet the Company's standards and requirements the Company shall have the right upon notice in writing to terminate this agreement and shall return to You any deposit and/or Initial Franchise Fee paid less the agreed deduction referred to in clause 8.

        4.1.7.3 The training and operations manual or manuals provided to You shall at all times remain the property of the Company and You agree to return them on demand.

    4.1.8 Advice on the initial advertising campaign and the opening of the business.

5. YOUR OBLIGATIONS

5.1 You will:

5.1.1 acquire the Premises;

5.1.2 ensure that adequate finance is available to You for the preparation of the Premises and by way of working capital;

5.1.3 [ensure that the Premises are altered, refurbished, equipped and fitted out in accordance with the Company's requirements;]

5.1.4 acquire such equipment books of account and any other items whatsoever that are necessary for the performance by You of Your obligations under the Franchise Agreement;

5.1.5 upon completion of the said training and the refurbishing fitting out and delivery and installation of the Start-up Package of the Premises to the satisfaction of the Company and within 7 days of the receipt by You from the Company of written notice execute and procure the execution by a person or persons who is acceptable to the Company as Guarantor of the Franchise Agreement in the agreed terms attached.

6. CONSEQUENCES OF DEFAULT IN PAYMENT

6.1 IF You make any default whatsoever in paying the purchase price or any instalment of it the Company will be entitled to suspend the provision and the making available of each and all of the above-mentioned services including the delivery and installation (where appropriate) of the Start-up Package until You have remedied such default and/or upon notice given to You to be released from each and all of its obligations under this agreement and without prejudice to any rights it may have to retake possession of any items of the Start-up Package delivered to the Premises but not attached to them.

7. ACKNOWLEDGEMENT AS TO ADVICE GIVEN

7.1 You acknowledge that the Company in giving advice to assist You in establishing a _____ business (including but without prejudice to the generality of the foregoing recommending equipment and materials and the assessment of Your suitability) bases its advice and recommendations on experience actually obtained in practice and is not giving any guarantees or warranties as to the success of Your _____ business.

7.2 It is hereby expressly agreed between the parties that this agreement contains the entire agreement between the parties other than the Franchise Agreement and/or any Head Lease or Underlease (if entered into) and that You acknowledge that no representation warranties inducement or promises made by the Company have been relied upon by You save as may have been notified by You to the Company in writing and are annexed to this agreement.

8. CONSEQUENCES OF NOT PROCEEDING

8.1 IF at any time before signing the Franchise Agreement

    8.1.1 You notify the Company in writing of Your intention to terminate this agreement; or

    8.1.2 the Company notifies You that it does not intend to enter into a Franchise Agreement with You

then in either such event this agreement will terminate.

8.2 In the event of termination under clause 8.1.1 any deposit paid to the Company will subject as provided below be repaid to You less an agreed deduction of £___ which is hereby agreed and acknowledged to be a genuine pre-estimate of the direct and indirect expenditure likely to have been incurred by the Company in providing services to You prior to Your starting Your _____ business.

8.3

    8.3.1 The Company will be entitled to rescind this agreement if You have not secured the Premises within the period of __ months from the date of the agreement whether by purchase lease or agreement for lease.

    8.3.2 In the event of such rescission the Company shall refund in full any deposit paid by You.

8.4 If You fail to perform any of Your obligations under this or any other agreement with the Company to the reasonable satisfaction of the Company (notwithstanding the provisions of clause 8.1) the Company may refuse to enter into the Franchise Agreement in which case no part of any deposit paid will be refunded to You.

8.5 It shall be a condition precedent of any return of the said deposit (less deduction) that You shall return complete whole undefaced and in good order and condition the Start-up Package and any training or operations manual or manuals loaned by the Company to You and will warrant to the Company (if it be the case) that their respective contents have not been divulged to any third party and (in any event) that You will not make whether directly or indirectly any use of the information which You have acquired by Your training, possession of the operations manual or association with the Company or any of its franchisees or employees.

9. ASSIGNMENT

9.1 This agreement is personal to You and is not assignable by You.

SCHEDULE

Start-up Package

Description of Item	Quantity	Price (excluding VAT)

SIGNED etc.

APPENDIX F (iii)

Sample Document: Outline of Franchise Agreement

This is NOT nor is it intended to be a legal document and should NOT be used as such.

The reader is strongly advised to seek legal advice before its use.

The author accepts no liability for its content or use.

PARTIES   Franchisor (1)

Franchisee (2)

Principal (3)

RECITALS

DEFINITIONS:

(A) Business

(B) Trade Name

(C) Trade Marks

(D) Products

(E) Services

1. RIGHTS GRANTED

1.1 Franchisor grants to Franchisee the right to:

   1.1.1 operate the system [and provide the services]

   1.1.2 use the trade name/trade mark

   1.3.3 use Franchisor's copyright material

   1.1.4 carry on the business only at agreed premises

Appendix F (iii): Sample Document: Outline of Franchise Agreement

2. TERM OF FRANCHISE

2.1 Term of Franchise to be __ years

3 RIGHT OF RENEWAL

3.1 Right of renewal for further period if Franchisee not then in breach and has substantially performed the terms of the agreement

3.2 Terms to be those on offer at time in Franchisor's standard agreement subject to Franchisee bringing business [and Premises] up to standard etc

4. LEASE OF PREMISES

4.1

    4.1.1 If Franchisor owns the freehold interest of the property Franchisor will grant to Franchisee a lease on terms to be specified in agreement

    4.1.2 If Franchisor owns a leasehold interest in the property Franchisor will grant to Franchisee an underlease on terms to be specified in agreement

    4.1.3 If Franchisor does not own any interest it will use reasonable endeavours to obtain a freehold or leasehold interest and will grant a lease or underlease

4.2 The parties will apply to the Court for an order that the security of tenure provisions of the Landlord and Tenant Act 1954 should not apply to the lease or underlease

4.3 The parties will apply for any licence which may be required from a superior landlord and Franchisee will supply references and other information as may be necessary

4.4 Allow for Franchisee to be allowed into possession pending completion of formalities

4.5 If Court order or consents not obtained within six months provision to be made for termination and the consequences

Appendix F (iii): Sample Document: Outline of Franchise Agreement

4.6 Completion to take place within four weeks after Court Order and consents obtained

4.7 Franchisee to procure execution of lease by guarantor if required

4.8 Franchisee to enter into any necessary licence permitting alterations under terms of lease or underlease

4.9 Franchisee to pay costs

4.10 Franchisor may waive requirement that Court Order is obtained

5. FRANCHISOR'S INITIAL OBLIGATIONS

5.1 The Franchisor will provide the following services and/or goods:

- **5.1.1.** Advice as to location suitability and acquisition of premises
- **5.1.2** Advice about conversion of premises
- **5.1.3** Use of standard plans and specifications
- **5.1.4** Advice with regard to fixtures and fittings
- **5.1.5** General supervision of conversion
- **5.1.6** Consultation and advice with Franchisor's executives on how to set up
- **5.1.7** Advice on initial stocking requirements
- **5.1.8** Advice on initial opening launch and advertising
- **5.1.9** Equipment fixtures and fittings listed in Schedule

6. FRANCHISOR'S CONTINUING OBLIGATIONS

6.1 The Franchisor shall:

- **6.1.1** provide Franchisee with an operations manual or manuals which remain the property and copyright of Franchisor
- **6.1.2** give Franchisee access to officers and executives of Franchisor for consultation and advice
- **6.1.3** provide know-how advice guidance relating to management finance promotion and methods of operation

Appendix F (iii): Sample Document: Outline of Franchise Agreement

    6.1.4 provide Franchisee with assistance in negotiating contracts and may enter into contracts with customers for the supply of services by the Franchisee

    6.1.5 provide telephone lines for use by Franchisee subscriber to be Franchisor

    6.1.6 provide Franchisee at his expense with stationery invoices quotation forms standard forms of contract and other documentation for use by Franchisee in his dealings with customers

    6.1.7 permit use of trade marks

    6.1.8 provide fascia signs on hire (terms to be specified)

7. LEASE OF EQUIPMENT

7.1 Provide for the leasing of any special equipment and set out terms

8. FRANCHISEE'S OBLIGATIONS

8.1 Franchisee shall:

    8.1.1 acquire the premises

    8.1.2 refurbish and equip premises without delay as required by Franchisor

    8.1.3 acquire necessary books of account and items of equipment

    8.1.4 ensure it has adequate finance including working capital

    8.1.5 operate the system as provided in the manual

    8.1.6 maintain standards associated with trade name

    8.1.7 display on premises vehicles and on all written material a notice to the effect that the business is operated under franchise

    8.1.8 not pledge credit of Franchisor or hold itself out as a party or agent of Franchisor

    8.1.9 not use trade name or trade marks as whole or part of its corporate title

Appendix F (iii): Sample Document: Outline of Franchise Agreement

8.1.10 use only signs and packaging in connection with sale etc. which contains trade name

8.1.11 operate business in accordance with the system only under trade name

8.1.12 decorate its vehicles with the livery specified by the Franchisor

8.1.13 not alter premises without Franchisor's consent

8.1.14 keep premises in proper state of repair and decoration

8.1.15 use only approved plant and machinery equipment fixtures and fittings

8.1.16 devote all its time to the business during business hours and use best endeavours to promote and extend the business and operate during hours specified by Franchisor

8.1.17 maintain and increase turnover of business

8.1.18 maintain adequate stock for protection of goodwill

8.1.19 obtain supplies of products from Franchisor or other suppliers approved or nominated by Franchisor

8.1.20 refund or replace bona fide defective goods

8.1.21 be free to determine its own prices notwithstanding that Franchisor may recommend prices

8.1.22 ensure staff are clean, polite and properly dressed in uniforms provided (if any) and ensure that staff receive any necessary special training

8.1.23 not employ as manager any person who has not passed training course and been approved by Franchisor

8.1.24 procure confidentiality undertakings from staff

8.1.25 not do anything which may bring the system into disrepute or which may damage the interests of Franchisor or other franchisees

8.1.26 permit Franchisor to speak to customers to ascertain if they are satisfied with the service or goods

Appendix F (iii): Sample Document: Outline of Franchise Agreement

8.1.27 use only such stationery for external use as Franchisor shall stipulate

8.1.28 provide Franchisor with copies of all contracts entered into by Franchisee

8.1.29 use telephone provided only for operating the system and to pay all bills relating to the provision and use of the phone

8.1.30 perform any contracts entered into by Franchisor on national basis

8.1.31 comply with all statutory requirements

8.1.32 at request of Franchisor provide potential franchisees with information reasonably requested

8.1.33 not carry on any other business

8.1.34 not poach employees from other Franchisees

8.1.35 not use or disclose know-how acquired under agreement except for the purpose of performing obligations under the agreement

9. TRAINING

9.1 Franchisor shall train Franchisee in the operation of the system and shall have right to terminate if Franchisee does not satisfy the Franchisor's training standards

9.2 Franchisor may require Franchisee to attend further training courses at Franchisee's expense if Franchisor considers it necessary

9.3 Franchisee shall establish a training programme for its staff

9.4 Principal or manager of Franchisee may attend if appropriate

10. IMPROVEMENTS

10.1 Both parties shall interchange ideas and innovations for benefit of all franchisees no improvement or innovation to be introduced by Franchisee without Franchisor's consent

10.2 Franchisor can use Franchisee's improvements without charge

Appendix F (iii): Sample Document: Outline of Franchise Agreement

11 INITIAL FRANCHISE AND MANAGEMENT SERVICES FEE

11.1 Franchisee to pay Initial Franchise Fee of £___ + VAT on signing agreement

OR

11.1 Franchisee to pay Initial Franchise Fee of £___ + VAT as to _____ on signing agreement _____ on starting training and as to the balance on supply of equipment fixtures and fittings or before opening for business

11.2 Franchisee to pay Continuing Franchise Fee of % of gross revenues

11.3 Specify payment interval and timing of payments

11.4 Gross revenues to be defined

11.5 Franchisee to pay interest of late payments

12. ACCOUNTING AND REPORTING

12.1 Franchisee shall:

12.1.1 use cash registers with no resetting device

12.1.2 maintain record of gross revenues and remit statement of gross revenues weekly/monthly or other periodic interval to Franchisor

12.1.3 maintain basic records for two years

12.1.4 carry out [one] two inventories per [month] year/periodic accounting interval

12.1.5 supply monthly profit and loss accounts monthly or once in each periodic accounting interval

12.1.6 supply two sets of accounts each year – one interim and one set audited

12.1.7 register for VAT and provide copy VAT returns

12.1.8 provide such further information relating to business as is required

13. ADVERTISING

13.1 Payment of advertising contribution to Franchisor to expend on advertising and promotional activities

13.2 Control of advertising and displays and signs etc by Franchisor

13.3 Display by Franchisee of advertising and promotional material supplied by Franchisor

13.4 Franchisor to arrange for annual audited statements and receipts and payments

14. INSURANCE

14.1 Franchisee to arrange full business insurance and cover Franchisor against third party claims

14.2 Franchisee to have Franchisor's interest noted on policies and/or furnish Franchisor with copies of policies and evidence of payment of premiums

15. TRADE MARKS

15.1 Protect position of unregistered marks

15.2 Provide for registered user agreement if trade mark registered

16. SALE OF BUSINESS

16.1 No right to assign franchise

16.2 Franchisor to grant new franchise agreement to acceptable purchaser

16.3 Right to sell business with consent subject to:

  16.3.1 purchaser being bona fide and at arm's length and meeting Franchisor's standards for acceptance as a Franchisee including executing a confidentiality undertaking or a franchise agreement and passing the training course

  16.3.2 payment of fee to Franchisor

  16.3.3 purchaser not being involved in a competing business

  16.3.4 purchaser having adequate financial resources

Appendix F (iii): Sample Document: Outline of Franchise Agreement

16.3.5 (if purchaser is a company) the individual or individuals controlling the company and company structure meeting Franchisor's standards for acceptance and the directors or shareholders entering into latest edition of Franchisor's standard franchise agreement

16.3.6 payment being made by Franchisee of all costs and obligations to Franchisor

16.4 Deemed release of parties from terms of Franchise Agreement save for these which by nature or effect survive termination

16.5 Provide protection for Franchisor against unauthorised transfer of shares if Franchisee is in company

16.6

16.6.1 Franchisee to submit to Franchisor copy of each written offer which Franchisee proposes to accept together with specified details

16.6.2 Franchisor to have rights of first refusal

16.6.3 If rights of first refusal in favour of Franchisor not exercised Franchisee may sell

17. DEATH OF FRANCHISEE

17.1 Within period of three months following death Franchisee's personal representatives must decide whether a relative or beneficiary of Franchisee wishes to be substituted as Franchisee subject to criteria to be laid down

17.2 If personal representatives wish to sell the business they must try to find a purchaser acceptable to Franchisor so that if Franchisor does not exercise rights of first refusal the business may be sold

17.3 Franchisor may provide management for period of three months following death of Franchisee on payment of costs and expenses (including manager's salary) plus 50%

17.4 If requested Franchisor may provide management on same terms for a further period of up to three months to enable personal representatives to arrange sale

Appendix F (iii): Sample Document: Outline of Franchise Agreement

17.5 If management fee not promptly paid Franchisor released from obligation to provide manager

17.6 If a sale or assignment not arranged within a six month period Franchisor may withdraw manager and terminate Franchise

OR

17. DEATH OF PRINCIPAL

17.1 Within period of three months following death of Principal the Franchisee must decide whether a relative or beneficiary of Principal wishes to qualify to be substituted as Principal subject to criteria to be laid down

17.2 If Principal not provided by Franchisee within a three month period Franchisee to seek purchaser acceptable to Franchisor so that if Franchisor does not exercise rights of first refusal the business may be sold

17.3 Franchisor may provide management for period of three months following death of Principal on payment of costs and expenses (including manager's salary) plus 50%

17.4 If requested Franchisor may provide management on same terms for *further period of up to three months to enable Franchisee to arrange sale*

17.5 If management fee not promptly paid Franchisor released from obligation to provide manager

17.6 If substitution of Principal or sale of business not arranged by Franchisee within specified period, Franchisor may withdraw manager and terminate franchise

18. TERMINATION

18.1 Termination by Franchisor if Franchisee:

    18.1.1 fails to commence business within stipulated period

    18.1.2 is in breach of any of the terms of the agreement

    18.1.3 fails to provide services to the Franchisor's standards

Appendix F (iii): Sample Document: Outline of Franchise Agreement

18.1.4 supplied false or misleading information in its franchise application

18.1.5 becomes insolvent makes any arrangement with creditors has a bankruptcy petition presented against it or has a receiver appointed of its assets (or if Franchisee is a company the Principal has a bankruptcy petition presented against him or becomes insolvent or makes any arrangement with creditors)

18.1.6 purports to assign agreement

19. CONSEQUENCES OF TERMINATION

19.1 The Franchisee:

19.1.1 must stop use of trade name and trade marks and must not thereafter hold itself out as being a franchisee of Franchisor

19.1.2 must pay to Franchisor all sums payable to Franchisor whether or not then due (No right to set off)

19.1.3 must return to Franchisor all manuals literature promotional material letter heads invoices or anything else which bears the trade name of or indicates any association with the Franchisor

19.2 The Franchisee:

19.2.1 must provide the Franchisor with a list of all customers and potential customers of which it is aware

19.2.2 must assign to Franchisor benefit of existing contracts

19.2.3 must join with Franchisor in cancellation of permitted use of trade marks

19.2.4 must cease use of telephone line [provided by Franchisor] [transfer it to Franchisor]

19.2.5 shall cease use of copyright material

19.3 The Franchisor to have an option to purchase the Franchisee's business on basis laid down

Appendix F (iii): Sample Document: Outline of Franchise Agreement

19.4 The Franchisee

    19.4.1 must not for a period of one year within [a radius of mile(s) from the premises] [Territory] compete with the Franchisor

    19.4.2 must not for the period of one year within [any Territory where] [a radius of mile(s) from any premises from which] Franchisor and any franchisee of Franchisor carries on business compete with the Franchisor or such franchisee

    19.4.3 must not for a period of one year solicit any customers of the Franchisor or the Franchisee

    19.4.4 shall not in future use or duplicate system

20. NO WAIVER

20.1 Failure to enforce or exercise rights not to be a waiver

21. SEVERABILITY

21.1 Agreement to survive illegality of any particular provision except if it affects the Franchisor's trade name or its rights to receive payment

21.2 Provisions relating to registration of franchise agreement under the Restrictive Trade Practices Act

22. ACKNOWLEDGEMENTS AS TO ADVICE GIVEN

22.1 Limitation of Franchisor's liability for advice given and explanation of system

23. FURTHER ACKNOWLEDGEMENTS

23.1 Acknowledgements by Franchisee as to justification for the imposition of restrictions by the Franchisor confirming reasonableness thereof and that it has been advised to take legal advice

24. NO WARRANTIES WITHOUT AUTHORITY

24.1 To limit liability of Franchisor for acts of Franchisee and to provide indemnities

Appendix F (iii): Sample Document: Outline of Franchise Agreement

25. PRINCIPAL'S GUARANTEE

25.1 Principal to guarantee performance by Franchisee of the agreement and to undertake to preserve confidentiality of Franchisor's trade secrets know-how etc.

26 ASSIGNMENT BY FRANCHISOR

26.1 Agreement to be assignable by Franchisor subject to assignee covenanting with Franchisee to perform all Franchisee's obligations

27. ARBITRATION

27.1 Arbitration clause (if and to the extent required)

28 NOTICES

28.1 Formal provisions

29. CLAUSE HEADINGS

29.1 Clause Headings not part of Agreement

<u>**SCHEDULE**</u>

APPENDIX F (iv)

Sample Document: Franchise Agreement

This is NOT nor is it intended to be a legal document and should NOT be used as such.
The reader is strongly advised to seek legal advice before its use.

The author accepts no liability for its content or use.

Contents

    Products

    Services

    Fast Food

1. Definitions and Interpretation
2. Rights Granted
3. Term of Agreement
4. Right to a New Franchise Agreement
5. Company's Initial Obligations
6. Company's Continuing Obligations
7. Your Obligations
8. Training
9. Improvements
10. Fees and Contributions
11. Accounting and Reporting
12. Advertising, Marketing and Promotions

Appendix F (iv): Sample Document: Franchise Agreement

13. Insurance
14. Trade Marks
15. Sale of Business
16. Death or Incapacity of You or Guarantor
17. Termination
18. Consequences of Termination
19. Waiver
20. Severability
21. Acknowledgments and Warranty
22. No Warranties without Authority and Indemnity
23. Guarantor's Obligations
24. Assignment by Company
25. Other Provisions
26. Arbitration

Disclaimer for Financial Projections

Operations Manual Receipt

Confidentiality Undertaking

The First Schedule – Start-up Package

The Second Schedule – Confidentiality Undertaking

The Third Schedule – Guarantee and Indemnity

The Fourth Schedule – Purchase Terms

Schedule A – Appointment of Sub-Contractor

Schedule B – Appointment of Agent

The Fifth Schedule – Option Deed

Appendix F (iv): Sample Document: Franchise Agreement

The Sixth Schedule – Equipment Package

The Seventh Schedule –Trade Marks

The Eight Schedule – Guarantee Procedures

The Ninth Schedule – Hire/Loan of Equipment

The Tenth Schedule – Software Licence

The Eleventh Schedule – Vehicle 82

[Additional clauses relating to anti-money laundering, anti-bribery, health and safety, data protection, child protection, liquor licensing etc.]

THIS AGREEMENT is dated the _____ and made **BETWEEN** You, the Guarantor and the Company and sets out the terms relating to the operation of Your **ZORCO BUSINESS**

IN THIS AGREEMENT:

1	**Advertising, Marketing and Promotions Contributions** means:	A sum equal to __% of the Gross Revenues (plus VAT)
2	**Advertising Spend** means:	£___ (inclusive of VAT)
3	**Approved Format** means:	_____@[internet service provider] or such other format as may be designated by the Company
4	**Approved Wording** means:	'This **ZORCO BUSINESS** is operated under franchise and independently owned by _____'
5	**Business Launch Spend** means:	£___ (inclusive of VAT)
6	**Commencement Period** means:	__ weeks/months from the date of this agreement
7	**Company** means:	_____ Limited (Company number _____) of _____
8	**Continuing Franchise Fee** means:	A sum equal to __% of the Gross Revenues (plus VAT)

Appendix F (iv): Sample Document: Franchise Agreement

9	**Equipment Package** means:	The fixtures and fittings goods and items of equipment described in the Sixth Schedule
10	**Equipment Package Price** means:	The price stated in the Sixth Schedule for the Equipment Package
11	**Guarantor** means:	_____ of _____
12	**Initial Franchise Fee** means:	£___ (plus VAT)
13	[**Occupation** means:	_____]
14	**Premises** means:	_____ or such [alternative] premises in _____ as may be approved by the Company
15	[**Property Management Fee** means:	a sum equal to __% of the annual rent payable by You for the Premises]
16	**Radius** means:	a radius of _____ mile(s) from the Premises
17	**Sign Hire Fee** means:	£___ per annum
18	**Start-up Package** means:	Such items as are specified in the First Schedule
19	**Start-up Package Price** means:	£___ (inclusive of VAT)
20	**Term** means:	__ years from the date of this agreement
21	**Territory** means:	The geographical area within the red edging on the map attached
22	**Trade Marks** means:	all those unregistered and/or registered marks details of which appear in the Seventh Schedule and/or such other marks in addition to or in substitution of any of them as may be specified by the Company from time to time

Appendix F (iv): Sample Document: Franchise Agreement

23	**Trade Marks Licence Fee** means:	£___ per annum
24	**Trade Name** means:	_____ and/or such other name or names in addition to or in substitution of any of them as may be specified by the Company from time to time
25	**Trading Period** means:	_____
26	**ZORCO BUSINESS** means:	the business of [selling the Products/providing the Services] (as specified in the Operations Manual from time to time) using the Intellectual Property
27	**ZORCO NETWORK** means:	all **ZORCO BUSINESSES** (including the Business)
28	**You**, **Your**, **Yours** and **Yourself** means:	_____ or _____ Limited (Company number _____) of _____ **We agree to abide by the attached Terms, Conditions and Obligations**

Signed by You .... Signed by the Guarantor ....
        Director

Independent Witness Independent Witness

Name .... Name ....

Address .... Address ....

Occupation .... Occupation ....

Signed for and on behalf of the   ....

Company   Director

WHEREAS

Appendix F (iv): Sample Document: Franchise Agreement

PRODUCTS

(A) The Company has expended time effort and money in developing and in obtaining and acquiring knowledge about the conduct of the **ZORCO BUSINESS** and has established a [substantial demand and] goodwill for the Products under, and a [substantial and exclusive] reputation and goodwill in, the Trade Name

(B) The System is the exclusive property of the Company and with the exception of the methods of merchandising and packaging of the Products and the decor colour scheme furniture and layout of the Premises, is secret and confidential

(C) The Trade Name is associated with uniformly high standards of distribution merchandising and promotion

(D) The Company operates and may from time to time grant franchises permitting others to operate businesses using the Intellectual Property to sell the Products at certain premises [and within certain areas]

(E) You desire to obtain the benefit of the Company's knowledge skill and experience and the right to sell the Products using the Intellectual Property [at] [from] the Premises [and within the Territory][and the Company has agreed to grant a franchise to You on the following terms]

(F) The Company is the owner of [and has applied for the registration of] the [registered] Trade Marks

SERVICES

(A) The Company has expended time money and effort in developing and in obtaining and acquiring knowledge about the conduct of the **ZORCO BUSINESS** and has established a [substantial demand and] goodwill, for the said business under, and a [substantial and exclusive] reputation and goodwill in the Trade Name

(B) The System is the exclusive property of the Company and with the exception of the methods of merchandising packaging decor colour scheme furniture and layout is secret and confidential

(C) The Trade Name is associated with uniformly high standards of service and quality of work

(D) The Company operates and may from time to time grant franchises permitting others to operate businesses providing the Services using the Intellectual Property in accordance with the System from certain premises [and within certain areas]

(E) You desire to obtain the benefit of the Company's knowledge skill and experience and the right to provide the Services using the Intellectual Property from the Premises [and within the Territory]

(F) The Company is the owner of [and has applied for the registration of] the [registered] Trade Marks

FAST FOOD

(A) The Company has expended time effort and money in developing the **ZORCO BUSINESS** and has established a [substantial demand and] goodwill for restaurants operating under, and a [substantial and exclusive] reputation and goodwill in, the Trade Name

(B) The System is the exclusive property of the Company and with the exception of the menus methods of merchandising packaging decor colour scheme furniture and layout is secret and confidential

(C) The Trade Name is associated with uniformly high standards of manufacture preparation service and merchandising of food and beverage products within the Menu Range

(D) The Company operates and may from time to time grant franchises permitting others to operate businesses using the Intellectual Property at certain premises

(E) You desire to obtain the benefit of the Company's knowledge skill and experience and the right to operate a business using the Intellectual Property at the Premises

(F) The Company is the proprietor of the copyright and design copyright in the designs of the fixtures and fittings plans and specifications for the Premises including colour schemes pattern of furnishings dress styles of staff and the like used in the System

(G) The Company is the owner of [and has applied for the registration of] [and the registered proprietor of] the Trade Marks

Appendix F (iv): Sample Document: Franchise Agreement

1. DEFINITIONS AND INTERPRETATION

1.1 **IN** this agreement the following words and/or expressions shall have the following meaning:

Accounting Reference Date:	_____ in each year of the Term or such other date as may be specified by the Company
Advertising, Marketing and Promotions Contribution:	(__%) of the first (£___) of Gross Revenues in any Trading Period (__%) of the next (£___) of Gross Revenues in any Trading Period (__%) of Gross Revenues in excess of (£___) in any Trading Period. The threshold amounts of Gross Revenues shall be increased annually in each Franchise Year on the Accounting Reference Date by the same proportion as any increase in the Retail Prices Index between the Accounting Reference Date on which such review is to take place and the immediately preceding Accounting Reference Date.
Affiliate:	persons and/or entities which directly or indirectly control are controlled by or are under the common control of the Company and in this regard 'control' means the power to direct or cause the direction of the management and policies of an entity
Approved Suppliers:	such supplier or suppliers of the Products as the Company shall nominate from time to time [and all franchisees of the Company]
Assets:	all [Vehicles] fixtures fittings and equipment employed in the Business the Residual Goodwill and Your interest in the Premises if they are commercial premises [and Your sound saleable stock of the Products]
Business:	the business carried on by You pursuant to and in accordance with this agreement

Appendix F (iv): Sample Document: Franchise Agreement

Confidentiality Undertaking:	an undertaking in the form set out in the Second Schedule or in such other form as may be supplied by the Company
[Continuing Franchise Fee:	(__%) of the first (£___) of Gross Revenues in any Trading Period (__%) on the next (£___) of Gross Revenues in any Trading Period (__%) of Gross Revenues in excess of (£___) in any Trading Period. The threshold amounts of Gross Revenues shall be increased annually in each Franchise Year on the Accounting Reference Date by the same proportion as any increase in the Retail Price Index]
DPA:	the Data Protection Act 1998 secondary legislation and guidance given by the Information Commissioner
Default Notice:	a written notice served by the Company setting out the nature of the default and giving You 7 days, in the case of a default relating to a failure to promptly make payment of any sums owing by You to the Company, and such period as the Company may specify in any other case PROVIDED that in the case of a Persistent Default You will not be entitled to any period of grace within which to remedy any such default neglect or failure
Direct or Local Advertising:	all advertising in [the Territory] solely for the benefit of the Business effected by means of such media as the Company in its discretion thinks fit
Franchise Transfer Fee:	a sum equal to __% of the sum then being charged by the Company to new franchisees by way of initial franchise fee or if the Company is not offering franchises at that time, a sum equal to __% of such initial franchise fee as was last charged by the Company adjusted for any

Appendix F (iv): Sample Document: Franchise Agreement

	increase in the Retail Price Index between the date such fee was last charged and the date of Your application for consent to the sale of the Assets [and if the Company has introduced the prospective purchaser a further __% of the sale price of the Assets]
[Franchise Year:	the period of 12 calendar months running from the _____ to _____]
Your Notice:	notice served by You pursuant to clause 15.2.1
Company's Notice:	notice served by the Company pursuant to paragraph (B) of the Purchase Terms
Guarantee and Indemnity:	a guarantee and indemnity in the form set out in the Third Schedule
Guarantor:	_____
Gross Revenues:	all gross sums receivable (whether or not payment is received) by You in or about the conduct of the Business arising directly or indirectly from whatever source including the assumed Gross Revenues for the purposes of any loss of profits insurance claims but excluding VAT
Initial Training:	the training provided by the Company to You in the operation of the System
Intellectual Property:	all or any of the following:

(A) the Trade Marks;

(B) the Trade Name;

(C) copyright and design copyright held by the Company in any material printed in writing or in computer code form (including but not limited to the Operations Manual and Software) designs or other work relating to the System;

Appendix F (iv): Sample Document: Franchise Agreement

	(D) designs (whether or not protected by copyright or registered) devised or acquired by the Company and applied in the manufacture assembly or sale of the Products and/or in the System; and
	(E) the System
Internet:	interactive multimedia, global communications network including all linking and framing and internet connections approved by the Company
[Menu Range:	such food and beverage products as are specified by the Company from time to time]
National Accounts:	customers with whom the Company has contracts for the [provision of the Services][supply of the Products]
National Accounts Terms:	the terms and conditions specified by the Company in relation to individual National Accounts
New Franchise Agreement:	the latest edition of the Company's standard form of franchise agreement being offered to its franchisees at the time of Your request for a new franchise agreement (appropriate for a corporate, partnership or sole proprietor franchisee) which may provide for other fees, higher continuing franchise fees and greater expenditures for advertising, marketing and promotion than are provided for in this agreement and may contain other terms materially different from the terms of this agreement
Offending Provision:	any term or provision referred to in clause 20.1
Operations Manual:	a manual or manuals which contain details of the Intellectual Property [(including but not limited to the Menu Range the Software the Products and the Services)] as may be updated by the Company from time to time

Appendix F (iv): Sample Document: Franchise Agreement

Option Deed:	a deed in the form set out in the Fifth Schedule
Participant:	any firm person or company who would be deemed to be a Participant under the provisions of Section 118 of the Fair Trading Act 1973 (as amended by the Trading Schemes Act 1996) and the regulations made under the said Acts
Periodic Accounting Interval:	the intervals in each year specified as such by the Company in the Operations Manual
Persistent Default:	a default neglect or failure by You and/or the Guarantor of the same agreement obligation or condition which has occurred more than twice in any period of 1 year as communicated to You
Purchase Terms:	the terms set out in the Fourth Schedule
Purchase Notice:	a notice served by the Company pursuant to the provisions of paragraph (D) of the Purchase Terms
[Products:	_____ and such other products in addition to, or in substitution of, them as may be specified in the Operations Manual from time to time]
[Range of Services:	such services as are specified by the Company from time to time]
Residual Goodwill:	the goodwill of the Business as a going concern but excluding the value of the goodwill derived from the use by You of the Intellectual Property
Retail Prices Index:	the General Index of Retail Prices which is Table 18.1 in the Monthly Digest of Statistics published in the United Kingdom by the Central Statistical Office or in its absence the nearest equivalent to it and if there is any change after the date of this agreement in the reference base used to compile the Retail Prices Index, the figure taken to be that at which the Retail Prices

Appendix F (iv): Sample Document: Franchise Agreement

	Index stands after such change will be the figure at which the Retail Prices Index would have stood if the reference base current at the date of this agreement had been retained
[**Services:**	_____ and such other services in addition to, or in substitution of, them as may be specified in the Operations Manual from time to time]
Software:	the computer software which You are required to use in the operation of the Business more particularly described in the Operations Manual
[**System:**	all of the following which are more particularly described in the Operations Manual:

    (A) the know-how and methods of distribution merchandising promotion and packaging used in or in connection with the sale of the Products under the Trade Name

    (B) the recognised design decor and colour scheme for the business premises occupied [and vehicles used] for the purposes of the **ZORCO BUSINESS**

    (C) the equipment, furniture, layout, service, format, and the standards of quality and uniformity of products and services offered by a **ZORCO BUSINESS**; and

    (D) the procedures for accounting inventory and management control used in the **ZORCO BUSINESS**]

[**System:**   all of the following which are more particularly described in the Operations Manual:

    (A) the know-how and methods used in or in connection with the provision of the Services under the Trade Name

(B) the recognised design decor and colour scheme for the business premises occupied [and vehicles] used in connection with the provision of the Services under the Trade Name

(C) the equipment, furniture, layout, service, format, and standards of quality and uniformity of products and services offered by a **ZORCO BUSINESS**; and

(D) the procedures for accounting inventory and management control used in the **ZORCO BUSINESS**]

[**System:** all of the following which are more particularly described in the Operations Manual:

(A) the restaurant format and the know-how and operating system utilising specialised [and] novel [and unique] techniques knowledge expertise skill and proprietary information relating to the development and operation of limited menu restaurants under the Trade Name

(B) the methods of preparation merchandising and packaging used in or in connection with the operation of the said restaurants under the Trade Name; and

(C) a recognised design decor and colour scheme for the restaurant premises kitchen and dining area, the equipment, layout, service, format, and standards of quality and uniformity of products and services offered and the ingredients recipes and procedures for inventory and management control used in the **ZORCO BUSINESS**]

Termination:	the expiry determination or termination of this agreement
VAT:	value added tax or its substitute
[Vehicle:	the vehicle [required to be] used by You in connection with Your conduct of the Business which is described in the Eleventh Schedule and such other vehicle or vehicles in addition to or in substitution of it as the Company may specify]

1.2 In this agreement where the context so requires or admits the singular includes the plural and the masculine includes the feminine and neuter and vice versa

1.3 The term 'Guarantor' and where You are a natural person the term 'You' will where the context so admits include Your or the Guarantor's personal representatives as the case may be

1.4 If You compromise 2 or more persons as parties to this agreement all covenants and agreements on Your part shall be deemed to be joint and several covenants

1.5 References in this agreement to 'set off' shall include legal and equitable set off

NOW IT IS HEREBY AGREED as follows:

2. RIGHTS GRANTED

2.1 **IN** consideration of Your paying the Initial Franchise Fee, the Advertising, Marketing and Promotions Contributions, the Sign Hire Fee, the Property Management Fee and the Continuing Franchise Fee promptly You have the right to use the Intellectual Property only in connection with the Business and subject to and in accordance with the terms of this agreement

2.2 For the avoidance of doubt it is hereby agreed and declared that:

    2.2.1 You have no right to and will not sub-licence sub-franchise or delegate any of the rights granted by this agreement

Appendix F (iv): Sample Document: Franchise Agreement

      2.2.2   except for the rights granted to You in this agreement and except for any rights granted by the Company to others, the Company reserves for itself all rights to all other territories

2.3   [Non-exclusive territory

      2.3.1   Before granting to any person a franchise to operate a **ZORCO BUSINESS** in the Territory, the Company will offer a **ZORCO** franchise to You and if You decline the Company's offer the Company shall be free to offer a **ZORCO** franchise to a third party **PROVIDED** such offer to a third party is on no more favourable terms than those offered to You

      2.3.2   If You fail to accept such offer within 21 days of its being made, You shall be deemed to have refused such offer]

3. TERM OF AGREEMENT

3.1   **THIS** agreement shall subject to the provisions for termination set out in this agreement subsist for the Term

4. RIGHT FOR A NEW FRANCHISE AGREEMENT

4.1   AT the end of the Term You will have the right to enter into a New Franchise Agreement with the Company **PROVIDED THAT ALL** of the following conditions are fulfilled

      4.1.1   such option may only be exercised by You by written notice to the Company which may only be given not more than 6 months nor less than 3 months before the expiry of the Term

      4.1.2   there must be no outstanding breach by You of any of the terms and conditions of this agreement or any other agreement with the Company

      4.1.3   You must have substantially observed and performed the terms and conditions of this agreement and any other agreement with the Company

4.1.4 You must agree to carry out, at its own expense, within a period of _____ days (or such longer period as may be specified by the Company) from the date You are notified by the Company, of the Company's requirements such works of renovation modernisation and refurbishment and replace such fixtures signs furnishings [Vehicles] and equipment as the Company considers to be necessary to bring the Premises and the Business up to the latest standards of the **ZORCO BUSINESS** and to comply with any relevant statutory or other requirements or regulations which apply to You the Premises and/or the Business

4.1.5 You and the Guarantor must sign a New Franchise Agreement with the Company save that:

4.1.5.1 [the New Franchise Agreement shall be for a period at least equal to the term granted by this agreement

4.1.5.2 You will not be required to pay any sum expressed to be by way of initial franchise fee;]

4.1.5.3 the Company will not be required to provide any of the initial or other obligations contained in such agreement which are appropriate to the establishment in business of a new franchisee;

4.1.5.4 any option in the New Franchise Agreement for You to enter into another franchise agreement or to renew any rights will not apply to You; and

4.1.5.5 You will pay all legal costs and expenses of the Company in connection with the New Franchise Agreement

4.1.6 if You and the Guarantor shall neglect or fail to execute and deliver to the Company the New Franchise Agreement within 21 days of being requested in writing by the Company to do so (such request not to be made earlier than 14 days following the receipt by You of the New Franchise Agreement) or if after the service of the notice referred to in clause 4.1.1 and before entering into the New Franchise Agreement You have failed to comply with any notice referred to in clause 4.1.4 or have committed a breach of this agreement such as to justify its termination or which may result in its termination Your right to enter into the New Franchise Agreement will at the option of the Company cease and be of no effect

4.2 Upon signing the New Franchise Agreement [You][parties] will be deemed to have released the [Company][each other] from all claims demands or liability under this agreement

5. COMPANY'S INITIAL OBLIGATIONS

5.1 THE Company will provide or make available the following to You:

- **5.1.1** consultation and advice as to the location suitability and acquisition of the Premises
- **5.1.2** consultation and advice with regard to alterations refurbishment renovation or other work necessary for converting the Premises into a typical outlet
- **5.1.3** the use on loan of standard plans drawings and specifications of a typical outlet
- **5.1.4** consultation and advice with regard to the way in which fixtures fittings and equipment are to be installed at the Premises
- **5.1.5** general supervision of the said conversion but not the day to day or immediate supervision which will be the responsibility of Your architect surveyor or shop fitter
- **5.1.6** consultation with the general management of the Company with regard to the purchase of materials the selection training and supervision of staff accounting book-keeping advertising and the day to day operation of the Business
- **5.1.7** advice on the amount mix and range of the initial stock of the Products to be purchased by You prior to its opening the Business for trading
- **5.1.8**
    - **5.1.8.1** advice on the initial advertising campaign to launch the Business

- 5.1.8.2 supply free of charge of window posters and leaflets announcing the opening of the Business

5.1.9 the Equipment Package at the Equipment Package Price

5.1.10 Initial Training [at the Company's head office or such other location as the Company may specify] for You any Guarantor and/or any proposed manager or such other member of Your staff as the Company may specify as soon as practicable after the date of this agreement

6. COMPANY'S CONTINUING OBLIGATIONS

6.1 **SUBJECT** to You and the Guarantor complying fully and promptly with all your respective obligations in this agreement, the Company shall during the subsistence of this agreement

- 6.1.1
  - 6.1.1.1 lend to You a copy of the Operations Manual which shall at all times remain the property of the Company
  - 6.1.1.2 provide You with updates to the Operations Manual containing details of any alterations and/or improvements in or to the System [or the Products and/or the Services]

6.1.2 provide You with reasonable access to the general management of the Company for consultation about the conduct of the Business with a view to enabling You to operate the System properly

6.1.3 provide You with advice know-how and guidance in such areas as management promotion and methods of operating the Business

6.1.4 provide You with advice in performing National Accounts contracts

6.1.5 provide You at Your expense with stationery invoices quotation forms contracts and other documentation for use by You in its dealings with customers and other third parties

6.1.6

    6.1.6.1 unless prevented by circumstances beyond its control use its best endeavours to supply the Products to You upon its terms and conditions of trade current from time to time

    6.1.6.2 nominate Approved Suppliers for the [Products]

6.1.7 where possible replace any goods which have been purchased from the Company and which are found to be genuinely defective or if replacement is not possible give credit for such goods provided they have been returned to the Company without delay

6.1.8 provide on hire and maintain at Your expense facias for signs on the Premises in the Company's distinctive style and all necessary plans for such signs

6.1.9 [subject to Your complying with clause 7.1.19.1 request a provider of telecommunications services to provide at the Premises 1 or more telephone lines for use by You exclusively in connection with the Business and of which the Company will be the official subscriber]

7. YOUR OBLIGATIONS

7.1 **You** will:

    7.1.1

        7.1.1.1 use Your best efforts to locate suitable premises and having obtained the Company's approval of them, acquire an interest in the Premises for a period at least equal to the Term

        7.1.1.2 if You enter into a lease for the Premises with a landlord who is not the Company, simultaneously enter into the Option Deed with the Company

    7.1.2 forthwith purchase the [Vehicles and the] Equipment Package at the Equipment Package Price and the initial stock of the Products referred to in clause 5.1.7

7.1.3 where appropriate ensure that the Premises [and the Vehicles] are without delay following acquisition altered refurbished decorated equipped and fitted out in accordance with the Company's requirements

7.1.4 acquire such other equipment books of account and any other items which are necessary for the performance by You of Your obligations under this agreement

7.1.5 ensure that You are creditworthy at all times and that adequate finance is available to You to enable You to perform Your obligations under this agreement and by way of working capital

7.1.6

   7.1.6.1 operate the System properly and strictly in accordance with the provisions of the Operations Manual as amended from time to time

   7.1.6.2 not make use of or disclose the Operations Manual for any purpose other than for the conduct of the Business

   7.1.6.3 not part with possession nor make any copies of the Operations Manual or any part of it

   7.1.6.4 ensure that the Operations Manual with which You are provided is kept up to date at all times

7.1.7

   7.1.7.1 use Your best endeavours to maintain the highest standards in all matters connected with the Business

   7.1.7.2 sell only the Products and provide only the Services and not sell anything or provide any service which does not conform with the standards associated with the Trade Name or of which it has not obtained the Company's prior written approval

7.1.8 comply with all instructions given to You by the Company with regard to the standard or quality of [the Services] [service and preparation of [the Products] products for sale (including display merchandising and packaging) [provided] in or about the conduct of the Business]

7.1.9

7.1.9.1 display the Approved Wording in such manner and upon such part or parts of the Premises [and or Vehicles] and place it upon all letter headings, bills, invoices and any other documents or literature employed by You in connection with the Business in such manner and in such place as the Company may direct

7.1.9.2 comply with the requirements of the Business Names Act 1985 and with the provisions of any statute which may repeal re-enact or amend such Act

7.1.9.3 at Your own expense obtain any consents which may be necessary from the landlord superior landlord local planning and/or building bylaw authority (as the case may be) for the display on the Premises of any signs specified by the Company, hoardings, parking facilities, access ways and the like and obtain the approval of police fire and any other relevant authorities and all licences required to carry on the Business in a lawful manner

7.1.10 pay to the Company in the form and manner specified in the Operational Manual from time to time

7.1.10.1 the Sign Hire Fee on each anniversary of the date of this agreement, the first such payment to be made on the signing of this agreement; and

7.1.10.2 the costs to the Company from time to time of maintaining such facias and/or the sign or signs such cost to be notified to You from time to time in writing and to be paid within 28 days following such notification

7.1.11

7.1.11.1 not pledge the credit of the Company, or represent Yourself as being the Company or a partner or agent of the

Company [save in the latter case where You are expressly authorised in writing to act as its agent in the performance of any National Accounts contract or part of it]

7.1.11.2 not permit any person connected in any way with You to represent himself or You in such a way that others dealing with him or You might regard him or You as a director officer employee agent or otherwise authorised to act on behalf of the Company

7.1.11.3 if You are a corporate entity, ensure that no part of the Trade Name or the Trade Marks form any part of Your corporate name

7.1.12

7.1.12.1 use only such signs and packaging materials for or in connection with the display [or] service [or sale] of the Products and/or the provision of the Services at the Premises [or on its Vehicles] as contain the Trade Name the Trade Marks or such other name and/or trade mark and/or symbol as may be designated by the Company from time to time

7.1.12.2 operate the Business only in accordance with the System and only under the Trade Name without any accompanying words or symbols of any nature (save as required by the provisions of this agreement) unless first approved in writing by the Company

7.1.12.3 not do anything which may bring the Trade Name or any of the Trade Marks into disrepute

7.1.12.4 [decorate all Vehicles with the livery specified by the Company and keep them in a good state of repair and clean condition]

7.1.12.5 affix only such notices to the Products or their packaging or advertising associated with the Business as the Company shall direct

7.1.12.6 not tamper with any markings or name plates or other indication of the source of origin of the Products which may be placed on them by or at the direction of the Company

7.1.12.7 not apply the Trade Mark or Trade Name or any part of them to any products [not obtained from] [unless expressly authorised by] the Company

7.1.12.8 without prejudice to any other rights or remedies of the Company, compensate the Company for any use by You of the Intellectual Property otherwise than in accordance with this agreement

7.1.12.9 indemnify the Company for any liability incurred to third parties for any use of the Intellectual Property by You (or by others with its consent) otherwise than in accordance with this agreement

7.1.12.10 not alter or convert the Premises in any way nor erect any new building of any kind on it nor install any fixtures or equipment of any kind in the Premises (whether by way of substitution or addition) and ensure that no sign or other medium of display or advertisement is erected or altered at the Premises without in every such case the previous written consent of the Company

7.1.12.11 carry out each authorised alteration erection and/or installation to the Premises only in accordance with plans drawings and specifications previously submitted to and approved by the Company at Your expense

7.1.12.12 at all times maintain the interior and exterior of the Premises and all parts of them clean orderly sanitary and in a good state of repair and decoration and forthwith at Your own expense comply with such requirements of the Company relating to the repair and decoration of the Premises as the Company may notify You in writing

7.1.13

7.1.13.1 use only such machinery equipment fixtures and fittings in the conduct of the Business as has been previously approved in writing by the Company

7.1.13.2 ensure that all machinery equipment fixtures and fittings are maintained in a condition which meets the operational standards specified in the Operations Manual

7.1.13.3 replace any machinery equipment fixtures and fittings as may become obsolete or inoperable with such item as meets the Company's then requirements of a new **ZORCO BUSINESS**

7.1.13.4 acquire and install for use within such reasonable period of time as may be specified by the Company such additional or different machinery equipment fixtures and fittings as may be specified by the Company as being necessary as a result of any change in or variation to the System or any part of it [provided always that the capital cost of such improvement or modification can be recovered by You during the Term]

7.1.14

7.1.14.1 continuously operate the Business at least upon such days and during such hours as the Company reasonably determines

7.1.14.2 devote the whole of Your time and attention to the Business during the hours of operation of the Business and during such other hours as are necessary to perform the administrative marketing promotional and accounting functions required in or about the conduct of the Business and in operating the System

7.1.14.3 diligently carry on the Business at the Premises and use Your best endeavours to promote the Business [within the Territory and not outside its boundaries]

7.1.14.4 [not in any way whether directly or indirectly solicit or tout for business to provide any Services [and or sell any of the Products] to or for anyone at any address which is outside the Territory]

7.1.14.5 ensure that there are employed in the Business such number of staff as in the opinion of the Company are sufficient to enable the Business to operate efficiently and to meet the demand for [the Products and or] the Services [in the Territory]

7.1.14.6 establish maintain and increase the turnover of the Business

7.1.14.7 at all times maintain such supply and stock [of the Products] [of ingredients and the Menu Range] [of such products and materials as are necessary to provide the Services in accordance with the System and in such quantities] as are sufficient to meet customer demand

7.1.14.8 obtain supplies of the Products only from the Company [and or Approved Suppliers] upon their respective terms of trade current from time to time

7.1.14.9 [purchase such of the Products as are described in the _____ Schedule only from the Company upon its standard terms and conditions current from time to time]

7.1.14.10 promptly and within the due time allowed make payment to all suppliers for goods and services sold or provided to You for the purposes of the Business

7.1.14.11 promote and preserve the goodwill and reputation associated with the Trade Name and/or the Trade Marks by promptly replacing where possible or if replacement is not possible, by refunding the cost of any goods supplied or sold by You to Your customers which are found to have been genuinely defective

7.1.14.12 follow the procedure specified in the Operations Manual in the event of any customer complaint

7.1.14.13 [make contracts with customers for the supply of the [Products and Services] on the standard terms and conditions set out in the Operations Manual but [(save in the case of National Accounts contracts)] You must determine Your own prices notwithstanding that the Company may recommend prices]

7.1.14.14 not enter into any agreement arrangement or concerted practice with any other franchisee of the Company or any other person whatsoever in relation to the prices at which You will sell [the Products] [products] or provide [the Services] any services

7.1.14.15 maintain a supply of and offer [to provide such range of the Services] [for sale such [Menu] Range of the Products] as the Company may specify or approve from time to time

7.1.14.16 not carry on, or permit to be carried on, any other business at the Premises nor extend the scope or range of the Business

7.1.14.17 not sub-contract the performance of any of Your obligations under this agreement

7.1.14.18 [sell the Products] [provide the Services] only to end users or other franchisees of the Company

7.1.14.19 comply with Your obligations under any other agreement between the Company and You

7.1.15

7.1.15.1 comply with the requirements of the Company with regard to Your cleanliness, clothing, appearance or demeanour and that of Your staff which in the opinion of the Company are necessary in order to maintain the

Appendix F (iv): Sample Document: Franchise Agreement

           uniformly high standards associated with the Trade Name

7.1.15.2   procure or ensure that any employee or prospective employee who performs or is to perform work which in the opinion of the Company requires special skill or knowledge receives such special training and/or takes part in such training course as may be notified to You by the Company

7.1.15.3   attend and if and as required by the Company procure that such of Your staff (including any Guarantor) as may be specified by the Company shall attend for such further training as the Company may prescribe

7.1.15.4   not employ as the manager of the Business any person who:

        7.1.15.4.1   has not successfully passed the Company's training course and

        7.1.15.4.2   has not been previously approved in writing by the Company

7.1.15.5

        7.1.15.5.1   procure from Your manager for the time being and from such categories of Your staff as are specified in the Operations Manual and such of Your other staff as the Company may specify from time to time a Confidentiality Undertaking;

        7.1.15.5.2   take such steps at Your own expense as the Company may require in order to enforce the Confidentiality Undertaking and/or to restrain any breach of its terms; and

        7.1.15.5.3   not permit any person to act or assist in the Business until such person has signed a Confidentiality Undertaking

Appendix F (iv): Sample Document: Franchise Agreement

7.1.16 not do nor permit to be done anything which may bring the System into disrepute or which may damage the interests of the Company or any member of the **ZORCO NETWORK**

7.1.17 permit the Company without any further or other authority other than that which You hereby irrevocably gives to the Company (and if necessary make arrangements to enable the Company) to speak and/or write to customers about the Services [and the Products] being provided to such customers by You so as to enable the Company to ascertain whether the standards associated with the System are being achieved and maintained

7.1.18

    7.1.18.1 use only such stationery invoices quotation forms contracts and other documentation and literature of whatever nature in Your dealings with third parties as the Company shall provide [at Your expense] stipulate or approve

    7.1.18.2 send to the Company a copy of each [contract entered into by You with customers] [invoice issued to Your customers and any spoilt invoices in numerically sequential order] [reports of sales of the Products [Services] future orders and other information in relation to the Business in accordance with the detailed procedures set out in the Operations Manual] and of all invoices for additional work performed from time to time

    7.1.18.3 [send to the Company such information as the Company may require to enable it to establish expand maintain and operate a database of **ZORCO** customers]

7.1.19

    7.1.19.1 [use the telephone line or lines provided by the Company exclusively for conducting and operating he Business and pay on demand for all charges made by the supplier of telecommunications services in connection with the installation continuance and use of any such line

7.1.19.2 not subscribe for any telephone lines the numbers of which are made public in any telephone fax or other directory of any nature whatsoever nor employ any other telephone lines in such manner as would associate such number with the Trade Name the Trade Marks or any of them or the Business]

7.1.20 Subject to clause 25.10.2, observe and perform such National Accounts contractual obligations as may be specified by the Company [in accordance with National Accounts Terms unless otherwise specified by the Company] and keep the Company fully and effectually indemnified against all claims demands damages costs or expenses which may be incurred or received by the Company resulting from any breach by You of the provisions of this clause or from any other act default or neglect of whatsoever nature on the part of You

7.1.21

7.1.21.1 comply with all statutory or other legal requirements and regulations which apply to You [the Premises and or] the Business

7.1.21.2 without limiting the generality of the provisions of clause 7.1.21.2 forthwith register and maintain Your registration under the Data Protection Act 1998

7.1.21.3 comply in all respects with the DPA and guidance given by the Information Commissioner when processing Personal Data and Sensitive Personal Data (as defined in the DPA)

7.1.21.4 not to revoke the consent You hereby give Us to disclose to or obtain from such third parties as We deem necessary to protect Our interests and/or those of any individual or member of the **ZORCO NETWORK** any of Your personal or Sensitive Personal Data (as defined in the DPA)

7.1.22 at all times be courteous and co-operative in all Your dealings with such prospective franchisees as the Company may specify and at the request of the Company provide such prospective franchisees with such information as they may reasonably and properly require but in so doing You must not disclose to them any trade secrets of the **ZORCO BUSINESS** nor any confidential information of the Company or any of its franchisees nor disclose to them any of the contents of the Operations Manual

7.1.23 [request a provider of telecommunications services approved by the Company to provide 1 or more telephone lines for the benefit of the Business at the Premises which You must use only in connection with the operation of the Business and You must ensure that the Company is the official subscriber for such line or lines]

7.1.24

    7.1.24.1 [if You are not already so registered forthwith make application to register with HM Customs and Excise for VAT before commencing the Business] [as and when required by law register with H M Customs and Excise for VAT] [and not commence the Business prior to such registration being obtained]

    7.1.24.2 [not do nor permit anything to be done whereby You cease to be registered for VAT]

7.1.25

    7.1.25.1 not during the Term enter into any transaction arrangement or agreement which causes the Trading Scheme Act 1996 to apply to the Company, You, the Business and/or the **ZORCO NETWORK** or any part of it

    7.1.25.2 not introduce any person firm or company to the Company for the purpose of their becoming a franchisee or a Participant nor accept nor receive any commission or other payment or benefit as a consequence of anyone becoming a franchisee or a Participant

Appendix F (iv): Sample Document: Franchise Agreement

      7.1.25.3 advise any person, firm or company enquiring about becoming a Participant or joining the **ZORCO NETWORK** to speak to and deal directly with the Company

      7.1.25.4 only sell the [Products] [and or Services] directly to customers of the Business and not sell or permit to be sold to any person firm or company any such [Products and/or Services] [for resale]

      7.1.25.5 not engage in the Business as a Participant anyone who is not registered and who does not continue to be registered for VAT

      7.1.25.6 cease using the services of a Participant immediately upon such Participant ceasing to be registered for VAT

      7.1.25.7 [not engage the services of anyone in the Business who is not Your employee except as an agent under the terms set out in Schedule B]

      7.1.25.8 [not engage in the Business any person firm or company other than employees except under the terms set out in Schedule A and ensure that all such persons have signed a contract with You in such form prior to engaging them]

7.1.26 attend and procure that the Guarantor any manager and such members of Your staff as the Company may specify attend the Initial Training and pay any travelling food and accommodation expenses which any Guarantor You and Your staff may incur during the period of training referred to in clauses 5 and 8

7.1.27 not during the subsistence of this agreement except with the prior written consent of the Company or under the terms of this agreement or any other agreement with the Company currently in force:

      7.1.27.1 be directly or indirectly engaged concerned or interested in any capacity whatsoever (except as the holder of not more than 5% of the shares in any company

Appendix F (iv): Sample Document: Franchise Agreement

whose shares are listed or dealt in on The Stock Exchange) in any business which is the same as or similar to the **ZORCO BUSINESS** [in the Territory] or in any territory [area] where it would compete with any member of the **ZORCO NETWORK** or the Company

7.1.27.2 at any time employ or seek to employ any person then employed by the Company or any of its franchisees nor shall it directly or indirectly induce any such person to leave his employment without the previous written consent of such person's employer nor will employ any such person without like consent within 6 months after the termination of such person's employment

7.1.27.3 [engage directly or indirectly in any capacity in any other business venture except with the prior written consent of the Company which will not be unreasonably withheld or delayed]

7.1.28 during the subsistence of this agreement and after Termination

7.1.28.1 not, except for the sole purpose of conducting the Business, divulge or use whether directly or indirectly for Your own benefit or for the benefit of any person firm or company other than the Company any information or knowledge concerning the System which may be communicated to You or which You may acquire in carrying out its obligations under this agreement

7.1.28.2 not use any confidential information provided to You by the Company for any purposes other than running the Business but this obligation shall cease after Termination if such confidential information becomes generally known or easily accessible otherwise than by Your breach

7.1.28.3 keep this agreement confidential and not disclose nor permit disclosure of any of its contents to anyone other than Your professional advisors and then only if You ensure that such disclosure is made to them in confidence and that no copies of the whole or any part of it are made

7.1.29 on entering into this or any other agreement or transaction with the Company during the Term or any continuation of it, make full disclosure of all material circumstances and of everything known to You in relation to the contract or transaction which would be likely to influence the conduct of the Company including, in particular, the disclosure of other agencies or franchises in which You are interested directly or indirectly

7.1.30 [to comply with the Company's Guarantee Scheme relating to the Products [and Services] from time to time set out in the Operations Manual whether the customer claiming under the guarantee purchased Products [or Services] from You or from any other franchisee of the Company]

7.1.31 if You are a corporate entity, ensure that there is no change in the beneficial ownership of Your issued share capital, or of Your de facto control, without the prior written consent of the Company

7.1.32 if You are a partnership, ensure that there is no change in the constitution of Your partnership, or in the terms of Your partnership agreement, without the prior written consent of the Company

7.1.33 ensure that there is no change in the beneficial ownership or of the de facto control of the Business without the prior written consent of the Company

8. TRAINING

8.1 THE Company shall have the right to require You any of your staff and any Guarantor to attend training courses (in addition to the Initial Training) at any time during the subsistence of this agreement if

8.1.1 it considers attendance at such courses to be advisable or

8.1.2 it wishes to train You and/or any of them in new and/or improved techniques which have been devised and which You and/or any of them will be required to put into effect in operating the System

8.2 Such additional training will be provided at Your expense

8.3 You must establish and maintain an initial and continuing training programmes for Your staff in accordance with the requirements contained in the Operations Manual

9. IMPROVEMENTS

9.1 **THE** Company shall use reasonable endeavours to conceive and develop new and improved methods of conducting a business in accordance with the System and other additions or modifications to the System which it may consider desirable

9.2 The Company agrees to make such improvements additions or modifications available to You at the earliest possible opportunity after it has in its opinion been fully developed and tested

9.3 You, for Your part, must notify the Company of any improvements in the method of operation of the System and/or the Business which You may consider would assist in the development of the System which the Company will evaluate

9.4 You must not introduce any improvement addition modification or innovation into the conduct of the Business or of the System without the prior written consent of the Company

9.5 ou must when required by the Company in writing, introduce any improvement addition modification or innovation to the System and the conduct of the Business at the time or times and in the manner specified in such written requirement and the System will thenceforth be deemed to have been varied as so specified

9.6 In order that You, the Company and its other franchisees may all benefit from the free interchange of ideas, You will permit the Company to introduce into the System and/or the Operations Manual any improvements which may have been notified by You to the Company without any payment being made for it by the Company or any of its franchisees to You

Appendix F (iv): Sample Document: Franchise Agreement

and will enter into a royalty free exclusive licence with the Company, in such reasonable form as may be submitted by the Company to You, for this purpose

10. FEES AND CONTRIBUTIONS

10.1 You will pay to the Company the Initial Franchise Fee upon signing this agreement

OR

10.1 You will pay to the Company the Initial Franchise Fee as follows:

    10.1.1 £___ upon signing this agreement

    10.2.2 £___ upon the commencement of Initial Training

    10.3.3 £___ [upon [delivery of] notification to You from the Company that the Company is ready able and willing to deliver] [the Equipment Package] [on or before the date upon which the Business is commenced]

    10.1.4 [£___ upon You acquiring an interest in the Premises]

10.2 During the subsistence of this agreement You must pay to the Company in the form and manner specified in the Operations Manual by not later than the [third] [first] working day of each Trading Period the Continuing Franchise Fee and the Advertising, Marketing and Promotions Contribution for the preceding Trading Period without any deduction or set off whatsoever

10.3 If You default in making any payment on the due date the Company may, in addition to all other remedies available to it, suspend the provision of all goods and services until payment is made

10.4 [The Advertising, Marketing and Promotions Contribution will be calculated as the relevant percentage specified in clause 1.1 applied to the Gross Revenues for the relevant calendar month so that the percentage applied to the whole of the Gross Revenues for the first calendar month will be ___% but once the aggregate Gross Revenues achieved since the previous

Appendix F (iv): Sample Document: Franchise Agreement

Accounting Reference Date exceed the first threshold then the percentage will reduce to __% and likewise (once the next threshold is achieved) again reduced to __%]

10.5 [The Continuing Franchise Fee which will normally be calculated as the percentage specified in clause 1.1 (which will remain fixed throughout the Term) applied to the Gross Revenues for the relevant calendar month but will be adjusted upwards to the Minimum Continuing Franchise Fee ('Minimum') for any month in which the Gross Revenues calculation yields a sum which is less than the Minimum

> 10.5.1 for the first 12 Trading Periods of the Term the Minimum will be the sum specified in Schedule _____
>
> 10.5.2 after the first 12 Trading Periods the Minimum for each monthly Trading Period during the Term will be the sum referred to in clause 10.5.1 increased (on the occasion of each anniversary of the date of this agreement in relation to the next 12 Trading Periods following) by applying the same percentage increase as the increase in the [Retail Prices] Index over its level 12 months previously; and whenever You pay a Minimum Continuing Franchise Fee in any calendar month he will claim back the difference between that Minimum and the Continuing Franchise Fee which would otherwise have been payable by deducting that difference from the Continuing Franchise Fee payable in the next calendar month, provided that the result will not be to reduce that month's Continuing Franchise Fee below the Minimum. Any difference not claimed back in the succeeding month will be carried forward into succeeding months until exhausted] [or if sliding scale used]

10.6 [The Continuing Franchise Fee will be calculated by applying the percentages specified for Continuing Franchise Fee in clause 1.1 and otherwise in accordance with 10.5 above]

10.7

> 10.7.1 You must remit to the Company the Property Management Fee in the form and manner specified in the Operations Manual and at the same time as payment is required to be made of the Continuing Franchise Fee

Appendix F (iv): Sample Document: Franchise Agreement

    10.7.2 The first payment of the Property Management Fee (or a proportionate part of it as the case may be) for the period from the date upon which You take possession or go into occupation of the Premises to the next following payment day, must be made on the signing of this agreement

10.8 You acknowledge and agree that it has no right to withhold payment of any fees because of Your dissatisfaction with the Company's performance of its obligations pursuant to this agreement and that if You are so dissatisfied You will pursue other remedies at law which may be available to You

10.9 [You will pay to the Company promptly upon demand a contribution towards the Company's costs of maintaining ISO 9002 accreditation which contribution shall be applied and charged equally amongst all of the **ZORCO BUSINESSES** and shall be calculated by dividing the costs of maintaining registration by the number of ZORCO BUSINESSES]

11. ACCOUNTING AND REPORTING

11.1 You must:

    11.1.1

        11.11.1.1 adopt the Accounting Reference Date as the end of Your financial year maintain a cash register approved by the Company which accumulates sales and which has no resetting devices and accurately record all transactions of the Business through such cash register

        11.1.1.2 keep all accounts and financial records of the Business separate from all other accounts and records

    11.1.2 maintain an accurate account and record of all Gross Revenues and prepare a statement of the Gross Revenues for each Trading Period in the form and manner specified in the Operations Manual and send it to the Company by fax followed by a hard copy by prepaid first class mail postmarked not later than the [third] [first] working day of the next following Trading Period

11.1.3

    11.1.3.1 maintain on the Premises in a form approved by the Company (and preserve them for at least 6 years after the end of the financial year to which they relate and thereafter for so long as any dispute shall remain outstanding between the parties) full and accurate books of account and all underlying or supporting records and vouchers [including the cash register rolls] relating to the Business and permit the Company (or any person firm or company nominated by the Company) during business hours to inspect the said books of account and records and to take copies of them

    11.1.3.2 without prejudice to any other rights which the Company may have (including but not limited to termination of this agreement) reimburse the Company for all costs incurred in conducting any inspection pursuant to clause 11.1.3.1 including (but without limiting the generality of the foregoing) travel, hotel, subsistence, salaries and fees incurred by the Company if during such inspection a discrepancy is found between the reported Gross Revenues and actual Gross Revenues for any Trading Period

11.1.4 [carry out not less than 2 full physical stock takes in each calendar year at 6 monthly intervals and supply copies of them in writing to the Company within 4 days after the date of completion of each such stock take]

OR

carry out a full physical stock take on the last day of each calendar month and supply copies of them in writing to the Company by the fourth day of the month following]

OR

carry out a full physical stock take on the last day of each Trading Period and supply copies of them in writing to the Company by the third day after the end of the said Trading Period]

11.1.5 [provide the Company by the third day from the end of each [Periodic Accounting Interval] [Trading Period] with a profit and loss statement for the preceding [Periodic Accounting Interval] [Trading Period] such statement to be completed in accordance with the instructions contained in the Operations Manual]

11.1.6 instruct a registered auditor to undertake a full annual audit of the Business, and ensure that no audit takes place more than 12 months from the date of the last audit or be finalised later than 3 months after the end of Your accounting year, and at Your expense provide the Company within 1 week of the completion of each annual audit a copy of the audited accounts certified each year by such registered auditor

11.1.7 [deliver to the Company on the due date for their submission to HM Customs and Excise a copy of Your return relating to Value Added Tax and deliver to the Company a copy of any assessment to Value Added Tax which may be raised by HM Customs and Excise in relation to the Business within 7 days of its receipt by You]

11.1.8 provide such further information relating to the Business as the Company may in its discretion think necessary to assist the Company in the discharge of its duties or the enforcement of its rights under the provisions of this agreement

11.1.9 in the event of any default in the payment of any sum which may be due from You to the Company pay to the Company interest at the rate of 2% per month calculated on a day to day basis on the amount of any sums due but not paid after judgement as before judgement

11.2

11.2.1 [You must comply with all Internet policies established from time to time by the Company including the payment to the Company of a monthly internet maintenance fee in an amount which will be determined by the Company from time to time, acting reasonably and representing a reasonable share of the costs of such service.

Appendix F (iv): Sample Document: Franchise Agreement

11.2.2 All e-mail addresses must be prepared in the following format: _____@[internet service provider] or such other format as may be designated by the Company]

12. ADVERTISING, MARKETING AND PROMOTIONS

12.1 **IN** consideration of Your paying to the Company the Advertising, Marketing and Promotions Contribution:

12.1.1 the Company agrees to conduct direct and indirect advertising, marketing and promotion of the Trade Name

12.1.1 [the Company shall pay an advertising, marketing and promotions contribution calculated on the same basis as that paid by You for each **ZORCO BUSINESS** operated by the Company]

12.1.3 [the Company will expend [half] of all the Advertising, Marketing and Promotions Contributions on Direct or Local Advertising and the Company has the right to apportion such expenditure between You and any other franchisees of the Company in the advertising or marketing area in which the Business is conducted in such manner as the Company thinks fit]

12.1.4 [the Company will expend the [balance of the] Advertising, Marketing and Promotions Contribution upon such advertising and/or marketing and promotional activities (including public relations) as the Company in its discretion thinks fit]

12.1.5 the Company will not be under any obligation to expend on advertising and promotion in each year any sum greater than the aggregate of the Advertising, Marketing and Promotions Contributions received from all its franchisees [plus its own contributions made pursuant to clause 12.1.2]

12.2 You must not conduct or carry on any advertising, marketing or promotions whatsoever without the prior written consent of the Company

12.3 [The Company will [make available for purchase by You] sell to You [at cost] such signs cards notices or displays as You reasonably require for the purpose of any advertising, marketing or promotions campaigns]

Appendix F (iv): Sample Document: Franchise Agreement

12.4 [You must co-operate with the Company in any advertising campaign sales promotion or other special activity which the Company may initiate and prominently display and maintain at Your own expense the advertising signs cards notices or displays supplied to You by or on behalf of the Company except that You shall not be obliged to participate in any marketing advertising research or promotional schemes involving the offer of reductions in price to customers of the Business]

12.5 You must not use or exhibit on or in connection with the Premises or the Business any signs cards notices or other display or advertising matter without the prior written consent of the Company and unless such materials have been obtained from a supplier approved by the Company who will not unreasonably withhold its consent or approval

12.6 All approved advertising matter must be installed and all advertising matter of whatever kind must be maintained at Your expense and it is Your responsibility to ensure that You obtain any necessary planning bylaw or other consents for them

12.7 Without prejudice to any other remedy of the Company including termination of this agreement, the Company may remove from the Premises [and or any Vehicles] without incurring any liability to You, any signs cards notices or other display or advertising matter which has not been supplied or approved by the Company, without Your consent except for the consent which You hereby irrevocably give to the Company and the Company may keep or destroy any such sign card notice or other display or advertising matter

12.8 Whenever so instructed by the Company You must remove from the Premises, temporarily or permanently as the case may be any advertising matter the removal of which, in the opinion of the Company, is necessary for the purpose or in consequence of any particular advertising or promotion campaign instituted by the Company

12.9 The Company will keep all advertising, marketing and promotion contributions received from its franchisees in an account separate from its other accounts and at the end of each of its financial years will arrange for its accountant to prepare a statement of the sums received and ex-

Appendix F (iv): Sample Document: Franchise Agreement

pended by the Company pursuant to the provisions of clause 12.1 the cost of which shall be paid out of such contributions

12.10 The Company will, on the written request from You, send You a chartered or certified accountant's certificate showing the total of such receipts and payments

12.11 If that account shows that the Company has either overspent or underspent the monies available, the amount overspent (including cost of money borrowed or advanced) may be recovered by the Company from the next year's contributions and the amount underspent will be added to the contributions for expenditure during the next financial year

12.12 The Company reserves the right to advertise recommended selling prices for the [Products and/or the Services] in response to general and specific commercial considerations **PROVIDED** that You will not be obliged to participate in any scheme advertising recommended selling prices and are free to determine Your own pricing structure

12.13 [You must not:

12.13.1 without the prior written consent of the Company set up any web-site in relation to the Business [the Products] [the Services] or to the **ZORCO BUSINESS** but shall contribute such information and details as the Company may require from time to time for the purposes of any web-site set up by the Company;

12.13.2 register, maintain, develop or operate any domain name or web site which makes any use of or contains any reference to any of the Trade Marks or the Trade Name or any part of any of them or anything confusingly similar to any of them;

12.13.3 create or permit any linking to or framing of any other web site from any web site developed or maintained by the Company without the express written consent of the Company and then subject only to any terms and conditions which the Company may impose;

12.13.4 use or permit the use of any of the Trade Marks or the Trade Name or any part of any of them or anything confusingly similar to any of them for or forming part of any domain name without the consent of the Company, and if the Company grants consent under the provisions of this clause it shall, nevertheless, be the absolute owner of any such domain name

12.13.5 If the Company provides consent under the provisions of this clause it will, nevertheless, be the absolute owner of any such domain name.

12.13.6 You must not cause or allow the Trade Name or the Trade Marks or any of them, to be used or displayed, in whole or in part, as an internet domain name, electronic mail or address, or in connection with any internet home page, web-site or other internet related activity without the prior written approval of the Company and then only in such manner and in accordance with such procedures, standards and specifications as the Company may establish.

12.13.7 You must contract with an internet service provider acceptable to the Company to provide and maintain access for You to the Internet

12.13.8 You must advertise through the Internet as prescribed by the Company in a form and content prescribed by the Company from time to time [either as a single franchisee for its Territory] or, [as a pro rata participant in a common and/or group advertisement with such other franchisees.] Pro rata costs shall be allocated based on the number of **ZORCO BUSINESSES**] within such area.]

13. INSURANCE

13.1 **You** must take out and maintain, at Your expense and with an insurance company approved by the Company, [keyman and other] insurance cover against loss (including loss of profits) damage and other risks and in such minimum sums as would be prudent under the circumstances from time to time against all liability (including product liability) of the Company and/or You and/or any supplier to You, to Your employees, customers and/or to members of the public

13.2 The Company will not incur any liability to You for recommending or not recommending any risks to be covered or minimum sums for which to be insured

13.3 You will use its best endeavours to procure that the Company's interest is noted on such policies and will furnish the Company from time to time, on demand with copies of the policies and evidence that the then current premiums therefor have been paid

13.4 You will use Your best endeavours to arrange with its insurers that no policy will be terminated or cancelled for whatever reason unless 14 days' notice of the insurers' intention has been given to the Company

13.5 You must not do nor permit to be done anything whereby any insurance policy is rendered invalid void or unenforceable

13.6 You must display an appropriate certificate of insurance in a public place at the Premises

14. TRADE MARKS

14.1 You must, when requested render to the Company, at the Company's expense, all reasonable assistance in obtaining registrations of the Trade Marks including the execution of any documentation which may be necessary to establish the Company as the owner of the Trade Marks

14.2 Subject to the provisions of the next sub-clause, in no circumstances must You apply for registration, as proprietor of any trade mark which is similar to the Trade Name or the Trade Marks or any or part of any of them or which would conflict with the Trade Name or the Trade Marks nor must You take any action or refuse or decline to take any action which may result in harm to the Trade Marks or put their registrations or any applications for their registration at risk

14.3 If at any time that the Company has applied for the registration of any of the Trade Marks, You are deemed in law to have rights in any of the Trade Marks You will at the request and expense of the Company make or proceed with (as the case may be) such application and do all things and execute such documents as may be necessary, for obtaining registration in

Appendix F (iv): Sample Document: Franchise Agreement

the name of You and upon such Trade Marks being registered, You will assign such registration to the Company for £1

14.4 You must, in all representations of any registered Trade Mark used by You [on the Products] [in the Business and in connection with the provision of the Services], append in a manner approved by the Company such inscription as is usual or proper for indicating that such Trade Mark is registered

14.5

14.5.1 You will at the request and expense of the Company do all acts and execute all documents for establishing You as a user of such of the Company's registered Trade Marks as the Company may specify and where applicable for the recordal of Your permitted use at the Trade Marks Registry and pay the Company the Trade Marks Licence Fee

14.5.2 You will not be entitled to exercise any of the rights granted by this agreement if You fail within 10 days after receipt of any document (referred to in clause 14.5.1) to execute it and return it to the Company

14.6 You must immediately notify the Company of all infringements or imitations of the Trade Marks the Trade Name or of any business which appears to or to be attempting to pass itself off as a **ZORCO BUSINESS** or a member of the **ZORCO NETWORK** which come to Your attention or any attempts to challenge Your right to use any of the Trade Marks or the Trade Name or to carry on the business as a **ZORCO BUSINESS** so long as this agreement subsists

14.7 The Company will, upon receiving advice from specialist Counsel that it is likely to succeed, take such action against such infringement challenge and/or imitation as it, in its sole discretion, considers appropriate and any rights which You may have under Section 30 of the Trade Marks Act 1994 are expressly excluded

14.8 You agree to provide such co-operation as the Company may request in the prosecution of any such action including the provision of evidence and being named as a party to any legal proceedings

Appendix F (iv): Sample Document: Franchise Agreement

14.9 The Company shall have the conduct of any such action and pay all legal expenses and costs which may arise from the joining of You as a party except such legal expenses and costs as You may incur by taking separate professional advice **PROVIDED THAT** the Company will not be liable to pay Your legal expenses and costs as set out above if it becomes necessary for such action to be taken to protect the Trade Marks as a direct or indirect result of any default or act or omission on Your part in relation to the Intellectual Property

14.10 Without prejudice to any right You may have to challenge the validity of the Trade Marks or the Company's ownership of any of them, You will not, without the prior written consent of the Company, take any action of whatever nature based upon the Trade Marks the Trade Name or any common law rights which You are licensed to use or exercise pursuant to this agreement or any trade mark licence entered into between the parties

14.11 No warranty express or implied is hereby given by the Company with respect to the validity of any of the Trade Marks

15 SALE OF BUSINESS

15.1 **You** do not have the right to assign this agreement nor to sell the whole or any part of the Business but You have the right to sell all (but not only a part) of the Assets (except in the normal course of business) with the prior written consent of the Company subject to the conditions listed in clause 15.4 and subject to the Company's option to buy the Assets set out below

15.2

    15.2.1 If You wish to sell the Assets You must forthwith notify Your intention to the Company in writing

    15.2.2 Upon receipt of Your Notice the Company will, in addition to its other rights under this agreement, have an option to purchase the Assets upon the Purchase Terms

Appendix F (iv): Sample Document: Franchise Agreement

15.3 If the Company does not exercise its option to purchase the Assets, it agrees to grant to a purchaser of the Assets who is acceptable to it, and subject to the conditions set out in clause 15.4, a franchise upon the terms and conditions contained in the New Franchise Agreement but neither the proposed purchaser nor You will be required to pay any sum expressed to be by way of initial franchise fee and the Company will not be obliged to provide any of the initial or other obligations (other than training) which are appropriate to the establishment of a new franchised business

15.4 The conditions which You are required to satisfy are as follows:

15.4.1 You must as soon as possible submit by notice in writing to the Company

15.4.11 a copy of each written offer received from any proposed purchaser to purchase the Assets from You which You propose to accept and any variation of the terms offered

15.4.1.2 a financial statement of affairs and the business history of the proposed purchaser

15.4.1.3 details of any other terms which may have been agreed between You and the proposed purchaser and

15.4.1.4 a warranty to the effect that to the best of Your knowledge and belief, the information provided pursuant to this sub-clause is complete and accurate in all respects and that no information has been withheld, such warranty is to be effective not only on the date upon which it is given but must also be repeated at the time of any sale of the Assets by You

15.4.2 any proposed purchaser must be bona fide at arms-length and shall submit its offer in writing and in good faith together with a properly completed application form and must meet the Company's standards with respect to business experience, probity, financial status, character, ability and compatibility with the Company and its staff and must successfully complete a programme of initial training by the Company

15.4.3

    15.4.3.1 the proposed purchaser may be required by the Company execute a confidentiality undertaking or the New Franchise Agreement prior to entering into any training

    15.4.3.2 You must not disclose any of the System or contents of the Operations Manual to any prospective purchaser and must ensure that no such prospective purchaser uses any of the Intellectual Property nor operates the whole or any part of the System without the express prior written consent of the Company and You will ensure that if requested by the Company any prospective purchaser shall sign a written confidentiality agreement in a form approved by the Company

15.4.4 You shall pay to the Company the Franchise Transfer Fee at the time of applying for consent and the Company's legal costs in connection with Your application for consent and the grant of a New Franchise Agreement to the proposed purchaser

15.4.5 neither You nor the Guarantor must, at the time of Your application for consent, be in breach of any of your respective obligations to the Company under the terms of this agreement or any other agreement with the Company

15.5.6 the proposed purchaser and any individuals referred to in clause 15.4.8.1 must not be engaged or concerned or interested in any way in any business which is the same as or similar to or which carries on a business which competes with any **ZORCO BUSINESS** or be a member of a group of companies one of whose members carries on such a business

15.4.7 the Company will need to be reasonably satisfied that the proposed purchaser has adequate financial resources, bearing in mind (amongst other things), the purchase price, to enable it to trade profitably and in so satisfying itself the Company must not be taken to be making any representations or giving any warranties to such proposed purchaser or to You

15.4.8 if the proposed purchaser is a company, the Company will require to be satisfied:

15.4.8.1 that the individual or individuals who will have effective voting or de facto control of such company meets the criteria set out in clauses 15.4.2 and 15.4.6;

15.4.8.2 with the suitability of the other persons who will be directors and/or shareholders in such company;

15.4.8.3 with the shareholding structure of such company; and

15.4.8.4 with the arrangements between the shareholders in such company

15.4.9 the proposed purchaser must procure that its directors any individuals having de facto control of it and all shareholders shall join it (in the capacity of guarantors and/or such other capacity as the Company may require) in entering into the New Franchise Agreement and must execute a Guarantee and Indemnity [and an Option Deed] in favour of the Company

15.4.10 payment must be made by You of all costs (including but not limited to the Franchise Transfer Fee) without any right of deduction or set-off and all Your obligations to the Company and any nominated suppliers must be discharged in full

15.4.11 [You and the prospective purchaser must both be registered with HM Customs and Excise for VAT at the time of the sale of the Assets]

15.5 Upon the Company exercising the option contained in clause 15.2 or approving and entering into a New Franchise Agreement with a proposed purchaser and upon the satisfaction of the conditions referred to in clause 15.4 including in particular the successful completion by the proposed purchaser of the Company's programme of initial training, the Company and You shall each be deemed to have released the other from the terms of this agreement except for those provisions which by their nature or effect survive termination

16. DEATH OR INCAPACITY

16.1 IF You (being a natural person) die during the subsistence of this agreement:

16.1.1 Your Personal Representatives and any surviving partner must together decide within a period of 3 months from the date of Your death whether they wish the Business to be carried on by a relative or beneficiary of Yours and any surviving partner

16.1.2 if it is so decided, then the said Personal Representatives must together with any surviving partner give written notice of their intention, within the said period of 3 months, to the Company giving the name or names (if that is the case) of such of Your relatives or beneficiaries and upon the Company being satisfied that such individual or individuals would be acceptable by applying the criteria set out in clause 15, the Company will not exercise its option contained in clause 15, but will consent to an assignment of this agreement to such individual or individuals and any surviving partner, subject to their entering into direct covenants with the Company to observe and perform the terms and conditions contained in this agreement

16.1.3 if the said Personal Representatives and any surviving partner wish to sell the Assets, then the provisions of clause 15 will apply and if the Company decides not to exercise its option referred to in clause 15 and a prospective purchaser acceptable to the Company by the criteria set out in clause 15 is found, the Assets may be sold to such purchaser within the period of 6 months from the date of Your death in accordance with the provisions contained in clause 15

16.1.4 if requested in writing by the said Personal Representatives and any surviving partner, the Company may (as soon as is reasonably practicable) provide a manager to manage the Business during the period of 3 months specified in clause 16.1.1

16.1.5 the Company will be entitled to a fee for the provision of any such manager equal to:

16.1.5.1 the normal salary of the manager;

16.1.5.2 the travelling accommodation and subsistence expenses of the manager; and

16.1.5.3 50% of the total of 16.1.5.1 and 16.1.5.2 plus Value Added Tax such fee to be paid at weekly intervals on the Tuesday of each week

16.1.6 the Company may also (as soon as is reasonably practicable) if requested by the said Personal Representatives and any serving partner provide such a manager for an additional period of up to 3 months upon the same terms and conditions so as to enable the Personal Representatives and any surviving partner to arrange for the sale of the Assets

16.1.7 if there is any failure promptly to pay to the Company any fee for the provision of the services of any manager, the Company will be released from any obligation to continue to provide a manager but without prejudice to its claim for payment of any sum due but not paid

16.1.8 if the said Personal Representatives and any surviving partner have not arranged to deal with the Business or to dispose of the Assets as provided in clause 16.1 within the relevant period referred to in clause 16.1 or intimate to the Company that neither course will be adopted, the Company will be entitled to withdraw the services of any manager and to terminate this agreement forthwith by notice in writing

16.2 If You are a corporate entity and any Guarantor dies during the subsistence of this agreement:

16.2.1 You must decide, within a period of 3 months from the date of death of such Guarantor, whether a relative or beneficiary of such Guarantor should sign an agreement with the Company substituting him or her for the deceased in the capacity of Guarantor under the terms of this agreement

16.2.1.1 if it is so decided, You must give written notice of it, within the said period of 3 months, to the Company giving the name and address of such relative or beneficiary together with such other information as the Company may require

16.2.1.2 on the Company being satisfied that such individual would be acceptable as a Guarantor by the criteria set out in clause 15 which apply to a proposed purchaser of the Business, and provided that the Company is satisfied as to the suitability of the other persons who will be Your shareholders, and with Your shareholding structure, and that such individual will have effective voting of or be in facto control of You, the Company will not exercise its option referred to in clause 15 and will enter into an agreement with You any surviving Guarantor and such individual substituting him or her in the place of the deceased Guarantor as Guarantor under the terms of this agreement subject to such individual signing such agreement and executing a Guarantee and Indemnity in favour of the Company

16.2.2 if You do not, within the said period of 3 months, produce an individual as Guarantor in accordance with and subject to the provisions of clause 16.2.1, then the provisions of clause 15 will apply and if the Company decides not to exercise its option referred to in clause 15 and a Purchaser acceptable to the Company by the criteria set out in clause 15 is found, the Assets may be sold to such purchaser within the period of 6 months from the date of the death of the deceased Guarantor in accordance with the provisions of clause 15

16.2.3 if requested in writing by You the Company may (as soon as is reasonably practicable) provide a manager to manage the Business during the period of 3 months specified in clause 16.2.1

16.3.4 the Company will be entitled to a fee for the provision of any such manager equal to:

16.2.4.1 the normal salary of the manager;

16.2.4.2 the travelling accommodation and subsistence expenses of the manager; and

Appendix F (iv): Sample Document: Franchise Agreement

16.2.4.3 50% of the total of 16.2.4.1 and 16.2.4.2 plus Value Added Tax such to be paid at weekly intervals on the Tuesday of each week

16.2.5 the Company may also (as soon as is reasonably practicable), if requested by You, provide such a manager for an additional period of up to 3 months upon the same terms and conditions so as to enable You to arrange a sale of the Assets

16.2.6 if there is any failure promptly to pay to the Company any fee for the provision of the services of any manager, the Company will be released from any obligation to continue to provide a manager but without prejudice to its claim for payment of any due sum but not paid

16.2.7 if You have not arranged a substitution for the deceased Guarantor within the said period of 3 months as provided in clause 16.2.1, or a sale of the Assets within the said period of 6 months as provided in clause 16.2.2 or intimate to the Company that neither course will be adopted, the Company will be entitled to withdraw the services of any manager and to terminate this agreement forthwith by notice in writing

16.2.8 You must, if requested by the Company, do all such acts and things and execute all such deeds and documents as may be necessary to give effect to the provisions contained in this clause

16.3 Any action taken by the Company under the provisions of clauses 16.1 or 16.2 on the instructions or with the approval of any person or persons claiming to be Your Personal Representatives or deceased Guarantor within the meaning of this agreement, will be binding on and not under any circumstances be open to challenge by Your Executor(s) or that of the Guarantor, even if he, she or they were not a party or parties to it and by their signing this agreement You and the Guarantor (as may be appropriate) expressly bind your Executor(s) to ratify and confirm all actions by such person or persons under this agreement, and to indemnify and free and relieve the Company of and from all liability and responsibility whatever in respect of such action as is referred to above

16.4 Any manager of the Business who is appointed pursuant to the provisions of clause 16.1 or 16.2 will act as the agent of the said Personal Representatives and any surviving partner in the case of an appointment under sub-clause 16.1, or Your agent in the case of an appointment under clause 16.2

16.5 [In the event of Your or any Guarantor's incapacity or unauthorised absence or that of any of Your directors, at any time, the Company has the right to appoint personnel (at the cost of You) to supervise the conduct of the Business to ensure that the Business is operated in a satisfactory manner to preserve the goodwill associated with the Business and the System and any such supervision will be subject to the provisions of clause 16.2.4 and 16.4]

16.6 In the event of any such incapacity lasting for a continuous period of [183 days] or a total period of [125] days in any period of [365] days, the Company may require You to dispose of the Business whereupon the provisions of clause 15 of this agreement shall apply]

17. TERMINATION

17.1 IF at any time during the Initial Training it becomes apparent to the Company that You or any Guarantor do not meet the Company's standards and requirements the Company has the right upon, notice in writing, to terminate this agreement forthwith

17.2 Upon such termination the Company will return to You any Initial Franchise Fee paid to the Company less a deduction of such sum as is equal to __% of the Initial Franchise Fee which sum will be deemed to be fully earned by the Company

17.3 The Company will be entitled to terminate this agreement if You, through no fault on your part, have not secured the Premises within the period of _____ months from the date of this agreement whether by purchase lease or agreement for lease, in which case the Company will refund in full any Initial Franchise Fee paid by You

17.4 It is a condition precedent for the return of the Initial Franchise Fee or any part of it that You or any Guarantor comply, so far as the same may be applicable, with the provisions of clause 18

Appendix F (iv): Sample Document: Franchise Agreement

17.5 The Company may, without prejudice to any other rights or remedies available to it, terminate this agreement forthwith by notice in writing to You, upon a material breach of this agreement and the following shall be deemed to be a material breach but the list shall not be deemed to be exhaustive, and upon such termination all Your rights under this agreement will cease:

17.5.1 if You fail to commence the Business within the period of _____ months from the date of this agreement; or

17.5.2 if Your lease or underlease of the Premises expires or is terminated or forfeit for any reason whatsoever; or

17.5.3 if You lose your right to occupy or conduct the Business from the Premises for any reason whatsoever; or

17.5.4 if You (being a natural person) or any Guarantor has in its franchise application or supporting details provided the Company with information which contains any false or misleading statements or omits any material fact which may make any statement misleading; or

17.5.5 if notwithstanding the provisions of clause 14.10 You or any Guarantor challenge the Company's ownership or the validity of any of the Intellectual Property or any other industrial or intellectual property rights of the Company; or

17.5.6 if You (being a natural person) or any Guarantor become insolvent make any arrangement or composition with Your, his or her creditors or have a bankruptcy petition presented against You, him or her have a receiver appointed of all or any part of Your, his or her assets or take any similar action in consequence of debt; or

17.5.7 if there is an assignment or a purported assignment of this agreement otherwise than in accordance with the provisions of clause 16; or

17.5.8 if there is a breach of any of the provisions of clauses 7.1.31, 7.1.32 or 7.1.33; or

Appendix F (iv): Sample Document: Franchise Agreement

    17.5.9 if You (being a corporate entity) become insolvent enter into liquidation whether compulsorily or voluntarily or if You make any arrangement or composition with Your creditors or have a Receiver (including an Administrative Receiver) appointed of all or any part of Your assets or take any similar action in consequence of debt; or

    17.5.10 if You or any Guarantor fail to comply with any Default Notice or are in Persistent Default; or

    17.5.11 [if the Software Licence is terminated or is determined for whatsoever reason; or]

    17.5.12 If any other agreement between the Company and You has been terminated by reason of any breach on the part of You or the Guarantor

17.6 Without prejudice to the generality of the provisions of clause 17.5 if the Company, on reasonable grounds, suspects that any information concerning the Company's business any of its franchisees, the System, this agreement or any part of it or particulars of any communication from the Company to You and/or to any Guarantor is being or has been communicated in any way to any third party or to any competitor of the Company or any of its franchisees, by You or any of Your employees or any Guarantor or any of Your shareholders (if any) or any other person associated with You, or such employee, Guarantor or shareholder, then the Company may forthwith without prejudice to any other rights or remedies available to it terminate this agreement and all Your rights under this agreement will thereupon cease

17.7

    17.7.1 This agreement will without prejudice to any rights or remedies of the Company automatically terminate immediately upon You taking any steps to cease or ceasing to be registered for VAT for whatsoever reason or if You fail to take any steps to prevent such event occurring, or upon You being in any breach of any of the clauses 2.2; 7.1.24; or 7.1.25

17.7.2 If this agreement is terminated pursuant to this sub-clause, the Company will be entitled to claim damages as if termination has occurred by virtue of Your breach of the agreement

18 CONSEQUENCES OF TERMINATION

18.1 UPON Termination You must

18.1.1 immediately discontinue conducting the Business, using the Intellectual Property, signs, cards, notices and other display or advertising matter indicative of the Company or of any association with the Company or of the Business or the Products [the Services]

18.1.2 make or cause to be made such changes in signs, cards, notices and other display or advertising matter Premises, [Vehicles], buildings and structures as the Company shall reasonably direct, so as effectively to distinguish the Business from its former public and marketing image, and if within 30 days of such direction You fail or omit to make or cause to be made any change, then the Company will have power (without incurring any liability to You), without the consent of You, except for the consent which You hereby irrevocably give, to enter upon the Premises (if they are commercial premises) [and or to take possession of the Vehicles] for the purpose of making and to make or cause to be made any such change at Your expense, which expense You must pay on demand

18.1.3 when demanded by the Company, deliver up to the Company at Your expense all stationery, literature, signs, cards, notices other display or advertising matter and any other article bearing the name of the Company or any Intellectual Property

18.1.4 return to the Company, at Your expense, all items which may have been loaned to You by the Company including the Operations Manual

18.1.5 forthwith pay to the Company [(without any deduction or right of set-off except where the Company itself is in breach or where there exists an indisputable or acknowledged debt or credit owing to You by the Company)] all sums of money which may be due or owing from You to the Company

18.1.6   forthwith prepare audited accounts of the Business for the period from the date when such accounts were last prepared up to and inclusive of the date of termination of this agreement and submit them to the Company within 30 days from the date of Termination

18.1.7   assign to the Company for the sum of £1 in such form as the Company reasonably requires, the benefit of such contracts with customers as the Company may specify and pay over to the Company any sums received on account of such contracts (without any deduction or right of set off)

18.1.8   join with the Company in cancelling any interest You may have in any of the Trade Marks which may have been recorded with the Registrar of Trade Marks, and if You fail to do so, the Company is hereby irrevocably appointed Your agent with full authority to give such notice to the Registrar of Trade Marks on Your behalf

18.1.9   cease using any e-mail address, internet domain name listing or registration relating to the Business the telephone lines and any other lines the numbers of which have been publicly associated with the Business and the Trade Name, and do all such acts and things including the signature of any document which may be necessary to ensure that the future use by the Company is assured and if You shall fail to do so, the Company is hereby irrevocably appointed Your agent, with full authority to give such notice to the relevant supplier of such communication services on Your behalf

18.1.10   cease the use of all material of whatever nature the copyright of which is vested in the Company or where its continued use would in any way infringe the Company's copyright

18.1.11 pay the Company's legal costs incurred in obtaining legal advice and in the preparation and service of the termination notice and all disbursements reasonably and properly incurred in relation to it

18.1.12 upon the payment of the sum of £1 by the Company provide the Company without delay with a list of all customers and (as far as it is aware) of prospective customers of the Business and there will be a deemed transfer of such customers and their goodwill to and for the benefit of the Company with effect from the date of payment of the said sum

18.1.13 the Company will have the option to purchase such of the sound saleable stock of Your Products as the Company may specify at cost [and any Equipment and Vehicles at their written down value]

18.1.14

18.1.14.1 [cease using any domain name incorporating any of the Trade Marks or the Trade Name or any part of any of them or anything confusingly similar to any of them and You must, at Your expense, do every act or thing necessary to ensure the full and unrestricted use and ownership of any such domain name by the Company]

18.1.14.2 cease using any or all of the Trade Marks, colour combinations, designs, symbols, or slogans, any and all domain names, electronic mail addresses and internet websites that display or use the Trade Marks or any such specific colour, combinations, designs, symbols or slogans and acknowledge that You have no further rights in any of them.

18.1.14.3 [Immediately cease to represent Yourself as a franchisee of the Company and discontinue the use of the Trade Marks, Trade Name and specific colour combinations, designs, symbols, or slogans of the Trade

Marks, any and all domain names, electronic mail addresses and internet websites that display or use the Trade Marks, Trade Name or any such specific colour combinations, designs, symbols or slogans, in any form or imitation, and refrain from identifying Yourself in name by any of the words [_____, _____ or _____] in any form or fashion;]

18.1.14.4 [Immediately make available to the Company copies of all Your past and current sales leads and records and all documents related to Your past and future operations that may exist including e-mail receiving agreements and all data and information relating to the foregoing stored in or retrieved or generated from computer or electronic system]

18.2 Upon Termination other than by reason of the sale of the Assets as permitted by this agreement, or the effluxion of time and the grant of a New Franchise Agreement to You by the Company pursuant to clause 4, the Company will have the option to purchase the Assets upon the Purchase Terms

18.3 Upon Termination neither You nor any Guarantor must

18.3.1 for a period of [1 year] after Termination be directly or indirectly engaged concerned or interested in any capacity whatsoever (except as the holder of not more than 5% of the shares in any company whose shares are listed or dealt in on The Stock Exchange) in any business which provides any products or services which compete with any of the Products or Services provided by the Company or any of its franchisees

18.3.1.1 from the Premises; or

18.3.1.2 within the Radius; or

18.3.1.3 within the Territory

18.3.2 [for a period of [1 year] after Termination be directly or indirectly engaged concerned or interested in any business which is conducted from any other premises in the United Kingdom if they are within a radius of _____:

18.3.2.1 from the premises of

18.3.2.1.1 any other You or prospective You of the Company; or

18.3.2.1.2 the Company from which it conducts or intends to conduct a **ZORCO BUSINESS** if it would compete with any of them; or

18.3.2.2 from any premises where a **ZORCO BUSINESS** is conducted or intended to be conducted by:

18.3.2.2.1 any You or prospective You of the Company; or

18.3.2.2.2 by the Company itself

18.4.2.3 if in any such case (referred to in clause 18.3.2.2.1 or 18.3.2.2.2) You shall have sold [the Products] [and or provide the Services] to customers whose place of business or residence is within any such radius]

18.3.3. [for a period of [1 year] after Termination be directly or indirectly engaged concerned or interested in any business which is conducted within any area in the United Kingdom

18.3.3.1 if it would compete with any **ZORCO BUSINESS** conducted or intended to be conducted by:

18.3.3.1.1. any other You or prospective You of the Company; or

18.3.3.1.2 the Company itself; or

18.3.3.2 where a **ZORCO BUSINESS** is conducted or intended to be conducted by:

18.3.3.2.1 any You or prospective You of the Company; or

18.3.3.2.2 by the Company itself

if in any such case (referred to in clause 18.3.3.2.1 or 18.3.3.2.2) You shall have sold [the Products] [and or provided the Services] to customers whose place of business or residence is within such area]

18.3.4 for the period of 1 year after Termination for the purpose of selling any products or services which are the same as or similar to any of the [Products] or the [Services] directly or indirectly solicit or tout for business from any person who was during the period of 1 year prior to Termination a customer of or in the habit of dealing with the Business

18.3.5 without prejudice to the foregoing provisions at any time after Termination be directly or indirectly engaged concerned or interested in a business which utilises the System or any significant part of it whilst the same remains confidential nor use the Trade Name or the Trade Marks or any name or mark likely to be confused with it

18.4 The parties agree that each of the covenants set out in sub-clause 18.3 is separate and severable and enforceable accordingly, and, whilst the restrictions contained in such covenants are considered by the parties to be reasonable in all the circumstances at present, it is acknowledged that restrictions of this nature may be invalid because of changing circumstances or other unforeseen reasons, and accordingly if any of the restrictions shall be adjudged to be void or ineffective for whatever reason, but would be adjudged to be valid and effective if part of its wording were deleted, or its period reduced, or its area reduced in scope, it shall then apply with such modifications as may be necessary to make it valid and effective

18.5 Termination shall be without prejudice to the accrued rights of the parties and any provision of this agreement which relates to or governs the acts of the parties to this agreement subject to Termination shall remain in full force and effect and shall be enforceable notwithstanding Termination

Appendix F (iv): Sample Document: Franchise Agreement

18.6 [If this agreement is terminated pursuant to this clause _____, You must pay to the Company, by way of liquidated damages, within 5 days of being notified in writing of the amount so payable, such sum as is calculated as follows:

$$E = A \times (\text{the higher of B or C}) \times D$$

- **A:** the number of months between the effective date of termination and the date this agreement would have terminated by effluxion of time;
- **B:** the average Continuing Franchise Fees receivable from You in the 3 months period prior to termination of this agreement;
- **C:** the average Continuing Franchise Fees receivable from You during the same period as is referred to in B;
- **D:** 60% representing a 40% discount by virtue of accelerated payment, the Company's duty to mitigate its loss and the Company not being required to perform its obligations hereunder;
- **E:** payment due from You]

19. WAIVER

19.1 You agree that except for any agreements entered into in writing between the parties to this agreement, this agreement contains the entire agreement between the parties and no representations warranties inducements or promises made by the Company and no other agreements whether oral or otherwise not embodied in this agreement shall add to or vary this agreement or be of any force or effect

19.2

19.2.1 You acknowledge that You have been told that if there are any representations warranties inducements or promises which You consider have been made to You which have induced You to enter into this agreement, You are obliged to submit a written statement of them to the Company so that an agreed form of such statement may be annexed to and form part of this agreement.

19.2.2 In the absence of such written annexure, You shall be deemed not to have relied upon any representation warranty inducement or promise made or given or purportedly made or given by the Company

19.3 No failure of the Company to exercise any power given to it under this agreement, or to insist upon strict compliance by You or by any Guarantor with any obligation under this agreement and no custom or practice of the parties at variance with the terms of this agreement, will constitute any waiver of any of the Company's rights under this agreement

19.4 All rights and remedies of the Company under this agreement are cumulative and may be exercised successively or concurrently and a waiver by the Company of any particular default by You or the Guarantor, will not affect or impair the Company's rights in respect of any subsequent default of any kind by You or the Guarantor, nor will any delay or omission of the Company to exercise any rights arising from any default by You or the Guarantor, affect or impair the Company's rights in respect of such default or any other default of any kind

20. SEVERABILITY

20.1 **IF** any term or provision or any part of any of it contained in this agreement shall be declared or become unenforceable invalid or illegal for any reason whatsoever, including but without derogating from the generality of the foregoing, a decision by any competent domestic court, the European Court of Justice the Commission of the European Union, an Act of Parliament, European Union legislation or any statutory or other bylaws or regulations or any other requirements having the force of law, the other terms and provisions of this agreement shall remain in full force and effect as if this agreement had been executed without the Offending Provision appearing in this agreement

20.2 If the exclusion of any Offending Provision adversely affects the Company's right to receive payment of fees or remuneration by whatever means payable to the Company (including but without prejudice to the generality of the foregoing the Company's right [exclusively] to supply You with the

Products and/or Services products and/or services) or materially adversely affects any of the Intellectual Property then the Company will have the right to terminate this agreement upon 30 days' notice in writing to You **PROVIDED** however that:

> 20.2.1 before the service of such notice the Company and You will use their best efforts, by good faith discussions, to agree within a period of 60 days from the date when the Company initiates such discussion process (time shall be of the essence for this purpose) upon alternative enforceable provisions which will have the same practical effect for the Company as the Offending Provision and

> 20.2.2 upon any agreement having been reached, the new provisions will be incorporated into this agreement and the Company will not be entitled to terminate this agreement under the provisions of this clause by reason of that particular event

20.3 If this agreement is subject to notification under the Competition Act, 1998 by reason of any provision of this agreement or by reason of any agreement or arrangement of which this agreement forms a part, then, unless it's a non-notifiable agreement as defined in that Act the following will apply:

> 20.3.1 any provision of this agreement by virtue of which it is subject to notification under the said Act will not take effect until the day after that on which this agreement and other relevant particulars of such agreement or arrangement will have been delivered by either party to the appropriate authorities in accordance with the provisions of that Act

> 20.3.2 You the Guarantor and the Company will use their respective best efforts to comply with the requirements of such Act relating to the delivery of such particulars

20.4 Notwithstanding any other provisions of this agreement, if it appears to the Company that this agreement or any part of it infringes or may infringe Article 81 of the EC Treaty or if the Company wishes any European Commission's Category Exemption regulation to apply to this agreement (including, but not limited to Regulation 2790/1999 of 22 December 1999) and deems it necessary or desirable to amend the terms and conditions of this agreement, so as to make it conform with provisions the of the said Article 81 and/or the requirements of such regulation it shall notify such amendments in writing to You whereupon within 28 days following such notification such amendments shall be incorporated into this agreement as if they had been expressly agreed between the Company and You

21. ACKNOWLEDGEMENTS AND WARRANTY

21.1 **You** and the Guarantor acknowledge that the Company in giving advice to and assisting You in establishing the Business [(including, but without prejudice to the generality of the foregoing, recommending equipment and materials advising on site selection and financial and/or profit projections] and the assessment of Your suitability (and where appropriate) that of the Guarantor) is not making or giving any representations guarantees or warranties

21.2 You acknowledge You have been advised by the Company to discuss Your intention to enter into this agreement with other franchisees (if any) of the Company and that You must decide on the basis of Your own judgement of what You have been told by the Company or such other franchisees whether or not to enter into this agreement

21.3 You and the Guarantor further acknowledge that the business venture contemplated by this agreement involves business risks and that Your success will be affected by Your and any Guarantor's business ability and commitment

21.4 You and the Guarantor acknowledge that you have both been advised by the Company to obtain independent legal advice before signing this agreement and that you are fully aware of all of the provisions of it and accept that the provisions of this agreement are fair and reasonable in all the circumstances known to or in the contemplation of each of you as at the date of this agreement

21.5 You hereby warrant that, prior to the signing of this agreement or any other **ZORCO** franchise agreement, You had no knowledge of the **ZORCO BUSINESS** or how to operate a business which is the same as or similar to the **ZORCO BUSINESS** or how to conduct the **ZORCO BUSINESS** or of the

Company's trade secrets know-how methods or the System other than any knowledge gained by virtue of its association with the Company prior to the date of this agreement

22. NO WARRANTIES WITHOUT AUTHORITY AND INDEMNITY

22.1 **You** must not make any statement, representation, or claims and must give no warranties to any customer or prospective customer in respect of [the Products sold by You] or the Services or the System or any of them except such as are implied by law, or may have been specifically authorised by the Company, such authority to be given either in writing or in the Operations Manual in its form current at the time of the making by You of such statement representation claim or the giving by You of such warranty

22.2 You hereby undertake with the Company to keep it fully and effectually indemnified against all claims demands losses expenses and costs which the Company may incur as a result of any breach by You of this provision or of any other provision contained in this agreement

23. GUARANTOR'S OBLIGATIONS

23.1 **IN** consideration of the Company entering into this agreement with You at the request of the Guarantor, the Guarantor hereby covenants and undertakes to the Company

  23.1.1 that You will duly observe and perform all Your obligations under this agreement

  23.1.2 that the Guarantor will (as a distinct and separate obligation) indemnify and render harmless the Company in respect of all losses damages claims costs and expenses which the Company may incur or suffer by reason of its entry into, continuation of, or termination (in any way) of this agreement

  23.1.3 that the Guarantor will devote his or her full time attention and effort to the management and operation of the Business except to the extent and in the manner expressly and previously agreed in writing by the Company

23.1.4 that the Guarantor will ensure that at all times You have not less than 2 directors (including himself)

23.1.5 that the Guarantor will not make use of any of the Intellectual Property (including the goodwill of the Company) and will not disclose to any third party or make use of any of the Company's trade secrets, know-how, the System or methods of which the Guarantor may acquire knowledge by virtue of the training he or she may have received from the Company, his or her involvement in the Business, his or her shareholding or directorship in You for any purpose other than the conduct of the Business

23.1.6 that the Guarantor will observe and comply with the provisions, mutatis mutandis, contained in clauses 7.1.25; 7.1.27; 7.1.28; 7.1.29; 7.1.31; and 7.1.33

23.1.7 that the Guarantor will forthwith execute the Guarantee and Indemnity and Option Deed in favour of the Company

23.1.8 [that the Guarantor will, if requested so to do by the Company, execute Your Lease or the Underlease to be granted to You pursuant to the provisions of the _____ Schedule as a surety for the performance by You of its obligations under Your Lease or the Underlease]

23.2 The Guarantor hereby warrants that prior to the signing of this agreement or any other **ZORCO** franchise agreement he or she had no knowledge of the **ZORCO BUSINESS** or how to operate a business which is the same as or similar to the **ZORCO BUSINESS** or how to conduct the **ZORCO BUSINESS** or of the Company's trade secrets know-how methods or the System other than any knowledge gained by virtue of any association with the Company prior to the date of this agreement

23.3. The Guarantor hereby acknowledges and agrees that:

23.3.1 liability under this clause shall not be in any way affected or impaired by the Company giving time or showing any indulgence whatsoever to You

23.3.2 if there are 2 or more persons as Guarantor as parties to this agreement all covenants and agreements on the part of the Guarantor shall be deemed to be joint and several covenants and obligations on their part

24 ASSIGNMENT BY COMPANY

24.1 THE Company may assign or otherwise deal with the benefit and burden of the whole or any part of this agreement, without any consent from You, and in the case of an assignment, if it procures that the assignee enters into a direct covenant with You to observe and perform all the Company's obligations contained in this agreement after such assignment, the Company will be released and discharged from all its obligations under this agreement

25. OTHER PROVISIONS

25.1 FOR the avoidance of doubt You hereby acknowledge that You have no claim to any copyright in the Operations Manual and that all goodwill associated with or arising from the use of the and Intellectual Property will at all times inure to the benefit of, belong to, and be vested in, the Company and that You only have the right to benefit from such goodwill to the extent and upon the terms provided by this agreement

25.2 In the event of any dispute the authentic text of the Operations Manual shall be the copy kept as such by the Company at its Head Office

25.3 The Operations Manual shall at all times remain the property of the Company

25.4 There shall be deemed to be incorporated into any option contained in this agreement for the purchase in certain circumstances by the Company of any interest of You in the Premises, the National Conditions of Sale (20th Edition), so far as they apply and are not varied by or inconsistent with the provisions of this agreement

25.5 Where under any of the provisions of this agreement the Company's consent or approval is required to be given or obtained, such consent or approval to be effective and binding on the Company, unless deemed by a provision in this agreement to have been given, must be in writing and signed by a director of the Company

25.6 Where in this agreement there is a reference to a requirement of the Company (however expressed) it shall be deemed to include any requirement contained in the Operations Manual

25.7

    25.7.1 where in this agreement there is reference to any matter to be specified by the Company, notice of such specified requirements may be communicated by way of amendment or addition to the Operations Manual

    25.7.2 the Company has the right to amend the Operations Manual from time to time and You must accept and incorporate such amendments into the copy of the Operations Manual in Your possession with effect from the Company's notification of such amendments to You

    25.7.3 The Company may transmit the Operations Manual and any amendments by electronic mail, internet or other electronic means. The Operations Manual, including all new pages and all superseded pages, all electronic copies (including disks, CD-ROM's or other copies stored by electronic means), and all information stored in or retrieved or generated from electronic or computer systems will be and remain the property of The Company.

25.8 Where in this agreement there is a duty imposed on You to send money reports or information to the Company by a certain day which for any reason (including but not limited to strikes or non-collection of post) You cannot perform, You are under an obligation to ensure that such money reports or information are received by the Company not later than during the second day after the day upon which such dispatch, remittance, transmission etc. could have taken place

25.9

    25.9.1 if it is necessary to amend the plans drawings and specifications referred to in clause 5.1.3 hereof to suit the Premises, You will at its own expense employ an architect or surveyor for the purpose

Appendix F (iv): Sample Document: Franchise Agreement

      25.9.2 no plans or drawings so amended must be used for any purpose until they shall have been approved in writing by the Company

25.10

      25.10.1 [the Company has the right to enter into contracts with National Accounts for the supply [of Services and/or the Products] by itself, You and/or any of its franchises on such terms as the Company in its discretion considers to be in the interests of **ZORCO NETWORK** as a whole

      25.10.2 if You do not wish to perform any National Accounts contractual obligations in any particular case and so inform the Company within 7 days from the date of the Company's request to You to perform such National Accounts contractual obligations, the Company may in its sole discretion, release You from Your obligations in so far as they relate to that particular National Accounts contract, in which case [notwithstanding the exclusivity granted by this agreement] the Company may perform such National Accounts contract itself or, at its option, nominate or sub-contract with a third party to do so]

25.11 notwithstanding anything to the contrary contained in this agreement, the Company and all members of the **ZORCO NETWORK** are entitled to [sell the Products][provide the Services] to [unsolicited] customers within the Territory]

25.12 All sums payable to the Company under or in connection with this agreement are quoted exclusive of VAT and You must in addition to any such sums pay to the Company VAT where applicable at the appropriate rate

25.13 Where You are required to purchase Products only from the Company [and or Approved Suppliers], and the Company fails to supply or procure that You be so supplied, You are entitled, so long as such failure continues, to obtain supplies of products which are as closely equivalent to the Products (which You is unable to obtain from the Company or Approved Suppliers) as possible, from alternative sources provided that You have obtained the prior written approval of the Company as to the quality of such products and such sources

25.14 The Operations Manuals forms a part of this agreement and if there is any conflict between the provisions of the Operations Manual and this agreement, the provisions of this agreement will prevail

25.15

    25.15.1 any notice required to be given under the agreement by the Company may be delivered personally or by sending it by first class prepaid post, if to You, at the Premises and if to the Guarantor, at his or her last known address

    25.15.2 any notice required to be given by You or the Guarantor may be given by leaving the same with the Company's company secretary at or by posting it by first class prepaid post to the Company's then registered office.

    25.15.3 Where a notice is sent by post under the provisions of this clause, service will be deemed to have been effected at the expiration of 72 hours (excluding bank holidays) after the same was posted whether or not it has been received

25.16 The parties to this agreement hereby warrant to each other that they have the power and authority to sign this agreement and any other document relating to any transaction contemplated by this agreement in the capacity in which they have signed this agreement

25.17 The clause headings to this agreement are solely for ease of reference and this agreement must not be construed by reference to them

25.18 In order to enable the Company to ascertain whether You are complying with the obligations imposed upon You under this agreement, and in order to enable the Company to enforce rights given to You by this agreement, the Company may at any time enter the Premises (if they are commercial premises) and/or as Your representative (which appointment You hereby irrevocably confirms during the Term and for the purposes only of giving effect to the provisions of this sub-clause) at any premises or location where You are supplying the Services and/or the Products and/or speak to any of Your customers without any other consent from

Appendix F (iv): Sample Document: Franchise Agreement

You except for the consent which You hereby give and which You hereby agree not to revoke

25.19 Except where the context otherwise requires, each of the restrictions contained in this agreement and in each clause and sub-clause of it shall be construed as independent of every other restriction and of every other provision of this agreement and the existence of any claim or cause of action by You against the Company whatsoever shall not constitute a defence to the enforcement by the Company of the said restrictions or of any of them

25.20

25.20.1 It is hereby expressly agreed amongst the parties to this agreement that having regard to the recitals and other provisions of this agreement, each of the restrictive covenants contained in this agreement and in each clause and sub-clause of it is reasonably necessary for the protection of the Company, the Intellectual Property, and the other franchisees of the Company and does not unreasonably interfere with the freedom of action of You

25.20.2 The parties agree that any such provisions shall be deemed to be altered and amended to the extent necessary to effect such validity and enforceability.

25.21

25.21.1 You acknowledge that the provisions in this agreement relating to the limits on Your right to make deductions or set offs (to which it may claim to be entitled) against payment of any sums fees or contributions due from You to the Company are fair and reasonable

25.21.2 You recognise that Your failure or refusal to make payments of such sums fees or contributions because of Your dissatisfaction with the Company's performance may result in Your continued involvement in the **ZORCO NETWORK** being subsidised by other franchisees who make payment of such fees and contributions

25.21.3 You also recognise that Your failure to pay such sums, fees or contributions will make it more difficult for the Company to continue to provide services to franchisees thus putting the **ZORCO NETWORK** in jeopardy and that this may cause severe problems for You in continuing to operate the Business

25.21.4 You accept that the remedies available to You which are not affected by the set off/deduction provisions of this agreement are sufficient for Your purposes including, as they do, a right to sue for damages and if appropriate acceptance of any repudiatory conduct on the part of the Company

25.22 This agreement must not be construed against the party preparing it, and must be construed without regard to the identity of the person who drafted it or the party who caused it to be drafted and must be construed as if all parties had jointly prepared the agreement and it must be deemed their joint work product, (except that copyright in it will remain vested in the Company or its solicitors as the case may be), and each and every provision of this agreement must be construed as though all the parties to it participated equal in its drafting; and any uncertainty or ambiguity shall not be interpreted against any one party. As a result of the foregoing, any rule of construction that a document is to be construed against the drafting party will not apply

25.23 You and the Guarantor agree jointly and severally to pay the Company's legal costs relating to this transaction and pay all the Company's costs charges and expenses incurred in or in contemplation of the enforcement of Your and/or Guarantor's obligations and You and the Guarantor shall jointly and severally keep the Company indemnified against all costs expenses claims and demands whatsoever in respect of the enforcement

25.24 Any reference in this agreement to a right of set off includes legal and equitable rights of set off

25.25 Nothing in this agreement shall constitute or be deemed to constitute any relationship of partnership, or relationship of employer and employee or that of principal and agent [(save as may be expressly authorised in writing by the Company)] between the Company and You or the Company and the Guarantor

25.26 This agreement shall remain in full force and effect notwithstanding the adoption by the United Kingdom of the euro

25.27 The parties to this agreement agree that any of the obligations of the Company may be performed by an Affiliate

25.28 If any exclusion of liability for negligent misrepresentation in this agreement fails the test of reasonableness applicable to such an exclusion, then liability for negligent misrepresentation will not be excluded

25.29 The parties do not intend any of the terms of this agreement to be enforceable by any third party pursuant to the provisions of the Contracts (Rights of Third Parties) Act 1999

25.30

> **25.30.1** [the provisions of the _____ Schedule [Lease Provisions] apply to this agreement
>
> **25.30.2** the Company hereby licenses the Software to You and You take the Software on licence from the Company upon the terms of the Software Licence]

26. ARBITRATION

26.1 **ANY** dispute or difference of any kind whatsoever which arises or occurs between the parties in relation to any thing or matter arising under out of or in connection with this agreement will be referred to arbitration under the Arbitration Rules of the Chartered Institute of Arbitrators by an arbitrator to be appointed by the President of the Chartered Institute of Arbitrators in London upon the application of any party **PROVIDED,** however, that not withstanding the application of arbitration to disputes or differences arising out of this agreement, the Company:

> **26.1.1** must not be prevented from terminating this agreement in accordance with clause [termination] and/or from applying to a competent court to enforce the provisions of clauses [Your Obligations] or [Consequences of Termination]; and
>
> **26.1.2** must be entitled to the entry of temporary and/or permanent injunctions and/or orders for specific performance enforcing the provisions of this agreement relating to the Company's con-

Appendix F (iv): Sample Document: Franchise Agreement

fidential information the Intellectual Property and/or the use of the System and/or any provisions contained in this agreement relating to the ownership or de facto control of You, any Guarantor or the Business or the assignment or purported or attempted assignment of this agreement

26.2 Neither You nor the Guarantor will be entitled in these circumstances to apply to any court for a stay of proceedings pending arbitration and you both hereby undertake not to do so

26.3 The costs of any arbitrator will be borne by the Company and You equally

26.4 The arbitrator will be required to carry out its deliberations in England

AS WITNESS the hands of the parties hereto the day and year first before written

Appendix F (iv): Sample Document: Franchise Agreement

Operations Manual Receipt

OPERATIONS MANUAL NO.

I/WE acknowledge receipt on loan of the above numbered operations manual in accordance with the terms of the franchise agreement entered into between us dated _____. I/We hereby acknowledge that I/we shall return this manual to You on demand and that I/we shall not make any copies of it or of any part of it nor shall I/we use it for any purpose other than for the purposes of conducting a business in accordance with the terms of the said franchise agreement.

IN WITNESS whereof this deed has been executed on the __ day of _____ 20__

SIGNED as a **DEED** by _____ in the presence of:

Witness:

Name:

Address:

Occupation:

Appendix F (iv): Sample Document: Franchise Agreement

Confidentiality Undertaking

[Add to your application form]

In consideration of Your agreeing to consider this application and to enter into discussions with me/us I/we hereby undertake to keep secret and confidential all information which You may provide to me/us or which I/we may discover in regard to Your business, Your business system, Your business methods, Your equipment, Your know-how and confidential information and not to disclose it to anyone else or use it myself/ourselves for any purpose whatsoever save to enable me/us to consider whether or not to become Your franchisee or, if we become a franchisee, under the terms of any franchise agreement which we may enter into with You

IN WITNESS whereof this deed has been executed on the ___ day of _____ 20__

SIGNED as a **DEED** by _____ in the presence of:

Witness:

Name:

Address:

Occupation:

Appendix F (iv): Sample Document: Franchise Agreement

The First Schedule

Start-Up Package

The Second Schedule

Confidentiality Undertaking

[To be issued to Your employees]

In consideration of the Company (as hereinafter defined) agreeing to the disclosure to me by the Employer of confidential information, know-how, systems and methods which are the property of the Company to enable me to perform my duties as an employee of the Employer

I, _____, undertake with [_____ Limited] of _____ ('Company') and with _____ ('Employer') to observe the following:

1 I shall not, during my employment (except with the prior consent of the Employer which consent will not be unreasonably withheld in the case of any business which is not similar to that carried on by the Employer) be concerned or interested directly or indirectly in any business which is similar to or which competes or which may compete with the business of the Employer or that of the Company or any of its franchisees otherwise than by the holding of securities quoted on a recognised stock exchange nor be personally employed or engaged in any capacity whatsoever in or in connection with any business other than the business of the Employer.

2 I shall not during my employment or at any time thereafter make any press, radio or television statements or publish in any form or medium or submit for publication any letter, article or book relating directly or indirectly to the business or affairs of the Employer or the Company without first obtaining consent in writing of the Employer and the Company.

3 During my employment or at any time thereafter:

    3.1 I shall not divulge or communicate to any person (other than those whose province it is to know the same or upon the instructions or with the approval of the Employer and the Company) nor use for my own purpose, or for the purposes other than the Employer's and the Company, any of the trade secrets know-how system any intellectual property methods or other confidential information of the Company and/or the Employer which I may have received or obtained, whether before, after, or while in the service of the Employer or the Company

3.2 I shall use my best endeavours to prevent the publication or disclosure by any other person of any of such trade secrets know-how system any intellectual property methods or other confidential information

3.3 In particular (but without derogating from the generality of the above) I shall not divulge or communicate to any person (other than those whose province it is to know the same or upon the instructions or with the approval of the Employer or the Company) nor use for my own purpose or for the purposes other than the Employer's or the Company's business, any of the lists of customers with whom the Employer deals which I may have received or obtained whether before, after, or while in the service of the Employer and shall use my best endeavours to prevent publication or disclosure by any other person of any of such lists of customers which I acknowledge constitute confidential information belonging to the Company, and of the Employer.

4 I shall hand over to the Employer and if the Employer has ceased to be a franchisee of the Company to the Company forthwith all documents, books, records, photographs, correspondence and other papers of whatsoever nature kept or made by me relating to the business of the Employer and any keys and other property whatsoever of the Employer which may then be in my possession or in my control upon the Employer's or the Company's request.

5 I undertake to observe the terms and conditions of the contract of employment with the Employer and its standard rules and regulations from time to time in force.

6 I undertake not, at any time during or within a period of 1 year from the termination of my employment, whether on my account or for any other person, firm or company, to endeavour to entice away from the Employer, solicit or interfere with, any person, firm or company who at any time during the period of 1 year preceding the date of termination of my employment or at the date of such termination was a customer or was in the habit of dealing with the Employer.

Appendix F (iv): Sample Document: Franchise Agreement

7   I undertake not to have any direct or indirect interest in any business which carries on a business similar to that carried on by the Employer (pursuant to its franchise agreement with the Company) the Company or any of its franchisees and whose premises or the geographical area of operations are sufficiently close to those of the Employer the Company or any of its franchisees, to compete with their business, or to assist such a competitor in any way for a period of 1 year from the termination of my employment without the Company's consent.

8   I undertake not to take part directly or indirectly in establishing a business which is the same as or similar to that conducted by the Employer pursuant to its franchise agreement with the Company during the term of my employment and the time the restraint on competition referred to in paragraph 7 is in force.

9   I undertake, upon the termination of my employment howsoever arising, and upon the request of the Employer, to resign from any office held by me with the Employer and I agree that should I fail to do so the Employer or the Company (if it so elects) is hereby irrevocably authorised to appoint some other person in my name and on my behalf to sign and do any document or things necessary or requisite to give effect thereto.

10   I acknowledge that

   10.1   each of the above provisions constitutes an entirely separate and independent restriction on me;

   10.2   the duration extent and application of each of the restrictions is no greater than is reasonable to protect the Employer and the Company, provided that if any such restriction shall be found wholly or partially to be void or unenforceable by a court of competent jurisdiction, but would be valid if some part thereof were deleted or its period or scope reduced or the geographical area limited, then such restriction shall apply with such modification as may be necessary to make it valid and effective; and

   10.3   I have been advised to obtain independent legal advice before signing this undertaking and that I am fully aware of all its provisions and accept that these provisions are fair and reasonable in all the circumstances known to or in the contemplation of the Employer, the Company or myself.

Dated the __ day of _____ 20__.

IN WITNESS whereof this deed has been duly executed day and year first before written

SIGNED as a **DEED** by _____ in the presence of:

Witness:

Name:

Address:

Occupation:

The Third Schedule

Form of Guarantee and Indemnity

This Deed is made the __ day of _____ 20__ **BETWEEN**

[_____] of _____ ('Company'); and

[_____] of _____ ('Guarantor')

WHEREAS

1. This agreement is supplemental to a Franchise Agreement ('Franchise Agreement') dated [_____] and made between [You ('You')] the Company and the Guarantor.

2. The Guarantor has agreed to guarantee the due performance of [Your] obligations under the Franchise Agreement.

NOW IT IS AGREED as follows:

1. If [You] fail to observe or perform any of the obligations under the Franchise Agreement and in particular but without prejudice to the generality of the foregoing shall fail to pay for any of the products or services supplied to [You] or to make payment when due of any fees contributions or any other sums which may be payable by [You] to the Company, the Guarantor will be liable for such default and shall make payment of any sums so due immediately upon demand being made by the Company.

2. The Guarantor will (as a distinct and separate obligation) indemnify and render harmless the Company in respect of all losses damages claims costs and expenses which the Company may incur or suffer by reason of its entry into, continuation of, or termination (in any way) of the Franchise Agreement.

3. The Guarantor hereby acknowledges and agrees that:

    3.1 Liability under this clause shall not be in any way affected or impaired by the Company giving time or showing any indulgence whatsoever to [You]

Appendix F (iv): Sample Document: Franchise Agreement

    3.2   If there are 2 or more persons as Guarantor as parties to this agreement all covenants and agreements on the part of the Guarantor shall be deemed to be joint and several covenants and obligations on their part.

IN WITNESS whereof this deed has been executed the day and year first before written.

EXECUTED as a deed by:

[_____] in the presence of _____

EXECUTED as a deed by:

[_____] in the presence of _____

The Fourth Schedule

Purchase Terms

1. The Company has the option to purchase the Assets on the following basis:
   - 1.1 such of the fixtures fittings and equipment, free from all encumbrances, employed in the Business as are specified by the Company at their current market value ('Current Market Value');
   - 1.2 the sound useable stock of the Products at cost or net realisable value ('Cost') whichever is the lower;
   - 1.3 Your interest in the Premises at a price ('Price') equal to its value with vacant possession in the open market with a willing vendor and willing purchaser, and in assessing the value in the open market there shall be disregarded (for the avoidance of any doubt) any value attributed to Your interest in the Premises by reason of:
     - 1.3.1 the occupation of the Premises by You;
     - 1.3.2 the goodwill of the Business carried on from it;
     - 1.3.3 any alterations and improvements carried out to the Premises; and
     - 1.3.4 the existence of the Franchise Agreement; and
   - 1.4 the Residual Goodwill at a value to be agreed
2. The Option may be exercised by the Company by notice in writing to You within 30 days from Termination or service of Your Notice
3.
   - 3.1
     - 3.1.1 The Company and You must attempt to reach agreement on the value of the Assets other than the said stock
     - 3.1.2 If agreement has not been reached within 30 days from the service of the Company's Notice, an independent valuer must be appointed at the joint expense of the Company and You to make a valuation of the Current Market Value the Residual Goodwill and the Price on the basis set out above ('Market Value'). The said valuer must be required to act as expert and not as arbitrator and such valuation will be binding on the Company and You

Appendix F (iv): Sample Document: Franchise Agreement

      3.1.3 If the Company and You are unable to agree on the valuer so to be appointed within 40 days from the service of the Company's Notice, the valuation must be made at the joint expense of the parties by a valuer to be nominated, at the request of either party, by the President for the time being at the Institution of Chartered Accountants of England and Wales and whose appointment must be on the basis set out in paragraph 3.1.2 of this schedule

      3.1.4 The valuer must be required by the parties to determine the Market Value as quickly as possible but in any event within 30 days following his or her appointment

4 If within 30 days after the determination of the Market Value the Company gives written notice to You of its intention to purchase the Assets at the Market Value and the Cost, then there will immediately come into force a binding contract ('Contract') for the sale and purchase of the Assets

5 The Contract shall incorporate the Edition of the National Conditions of Sale current at the date of service of the Purchase Notice or (if the said National Conditions are no longer published) the 20th Edition of the National Conditions except to the extent that the said Conditions are inconsistent with the terms of this agreement and in any event:

    5.1 no deposit shall be payable;

    5.2 the contractual completion date shall be 28 days from the service of the Purchase Notice or in the case of the purchase of a leasehold interest 7 days from the date upon which the landlord's licence to assign shall have been obtained (whichever is the later) ('Completion')

    5.3 Title shall be deduced:

        5.3.1 in accordance with Section 110 of the Land Registration Act 1925 (in the case of sale of registered land)

        5.3.2 and in the case of a sale of freehold unregistered land shall commence with a Conveyance on sale completed at least 15 years before the service of the Purchase Notice and

        5.3.3 in the case of a sale of leasehold unregistered land shall Commence with the lease under which the Premises are held

6   The sale shall be with vacant possession of the Premises on completion
7   You will sell with Full Title Guarantee;
8   On Completion You will assign the Assets of the Company and
   8.1   the Company will pay to You:
      8.1.1   the Market Value;
      8.1.2   (as soon as it is ascertained) the Cost to be agreed between the Company and You or in default of agreement such Cost as may be certified by the valuers normally employed by the Company who will act as experts and not as arbitrators; and
   8.2   You together with the Guarantor will jointly and severally:
      8.2.1   covenant with the Company that neither You nor the Guarantor will at any time for a period of 1 year from Completion be directly or indirectly engaged interested or concerned in any business which is the same as similar to:
         8.2.1.1   the Business [from the Premises][within the Territory][or within the Radius];
         8.2.1.2   or which competes with any ZORCO BUSINESS in the United Kingdom;
      8.2.2   warrant to the Company that the items referred to in paragraphs 1.1 and 1.2 above are Your sole and unencumbered Property; and
      8.2.3   agree not to directly or indirectly solicit or tout for business from any [National Account customer] or any other customer or any person who, during the period of [1 year] prior to Completion was a customer of or in the habit of dealing with the Business for the purpose of selling any [services and/or products] which are the same as or similar to any of the [Services and/or Products]
9   In the case of the sale of a lease, the Contract will be conditional upon Your obtaining consent to the proposed assignment of Your lease by all requisite reversioners (unless this requirement is waived by the Company)
10 You must, if the Company so requests, from the date of Termination and until the expiration of such period (not exceeding 30 days) as the Company

may specify from that date, and as from the date of service of any Notice or the Purchase Notice and pending Completion, be obliged to continue operating the Business in accordance with the terms of this agreement

11 You will keep the Company fully and effectually indemnified against all breaches of this agreement

12 You will indemnify the Company and keep the Company indemnified on demand against all liabilities costs claims proceedings fines penalties compensation Court or tribunal order, awards and demands arising from any liability or obligation of Yours in any way connected with or relating to the employment of the Guarantor and any of Your employees in the Business or the termination of such employment (including statutory obligations and contractual rights and obligations) which may be transferred to the Company pursuant to the Transfer of Undertaking (Protection of Employment) Regulations 1981.

13 For the avoidance of doubt, nothing in this schedule shall confer on any third party any benefit or the right to enforce any term of this agreement.

Appendix F (iv): Sample Document: Franchise Agreement

Schedule A

Appointment of Sub-Contractor

(VAT Registered)

[On Your headed notepaper]

Date:

[Sub-contractor details]

Dear [_____],

We hereby appoint You as an independent contractor to provide us or for us the [goods] [services] and upon the terms agreed by us from time to time, but subject to the following conditions:

1   You agree to comply with such directions as we advise You.

2   You agree not to do anything which may damage our reputation, goodwill, intellectual property rights or business, or that of [Company] of [_____] ('X')

3   ou confirm that You are registered for and will continue to be registered for VAT

4   You agree to make full payment for all goods and/or services provided by us to You without any deductions whatsoever and in accordance with any payment terms agreed between us.

5   You agree to indemnify us and X for any loss suffered by us or X as a result of Your actions.

This appointment will cease automatically if You breach any of the above conditions.

Please signify Your acceptance of these terms by signing and returning one copy of this letter to us.

Yours sincerely,

....

DIRECTOR/YOU

Appendix F (iv): Sample Document: Franchise Agreement

Schedule B

Appointment of Agent

[On Your headed notepaper]

Date:

[Details of Agent]

Dear [_____],

We hereby appoint You as our agent in connection with the provision on our behalf of the [goods] [services] and upon the terms agreed between us from time to time but subject to the following conditions:

You agree:

1 to comply with such directions as we advise You and You agree not to do anything which may damage our reputation, goodwill, intellectual property rights or business or that of [Company] of [_____] ('X')

2 to indemnify us and X for the value of [all products provided by us to You] [the services provided by You on our behalf] and for any loss suffered by us or X as a result of Your actions.

Please signify Your acceptance of these terms by signing and returning one copy of this letter to us.

Yours sincerely,

....

DIRECTOR/YOU

The Fifth Schedule

Option Deed

THIS DEED is made the ___ day of _____ 20__ **BETWEEN** _____ **LIMITED** whose registered office is at _____ ('You') of the one part and _____ **LIMITED** of _____ ('Company') of the other part

THIS DEED IS SUPPLEMENTAL TO:

(A) Franchise Agreement dated the ___ day of _____ 20__ made between the Company of the one part and You of the other part ('Franchise Agreement')

(B) lease dated _____ made between (1) _____ Limited of _____ and (2) You ('Lease') whereby the premises known as _____ ('Premises') were demised to You

NOW THIS DEED WITNESSETH as follows:

1 IN consideration of the approval by the Company of the Premises for the purposes of a _____ franchise You hereby covenants with the Company:

   1.1 not to assign underlet part with or share possession or occupation of the whole or any part of the Premises otherwise than in accordance with the following provisions

   1.2 You shall first by notice in writing offer to assign the Lease to the Company

   1.3 the said notice shall contain full particulars of the disposition proposed by You

   1.4 the said offer shall be capable of unconditional acceptance by the Company within 45 days after receipt of such notice

   1.5 if the said offer is accepted then completion of the assignment of the Lease shall take place on the date falling 28 days after such acceptance (or if that day is not a working day then the next following working day)

   1.6 if the said offer is not accepted within the said period of 45 days then You shall be entitled to complete within 120 days of Your said notice the said disposition proposed by You

Appendix F (iv): Sample Document: Franchise Agreement

2   **You** shall be under no obligation to offer to assign the Lease to the Company in the following circumstances:

   2.1   in the event of You wishing to relocate to other premises within the terms of the Franchise Agreement and such premises have previously been approved in writing by the Company and the Company and You have executed a deed in relation to such other premises in the same form as this deed (subject to any reasonable variations required by the Company) and the Company and You have agreed in writing that the Franchise Agreement shall apply to such other premises

   2.2   in the event of You wishing to assign the Premises to a new You of the Company who executes a deed in relation to the Premises in the same form as this deed (subject to any reasonable variations required by the Company) at the same time as he completes the assignment

3   **You** further covenant with the Company that You shall not use the Premises for any purpose other than for the Business as defined in the Franchise Agreement

4

   4.1   **IN** the event that the Franchise Agreement shall be determined or terminated for any reason or shall expire and not be renewed the Company shall be entitled on or at any time thereafter to serve on You notice requiring You to assign the Lease to the Company

   4.2   the said notice shall specify the date for completion of the said assignment which date shall be the date of or any date within 28 days after the termination of the Franchise Agreement (at the absolute discretion of the Company) and You shall assign the Lease to the Company on the date so specified by the Company

5   **THE** following provisions apply to any assignment made pursuant to the provisions of this Deed:

   5.1   You assign with full title guarantee

   5.2   title shall commence with the Lease or (if registered) shall be deduced pursuant to s.110 of the Land Registration Act 1925

   5.3   the said assignment shall be in the form annexed hereto and executed in escrow by the parties hereto

Appendix F (iv): Sample Document: Franchise Agreement

5.4 the Lease shall be assigned with vacant possession

5.5 the National Conditions of Sale (20th Edition) shall apply to the said assignment save that Condition 11(5) shall not apply but You shall in any event use Your best endeavours to obtain the consent of the Landlord of the Premises both before and after completion of the assignment

6 **THE** provisions of s.196 of the Law of Property Act 1925 as amended by the Recorded Delivery Services Act 1962 shall apply to any notice under this deed

7 **WHERE** there are two or more persons included in the expression 'You' the covenants undertaken herein which are expressed to be made by them shall be deemed to be made jointly and severally and unless the context otherwise admits the singular shall include the plural and the masculine shall include the feminine or neuter genders and vice versa

IN WITNESS whereof this deed has been executed by the parties hereto the day and year first before written

SIGNED as a **DEED** by _____ **LIMITED** acting by a director and secretary or by two directors

....
         Director   Director/Secretary

SIGNED as a **DEED** by _____ **LIMITED** acting by a director and secretary or by two directors

....
         Director   Director/Secretary

THIS ASSIGNMENT is made the __ day of _____ One thousand nine hundred and twenty _____ **BETWEEN** _____ **LIMITED** whose registered office is at _____ ('Vendor') of the

one part and _____ **LIMITED** of _____ ('Purchaser') of the other part

Appendix F (iv): Sample Document: Franchise Agreement

WHEREAS:

(A) By a lease ('Lease') dated the [_____ 20__] made between _____ Limited of _____ and the Vendor and _____ the property known as _____ ('Property') **TOGETHER WITH** but **EXCEPT AND RESERVED** as mentioned in the Lease was demised to the said Vendor for the term of years therein specified at the yearly rent thereby reserved and upon the covenants agreements and conditions therein contained

(B) The residue of the said term of years is vested in the Vendor

(C) The Vendor has agreed with the Purchaser for the assignment to the Purchaser of the Lease for the residue of the said term of years and subject to the said rent thereby reserved and the covenants agreements and conditions therein contained

NOW THIS DEED WITNESSETH as follows:

1 **IN** pursuance of the said agreement and in consideration of the sum of £1 paid by the Purchaser to the Vendor (receipt of which the Vendor hereby acknowledges) the Vendor as beneficial owner **HEREBY ASSIGNS** unto the Purchaser with full title guarantee **ALL THAT** the Lease **TO HOLD** the same unto the Purchaser for all the residue now unexpired of the said term of years subject henceforth to the payment of the rent thereby reserved and to the covenants agreements and conditions therein contained and on the part of the tenant to be observed and performed

2 **THE** Purchaser hereby covenants with the Vendor that the Purchaser will henceforth at all times duly pay all rent becoming due under the Lease and observe and perform all covenants conditions and other matters contained in or referred to in the Lease and on the part of the tenant to be observed and performed and will indemnify the Vendor against all costs charges actions and proceedings arising as a result of any breach or non-observance of the said covenants agreements and conditions

3 **IT IS HEREBY AGREED AND DECLARED** that notwithstanding the covenants implied by reason of the Vendor being expressed to sell herein with full title guarantee the said covenants shall nevertheless not be deemed to imply that the covenants in the Lease for the repair and decoration of the

Property have been observed and performed up to the date hereof and the Vendor hereby covenants with the Purchaser to indemnify the Purchaser against all costs charges actions and proceedings arising as a result of any breach, non-observance or non-performance of any of the said covenants agreements and conditions

4 **IT IS HEREBY CERTIFIED** that the transaction hereby effected does not form part of a larger transaction or series of transactions in respect of which the amount or value or the aggregate amount or value of the consideration exceeds Sixty Thousand Pounds (£60,000.00)

IN WITNESS whereof the parties hereto have duly executed this deed the day and year first above written

SIGNED as a **DEED** and **DELIVERED** by the said _____ **LIMITED** acting by its director and secretary or by two directors

        ....

        Director   Director/Secretary

SIGNED as a **DEED** by _____ **LIMITED** acting by its director and secretary or by two directors

        ....

        Director   Director/Secretary

Appendix F (iv): Sample Document: Franchise Agreement

The Sixth Schedule

Equipment Package

Appendix F (iv): Sample Document: Franchise Agreement

The Seventh Schedule

Trade Marks

Appendix F (iv): Sample Document: Franchise Agreement

The Eighth Schedule

Guarantee Procedures

1 **YOU** shall follow the administrative procedures established from time to time in the Operational Manual for the preparation and issue of guarantees and for dealing with any claims which may be made by Your customers

2 **UNLESS** specifically authorised in writing so to do You shall not issue any guarantees to any customer and then only to the extent and in the manner provided by such authority

3 **You** shall when required by the Company provide the Company with access to premises at which work is being carried out and with such information as the Company may require to satisfy itself that work is being or has been performed to the standard required for the issue of a guarantee

4 **THE** Company having undertaken responsibility as between itself and You to deal with claims from Your customers upon the terms contained in this clause You shall at the same time each week as payment is made of the Continuing Franchise fee pay to the Company a sum equal to 1% of Your gross sales (as defined in clause _____ hereof) The sum so received by the Company from You shall together with all sums paid to the Company by all its franchisees be placed into a guarantee fund (the 'Fund'). The Fund shall be the beneficial property of the Company which shall have complete discretion over the application of the Fund

5 **WITHOUT** prejudice to the generality of the foregoing and with like discretion the Company may apply the fund or any part thereof:

> 5.1 in the payment of any insurance premium which may be payable in respect of any insurance cover which the Company may be able to arrange to provide indemnity to You as well as the Company for claims which may be made
>
> 5.2 in the payment of any excess sum which may have to be borne under the terms of such insurance cover
>
> 5.3 in the payment of the cost of any remedial work (by whomever it may be carried out) or claims which may arise against the Company

Appendix F (iv): Sample Document: Franchise Agreement

and/or any of its franchisees and which may not have the benefit of such insurance cover or which it may be prudent to settle on commercial rather than legal grounds

5.4 in the payment of all administrative expenses incurred by the Company in dealing with claims made against the Company and/or its franchisees

6 IN the event that the fund is inadequate for the purpose of meeting all such claims costs and expenses incurred You shall pay to the Company such additional sums (in common with other franchisees of the Company) as may be required to cover the additional claims costs and expenses so incurred

7 You shall not do anything which may cause any Insurance Policy to be vitiated or renewal thereof to be refused or the premium to be increased

8 IF You shall in any 1 year be responsible for claims which in aggregate value exceed a sum equal to 1% of its gross sales (as defined in clause _____ hereof) he (it) shall be obliged

8.1 to undergo retraining

8.2 to have his (its) staff retrained

8.3 to terminate the employment of any staff member whose record in this respect and whose response in retraining is such that the Company in its absolute discretion considers him unsuitable to continue with his then responsibilities

9 IN the event that in any 1 year such claims shall be in excess of a sum equal to 1½% of Your gross sales (as defined in clause _____ hereof) You shall if so required and to the extent stipulated by the Company make additional contributions to the fund within 7 days after the same shall have been demanded

10 FOR the avoidance of doubt it is hereby agreed and declared:

10.1 that the Fund is the beneficial property of the Company and no trust arises in respect of the Fund or any accretions thereto

10.2 the Company shall not be under any obligation to make any refunds or repayments to You upon termination (for any reason) of this agreement or otherwise

Appendix F (iv): Sample Document: Franchise Agreement

10.3 that the Company will not charge the Fund for remedial work carried out by the Company more than the full commercial rate at which the Company charges its customers for like work

10.4 that in respect of claims arising out of work done or advice or survey reports given or made by You You are primarily liable to the customer

The Ninth Schedule

Hire/Loan of Equipment

1. **THE** Company agrees to hire [loan] to You [free of charge] the Equipment and You agree to take the Equipment on hire [loan] from the Company [upon the terms as to payment set forth in Part II of the _____ Schedule and] upon the following terms

2. **You** must not sell or offer for sale mortgage or pledge underlet lend or otherwise deal with or part with the possession of the Equipment

3. **You** must not interfere with or adjust the Equipment except as specifically authorised in the (manufacturers manual) Operations Manual

4. **You** will keep the Company indemnified against all loss and damage to the Equipment caused by the wilful or negligent misuse thereof

5. **THE** Company may affix to the Equipment or any part of it such labels, plates or other marks indicating the owner of the Equipment and You must not obliterate deface or cover them and must ensure that the Company at all reasonable times has access to the Equipment for the purpose of inspecting the Equipment and such labels and/or plates and keeping them in good repair

6. **You** must ensure that the Equipment is not used or permitted to be used for any purpose other than in the Business and as provided in the Operations Manual

7. **You** must not pledge, charge or offer the Equipment as security nor will You permit any lien or other encumbrance to affect the Equipment

8. **You** must inform any person to whom a debenture or any charge over any part of Your assets is to be granted that the Equipment is not Your property

9. **You** must at all times keep the Equipment insured in the joint names of Yourself and the Company in its full value and against such risks as are usual and appropriate or as are specified by the Company with an insurer previously approved in writing by the Company

10. **You** must, at Your expense, promptly return to the Company the Equipment in good working order and in a good state of repair upon the termination of this agreement

Appendix F (iv): Sample Document: Franchise Agreement

The Tenth Schedule

Software Licence

THE Company hereby grants [hires/loans] to You [free of charge] a licence to use the Software and the Computer Equipment and You agrees to take the Software and the Computer Equipment on [licence] [hire] [loan] from the Company [upon the terms as to payment set forth in the _____ Schedule] and upon the following terms:

1 **You** must not sell or offer for sale mortgage or pledge underlet sub-licence lend or otherwise deal with or part with the possession of the Computer Equipment or the Software

2 **You** must not interfere with or adjust the Software or the Computer Equipment except as specifically authorised in the Operations Manual

3 **You** will keep the Company indemnified against all loss and damage to the Software or the Computer Equipment caused by the wilful or negligent misuse of it

4 **THE** Company may affix to the Software and the Computer Equipment or any part of it such plates, labels or other marks indicating the owner of the Software and the Computer Equipment and You must not obliterate deface or cover up any of them and the Company must at all reasonable times have access to the Software and the Computer Equipment for the purpose of inspecting such plates and/or labels and keeping them in good repair

5 **You** must not use nor permit the Software or the Computer Equipment to be used for any purpose other than in the Business as provided in the Operations Manual

6 **You** must not charge or offer the Software or the Computer Equipment as security nor must You permit any lien or other encumbrance to affect the Software or the Computer Equipment

7 **You** must inform any person to whom a debenture charge or lien over any part of Your assets is to be issued that the Software and Computer Equipment is not Your property

8 **You** must at all times keep the Software and the Computer Equipment

Appendix F (iv): Sample Document: Franchise Agreement

insured in the joint names of Yourself and the Company to its full value against such risks as are usual and appropriate or as are specified by the Company with an insurer previously approved in writing by the Company

9   You must at Your own expense return to the Company the Software and the Computer Equipment in good working order and in a good state of repair upon the expiry determination or termination of this agreement for whatsoever reason

10 You must only use computer hardware approved by the Company in operating the Software and You must not use the approved hardware to operate any other software

11 THE Company will supply to You the keywords and any Software renewal keywords necessary to permit continued use of the Software so long as You are not in breach of any of the terms of this agreement

12 You must upon the expiry determination or termination of this agreement for whatsoever reason furnish the Company with a certificate certifying that no copy of the Software has been retained by You nor (to its knowledge) by any other person

13 You undertake with the Company:

   13.1 not to copy (except to provide data backup and then so that no more than 1 copy of the Software plus the original is held by You), reproduce, translate, adapt, vary or modify the Software nor to communicate the same to any third party without the Company's prior written consent

   13.2 to reproduce and include the copyright notice of the owner of the Software on all and any copies, whether in whole or in part, in any form

   13.3 not to provide or otherwise make available the Software in whole or in part, in any form to any person other than Your employees without prior written consent from the Company

   13.4 not to modify, enhance or otherwise improve the Software nor incorporate the Software whether in its original or any improved form within any other software

Appendix F (iv): Sample Document: Franchise Agreement

    13.5 to allow the Company full access to the Software and (but without limiting the generality of the foregoing) to permit the Company to enter the Premises without any other consent save that which You hereby give and which You hereby agree not to revoke at any time during business hours for the purposes of inspecting the Software and otherwise employ any technique it may consider appropriate to enable it to supervise the use by You of the Software

14 **THE** Company shall not be liable to You for any loss, damage, costs, legal costs, professional or other expenses incurred or suffered by You whether direct or consequential (including any economic loss or other loss of turnover, profits or goodwill) by reason of any fault of the Software the Computer Equipment or any computer hardware used by You in the Business

15 **THIS** licence will terminate upon the expiry determination or termination of this agreement

Payment Terms

The annual sum of £___ (plus VAT) payable in advance commencing on the ___ day of _____ 20__

Appendix F (iv): Sample Document: Franchise Agreement

The Eleventh Schedule

Vehicle

APPENDIX F (V)

Sample Document: Outline of International Master Franchise Agreement

This is NOT nor is it intended to be a legal document and should NOT be used as such.

The reader is strongly advised to seek legal advice before its use.

The author accepts no liability for its content or use.

PARTIES

(A) Franchisor

(B) Sub-Franchisor

PRELIMINARY

(A) Establish and define the System Trade Name Trade Marks copyright and their ownership

(B) Agreement of parties to establish a franchise on terms set out

1 RIGHTS GRANTED

1.1 THE Franchisor grants licence to Sub-Franchisor to:

    1.1.1 operate the System

    1.1.2 use the Trade Name

    1.1.3 use the Trade Marks

    1.1.4 use the Franchisor's copyright material within Scotland, Wales, Northern Ireland, the Channel Islands, the Isle of Man and England but excluding the area in England shown edged in red on the map attached ('Territory')

Appendix F (v): Sample Document: Outline of International Master Franchise Agreement

1.2 The Sub-Franchisor may operate company-owned unit and may sub-franchise to third parties. (Company owned unit shall be conducted by a wholly-owned subsidiary of the Sub-Franchisor)

1.3 Each operational outlet shall be subject to a franchise agreement between the Sub-Franchisor and its wholly owned subsidiary or franchisees as the case may be in the form annexed hereto ('Franchise Agreement')

1.4

    1.4.1 Notwithstanding the rights granted no part of the Trade Name or Trade Marks shall form part of the Sub-Franchisor's corporate name

    1.4.2 The Sub-Franchisor shall not hold itself out as being the agent or partner of the Franchisor or entitled to pledge the credit of the Franchisor and will identify itself as the licensee of the Franchisor in dealings with third parties

2. TERM OF LICENCE

2.1 **TERM** to be 25 years subject to provisions for termination contained in this Agreement

3. RIGHTS OF RENEWAL

3.1 **RENEWAL** on notice if no outstanding breach of this Agreement and the Sub-Franchisor has substantially observed Agreement

3.2 New Agreement on current form

[exclude another initial fee?]

[provide a new development schedule?]

3.3 The Sub-Franchisor to give release to the Franchisor on entering into new Agreement

Appendix F (v): Sample Document: Outline of International Master Franchise Agreement

4. SUB-FRANCHISOR'S OBLIGATIONS

4.1 THE Sub-Franchisor shall:

- 4.1.1 Ensure that it has adequate finances including working capital to discharge its obligations
- 4.1.2 Operate the System as instructed only under the Trade Name and Trade Marks
- 4.1.3 Appoint as General Manager ('General Manager') from time to time in charge of the business hereby franchised such person as is reasonably acceptable to the Franchisor and train him to the standards required by the Franchisor
- 4.1.4 Maintain the standards associated with the Trade Name and Trade Marks
- 4.1.5 Use best endeavours to increase turnover
- 4.1.6 Not bring System or Trade Marks/Trade Name into disrepute
- 4.1.7 Ensure that all units disclose their obligations under the Franchise Agreements and in particular correctly return gross sales figures
- 4.1.8 Keep the Franchisor informed of all enforcement action taken
- 4.1.9 Arrange for the Franchisor to inspect franchised units
- 4.1.10 Ensure that all statutory and other relevant regulations which apply within the Territory to this Agreement or the business or franchising or the units and their manner of operation are complied with
- 4.1.11 Ensure that only equipment and products approved by the Franchisor are used by the units
- 4.1.12 Obtain confidentiality undertaking from employees and enforce its observance
- 4.1.13 Train its own staff and franchisees in the operation of the System in all its aspects, in the case of franchisees to such standards as are specified by the Franchisor as will discharge the training obligations of the Franchisor under the Franchise Agreement

Appendix F (v): Sample Document: Outline of International Master Franchise Agreement

4.1.14 Provide the Franchisor with a copy of all operational agreements within 10 days after they are executed

4.1.15 Permit the Franchisor and other franchisees of the Franchisor to attend franchise conventions seminars and meetings

4.1.16 Take on loan from the Franchisor the computer software described in Part I of the Schedule attached upon the terms set out in Part II of the said Schedule

5. INITIAL and CONTINUING FRANCHISE FEES

5.1 THE Sub-Franchisor shall pay to the Franchisor the sum of £___ by way of Initial Franchise Fee upon the signing of this Agreement

5.2 The Sub-Franchisor shall pay to the Franchisor a Management Services Fee equal to __% of the gross network sales of the franchisees plus VAT

5.3 Define 'gross network sales'

5.4 Fees to be paid monthly by the 10th day of the month following the month to which fees relate

6. ACCOUNTANCY

6.1 THE Sub-Franchisor shall:

    6.1.1 remit monthly return of gross sales of all units

    6.1.2 monitor the financial performance and accuracy of gross sales returns of all units

    6.1.3 collect and submit to the Franchisor audited monthly statements (in the form specified) from each unit

    6.1.4 submit to the Franchisor each year within 120 days after the end of its financial period balance sheets and profit and loss accounts certified by an independent accountant (approved by the Franchisor) relating to the franchised business

6.1.5 collect from all franchisees within 120 days after the end of each financial period of one year a balance sheet and profit and loss account certified by an independent accountant and forward the same to the Franchisor

7. PROMOTION & ADVERTISING

7.1 THE Sub-Franchisor shall:

7.1.1 establish an Advertising and Promotion Fund for the promotion of the System within the Territory

7.1.2 collect __% of gross network sales from franchisees for payment into the fund

7.1.3 only use advertisements and promotions approved by the Franchisor

7.1.4 Actively advertise and promote the System the Trade Marks and the Trade Name within the Territory

8. TRADE MARKS

8.1 MAKE appropriate provision for licensing of use of Trade Marks

8.2 Provide that the Sub-Franchisor holds use of Trade Marks for benefit of the Franchisor and will assign to the Franchisor any rights it may acquire

8.3 Provide for the grant of a registered user agreement (if applicable)

8.4 The Sub-Franchisor to join in defence of Trade Marks or assertion of rights in event of infringement

8.5 The Franchisor gives no warranty that Trade Marks cannot be challenged or set aside

Appendix F (v): Sample Document: Outline of International Master Franchise Agreement

9. SALE OF BUSINESS

9.1 THE Franchisor may assign this Agreement subject to the Sub-Franchisor's approval not to be unreasonably held or delayed

9.2 The Sub-Franchisor can assign this Agreement to a third party of whom the Franchisor approves subject to the provision of the following information:

    9.2.1 name and address of the proposed assignee

    9.2.2 the proposed assignee's business experience, present occupation, references

    9.2.3 evidence of financial capacity

    9.2.4 proposed ownership interest

    9.2.5 proposed term of assignment

    9.2.6 confirmation of proposed assignee's willingness to complete training

    9.2.7 confirmation of proposed assignee's willingness to execute a novation agreement

9.3 The following conditions must also be satisfied:

    9.3.1 the proposed assignee must be bona fide at arm's length and meet the Franchisor's standards for acceptance

    9.3.2 the payment of a fee to the Franchisor to cover costs incurred

    9.3.3 there being no outstanding breaches of this Agreement by the Sub-Franchisor

    9.3.4 the assignee to sign a novation agreement

    9.3.5 the Franchisor not exercising a right of first refusal on same terms as offer

    9.3.6 the assignee successfully completing a training programme to the Franchisor's satisfaction

Appendix F (v): Sample Document: Outline of International Master Franchise Agreement

10. TERMINATION

10.1 **TERMINATION** by the Franchisor if the Sub-Franchisor

 10.1.1 is in breach of any of the terms of this Agreement (allow time to remedy breaches capable of remedy so long as not persistent defaults)

 10.1.2 fails to maintain the Franchisor's standards

 10.1.3 if it is found that pre-contract or pre-novation information supplied by the Sub-Franchisor or any proposed assignee (as the case may be) is false or misleading

 10.1.4 goes into liquidation or is insolvent

11. CONSEQUENCES OF TERMINATION

11.1 **ON** termination the Sub-Franchisor must:

 11.1.1 stop use of the Trade Name copyrights and Trade Marks (and do whatever has to be done to clear any registered user agreements in respect of the Trade Marks)

 11.1.2 pay to the Franchisor all monies payable whether or not otherwise due without any right of deduction or set off

 11.1.3 return to the Franchisor all manuals book-keeping and accounting procedures

 11.1.4 cease use of the Franchisor's copyright material

 11.1.5 cease holding himself out as franchisee (or Sub-Franchisor) of the Franchisor

 11.1.6 assign to the Franchisor the benefit (subject to the Franchisor assuming the burden in future) of such of the Franchise Agreements as the Franchisor may specify

 11.1.7 not make use of or disclose any confidential information relating to the System or any of its component parts or the business conducted utilising the System

Appendix F (v): Sample Document: Outline of International Master Franchise Agreement

    11.1.8   shall not for a period of one year compete with the Franchisor or its franchisees in the Territory

    11.1.9   shall not at any time solicit customers of the Sub-Franchisor or the franchisees

    11.1.10   shall not at any time use or duplicate the System or any part thereof

12. WAIVER

12.1 **FAILURE** to enforce rights not to be a waiver

13. SEVERABILITY

13.1 **THIS** clause to rectify illegality of any particular provision except if it affects the Franchisor's Trade Marks or right to be paid fees, when this Agreement may be terminated

14. LIMITATION OF LIABILITY

14.1 **LIMITATION** of Franchisor's liability for advice given

15 NOTICES

15.1 **FORMAL** provisions

Signed, etc.

Appendix F (v): Sample Document: Outline of International Master Franchise Agreement

The Schedule

Computer Software

PART I

Description of Software

PART II

Terms of Hire

APPENDIX F (vi)

Sample Document: International Master Franchise Agreement

This is NOT nor is it intended to be a legal document and should NOT be used as such.

The reader is strongly advised to seek legal advice before its use.

The author accepts no liability for its content or use.

Contents

A. Parties	00
B. Recitals	00
1. Retailing	00
2. Rights Granted	00
3. Term	00
4. Right of Renewal	00
5. Language of Communication	00
6. Franchisor's Initial Obligations	00
7. Sub-Franchisor's Obligations during the Initial Development Period	00
8. Franchisor's Obligations during the Initial Development Period	00
9. Franchisor's Continuing Obligations	00
10. Sub-Franchisor's Obligations	00
11. Initial Training	00
12. Continuing Training	00

Appendix F (v): Sample Document: Outline of International Master Franchise Agreement

13. Financial Provisions	00
14. Accounting and Reporting	00
15. Promotion and Advertising	00
16. Trade [Service] Mark	00
17. Sale of Business	00
18. Termination	00
19. Consequences of Termination	00
20. Failure to Exercise Rights not to be a Waiver	00
21. Severability	00
22. Acknowledgement as to Advice Given	00
23. Assignment by Franchisor	00
24. Guarantor Provisions	00
25. Registrations and Approvals	00
26. Arbitration	00
27. Definitions	00
28. Notices	00
29. Applicable Law	00
30. Marginal Notes not part of Agreement	00
The First Schedule	00
The Second Schedule	00

Appendix F (v): Sample Document: Outline of International Master Franchise Agreement

THIS AGREEMENT is made the day of Two Thousand and Twenty _____
BETWEEN _____ (Company Registration Number _____) of _____ ('Franchisor') and _____ of _____ ('Sub-Franchisor') and _____ of _____ ('Guarantor')

WHEREAS:

1. RETAIL

1.1 The Franchisor has expended time effort and money in developing obtaining and acquiring knowledge about the conduct of the business ('_____ BUSINESS') of the distribution merchandising and promotion of _____ ('Products') and has established a reputation in the name _____ ('Trade Name')

1.2 The methods ('System') of distribution merchandising promotion and packaging used in or in connection with the sale of the Products under the Trade Name are secret and confidential and are the exclusive property of the Franchisor

1.3 The System includes methods of selecting stock assessing required levels of stock methods of merchandising preparation and packaging dealing with customers and suppliers used in or in connection with the operation of the _____ BUSINESS and a recognised design decor and colour for the business premises occupied for the purposes of the _____ BUSINESS, staff recruitment, training and management, equipment furniture layout service format standards of quality and uniformity of products and services offered and procedures for accounting inventory and management control

1.4 The Trade Name is associated with uniformly high standards of service and quality of products

1.5 The Franchisor is the owner of the trade mark _____ which has become associated with the Products and services which are provided in the course of the conduct of the _____ BUSINESS in accordance with the System ('Trade Mark') and has or may cause application to be made in the area described in the _____ Schedule ('Territory') to register the Trade Mark. The Franchisor will enter into a Registered User Agreement with the Sub-Franchisor authorising the use by the Sub-Franchisor of the Trade Mark

Appendix F (v): Sample Document: Outline of International Master Franchise Agreement

which the Sub-Franchisor will be required to use in connection with its conduct of the Said Business (as hereinafter defined) and has also agreed so far as may be necessary for the protection of the Trade Mark to enter into Registered User Agreements with Sub-Franchisees of the Sub-Franchisor

1.6 [There is some doubt as to the registerbility of the Trade Name as a trade mark and/or service mark in the Territory. If it is decided to use another name in the Territory the Franchisor shall select such name and the Sub-Franchisor shall use it pursuant to the provisions hereinafter contained]

1.7 The Sub-Franchisor desires to obtain the benefit of the Franchisor's knowledge skill and experience and the right to operate and/or sub-franchise others ('_____ NETWORK') to operate the System under the Trade Name and utilising the Trade Mark by opening _____ ('_____ OUTLETS') at premises the Sub-Franchisor may nominate within the Territory upon the terms and conditions appearing below

1.8 The Guarantor has agreed to join in this Agreement to guarantee the performance of its obligations by the Sub-Franchisor

NOW IT IS HEREBY AGREED AS FOLLOWS:

2. RIGHTS GRANTED

2.1 **SUBJECT** to and in accordance with the terms hereof the Sub-Franchisor shall within the Territory have the [exclusive] right to use in the Said Business (as hereinafter defined)

    2.1.1 the System

    2.1.2 the Trade Name the Trade [Service] Mark and other symbols insignia distinctive designs and plans or specifications owned by the Franchisor together with the benefit of the Franchisor's accumulated experience and knowledge relating to the System

    2.1.3 the copyright of the Franchisor in any printed matter distinctive features marks decor fabric designs and drawings and any other relevant matters or material

    2.1.4 the Franchisor's secret formulae specifications recipes processes methods of merchandising preparation and packaging

Appendix F (v): Sample Document: Outline of International Master Franchise Agreement

2.2

2.2.1 The Sub-Franchisor shall have the right to grant sub-franchises to others within the Territory permitting such others ('Sub-Franchisees') to operate a _____ OUTLET or _____ OUTLETS utilising the System and under the Trade Name Agreements (hereinafter defined)

2.2.2 If the Sub-Franchisor wishes to operate any _____ OUTLETS it shall not do so but shall establish a wholly owned subsidiary ('the Subsidiary') for the purpose

2.2.3 The operation of each _____ OUTLET shall be subject to a Franchise Agreement (a 'Unit Franchise Agreement') to be entered into between the Sub-Franchisor and as the case may be a Sub-Franchisee or the Subsidiary in the form of the draft Agreement hereto annexed with such amendments only as may be necessary to comply with the laws of the Territory or business practices in the Territory to which the Franchisor may in its absolute discretion agree provided however that such amendments shall only be for the purpose of giving substantial effect to the provisions which are proposed to be amended. The Franchisor will discuss with the Sub-Franchisor and consider any other amendments which the Sub-Franchisor may from time to time propose would be advisable

2.2.4 The Sub-Franchisor shall not enter into other agreements with any Sub-Franchisee or the Subsidiary unless the terms thereof shall have first been approved by the Franchisor

2.3 No part of the Trade Name or the Trade Mark shall form part of the Sub-Franchisor's the Subsidiary's or any Sub-Franchisee's corporate name

2.4 The Sub-Franchisor shall not pledge the credit of the Franchisor or represent itself as being the Franchisor or an agent or partner of the Franchisor. The Sub-Franchisor shall not permit any person connected in any way with the Sub-Franchisor to represent himself or the Sub-Franchisor in such a way that others dealing with him or the Sub-Franchisor might regard him or the Sub-Franchisor as a director officer employee agent or otherwise authorised to act on behalf of the Franchisor

Appendix F (v): Sample Document: Outline of International Master Franchise Agreement

2.5 The Sub-Franchisor shall in all dealings with third parties give clear indication by inscription on all business documents that the Said Business is being operated under licence from the Franchisor

2.6 For the avoidance of doubt the Sub-Franchisor hereby acknowledges that all goodwill associated with or arising from the use of the System, the Trade Name, the Trade Marks or any other industrial or intellectual property rights of the Franchisor shall at all times belong to and be vested in the Franchisor and that the Sub-Franchisor only has the right to benefit from such goodwill to the extent and upon the terms provided by this agreement

3. TERM

3.1 THIS Agreement subject to the provisions for determination hereinafter contained [shall subsist for the period of __ years from the date of this agreement

   3.1.1 [Shall subsist for the period ('the Initial Development Period') from the date of this agreement until _____ and

   3.1.2 if the Sub-Franchisor serves the notice referred to in clause _____ shall continue thereafter until _____] and the Sub-Franchisor shall have the benefit of the right of renewal hereinafter contained

4. RIGHT OF RENEWAL

4.1 THE Sub-Franchisor shall have the right to renew the rights granted in this Agreement at the expiration of the Term upon the following terms and conditions:

   4.1.1 Subject to the following conditions precedent such right may only be exercised by the Sub- Franchisor by notice in writing to the Franchisor given not more than twelve months nor less than six months before the expiration of the Term. The conditions precedent are that

      4.1.1.1 there shall be no outstanding breach by the Sub-Franchisor of the terms of this Agreement; and

Appendix F (v): Sample Document: Outline of International Master Franchise Agreement

        4.1.1.2   the Sub-Franchisor shall have substantially observed and performed the terms and conditions hereof

        4.1.1.3   the payment by the Sub-Franchisor to the Franchisor of a renewal fee of a sum equal to [the aggregate amount of Continuing franchise fees payable by the Sub-Franchisor to the Franchisor during the period of twelve months immediately preceding the service of the notice]

4.1.2   Upon the valid exercise of the right of renewal and upon the expiration of the Term the Sub-Franchisor shall execute a new International Master Franchise Agreement ('New International Master Franchise Agreement') with the Franchisor for a period at least equal to the Term Subject to

        4.1.2.1   such amendments as the Franchisor shall have found to be necessary in the light of its experience with other sub-franchisors of the Franchisor; and

        4.1.2.2   the Franchisor not being obliged to provide any of the initial or other obligations contained in such Agreement which are appropriate to the establishment in business of a new sub-franchisor; and

        4.1.2.3   the Sub-Franchisor shall be obliged to maintain in operation in the Territory throughout the term of the New International Master Franchise Agreement the minimum number of _____ **OUTLETS;** and (iv) the New International Master Franchise Agreement may not contain a right of renewal

4.1.3   The Sub-Franchisor shall upon the execution of the New International Master Franchise Agreement be deemed to have released and discharged the Franchisor from and against all claims and demands whether or not contingent which the Sub-Franchisor may have against the Franchisor arising from this Agreement or otherwise in any way out of the relationship between the Franchisor and the Sub-Franchisor

Appendix F (v): Sample Document: Outline of International Master Franchise Agreement

4.1.4 Provided further that if after the service of the notice referred to in sub-clause 4.1.1 and prior to the entry into the New International Master Franchise Agreement the Sub-Franchisor shall commit a breach of this Agreement such as to justify the termination hereof or which may result in the termination hereof the Sub-Franchisor's right to a New International Territorial Licence shall cease and be of no effect and the Sub-Franchisor shall not be entitled to any refund or repayment whether wholly or partly of any sum paid to the Franchisor in respect of the exercise of the right of renewal

5. LANGUAGE OF COMMUNICATION

5.1 THE language of communication between the parties hereto shall be the English language

5.2 The Sub-Franchisor shall be responsible for the translation into the language or languages of the Territory of the Printed Items (as hereinafter defined) provided by the Franchisor to the Sub-Franchisor

5.3 The Sub-Franchisor will do all such things and take all such steps as may be necessary to vest the copyright in all such translations in the Franchisor

5.4 In the event of any conflict between the text in the language or languages of the Territory and the English the English version shall prevail

6. FRANCHISOR'S INITIAL OBLIGATIONS

6.1 IN addition to the training to be given pursuant to clause _____ the Franchisor will so soon after the date hereof as may be practicable and agreed between the parties provide the following services and items to the Sub-Franchisor:

6.1.1 Advice with regard to the adaptation of the System having regard to the conditions prevailing within the Territory which may affect the System. The Sub-Franchisor may propose changes in the Operations Manual for use in the Territory to reflect legal business and operational differences which the Sub-Franchisor considers

Appendix F (v): Sample Document: Outline of International Master Franchise Agreement

      exist between the Territory and the United Kingdom. The Franchisor will consider such proposals in consultation with the Sub-Franchisor and will determine (in its discretion) what changes ought properly to be made. The Sub-Franchisor shall not introduce any changes except with the prior written approval of the Franchisor and upon such approval being given the Operations Manual shall be varied in the terms of such approval

    6.1.2 Operational support in accordance with the provisions of clause _____

    6.1.3 A copy on loan of the Franchisor's Operations Manual

    6.1.4 A copy on loan of all other manuals and written materials relating to the operation of the System which the Franchisor issues to its franchisees from time to time

6.2 It is hereby acknowledged by the Sub-Franchisor that the copyright in the items mentioned in sub-clauses 6.1.1, 6.1.3 and 6.1.4 and any additions or amendments thereto ('the Printed Items') belongs to the Franchisor

7. SUB-FRANCHISOR'S OBLIGATIONS DURING THE INITIAL DEVELOPMENT PERIOD

7.1 **DURING** the first twelve months of the Initial Development Period the Sub-Franchisor shall be obliged to open for trade not less than __ nor more than __ _____ **OUTLETS** ('the Initial Outlets') within the Territory as hereinafter provided

7.2 The sites for or as the case may be the territory allocated to the Initial Outlets to be opened pursuant to sub-clause 7.1 shall be selected by mutual agreement between the parties and shall be representative of trading positions styles locality and catchment areas

7.3 The Sub-Franchisor shall within the period of _____ months from the date hereof open for business not less than _____ Initial Stores (time being of the essence)

Appendix F (v): Sample Document: Outline of International Master Franchise Agreement

7.4   Not later than _____ (time being of the essence) the Franchisor shall by notice in writing given to the Sub-Franchisor indicate whether or not it is satisfied that the Initial Outlets are successful and if it is so satisfied or if the Sub-Franchisor shall not have served such notice then this agreement shall continue until _____ as provided in clause _____

7.5   If the Sub-Franchisor shall indicate in the notice referred to in sub-clause 7.4 that it is not satisfied that the Initial Outlets are successful then this agreement shall cease and determine

8. FRANCHISOR'S OBLIGATIONS DURING THE INITIAL DEVELOPMENT PERIOD

8.1   **DURING** the period of _____ from the date hereof the Franchisor shall make available a senior executive who will be [based in the Territory] [available in England] for consultation and assistance with the training provided to the Sub-Franchisor pursuant to clauses _____ or _____ hereof. The Franchisor shall have the right to nominate which of its senior executives will be made available for this purpose bearing in mind the services and experience which may be required or appropriate from time to time. The Franchisor shall be responsible for the payment of the salary of the senior executives provided as aforesaid and the Sub-Franchisor shall be responsible for the payment of the cost of travel between England and the Territory accommodation and transportation costs within the Territory

8.2   The Franchisor shall be available for consultation with the Sub-Franchisor in regard to the siting of the Initial Outlets and shall discharge the initial obligations set forth in clauses _____ and _____

8.3   The Franchisor will evaluate the trading performance of each of the Initial Outlets and following detailed consultation with the Sub-Franchisor will determine what changes should be made in order to achieve the most effective format for the future operation of the System in the Territory. The Franchisor will notify the Sub-Franchisor in writing of the changes so to be made to the System not later than _____

Appendix F (v): Sample Document: Outline of International Master Franchise Agreement

9. FRANCHISOR'S CONTINUING OBLIGATIONS

9.1 IN addition to the training to be given pursuant to clause _____ the Franchisor will during the term of this Agreement provide the following services and items to the Sub-Franchisor:

> 9.1.1 details of alterations and/or improvements in or to the System in a form which will enable the Sub-Franchisor to keep the Printed Items up to date
>
> 9.1.2 copies of such United Kingdom marketing materials which the Franchisor may consider capable of adaptation for use within the Territory
>
> 9.1.3 after the conclusion of the Initial Development Period the Franchisor shall if required so to do by the Sub-Franchisor provide the services in the Territory of a senior executive of the Franchisor whom the Franchisor after consultation with the Sub-Franchisor considers suitably experienced for the purpose:
>
>> 9.1.3.1 during the first _____ years thereafter for _____ Working Days within the Territory in each period of three months; and
>>
>> 9.1.3.2 thereafter for _____ Working Days within the Territory within each period of six months
>
> The Franchisor shall pay the salary of such person for each of such visits. The Sub-Franchisor shall in respect of such person pay the cost of travel between England and the Territory first class hotel accommodation plus other expenses (including food and ground transportation) For the avoidance of doubt the expression 'Working Day' shall mean the normal hours of operation of the Sub-Franchisor and the time taken in travel to and from the Territory shall not be taken into account in calculating a number of working days pursuant to this Clause

Appendix F (v): Sample Document: Outline of International Master Franchise Agreement

10. SUB-FRANCHISOR'S OBLIGATIONS

10.1 THE Sub-Franchisor shall:

   10.1.1 ensure that it has adequate finances (including working capital) available to it to enable it to discharge its obligations under this agreement

   10.1.2 operate the System properly and strictly in accordance with the provisions of the Printed Items current from time to time

   10.1.3 not make use of the Printed Items nor make or cause to be made any copies of any of the Printed Items or any part thereof except for the purposes of conducting the Said Business

   10.1.4 ensure that the Printed Items with which it is provided are kept up to date at all times

   10.1.5 establish not less than __ _____ **OUTLETS** within the Initial Development Period and thereafter to open for business either through the Subsidiary or Sub-Franchisees and maintain in operation the number of _____ **OUTLETS** shown in the Second Schedule hereto against each year of the term of this agreement

   10.1.6 appoint and ensure that at all times during the subsistence of this agreement there is appointed as general manager of the Said Business and of the Subsidiary such person ('General Manager') as is reasonably acceptable to the Franchisor and who passes as may be appropriate the training course referred to in clauses _____ or _____

   10.1.7 appoint and ensure that at all times during the subsistence of this Agreement there are appointed as senior executives ('Senior Executives') _____ persons who together with the General Manager will have responsibility for _____ The Senior Executives shall be persons reasonably acceptable to the Franchisor and who pass as appropriate the training course referred to in clauses _____ or _____

   10.1.8 procure that the managers of the first __ _____ **OUTLETS** are selected for their managerial ability and each of them will be

Appendix F (v): Sample Document: Outline of International Master Franchise Agreement

         required to pass the store manager's training course established by the Franchisor

10.1.9   use its best endeavours to maintain the highest standards in all matters connected with the Said Business

10.1.10   use its best endeavours to establish maintain and increase the turnover of the Said Business and of the _____ **OUTLETS**

10.1.11   not do or permit to be done anything which may bring the System and/or the Trade [Service] Mark and/or the Trade Name into disrepute or which may damage the interests of the Franchisor or the Sub-Franchisees

10.1.12   ensure that the Subsidiary and the Sub-Franchisees operate their respective businesses strictly in accordance with the System and promptly perform and discharge their respective obligations under the Unit Franchise Agreements and in particular (without derogating from the generality of the foregoing) accurately make returns to the Sub-Franchisor of Gross Revenues and payment of all sums which may be due to the Sub-Franchisor

10.1.13   make arrangements for the Franchisor to inspect the units operated by the Subsidiary and the Sub-Franchisees so as to ensure that the Franchisor's standards are being achieved and the System correctly operated

10.1.14   observe and perform and ensure that the Subsidiary and all Sub-Franchisees observe and perform all statutory or other legal requirements and regulations of municipal or other authorities which are required to be observed and performed in the operation of the Said Business or the _____ **OUTLETS** as the case may be

10.1.15   use only and ensure that the Subsidiary and all Sub-Franchisees use only such equipment fixtures and fittings in the operation of the System as shall meet the quality standards and specifications contained in the Printed Items or as may otherwise from time to time be approved by the Franchisor

Appendix F (v): Sample Document: Outline of International Master Franchise Agreement

10.1.16 procure from all its staff an undertaking in a form to be approved by the Franchisor not to use or disclose to any third party any information or knowledge concerning the business of the Franchisor the Said Business or the System which may be communicated to such staff or which such staff may acquire pursuant to the discharge of their obligations to the Sub-Franchisor and shall take such steps at its own expense as the Franchisor may require in order to enforce the said undertaking or to restrain any breach of its terms

10.1.17 train its own staff the Sub-Franchisees and the Subsidiary in the operation of the System in all respects

10.1.18 maintain facilities suitable for training Sub-Franchisees to such extent as will discharge the Sub-Franchisor's obligations in regard to training under the Unit Franchise Agreements

10.1.19 within 10 days after the entry by the Sub-Franchisor into an Unit Franchise Agreement or any other agreement with a Sub-Franchisee or the Subsidiary provide the Franchisor with such information in relation thereto (including signed copies) as may be required from time to time by the Franchisor

10.1.20 keep the Franchisor informed of market developments in the Territory and of any material plans or developments in the Said Business which could have an effect beneficial or adverse upon the operation of _____ **OUTLETS** in the Territory

10.1.21 keep the Franchisor fully and effectually indemnified against all claims demands damages costs and expenses which the Franchisor may incur resulting from any alleged breach by the Sub-Franchisor of Unit Franchise Agreements or from third parties for any reason whatever including (not by way of limitation) vicarious liability

10.1.22 at its own expense take out and maintain full insurance cover against all such risks as shall be appropriate and in particular shall ensure that the Franchisor is fully covered in the Territory against product and third party liability claims

Appendix F (v): Sample Document: Outline of International Master Franchise Agreement

10.1.23 provide the Franchisor with a copy of the insurance policies and evidence that the policies are in force

10.1.24 if requested by the Franchisor increase the range of risks covered and the sums insured if the Franchisor considers that the insurance cover arranged by the Sub-Franchisor is not adequate in any respect

11. INITIAL TRAINING

11.1 **THE** Franchisor will train in England the Sub-Franchisor's initial General Manager the Senior Executives and the managers of the first _____ Initial Outlets in the operation of the System

11.2 There will be no further charge for such training and the Sub-Franchisor will be responsible for the payment of salaries fares to and from the Territory hotel accommodation food ground transportation and other expenses of such General Manager Senior Executives or other staff of the Sub-Franchisor while being trained under the provisions of this clause

11.3 The Franchisor may at any time during training by notice in writing inform the Sub-Franchisor that any person submitted for training is not suitable and in its judgment (as to which the Franchisor shall have a complete discretion) will not pass (or has not passed) the training course In such event the Franchisor's obligations in respect of such trainee under this clause shall be regarded as discharged and any further training for any replacement for such trainee shall be provided under the provisions of clause _____

12. CONTINUING TRAINING

12.1 **THE** Franchisor will train in England at the expense of the Sub-Franchisor any subsequent General Manager Senior Executives or replacement for any trainee of the Sub-Franchisor

12.2 The Sub-Franchisor will be responsible for the payment of salaries fares to and from the Territory hotel accommodation food ground transport and other expenses of such staff while being trained under the provisions of this clause

12.3   The Franchisor may suspend or terminate training at any time if in its judgment (as to which the Franchisor shall have a complete discretion) any person submitted for training is not suitable for the purpose for which it is proposed he is to be employed and will not pass (or has not passed) the training course

13. FINANCIAL PROVISIONS

13.1   ON the execution of this Agreement the Sub-Franchisor shall pay to the Franchisor the sum of _____

13.2   Unless the Sub-Franchisor shall have served notice pursuant to the provisions of clause __ hereof that it wishes this agreement to continue, or if the Sub-Franchisor shall not serve such notice when this Agreement shall be deemed to continue until _____ the Sub-Franchisor shall pay to the Franchisor the sum of _____

13.3   The sums paid pursuant to sub-clauses 13.2 and 13.3 shall be deemed fully earned on payment and no part thereof shall be repayable in any circumstances

13.4   During the subsistence of this agreement the Sub-Franchisor shall pay to the Franchisor a continuing franchise fee in respect of each [Trading Period] [month] during the Term such sum as is equal to _____ of the Gross Network Revenue of the Subsidiary and of the Sub-Franchisees during such [Trading Period] [month]

13.5   In this agreement the expression 'Trading Period' shall mean either a calendar month or a period of four weeks corresponding with thirteen four week periods specified in each year by the Franchisor in the Printed Items

13.6   The expression 'Gross Network Revenue' in this Agreement shall mean the aggregate of the Gross Revenue (as that expression is defined in the Unit Franchise Agreement) of the Subsidiary and of Sub-Franchisees under Unit Franchise Agreements

13.7   All fees and payments to be made under the provisions of sub-clause 13.4 shall be made not later than the _____ day of the [Trading Period] [month] following the [Trading Period] [month] upon whose Gross Network Revenue the payment is based

Appendix F (v): Sample Document: Outline of International Master Franchise Agreement

13.8 All payments to be made hereunder to the Franchisor shall be made in Pounds Sterling ('the Specified Currency') by telegraphic transfer or such other means as the Franchisor may from time to time specify into such bank account as the Franchisor shall in writing direct The conversion rate shall be the [official] exchange rate in the currency of the Territory for the purchase of the Specified Currency applicable on the due date for the payment quoted by the Foreign Exchange department in [London] of _____ Bank

13.9 If at any time any legal restrictions shall be imposed in the Territory upon the purchase of the Specified Currency or the transfer to or credit of a non-resident corporation with payments in the Specified Currency the Sub-Franchisor shall notify the Franchisor immediately the Sub-Franchisor shall use its best endeavours to obtain any consents or authorisations which may be necessary in order to effect payment The Franchisor may direct the Sub-Franchisor to make payment to the Franchisor in such other currency and in such other territory or jurisdictions as the Franchisor may select The acceptance by the Franchisor of payment in a currency other than the Specified Currency shall not relieve or release the Sub-Franchisor of or from its obligation to make future payments in the Specified Currency to the extent permitted by law Provided always that if having used its best endeavours the Sub-Franchisor is unable to obtain consent to or authorisation of a method and manner of payment acceptable to the Franchisor then the Franchisor may by notice in writing to the Sub-Franchisor forthwith determine this Agreement without any claim being made by either party against the other in respect of such termination but subject to the provisions of this Agreement which expressly or by implication become effective or continue in effect subsequent to such termination

13.10 [If the laws of the Territory require the Sub-Franchisor to withhold tax on any payment which the Sub-Franchisor is obliged to make to the Franchisor the Sub-Franchisor shall:

13.10.1 obtain a proper receipt and discharge for the tax so deducted and forward it without delay to the Franchisor and

545

13.10.2 do all such other things and take such other steps as may be reasonably required to enable the Franchisor to obtain any tax credit which may be available to it

13.10 [if the laws of the Territory require the Sub-Franchisor to withhold tax on any payment which the Sub-Franchisor is obliged to make to the Franchisor the Sub-Franchisor shall not withstanding such requirement and in addition to the net sum payable be obliged to make payment to the Franchisor of a sum or sums equal to the amount which is required to be withheld]

13.11 In the event that the laws of the Territory require the payment by the Sub-Franchisor or the charge by the Franchisor of a sales or similar tax a value added tax or transactional tax then the Sub-Franchisor shall when making payment to the Franchisor under any of the provisions of this Agreement make payment of such tax at such rate as may from time to time be appropriate

13.12 In the event of any default in the payment of any sums which may be due from the Sub-Franchisor to the Franchisor the Sub-Franchisor shall pay to the Franchisor interest at the rate of five per cent. (5%) per annum over the prime or equivalent rate then applicable in the Territory or if lower the highest rate permissible at law in the Territory on a day to day basis until payment is made notwithstanding that the Franchisor may have obtained judgment for any overdue payments

14. ACCOUNTING AND REPORTING

14.1 THE Sub-Franchisor shall:

14.1.1 provide the Franchisor with a statement of the Gross Network Revenue by the _____ day of the [Trading Period] [month] following the [Trading Period] [month] to which the Gross Network Revenue relates

14.1.2 monitor the financial performance and verify the accuracy of the Gross Network Revenue reports of the Subsidiary and the Sub-Franchisees and provide the Franchisor with such information as may be required by the Franchisor based upon

Appendix F (v): Sample Document: Outline of International Master Franchise Agreement

        information available to the Sub-Franchisor under the provisions of the Unit Franchise Agreements

14.1.3   collect from the Subsidiary and each Sub- licensee financial statements relating to each [Trading Period] [month] (in the form required by the Franchisor) and submit summaries thereof in the form required by the Franchisor to the Franchisor by the _____ day of the [Trading Period] [month] following the [Trading Period] [month] to which the statements relate

14.1.4   submit to the Franchisor within _____ days after the end of the Sub-Franchisor's financial year a balance sheet and profit and loss account in respect of the Said Business certified by an independent [chartered][certified public] accountant

14.1.5   collect from the Subsidiary and each Sub-licensee within _____ days after the end of each of their respective financial periods of one year a balance sheet and profit and loss account in respect of its business as the operator of a _____ OUTLET or _____ OUTLETS certified by an independent [chartered] [certified public] accountant and forward a copy thereof to the Franchisor if requested so to do. The Sub-Franchisor has the responsibility to satisfy itself that the gross revenue shown in such accounts correspond with those in the periodic statements submitted during the relevant financial period and shall forthwith take such action as may be necessary to collect any unpaid fees and in any event shall forthwith remit to the Franchisor any consequentially unpaid fees due pursuant to clause _____ hereof together with interest thereon in accordance with clause _____ hereof from the date upon which payment should have been made to the date upon which payment is made

15. PROMOTION AND ADVERTISING

15.1   THE Sub-Franchisor shall be responsible for the advertising and promotion of the _____ NETWORK within the Territory and shall establish an advertising and promotional fund for the purpose

Appendix F (v): Sample Document: Outline of International Master Franchise Agreement

15.2 The Sub-Franchisor will collect from the Subsidiary and all Sub-Franchisees at least __% of their gross revenue and pay such sum into the said advertising and promotional fund

15.3 The Franchisor will establish and publish in the Printed Items criteria for advertising and promotion which if observed will not require any consent from the Franchisor. All other advertising and promotional activities conducted by the Sub-Franchisor shall be subject to the prior written approval of the Franchisor which approval will not be unreasonably delayed

15.4 The Sub-Franchisor will upon being requested to do so provide the Franchisor with details of its proposed advertising and promotional activities

16. TRADE MARK

16.1

16.1.1 THE Sub-Franchisor shall render to the Franchisor all reasonable assistance (including but not limited to evidence of user) in obtaining registrations in the Territory of the Trade [Service] Mark

16.1.2 in no circumstances shall the Sub-Franchisor apply for registration as proprietor of any trade mark in respect of the Trade Name the Trade [Service] Mark or any or part of them or which would conflict with the Trade Name or the Trade [Service] Mark

16.1.3 if at the time the Franchisor desires to apply for registration of a trade mark or a service mark and has so applied the Sub-Franchisor is deemed in law to have rights in the trade mark or service mark so as to make it necessary for an application to be proceeded with in the name of the Sub-Franchisor the Sub-Franchisor shall at the request and expense of the Franchisor make and proceed with such application and do all acts and execute all documents necessary for obtaining registration in the name of the Sub-Franchisor and thereupon the Sub-Franchisor shall assign such registration to the Franchisor or as the Franchisor shall direct

Appendix F (v): Sample Document: Outline of International Master Franchise Agreement

16.1.4 the Sub-Franchisor shall be entitled to the like rights in respect of any registered trade marks or service marks of the Franchisor (including the Trade [Service] Mark) used in the _____ BUSINESS registered in the Territory as are granted by this Agreement [and the Sub-Franchisor] _____ shall at the request and expense of [the Franchisor] do all acts and execute all documents for establishing the Sub-Franchisor the Sub-Franchisees and the Subsidiary respectively as a user thereunder and where applicable for the registration of the Sub-Franchisor's the Sub-Franchisees and the Subsidiary's permitted use at the Trade Marks Registry in the Territory. The registered user agreement shall (inter alia) contain the right of the Franchisor to control the specifications and quality of products [services] and the rights given to the Sub-Franchisor shall be limited to use in the Said Business and to the Sub-Franchisee and the Subsidiary shall be limited to use pursuant to the Unit Franchise Agreements and in such other ways as required by the Franchisor consistent with this Agreement. The Sub-Franchisor and/or any Sub-Franchisee and/or the Subsidiary shall not following such request be entitled to exercise any of the rights herein granted if it shall have failed within 10 days of the receipt of such document to have executed and returned it to the Franchisor as the case may be.] The Sub-Franchisor the Sub-Franchisees and the Subsidiary shall pay to the Franchisor under the terms of the registered user agreement the sum of _____ [(£___)] per annum for the use of the Trade [Service] Mark or any other registered trade mark and service marks of the Franchisor

16.1.5 The Sub-Franchisor shall and shall procure that the Subsidiary and the Sub-Franchisees shall in all representations of the Trade [Service] Mark used by them append in a manner approved by the Franchisor such inscription as is usual or proper for indicating that the Trade [Service] Mark is registered

16.2 The Sub-Franchisor shall immediately notify the Franchisor of all infringements or imitations of the Trade Name or the Trade [Service] Mark or any business which appears to or to be attempting to pass itself off as

Appendix F (v): Sample Document: Outline of International Master Franchise Agreement

the _____ **BUSINESS** or a _____ **OUTLET** which may come to its attention or any attempts to challenge its right to use the Trade Name or the Trade [Service] Mark or to carry on the Said Business so long as this Agreement shall subsist. The Franchisor shall take such action as in its sole discretion it considers appropriate. The Sub-Franchisor agrees to provide such co-operation in the prosecution of any such action including the provision of evidence and being named as a party to any legal proceedings as the Franchisor shall require. The Franchisor shall have the conduct of any such action and the Franchisor shall pay all legal expenses and costs which may arise from the joining of the Sub-Franchisor as a party save for such legal expenses and costs which the Sub-Franchisor may incur by taking separate legal advice. The Sub-Franchisor shall not without the prior written consent of the Franchisor take any action of whatever nature based upon the Trade Name Trade Mark or any other legal rights which the Sub-Franchisor is licensed to use or exercise pursuant to this Agreement [or any registered user agreement entered into between the parties]

16.3 No warranty expressed or implied is hereby given by the Franchisor with respect to the validity of the Trade [Service] Mark. If it shall not be possible for the Franchisor to secure registration of the Trade [Service] Mark in the Territory and it shall be considered inadvisable to continue to use the Trade Name the Franchisor shall at its own expense in co-operation and consultation with the Sub-Franchisor devise an alternative trade name and/or trade marks and service marks as similar as possible to the Trade Name and Trade [Service] Mark and utilising similar or the same colours. The Franchisor shall be responsible for all costs and expenses which may be incurred by it in effecting such registration as may be possible and upon the introduction of a new trade name trade mark and/or service mark the expressions 'Trade Name' and 'Trade [Service] Mark' herein defined shall apply to them as if they had been in existence at the date of this Agreement. None of the Sub-Franchisees the Subsidiary and the Sub-Franchisor shall have any claim against the Franchisor of whatever nature in the event that such changes are required to be made and the Sub-Franchisor shall keep the Franchisor fully and effectually indemnified against all claims demands damages costs and expenses which may be made against or suffered by the Franchisor in respect of the introduction of a new trade name trade mark and/or service mark

17. SALE OF BUSINESS

17.1 THE Sub-Franchisor shall not have the right to assign this Agreement but it shall have the right to sell the Said Business with the prior written consent of the Franchisor and subject to the conditions listed in sub-clause 17.3

17.2 The Franchisor hereby undertakes to grant to a purchaser of the Said Business who is acceptable to it pursuant to the terms thereof an International Master Franchise Agreement for the Territory for a period equal to the unexpired term granted by this Agreement commencing with the date of the sale of the Said Business excluding the payment of any sum initial fee but otherwise upon similar terms and conditions to those herein contained

17.3 The conditions required to obtain the written consent of the Franchisor to the sale of the Said Business by the Sub-Franchisor shall be:

17.3.1 any proposed purchaser shall be bona fide and at arm's length and shall meet the Franchisor's standards with respect to business experience financial status and ability and shall provide as the General Manager and as Senior Executives for the said Business such persons who shall successfully complete a programme of initial training by the Franchisor and who shall otherwise be acceptable by the criteria established by the Franchisor from time to time for suitability as a Sub-Franchisor. Before making any binding commitment regarding a sale of the Said Business the Sub-Franchisor shall notify the Franchisor in writing

17.3.1.1. the proposed purchaser's name address and telephone number

17.3.1.2 the proposed purchaser's business experience present occupation and references

17.3.1.3 evidence of its financial capability including personal and business financial statements

Appendix F (v): Sample Document: Outline of International Master Franchise Agreement

    17.3.1.4 capital and ownership interests in the proposed purchaser

    17.3.1.5 proposed terms of sale

    17.3.1.6 evidence of the proposed purchaser's willingness to complete the Franchisor's training programme

    17.3.1.7 evidence of the proposed purchasers willingness to execute an agreement with the Franchisor upon the terms set forth in sub-clause 17.2 and the Sub-Franchisor shall have obtained the Franchisor's prior written approval

17.3.2 the Sub-Franchisor shall pay to the Franchisor a sum equal to the cost to the Franchisor of dealing with the application for consent and the training of the proposed purchaser and its General Manager and Senior Executives including such cost where the prospective purchaser does not proceed for any reason

17.3.3 the Sub-Franchisor must at the time of its application for consent not be in breach of any of its obligations to the Franchisor under the terms of this Agreement

17.3.4 the proposed purchaser shall not be engaged or concerned or interested in any way in any business which carries on a business which competes with the business of _____ or with the _____ **BUSINESS** or which is a member of a group of companies one of whose members carries on such a business

17.3.5 if the proposed purchaser is a corporation the shareholders and officers must be persons acceptable to the Franchisor according to the criteria set out in sub-clause 17.3 and shall if so required undertake to the Franchisor in writing to guarantee the observance and performance by the proposed purchaser of its obligations as sub-franchisor

17.3.6 payment by the Sub-Franchisor of all costs and the discharge of all obligations by or of the Sub-Franchisor to the Franchisor including any sum due under sub-clause 17.3 without any right of deduction or set-off

17.4

    17.4.1 The Sub-Franchisor shall as soon as possible submit to the Franchisor a copy of the proposed purchaser's written offer to purchase the Said Business together with the following information:

        17.4.1.1 a financial statement of affairs and the business history of the proposed purchaser and

        17.4.1.2 details of any other terms which may have been agreed between the Sub-Franchisor and the proposed purchaser

    17.4.2 Upon receipt of such notice accompanied by the said information the Franchisor shall in addition to its other rights hereunder and subject to obtaining any consents which may be required and complying with any other relevant requirements under the laws of the Territory have an option to purchase the Said Business for the same amount and upon the same terms as the proposed purchaser has offered

    17.4.3 The Franchisor shall have a period of thirty (30) days after receipt of such written notice and the said information to exercise its option to purchase by notice in writing to the Sub-Franchisor in which event the sale and purchase shall be completed within 20 days following the service of such notice

17.5 Upon the Franchisor completing the purchase of the Said Business following the exercise of the option contained in sub-clause 17.4 or entering into an International Master Franchise Agreement with an approved purchaser of the Said Business and upon the satisfaction of the conditions referred to in sub-clause 17.3 in particular and (without derogating from the generality of the foregoing provisions) the successful completion by the prospective purchaser's General Manager and Senior Executive of the Franchisor's programme of initial training the Franchisor and the Sub-Franchisor shall each be deemed to have released the other from the terms of this Agreement save for those provisions which by their nature survive termination. In addition the Sub-Franchisor shall be deemed to have released and discharged the Franchisor from and against all claims and demands whether or not contingent which the Sub-Franchisor may have against the Franchisor arising from this Agreement or otherwise in any way out of the relationship between the Franchisor and the Sub-Franchisor

17.6 For the purpose of this clause any change in the beneficial ownership of the issued share capital or stock or of the de facto control of the Sub-Franchisor [or of the Guarantor] to which the Franchisor has not previously consented in writing shall be deemed to be assignment

18. TERMINATION

18.1 IF the Sub-Franchisor shall:

18.1.1 fail to commence the Said Business within the period of six months from the date hereof or

18.1.2 neglect or fail to perform or observe any of the agreements or conditions on its part to be performed or observed hereunder or

18.1.3 fail to ensure that the Subsidiary or any Sub-Franchisee operate the System to the standards required by the Franchisor as set out in the Printed Items and otherwise in compliance with the Unit Franchise Agreement

and in any such case shall fail to remedy such default neglect or failure (where capable of remedy) to the Franchisor's satisfaction within thirty days after written notice thereof from the Franchisor **PROVIDED** however that in the case of persistent default neglect or failure the Sub-Franchisor shall not be entitled to any period of grace within which to remedy any default neglect or failure. A persistent default neglect or failure shall be a default neglect or failure of the same agreement or condition or obligation which has occurred more than twice in any period of one year

Appendix F (v): Sample Document: Outline of International Master Franchise Agreement

OR if the Sub-Franchisor shall in the negotiations preceding the signing of this Agreement have provided the Franchisor with information which contains any false or misleading statements or omits any material fact which may make any statement misleading

OR if the Sub-Franchisor [or the Guarantor] shall have become insolvent entered into liquidation whether compulsorily or voluntarily otherwise then for the purpose of amalgamation or reconstruction or if the Sub-Franchisor shall make any arrangement or composition with its creditors or shall have a receiver appointed of all or any part of its assets or if the Sub-Franchisor takes any similar action in consequence of debt

OR if there shall be a purported or deemed assignment of this Agreement

OR if there shall be a purported or deemed sale of the Said Business or any change in the beneficial ownership of or the de facto control of the Sub-Franchisor or the Subsidiary without the prior written consent of the Franchisor

THEN the Franchisor may without prejudice to any other rights or remedies available to it terminate this Agreement and all rights of the Sub-Franchisor hereunder shall thereupon cease

18.2 Without prejudice to the generality of the provisions of the preceding sub-clause if the Sub-Franchisor makes any default in making any payment under any of the provisions of this Agreement or in remitting or supplying any statement or copy contracts or reports or information due under the terms of this Agreement within 10 days after the same shall be due or if the Franchisor shall on reasonable grounds suspect that any information concerning the Franchisor's business or particulars of any confidential communication from the Franchisor to the Sub-Franchisor is being or has been communicated in any way to any competitor of the Franchisor then the Franchisor may forthwith without prejudice to any other rights or remedies available to it terminate this Agreement and all rights of the Sub-Franchisor hereunder shall thereupon cease

OR

Appendix F (v): Sample Document: Outline of International Master Franchise Agreement

18.2 [This Agreement may be terminated forthwith by the Sub-Franchisor upon written notice to the Franchisor in the event that:

18.2.1 The Franchisor ceases the business of operating or franchising others to operate the _____ **BUSINESS**

18.2.2 The Franchisor shall neglect or fail to perform or observe any of the agreements and conditions on its part to be observed or performed hereunder and shall fail to remedy such neglect or failure (where capable of remedy) to the Sub-Franchisor's reasonable satisfaction within such period as is reasonable in all the circumstances but not in any event less than thirty days after written notice thereof from the Sub-Franchisor or

18.2.3 The Franchisor shall become insolvent or shall have a winding up or administration order made against it]

19. CONSEQUENCES OF TERMINATION

19.1

19.1.1 **UPON** the termination of this Agreement for any cause the Sub-Franchisor will immediately discontinue the use of the Trade Name the Trade [Service] Mark signs cards notices and other display or advertising matter indicative of the Franchisor or of any association with the Franchisor or of the Said Business and will make or cause to be made such changes in signs cards notices and other display or advertising matter buildings and structures as the Franchisor shall reasonably direct so as effectively to distinguish the Said Business from its former public and marketing image

19.1.2 The Sub-Franchisor shall also when demanded by the Franchisor and (except in the case of items supplied to the Sub-Franchisor free of charge) upon payment of the reasonable market value thereof deliver up to the Franchisor all stationery literature signs cards notices other display or advertising matter and any other article bearing the name of the Franchisor or the

Appendix F (v): Sample Document: Outline of International Master Franchise Agreement

                Trade Name or the Trade [Service] Mark which may be the property of the Sub-Franchisor

      19.1.3   All items which may have been loaned to the Sub-Franchisor by the Franchisor including the Printed Items shall be returned to the Franchisor at the Sub-Franchisor's expense

      19.1.4   The Sub-Franchisor shall also forthwith pay to the Franchisor (without any deduction or right of set-off) all sums of money which may be due from the Sub-Franchisor to the Franchisor

19.2   The Sub-Franchisor shall further and forthwith upon such termination:

      19.2.1   at the request of the Franchisor and subject to compliance with any requirements of the law of the Territory assign all Unit Franchise Agreements (other than those with the Subsidiary) to the Franchisor in such form as the Franchisor shall reasonably require

      19.2.2   [at the option of the Franchisor forthwith transfer the whole of the issued share capital of the Subsidiary to the Franchisor or to whomsoever it may direct]

      19.2.3   join with [the Franchisor] or _____ in cancelling any permitted user of the Trade [Service] Mark. If the Sub-Franchisor shall fail so to do the Franchisor is hereby irrevocably appointed the agent of the Sub-Franchisor with full authority to give such notice to the Registrar of Trade Marks on behalf of the Sub-Franchisor

      19.2.4   cease using the telephone lines the numbers whereof have been publicly associated with the Said Business and shall do all such acts and things including the signature of any document which may be necessary to ensure that the future use of such telephone lines by the Franchisor is assured

      19.2.5   cease the use of all material of whatever nature the copyright whereof is vested in the Franchisor or where the continued use thereof would in any way infringe the Franchisor's copyright

19.3 The Sub-Franchisor hereby irrevocably appoints the Franchisor as its agent or attorney with full authority to sign and execute all contracts assignments deeds notices and other documents which may be necessary to give effect to any of the provisions of this clause in the event of the failure of or refusal by the Sub-Franchisor to observe and perform its obligations under this agreement

19.4 Upon the termination of this Agreement for any cause:

19.4.1 the Sub-Franchisor shall not for a period of __ [months] [year] thereafter directly or indirectly be engaged concerned or interested in a business which competes with the _____ **BUSINESS** or the _____ **NETWORK** within the Territory

19.4.2 the Sub-Franchisor shall not at any time thereafter solicit or tout for business from any person who was during the period of two years prior to such termination a Sub-Franchisee or a customer of or in the habit of dealing with the Said Business

19.4.3 the Sub-Franchisor shall not at any time thereafter directly or indirectly be engaged concerned or interested in a business which utilises or duplicates the System or any significant part thereof or use the Trade Name or the Trade Mark or any name or mark likely to be confused therewith

20. FAILURE TO EXERCISE RIGHTS NOT TO BE A WAIVER

20.1 **THIS** Agreement contains the entire agreement between the parties and no representations warranties inducements or promises made by the Franchisor whether oral or otherwise and no other agreements whether oral or otherwise not embodied herein and no custom or practice of the parties or either of them at variance with the terms hereof shall add to or vary this Agreement or be of any force or effect

20.2 No failure of the Franchisor to exercise any power given to it hereunder or to insist upon strict compliance by the Sub-Franchisor with any obligation hereunder and no custom or practice of the parties at variance with the terms hereof shall constitute any waiver of any of the Franchisor's rights under this Agreement

20.3 Waiver by the Franchisor of any particular default by the Sub-Franchisor shall not affect or impair the Franchisor's rights in respect of any subsequent default of any kind by the Sub-Franchisor nor shall any delay or omission of the Franchisor to exercise any rights arising from any default of the Sub-Franchisor affect or impair the Franchisor's rights in respect of the said default or any other default of any kind

21. SEVERABILITY

21.1 IF any term or provision or any part thereof (in this clause called 'the offending provision') contained in this Agreement shall be declared or become unenforceable invalid or illegal for any reason whatsoever including but without derogating from the generality of the foregoing a decision by any competent domestic or the European Court of Justice the Commission of the European Committee an Act of Parliament European Community legislation or any statutory or other bylaws or regulations or any other requirements having the force of law the other terms and provisions of this Agreement shall remain in full force and effect as if this Agreement had been executed without the offending provision appearing herein. In the event that the exclusion of any Offending Provision shall adversely affect the Franchisor's right to receive payment of fees or remuneration by whatever means payable to the Franchisor (including but without prejudice to the generality of the foregoing the Franchisor's right [exclusively] to supply the Franchisee with the Products and/or Services) or materially adversely affect the Trade [Service] Marks the Trade Name trade secrets know-how methods or the System then the Franchisor shall have the right to terminate this Agreement upon 30 days' notice in writing to the Franchisee Provided however that before the service of such notice the Franchisor and the Franchisee shall use their best efforts by good faith discussions to agree within a period of 60 days from the date when the Franchisor initiates such discussion process (time in this respect shall be of the essence) upon alternative enforceable provisions which will have the same practical effect as the Offending Provision. Upon any agreement having been reached the new provisions shall be incorporated in this Agreement and the Franchisor shall not be entitled to terminate this Agreement under the provisions of this clause by reason of that particular event

22. ACKNOWLEDGEMENT AS TO ADVICE GIVEN

22.1   IT having been agreed between the parties that this Agreement contains the entire agreement between the parties the Sub-Franchisor acknowledges that no representation warranties inducement or promises made by the Franchisor have been relied upon by it save such as may have been notified by the Sub-Franchisor to the Franchisor in writing and are annexed to and incorporated in this Agreement In particular the Sub-Franchisor acknowledges that it recognises that the business venture contemplated by this Agreement involves business risks and will be affected by its business ability and commitment

22.2   Except where the context otherwise requires each of the restrictions contained in this Agreement and in each clause and paragraph thereof shall be construed as independent of every other restriction and of every other provision of this Agreement and the existence of any claim or cause of action of the Sub-Franchisor against the Franchisor whatsoever shall not constitute a defence to the enforcement by the Franchisor of the said restrictions or of any of them

22.3   It is hereby expressly agreed between the parties hereto that having regard to the recitals and other provisions of this Agreement each of the restrictive covenants contained in this Agreement and in each clause and paragraph thereof is reasonably necessary for the protection of the Franchisor's industrial and intellectual property rights the Trade Name the Trade Mark and does not unreasonably interfere with the freedom of action of the Sub-Franchisor

22.4   In order to enable the Franchisor to ascertain whether the Sub-Franchisor is complying with the obligations imposed upon it by this Agreement and in order to enable the Franchisor to enforce rights given to it by this Agreement the Franchisor may at any time during normal business hours enter the Sub-Franchisor's and the Subsidiary's premises without any consent of the Sub-Franchisor save that which is hereby given and which the Sub-Franchisor hereby agrees not to revoke

23. ASSIGNMENT BY FRANCHISOR

23.1 THE Franchisor may in connection with an internal reorganisation or sale of a substantial part or the whole of its undertaking assign (or otherwise deal with) the benefit and burden of this Agreement without the consent of the Sub-Franchisor subject to the assignee entering into a direct covenant with the Sub-Franchisor thereafter to observe and perform all the Franchisor's obligations herein contained

23.2 The submission by the assignee of a covenant to the above effect duly executed by the assignee shall be deemed to be in compliance with the requirements of this clause and the Franchisor herein named shall thenceforth be discharged from all obligations under this Agreement

24. GUARANTOR PROVISIONS

24.1 THE Guarantor hereby covenants and undertakes with the Franchisor

24.1.1 that the Sub-Franchisor will duly observe and perform all the obligations herein contained on the Sub-Franchisor's part to be observed and performed

24.1.2 if the Sub-Franchisor shall fail to observe or perform any of the said obligations or fail to make payment when due of continuing franchise fees or any other sums which may be payable by the Sub-Franchisor to the Franchisor under this Agreement the Guarantor will be liable for such default and shall make payment of any sums so due upon demand being made by the Franchisor

24.1.3 the Guarantor will (as a distinct and separate obligation) indemnify and render harmless the Franchisor in respect of all losses damages claims costs and expenses which the Franchisor may incur or suffer by reason of its entry into, continuance of, or termination (in any way) of this Agreement

24.1.4 that the Guarantor will not make use of any of the Franchisor's industrial and intellectual property rights of whatsoever nature (including goodwill) and will not disclose to any third party or make use of any of the Franchisor's trade secrets methods know-how the system of which the Guarantor may acquire knowledge by virtue of its involvement in the Said Business or its shareholding in the Sub-Franchisor

24.1.5 the liability of the Guarantor under this clause shall not be in any way affected or impaired by the Franchisor giving time or showing any indulgence whatsoever to the Sub-Franchisor

24.1.6 and warrants that prior to the execution of this Agreement he had no detailed knowledge of the _____ BUSINESS or how to operate a business similar to the _____ BUSINESS or how to conduct the _____ BUSINESS or of the Franchisor's trade secrets know-how methods or the System

25. REGISTRATION AND APPROVALS

25.1 IF this agreement is subject to effective registration or the obtaining of approvals of the appropriate government or other regulatory authorities federal state or provincial in the jurisdiction in which the Sub-Franchisor shall be carrying on the said business:

25.1.1 the Sub-Franchisor shall forthwith make application and if application is required by such authorities to be made by the Franchisor the Franchisor shall forthwith make application to the appropriate authorities for such registration and approvals as aforesaid

25.1.2 the Franchisor and the Sub-Franchisor shall each use its best endeavours to procure effective registration and the necessary approvals and shall do all such things and take all such steps as may reasonably be required in order to effect such registration or to obtain such approvals Provided however that the cost of registration and of obtaining such approvals shall be borne by the Sub-Franchisor including the cost of application and of prosecuting the applications

Appendix F (v): Sample Document: Outline of International Master Franchise Agreement

25.2 If in granting registration and in giving such approvals conditions are imposed upon the Franchisor which in its reasonably held opinion

    25.2.1 may result in the loss of or loss of control of its Trade Marks Trade Names know-how trade secrets or other industrial and intellectual property rights of whatsoever nature

    25.2.2 may place in jeopardy its right to receive the agreed level of gross compensation (however it may be calculated or charged) for the use of such Trade Marks Trade Name know-how trade secrets and other industrial and intellectual property rights of whatsoever nature

    25.2.3 may otherwise limit or restrict the right of the Franchisor to exercise proper control over the operator of the System

the Franchisor shall have the right forthwith to terminate this agreement by notice in writing given to the Sub-Franchisor without prejudice to the continuation in full force and effect of those provisions which are intended to continue in effect after the termination of this agreement

26. ARBITRATION

26.1 ANY dispute or difference of any kind whatsoever which arises or occurs between the parties in relation to any thing or matter arising under out of or in connection with this Agreement shall be referred to arbitration in accordance with _____ Provided however that notwithstanding the application of arbitration to disputes or differences arising out of this Agreement the Franchisor shall not be prevented from terminating this Agreement in accordance with Clause _____ hereof or from enforcing the provisions of Clause _____ hereof and/or from applying to a competent court to enforce the provisions of Clause _____ hereof. The Franchisee shall not be entitled in these circumstances to apply to any court for a stay of proceedings pending arbitration and the Franchisee hereby undertakes not to do so

Appendix F (v): Sample Document: Outline of International Master Franchise Agreement

27. DEFINITIONS

27.1 IN this Agreement the expression 'Said Business' shall mean the business carried on by the Sub-Franchisor in exercise of the above rights and pursuant to and in accordance with this Agreement

27.2 If there are two or more persons as Sub-Franchisor as parties to this Agreement all covenants and agreements on the part of the Sub-Franchisor shall deemed to be joint and several covenants and agreements on their part

27.3 Where under any of the provisions of this Agreement the Franchisor's consent or approval is required to be given or obtained such consent or approval to be effective and binding on the Franchisor unless deemed by a provision in this agreement to have been given must be in writing and signed by a director of the Franchisor

27.4 Where in this Agreement there is a reference to a requirement of the Franchisor (however expressed) it shall be deemed to include any requirement contained in the Operations Manual

27.5 Where in this Agreement there is reference to any matter to be specified by the Franchisor notice of such specified requirements may be communicated by way of amendment or addition to the Operations Manual

27.6 In this Agreement where the context so requires or admits the singular shall include the plural and the masculine shall include the feminine and neuter and vice versa

27.7

    27.1.1 In the event of any dispute the authentic text of the Printed Items shall be the copy kept as such by the Franchisor at its principal business office

    27.7.2 The Printed Items translations thereof and the copyright therein shall at all times remain the property of the Franchisor

27.8 The Sub-Franchisor hereby warrants that prior to the execution of this Agreement it had no detailed knowledge of the _____ **BUSINESS** or how to operate a business similar to the _____ **BUSINESS** or how to

Appendix F (v): Sample Document: Outline of International Master Franchise Agreement

conduct the _____ **BUSINESS** or of the Franchisor's trade secrets know-how methods or the System

28. NOTICES

28.1 **ANY** Notice required to be given hereunder by the Franchisor may be delivered personally or by sending it by first class prepaid post if to the Sub-Franchisor at its last known business address in the Territory and any notice required to be given by the Sub-Franchisor or the Guarantor may be given by leaving the same at or posting it by first class prepaid post to the Franchisor's principal place of business

28.2 Where a notice is sent by post under the provisions of this clause service shall be deemed to have been effected at the expiration of fourteen (14) days (excluding public holidays in the Territory and in the Country in which the Franchisor's said office is situate) after the same was posted whether or not it shall have been received

29. APPLICABLE LAW

29.1 **SUBJECT** to sub clause (B) this Agreement shall be construed and enforced according to the laws of _____. The parties hereto submit to the non-exclusive jurisdiction of the _____ Courts

29.2 The law of the Territory shall apply to disputes relating to the Trade and Service Marks and any other industrial and intellectual property of the Licensor and in relation to any other matters to which such law shall be applied by the application of the rules of conflict of laws in the Territory for the purposes of the enforcement of this Agreement to the exclusion of _____ law by the application to it of the applicable law of the Territory

30. MARGINAL NOTES NOT PART OF AGREEMENT

30.1 The marginal notes to this Agreement are solely for ease of reference and this Agreement shall not be construed by reference thereto

AS WITNESS etc.

Appendix F (v): Sample Document: Outline of International Master Franchise Agreement

The First Schedule

The Territory

Appendix F (v): Sample Document: Outline of International Master Franchise Agreement

The Second Schedule

Targets and Openings

References

British Franchise Association. (2015). 2015 NatWest/British Franchise Association Survey.

Groves, P. (1997). *Sourcebook on Intellectual Property Law*. London: Cavendish.

Hewitt, C M. (1956). *Automobile Franchise Agreements*. Homewood, IL: Richard D Irwin.

Price, S. (1997). *The Franchise Paradox: New Directions, Different Strategies*. London: Cassell.

Smith, B. (n.d.). Assessing the option. How to Franchise Your Business, Hotel Café Royal, London.

Stanworth, J, Purdy, D, and Price, S. (1997). Franchise growth and failure in the US and the UK: A troubled dream-world revisited. *Franchising Research: An International Journal 2*(2): 75–94.

Wiessner, D. (2016, October 31). McDonald's to pay $3.75 mln in 1st settlement with franchise workers. Reuters. Retrieved from https://www.reuters.com/article/mcdonalds-settlement/mcdonalds-to-pay-3-75-mln-in-1st-settlement-with-franchise-workers-idUSL1N1D10XB